USA
Immigration &
Orientation

Third Edition, Revised

Book 1 - Getting In
Solving the Immigration Process

Book 2 - Getting Settled
Adjusting to U.S. Living

Bob & Mary McLaughlin

Wellesworth Publishing
Satellite Beach, Florida

Published by:

Wellesworth Publishing
P.O. Box 372444
Satellite Beach, FL 32937-2444
U.S.A.

McLaughlin, Bob
  USA Immigration & orientation / Bob & Mary McLaughlin
  Includes bibliographical references and index.
  1. United States--Emigration and immigration
  2. Naturalization--United States--Handbooks, manuals, etc.
  I. McLaughlin, Mary   II. Title
JV6543.M44   2000

ISBN 0-9657571-4-5

Library of Congress Catalog Card Number: 99-75880
325.73--dc21

Printed in the United States of America
Third Edition, Revised, Fifth Printing

Contents

Foreword vii
Preface viii
Acknowledgments ix
Disclaimer x
Book 1 - Getting In - Introduction 1
I - Immigration Laws 3
    1 - Making and Publishing Immigration Laws 5
    2 - The Administration of Immigration Laws 7
II - Temporary Status 12
    3 - Visitor Classifications 29
        VWPP - Visa Waiver Pilot Program 30
        B - Temporary Visitor for Business or Pleasure 33
        Border Crossing Card - Mexicans and Canadians 40
        C-1/D - Alien in Transit/Crew member, Sea or Air 42
        Advance Parole 46
        TWOV - Transit WithOut Visa 49
    4 - Educational Classifications 50
        F - Academic Student 51
        J - Exchange Visitor 65
        M- Vocational or Non-Academic Student 84
    5 - Business Professionals 90
        E - Treaty Trader or Investor 91
        H - Professional, Temporary Worker or Trainee 99
        L - Intra-Company Transferee 123
        TN - Treaty NAFTA Professional 132
    6 - Extraordinary/Internationally-Recognized Persons 140
        O - Aliens of Extraordinary Ability in the Sciences, Arts, Education,
            Business, Athletics 141
        P - Internationally-Recognized Athlete and Entertainer 148
    7 - Special Purpose Classifications 155
        I - Foreign Information Media Representative 156
        K - Marriage to U.S. Citizen 159
        Q-1/Q-2 International Cultural Exchange Program/
            Irish Peace Process Cultural and Training Program . . . 167
        R - Alien in a Religious Occupation 172
        S - Alien Witness and Informant 178
        Other Status - Humanitarian Parole/Retirement Visa 180

8 - Foreign Government and Organization Representative 181
    A - Senior Government Official 183
    C-2/C-3 - Alien in Transit to United Nations (C-2) and Foreign
        Government Official (C-3) 188
    G - Government Representative to International Organization . 189
    N - International Organization Family Member 195
    NATO - Representative of Member State 197
III - Green Cards 201
    9 - Family-Sponsored Preferences 216
    10 - Employment-Based Preferences 224
    Employment-Based First Preference (EB1) 233
    Employment-Based Second/Third Preference (EB2/EB3) 242
    Employment-Based Fourth Preference (EB4) 260
    Employment-Based Fifth Preference (EB5) 268
    11 - Diversity (DV) Lottery 274
    12 - Refugee/Asylee 281
IV - U.S. Citizenship 292
    13 - Derivative Status 295
    14 - Dual Nationality 297
    15 - Naturalization *with Test Questions* 299
V - Research Resources 314
    16 - Legal Assistance 315
    17 - New Legislation 317
    18 - United States Government Resources 338
Book 2 - Getting Settled - Introduction 345
I - Governmental Procedures 348
    19 - U. S. Customs Service 349
    20 - Social Security 355
    21 - Selective Service 361
    22 - Buying or Leasing a Car - License & Registration 364
    23 - Employment Benefits and Compensation 368
II - Finance 371
    24 - Taxation 372
    25 - Banking and Financial Transactions 375
    26 - Buying or Renting a Home 380
    27 - Mortgages 394

III - Insurance 405
    28 - Homeowner's Insurance 406
    29 - Health Insurance 410
        Health Care Legislation 411
        Points to Consider When Choosing a Provider 413
        Options For Health Insurance Coverage 415
        Health Insurance Definitions 424
    30 - Automobile Insurance 428
IV - Community 432
    31 - Primary and Secondary Education 433
    32 - Social Activities 437
    33 - Marriage Procedures 440
V - Post-Naturalization Rights 443
    34 - Voting 444
    35 - Passport 447
Appendix A - Immigration And Naturalization Service (INS) Forms and Fees .. 455
Appendix B - Affidavit of Birth 457
Appendix C - Information Telephone Numbers 458
Appendix D - Credential Evaluators 460
Appendix E - Dictionary of Occupational Titles (DOT) 462
Appendix F - Department of Labor -ETA - Regional Offices 466
Glossary 469
References 473
Index 477
Order Form 486

Foreword

America is not only a nation of immigrants, but a nation that continues to rekindle its basic spirit with new immigrants who look for opportunity in their new country. As the world leader, the United States is a desirable home for many families around the globe seeking freedom, business and educational opportunities, and the security provided by a nation of laws. We cannot accept all of those who desire to enter through our ports, and as a result, a complex body of laws, rules and regulations has evolved in order to admit immigrants who serve the national interest.

Bob and Mary McLaughlin have, through extensive research and recent editing to incorporate the new immigration laws, produced a very comprehensive and useful immigration reference book.

The McLaughlins have presented the material in a well organized and easily understandable manner which can be followed by the non-lawyer. The book outlines immigration law, policy and practice in such a way that the general theory behind immigration law can be understood, while also giving specific information about substantive areas of law.

During my term as Commissioner of the Immigration and Naturalization Service, one of our goals was to simplify immigration procedures so that all persons would be able to avail themselves of immigration benefits without the need of an attorney. With the enactment of reform measures in 1986, 1990 and 1996, however, immigration laws have become more complicated and procedures more complex so that now, the immigration lawyer may be more necessary than before. While a reader with a specific immigration purpose should contact an immigration lawyer for advice, the McLaughlin book is well written and gives the reader a good idea where to start and how to negotiate the twists and turns necessary to achieve the benefits and opportunities available.

The subject of immigration is rapidly rising to the top of the world's agenda. This book represents a real service to many who are interested in this expanding and important field. It will certainly find its way, to the desks of many practitioners who specialize in immigration law. I recommend *USA Immigration & Orientation* to the reader, and commend the McLaughlins for their practical treatment and excellent organization of the immigration laws and procedures.

Gene McNary
Former Commissioner, Immigration and Naturalization Service
Attorney at Law
McNary, Morris & Smalley LLP.
Saint Louis, Missouri

Preface

USA Immigration & Orientation is packed with 500 pages of vital information including many important 1999 and early 2000 procedural changes to help you navigate through the very complex processes of immigrating and adjusting to U.S. living.

In fact, **USA Immigration & Orientation** is actually two books for the price of one. Both are written by people who have lived the immigration experience first hand and have written the book to share what they have learned with others who are about to follow. This is truly a layman's guide, by and for the layman.

The book provides information the authors wish they had been aware of both during and after the immigration formalities. Without knowing where to turn for answers, one can easily form the impression that the system has no answers or compassion. Yes, it is complex and often prolonged. It is also both thorough and fair. So, don't be discouraged and don't try shortcuts.

This book is our way of thanking the many civil servants whose patience and understanding turned our immigration process into an adventure with a happy ending. Countless hours of intensive interviews with experienced members of the Immigration and Naturalization Service (INS) and the Department of State (DOS) confirmed that the roles of these bodies are both independent and interdependent.

The patience and understanding of the DOS and INS officers have provided us with the basics of Book 1, Getting In which identifies all the immigration classification options and explains what is necessary to qualify for each. It also puts in perspective the role of the participating government agencies in the processing of applications for each classification.

Equal emphasis was placed on the many agencies in both the private and public sector which play a role in the adjustment to life in the United States. What you will read in Book 2, Getting Settled, is the result of the explanations of patient and helpful practitioners and participants in many fields.

Book 2, Getting Settled, deals with the social and administrative aspects of life in the United States. Health care, banking, taxation, buying or renting a home and many other important topics are explored.

Taken together, Book 1 and Book 2 offer a comprehensive reference about the intricacies of getting in and getting settled in the United States. Both are divided into five parts to help you concentrate on your most important needs.

The authors hope that **USA Immigration & Orientation** will save you both time and frustration as do your own research, identify your priorities, pick your classification, develop a realistic plan and decide whether you need to hire professionals who can help you deal with the specifics of your case, for a fee.

The authors welcome your input for use in future editions.

Acknowledgments

In compiling this reference book, the authors have interviewed expatriates from many countries, officials in government departments across the continent and experts in many other fields.

We would like to thank all who have contributed information and, in particular, the following persons and organizations without whose expertise this book would not be possible.

Barbara Artz	Parent, Brevard County, Florida
Susan Brandt	Department of State
John Bulger	Immigration and Naturalization Service
Joe Carroll	WKMG-TV
Marisa Carroll	Student, Brevard County, Florida
Mary Ann Carroll	Ribbitt Productions
Edward Christensen	Certified Public Accountant
Dan Dease	Xerographic
Karen Eckert	Immigration and Naturalization Service
Sally Gober	Department of State
Bill Greer	Space Coast Writers Guild
John Hogan	Immigration and Naturalization Service
Stella Jarina	Immigration and Naturalization Service
Krissa Jensen	
Bill Johnson	Board of Education, Brevard County, Florida
Neal Johnson	Barnett Bank
James Krampen	Specialty Risk International Insurance
Harvey Kahan	Kahan Associates Insurance Agents
Gary McLaughlin	WCCB-TV
James McLaughlin	Computall Services
Edward Odom	Department of State
Thomas Petersen	Petersen International Insurance Brokers
Dale Rumbarger	Department of State
Joan Smith	Department of State
Jean Sparks	Florida Institute of Technology
Samuel Tiranno	Immigration and Naturalization Service
Lemar Wooley	Immigration and Naturalization Service

Disclaimer

USA Immigration & Orientation is sold with the understanding that the publisher and authors are not engaged in rendering individual financial, legal or any other professional advice. If formal assistance is required, the services of a competent professional should be sought.

The authors of **USA Immigration & Orientation** have made every effort to research, refine and verify the information in this book, to make it as complete and accurate as possible and to present it from the layman's perspective.

Since U.S. immigration procedures and many aspects of everyday U.S. living are constantly changing, each situation may be unique and thus open to interpretation. Consequently, the publisher and authors assume no liability or responsibility to any person or entity with respect to any loss or damage caused, or alleged to be caused, directly or indirectly, by reading and acting on the information contained herein.

If you do not wish to be bound by the above, you may return this book with your sales receipt to the publisher for a refund of your purchase price.

Book 1

Getting In

Solving the Immigration Process

Book 1

Introduction

Book 1 of **USA Immigration & Orientation** is devoted to helping you–understand the complexities of immigration and selecting the process which best meets your aspirations. Book 1 also shows you how several U.S. government agencies work together to assess your situation and determine whether you and your adoptive country are right for each other.

As an indication of the extent of U.S. immigration, here are a few statistical surprises. The Immigration and Naturalization Service (INS):

In Fiscal Year 1999:

- Naturalized 872, 485 new citizens   *Ref: INS, October 28, 1999*
- Removed 176,900 people

In Fiscal Year 1998:

- Admitted 660,477 new immigrants (Green Card holders)
  - 357,037 were processed by the State Department abroad
  - 303,440 were processed by the INS in the United States

In Fiscal Year 1996:

- Counted 24. 8 million nonimmigrant admissions
- Estimated 5 million illegal aliens

After many meetings with helpful and knowledgeable practitioners from the Department of State (DOS) and the Immigration and Naturalization Service (INS), the authors are pleased to include several of their useful suggestions on this very first page.

Do:
- Follow both the spirit and the letter of the law
- Be wary of anyone who promises to get you a visa
- Be over-prepared for all interviews
- Make copies of every document you submit
- Take as much documentation as possible to support your case including previously submitted evidence

- Carefully read and follow the requirements for each application
- Try to process your application in the off-season (avoid summers if possible)
- Send all mail certified, return receipt requested

Don't:
- Try to beat the system, you won't win
- Accept free advice from friends, neighbors and non-professionals
- Delay the processing of other cases by calling the INS or DOS to ask questions which are answered by documents you have obtained

Book 1, Getting In, is set out in five parts which introduce you to the intent and structure of the immigration process as well as the various options available for both temporary and permanent residence in the United States.

Part I - Immigration Laws

Part I explains how laws in general and immigration laws in particular are made and implemented in the United States. Also included is a detailed explanation of the role of the principal players, the U.S. Departments of Justice, State and Labor.

Part II - Temporary Status

Part II is a major examination of the rationale and criteria for all of the available temporary or nonimmigrant visa classifications.

This part is divided into six chapters devoted to a groups of similar classifications which were each created to meet a specific need. The means to qualify for each classification is described on a step-by-step basis.

Part III - Green Cards

Part III contains four chapters which explain how to qualify for a Green Card.
- Family-Sponsored
- Employment-Based
- Diversity (DV) Lottery
- Refugee/Asylee

Part IV - U.S. Citizenship

Part IV discusses the acquisition, advantages and responsibilities of U.S. citizenship with 100 naturalization interview test questions.

Part V - Research Resources

Part V introduces sources of research information available to those who wish to further explore the particular aspect of the immigration process relevant to them.

Part I

Immigration Laws

The immigration laws of the United States control the admission of aliens and the distribution of benefits to qualified recipients.

A Brief History of Immigration Laws

The cornerstone of immigration and nationality laws has been, and remains, the Immigration and Nationality Act (INA or the Act) of June 27, 1952 which took effect on December 24, 1952. The INA, as it will be identified in this book, was a major revision of existing laws such as the earlier acts of 1917, 1924 and 1950.

Since 1952, a series of new laws has served to amend the INA without taking away from its status as the preeminent U.S. immigration and nationality legislation.

Some of the more notable amendments to the INA include:

- Immigration Reform and Control Act of 1986 (IRCA)
- Immigration Act of 1990 (IMMACT90)
- Miscellaneous and Technical Immigration and Naturalization Amendments of 1991 (MTINA)
- Technical Corrections Amendments Act of 1994
- Illegal Immigration Reform and Immigrant Responsibility Act of 1996 (IIRIRA96)
- American Competitiveness and Workforce Improvement Act of 1998

The Illegal Immigration Reform and Immigrant Responsibility Act of 1996 (IIRIRA96) contained several key provisions, some of which may not be implemented. Many are reported throughout Book 1 and summarized in Chapter 17. They include:

- Increased penalties for violations, and
- The tightening of procedures for:
  - employment verification
  - border security
  - recording the whereabouts of violators and legal aliens alike
  - education of the children of illegal immigrants

Changes are being phased in gradually, including several on April 1, 1997. Some of the changes relate to deportation and removal.

Also reported in Chapter 17 are the key provisions of the American Competitiveness and Workforce Improvement Act which was enacted in response to the 1998 H-1B crisis. The Act was designed to:

- Protect U.S. workers
- Temporarily increase the annual quota of H-1B workers until 2001
- Increase H-1B fees
- Tighten recruitment rules for H-1B-dependent employers
- Establish major penalties for employers who abuse the H-1B program
- Designate fees for job training of U.S. workers

To help you better understand the immigration process, Part I explores how immigration and other U.S. laws are made, published and regulated.

Chapter 1 - Making and Publishing Immigration Laws
- The origin and promulgation of immigration law

Chapter 2 - The Administration of Immigration Laws
- The agencies which regulate immigration law

Chapter 1

Making and Publishing Immigration Laws

Immigration is one of many areas of legal specialization with which the United States Congress must deal. To facilitate the reader's understanding of how immigration and other laws are created and enforced, the following brief overview of the process is included.

Public and Private Bills

Congress generates both public and private bills.

Public Bills

Public bills relate to public matters and deal with individuals only by classes.

Private Bills

Private legislation such as immigration and naturalization bills and claims against the government provide relief to individuals and institutions from the unanticipated implications of existing public laws.

There has been a dramatic decrease in private bills in recent years because Congress has given executive agencies increased authority to act on private matters.

How a Bill Becomes Law

Immigration and other private measures are referred to House and Senate subcommittees for processing.

After a private bill is reported out of committee, the floor action which takes place is reflected in the Congressional Record. It is signed by the Speaker of the House and the President of the Senate and sent to the President for signature into law or veto.

A bill may become law without the President's signature if he does not veto it within 10 days of being presented to him. However, if the Congress adjourns before that 10-day period ends, a "pocket veto" occurs and the bill does not become law.

In a regular veto, the President returns the bill to its originating chamber with his stated objections. A two-thirds vote in both chambers is needed to override the veto.

Publishing Laws

A **Slip Law** is published as an unbound pamphlet by the Office of the Federal Register. A number is assigned for public and private laws, and this notation runs sequentially through a Congress. Slip laws are competent evidence in all courts, tribunals and public offices.   *Ref: 1 USC 113*

Statutes at Large are a chronological arrangement of slip laws bound as sessional volumes and published at the end of each session. Immigration and other private laws are published in separate sections. These are also legal evidence of the laws contained in them.

The **United States Code (USC)** contains a consolidation of the general and permanent laws of the United States arranged according to subject matter under 50 title headings. The purpose of the USC is to present the laws in a concise and usable form without requiring recourse to the many volumes of the Statutes at Large containing the individual amendments. Title 8 of the United States Code is devoted to immigration matters.

The **Federal Register (FR)** publishes the general and permanent rules of the Executive departments and agencies of the Federal Government.

The **Code of Federal Regulations (CFR)** codifies all current orders, rules and regulations published in the Federal Register under 50 titles representing broad areas subject to Federal regulation.

As in the United States Code, Title 8 is devoted to immigration. It contains all current regulations issued by the Immigration and Naturalization Service, Department of Justice and is revised at least once per calendar year, as of January 1.

Title 8 of the Code of Federal Regulations, 8 CFR, is used as the main operating reference manual by INS officers in the field. It is kept up to date by the individual issues of the Federal Register. These two publications must be used together to determine the latest version of any given rule.

Title 22 of the Code of Federal Regulations, 22 CFR.40 et al is known as the State Department's **Foreign Affairs Manual (FAM)**. Volume 9 - Visas, referred to as 9 FAM throughout the book, serves as the basic policies and procedures source of the State Department, its major resource to meet its responsibility for the administration of immigration affairs overseas.

The FAM is updated on a regular basis and Transmittal Letters are issued to reflect the changing administrative guidelines in the Department of State.

Chapter 2

The Administration of Immigration Laws

The Immigration and Nationality Act (INA) regulates the admission of aliens into the United States and designates the Attorney General and the Secretary of State as the principal administrators of its provisions.   *Ref: 8 USC 1101 et seq.*

The INA also provides that an alien who seeks admission or status in certain immigrant or nonimmigrant classifications shall be excluded unless certification from the Secretary of Labor is received.

Each of the U.S. Government departments charged with administering the immigration and naturalization of aliens has a specific well-defined role to play.

Department of State (DOS)

The State Department advises the President on the formulation of foreign policy. As Chief Executive, the President has overall responsibility for the foreign policy of the United States.

The Secretary of State is the ranking member of the cabinet and fourth in line of presidential succession.   *Ref: DOS Fact Sheet, May 26, 1995*

The Department of State's Bureau of Consular Affairs, under the direction of one of 19 Assistant Secretaries, is responsible for:

- The administration and enforcement of the immigration and nationality laws which concern the State Department and its Foreign Service
- The protection and welfare of American interests abroad
- The protection and welfare of American citizens traveling or living abroad
- The issuance of passports to U.S. citizens
- The issuance of visas and related services to foreign nationals who wish to visit or reside in the U. S.   *Ref: DOS Fact Sheet, May 26, 1995*

The consular offices of the Department of State throughout the world are generally the initial contact for aliens who wish to come to the United States. DOS determines the type of visas for which aliens may be eligible and issues those visas.

The DOS uses the Foreign Affairs Manual (FAM) as its working procedures and interpretation reference manual in the administration of the immigration laws for which it is responsible. 9 FAM deals with immigration matters. *Ref: 22 CFR.40 et al.*

Department of Labor (DOL)

The Department of Labor is a vital component of the immigration process.

Since immigration law serves as a protection to U.S. workers, the DOL must determine whether an adequate pool of U.S. workers is available to meet the needs of U.S. commerce. Where a shortage of available qualified U.S. workers exists, the DOL must ensure that alien workers seeking admission are fully qualified and appropriately compensated.

Immigration law requires that the DOL be involved in the processing of cases involving certain temporary and permanent classifications. Depending on the classification, the process is called either Labor Certification or Labor Condition Application.   *Ref: INA 212(a)(5)(A)*

Department of Justice

While the first immigration office was created as far back as 1864, it was not until March 3, 1891 that President Benjamin Harrison signed the Immigration Act of 1891 into law thus establishing the first Federal immigration agency. The Naturalization Act of 1906 created the Bureau of Immigration and Naturalization with responsibility for administering and enforcing immigration laws, for supervising the naturalization of aliens and for keeping naturalization records. While the two functions were separated in 1913, they were reunited to stay in 1933 with the creation of the Immigration and Naturalization Service within the Labor Department. Finally, in 1940, the INS moved to the Justice Department where it remains.

Attorney General

As head of the Justice Department and responsible for the Immigration and Naturalization Service, the Attorney General is charged with the administration and enforcement of the Immigration and Nationality Act of 1952 with all of its amendments as well as all other laws relating to the immigration and naturalization of aliens, except the powers, functions, and duties conferred upon:

- The President
- The Secretary of State
- Officers of the Department of State
- Diplomatic or consular officers

Immigration and Naturalization Service (INS)
The INS mission is divided into four major functional areas:

- Facilitating the entry of legal visitors or immigrants
- Providing assistance to those seeking permanent resident status or naturalization
- Preventing unlawful entry, employment, or receipt of benefits
- Apprehending or removing those aliens who enter or remain illegally

The Attorney General has delegated to the Commissioner, the principal officer of the Immigration and Naturalization Service, authority to administer and enforce the Immigration and Nationality Act and all other laws relating to immigration and nationality as prescribed by 28 CFR 0.105.

The **Commissioner** shall be a citizen of the United States appointed by the President, by and with the advice and consent of the Senate.

Ref: INA 103; 8 USC 1103

The INS is divided into operational and management functions. Overall, policy and executive direction flows from INS headquarters at 425 I Street N.W., Washington, DC 20536 to 33 districts and 21 border patrol sectors throughout the United States. For operational purposes, the INS maintains four regional Service Centers to control the entry of aliens and three regional sectors which provide administrative support to the field offices as well as refugee offices in several foreign countries.

Ref: 48 FR 8039, February 25, 1983

The INS had 28,400 permanent full-time employees and an annual budget of nearly $4 billion in Fiscal Year 1999. It is the largest federal law enforcement agency.

The agency is governed by the Code of Federal Regulations and Operational Instructions. While the INA is the law, 8 CFR serves as the INS reference manual of working procedures and interpretations of laws within its jurisdiction.

Other Agencies

Several other federal government agencies such as the Customs Service, Selective Service, and the Internal Revenue play a major role after the formal immigration proceedings have been completed. Book 2 explains their functions in detail.

The Immigration Process - Step By Step

Parts II and III describe the role of these federal bodies in the processing of petitions and applications for both nonimmigrant or temporary status in Part II and immigrant or permanent status in Part III.

To help you understand the normal sequence of events, information is presented throughout Book 1 in the following chronological format.

Step 1 - Clearing the Department of Labor (DOL) in the U.S.

Some aliens require pre-clearance from the U.S. **Department of Labor (DOL)** if they wish to work in certain designated temporary or permanent immigration classifications. This usually involves verification of the aliens's credentials, willingness to pay the going rate for the type of work involved, and sometimes, the employer's inability to find qualified U.S. workers.

Step 2 - Clearing the Immigration and Naturalization Service (INS) - Initial Petition

Usually, a prospective employer or a family member will file a petition with the **Immigration and Naturalization Service (INS)** in the United States. However, in some cases, an alien may file a personal application and refugee candidates may file with the INS outside the United States.

Step 3 - Clearing the Department of State (DOS) Abroad

An alien may apply for a visa from the **Department of State (DOS)** at a U.S. Embassy or Consulate serving his or her home outside the United States. However, the consul who handles the application is not bound by an approved INS petition.

When approved, a visa signifies that an alien has been pre-screened abroad and found to be eligible to apply for admission in a specific classification.

Step 4 - Clearing the INS at a U.S. Port of Entry

When an alien arrives with a visa at a U.S. port of entry, jurisdiction switches from the State Department to the **Immigration and Naturalization Service**. At that point, an Immigration Inspector must be satisfied that the alien has the right type of visa and intends to engage in activities which are both permitted and consistent with the limitations of the visa. If satisfied, the inspector will grant entry into the United States in a particular "status" which sets out:

- One of the applicable temporary or permanent classifications
- A maximum duration of stay

To avoid confusion, both the "visa" issued abroad by the DOS and the "status" approved by the INS within the United States bear the same name. For example, a E visa issued abroad has the same effect and the same name as E status acquired on entry into the United States.

Step 5 - Extension or Change/Adjustment of Status

Depending on the classification, aliens living in the U.S. may be able to obtain an INS change or adjustment of status or extension, or a State Department visa extension without leaving the United States, if they are *In Status* when applying.

Status may be violated and deportation may result if an alien does any of the following:

- Remains beyond the expiration date of the status granted by the INS
- Engages in employment without authorization
- Engages in an activity which is not consistent with the status under which he or she was admitted

Part II

Temporary Status

M ost temporary classifications or categories are identified by a single letter identifier. Every letter from A to S is used plus extras such as NATO and TN (NAFTA). All are described in Part II.

Each classification has been created to meet a unique combination of needs and goals of aliens, employers and government alike. Employment is permitted in some, not all, classifications. So, choose your classification carefully.

When considering your classification, it is important to understand that U.S. immigration law is based on the premise that every alien shall be presumed to be an immigrant until he or she establishes entitlement to a nonimmigrant visa to the satisfaction of the consular officer or immigration inspector. H-1 and L visas do not require that commitment.   *Ref: INA 214(b)*

Applicants for entry usually must prove that they have a permanent residence and other strong ties abroad that would compel them to leave the United States when their temporary stay ends.   *Ref: DOS Publication 9772, June, 1990*

The State Department considers that the longer an applicant has been out of status, the greater the presumption of immigration. *Ref: DOS Policy March 20, 1996*

Try to find out as much as possible before starting an immigration application procedure. USA Immigration & Orientation identifies many sources of information including the internet. It may also be possible to call or meet an officer at certain times in an INS or consular office.

When phoning the INS or the State Department, have your file number or document identification number available along with a pencil and paper to take full notes of any instructions received.

How Nonimmigrant Classifications are Grouped in Part II

It is vital that you choose the classification which is best for you.

To make your choice easier, Part II has been grouped into six chapters. Each chapter assembles all the current nonimmigrant or temporary immigration classifications which address a similar need.

First, review the following list of chapters and the nonimmigrant classifications which they include to help you decide which best meets your needs and qualifications. Then, turn to the classifications which you feel may be the most suitable.

Chapter 3 - Visitor Classifications

- VWPP   Visa Waiver Pilot Program
- B-1/B-2   Temporary Visitor for Business or Pleasure
- Border Crossing Card - Mexicans and Canadians
- C-1/D   Alien in Transit / Crew member, Sea or Air
- *   Advance Parole
- TWOV   Transit Without Visa

Chapter 4- Educational Classifications

- F   Academic Student
- J   USIA Exchange Visitor
- M   Vocational or Non-Academic Student

Chapter 5- Business Professionals

- E   Treaty Trader or Investor
- H   Professional, Temporary Worker or Trainee
- L   Intra-Company Transferee
- TN   Treaty NAFTA Professional

Chapter 6 - Extraordinary/Internationally-Recognized Persons

- O   Alien of Extraordinary Ability in the Sciences, Arts, Education, Business, or Athletics
- P   Internationally-Recognized Athlete or Entertainer

Chapter 7 - Special Purpose Classifications

- I   Foreign Information Media Representative
- K   Marriage to U.S. Citizen
- Q   International Cultural Exchange Program Participant
- R   Alien in Religious Occupation
- S   Alien Witness and Informant
- *   Other Status (Humanitarian Parole, Retirement Visa)

Chapter 8 - Foreign Government Representative Classifications

- A   Senior Government Official
- C-2/C-3   Alien in Transit to United Nations and Foreign Government Official
- G   Government Representative to International Organization
- N   International Organization Family Member
- NATO   Representative of Member State

Admission Process

As noted in Part I, the process is usually carried out in several steps. What follows is a general overview of how the process evolves for a candidate for nonimmigrant status. For detailed information, you should refer to the section devoted to the specific nonimmigrant classification of interest to you.

Unless you are seeking H-1B or L status, be prepared to prove that you are not an intending immigrant and that you are entitled to a nonimmigrant visa. If you are unable to prove nonimmigrant intent, it may be necessary to post a bond with the Attorney General.   *Ref: 9 FAM 41.11*

Step 1 - Pre-clearance

Some classifications require pre-clearance before a petition may be filed.

An employer must apply for DOL approval before proceeding with petitions for H-1B, H-2 and some D visas. In those cases, an employer must apply for Labor Condition Application (LCA) for H-1B candidates, Labor Certification for H-2 candidates or file an attestation to allow foreign vessel crew members to do longshore work in Alaskan ports. In all cases, the DOL must be convinced that there is a need to admit an alien to carry out a temporary job, that there are no U.S. qualified citizens or residents available, that the going rate will be paid and the U.S. job market will not be adversely affected.

Aliens wishing to study in the United States also require a form of pre-clearance. There are three classifications from which to choose. Prior acceptance is required from an accredited institution in each case.

Step 2 - Clearing The Immigration and Naturalization Service (INS) - Initial Petition

If DOL clearance is not required, this is usually the first step. However, Canadian applicants for TN - NAFTA status may skip this step and file directly at a U.S. port of entry. Several INS fees were amended effective October 13, 1998.   *Ref: 63 FR 157*

Regardless, in this step, the employer or sponsor must usually file a petition and specified supporting documentation with the appropriate INS regional Service Center. Forms may be ordered from the INS by calling (800) 870-3676 or downloaded from the internet at http://www.ins.usdoj.gov/graphics/formsfee/forms

Documentation and supporting evidence includes:

- *INS forms*
    - nonimmigrant status, or
    - immigrant status
- *Fees*
    - appropriate fee(s) for classification being petitioned for
- *Passports and photographs*
    - passport valid for at least six months beyond intended stay
    - photographs 1½" square (37 mm square) showing right ear without head covering against a light background
- *Current and prior immigration status*
    - such as I-94
- *DOL approvals*
    - such as Labor Certification or Labor Condition Application
- *Professional credentials*
    - such as degrees and/or professional status
- *Employer's supporting documentation*
    - supporting letter confirming salary, function and source of funds
- *Proof of financial support or solvency*
    - Form I-134, Affidavit of support from family sponsor
    - own funding
- *Civil documents, including dependents*
    - birth
    - marriage
    - divorce
    - death of spouse
- *Police clearance*
    - verification of local police records which may include fingerprinting
- *Medical clearance*
    - if history of medical ineligibility
    - consular medical examination
- *Evidence that U.S. stay is temporary (intent to depart)*
    - binding family ties
    - return tickets
    - no intention to abandon residence abroad

The INS will now accept copies of certain documents such as diplomas and certificates if you submit a signed Form ER 750 which certifies that:

- Copies of original documents are exact and unaltered, and
- You will submit original documents if required

On approval, the INS will issue a Form I-797, Notice of Approval to the petitioner and notify the appropriate consulate if the case is to be processed abroad.

Aliens who are ineligible for entry as a nonimmigrant because of a drug conviction, criminal record, or other reason must file Form I-192, Application for Advance Permission to Enter as a Nonimmigrant with the $170 filing fee, 90 to 120 days in advance of their planned entry. A typical example is a long distance trucker with a drug conviction who must make trips into the United States as part of his or her job. It is important to remember that the United States does not recognize a pardon from a foreign country.   *Ref: INA 212(d)(3)*

Step 3 - *Clearing The Department Of State (DOS) Abroad*

Virtually all nonimmigrant visa classifications may be processed at U.S. Embassies or Consulates abroad.

Every alien seeking a nonimmigrant visa is required to apply in person before a consular officer except:

- Child under 14 years of age
- A, C-2, C-3, G or NATO
- Applicant for diplomatic or official visa
- B, C-1, H-1 or I
- J-1 who is a leader in a field of specialized knowledge or skill
- D ship or aircraft crew member with a qualifying employer's letter
- Any nonimmigrant category where the consular officer determines that a waiver of personal appearance is warranted   *Ref: 9 FAM 41.102*

The requirement to file Form OF 156 may be waived if the interview has been waived.   *Ref: 9 FAM 41.103*

The State Department has introduced a new rule which may allow aliens to select any consulate in their home country to process their visa application.

The usual application form required by the DOS is Optional Form 156 or OF 156, Nonimmigrant Visa Application. This may change as new legislation provides for the introduction of separate application forms for various classes of nonimmigrant admissions.   *Ref: IIRIRA96.634*

Form OF 156 is available in English, Spanish, German, French, Dutch, Korean, Thai or Indonesian from http://travel.state.gov/visa_services.html#*of156* and for use in Canada, the Philippines and the Netherlands.

Documentation and supporting evidence includes:

- *DOS form*
  - OF 156, Nonimmigrant Visa Application
- *Fees*
  - $45 non-refundable Machine-Readable Visa (MRV) fee collected at posts which issue MRVs
  - visa reciprocity fee equating to fees charged in similar circumstances in alien's home country (A, G, C-2/3, NATO exempt) (see http://travel.state.gov/reciprocity/index.htm for reciprocity fees)
  - visa filing fee may be waived by the Secretary of State for a nonimmigrant alien engaged in charitable activities in the U.S.
- *Passports and photographs*
  - passport valid for at least six months beyond intended stay (A, C-3, NATO exempt)
  - every applicant must furnish photograph(s) in the quantity required 1½" (37 mm) square in reasonable likeness showing full face (head covering may be permitted) against a light background signed on reverse   *Ref: 22 CFR 41.105 (a) (3)*
- *Current and prior immigration status*
  - such as I-94
- *Prior INS, DOL, USIA, academic approvals*
  - such as INS I-797, DOL Labor Certification or Labor Condition Application, I-20, IAP-66
- *Professional credentials*
  - such as degrees and/or professional status
- *Employer's supporting documentation*
  - letter confirming:
    - salary and source of funding
    - function
    - period of employment
- *Additional evidence*
  - purpose of trip
  - document outlining plans in U.S.
- *Proof of financial support or solvency*
  - arrangements to cover expenses in U.S. such as:
    - Form I-134, Affidavit of Support from family sponsor
    - own funding
- *Civil documents, including dependents*
  - birth
  - marriage
  - divorce
  - death of spouse

- *Police clearance*
  - police certificate if the consular officer has reason to believe that a police or criminal record may exist (A-1/2, C-3, G-1 to G-4, NATO-1 to NATO-4 and NATO-6 exempt)
- *Medical clearance:*
  - if history of medical ineligibility
  - if applying for K visa
  - if entering for medical treatment   *Ref: 9 FAM 41.108*
- *Evidence that U.S. stay is temporary (intent to depart)*
  - binding family ties
  - return tickets
  - no intention to abandon residence abroad

Unless the requirement is waived, each applicant for a nonimmigrant visa must be interviewed by a consular officer abroad. Based on the documentation presented, the consular officer shall determine the proper nonimmigrant classification and the alien's eligibility to receive a visa.   *Ref: 9 FAM 41.102*

Information on obtaining or renewing nonimmigrant visas may be obtained by calling (202) 663-1225. You may speak with a Visa Information Officer between 8:30 am and 5:00 pm, Eastern Time, Monday to Friday. You may also take advantage of the Auto-fax system by calling (202) 647-3000.

K interviews may not be waived.

Fingerprints are no longer taken at U.S. Consulates on a regular basis. The pilot fingerprint program sunsetted on May 1, 1998. Fingerprints will be taken if a criminal record comes up in a regular search of law enforcement database sources, at the request of the INS or if there is no other way to confirm the identity of an applicant.

Officers may refuse to accept applications for reasons unclear to the applicant. Don't be surprised and don't give up if you believe you are right.

When arriving for interviews at consular or INS offices, do not be afraid to ask for directions if you find the signs are confusing or not helpful. Be prepared to leave briefcases with security. As there may be a long wait, take a good book such as this one to read.

Grounds for Denial

Aliens are ineligible to obtain visas if the consular officer believes that any of the following impediments apply:

Examples	**Grounds**
• Physical or mental disorder posing a threat	• Health-related

- Criminal activity, convictions, prostitution
- Terrorist activity, adverse effect on foreign policy, past memberships
- Likely to become a public charge
- Lack of determination by Secretary of Labor
- Previously deported, stowaways
- Smugglers
- Draft dodgers

- Polygamists, international child abductors

- Criminal and related
- Security and related

- Public charge

- Labor certification

- Illegal entrants and immigration violators
- Missing required documents
- Permanently ineligible for citizenship
- Miscellaneous

State Department officials discourage dealing with U.S. Embassies and Consulates in third countries such as Mexico and Canada as they do not have the time or resources to verify information with authorities in your home country. You may be better served by dealing with a U.S. Embassy or Consulate in your country of residence or physical presence if you are living there or when you are home for a visit.

At a cost of $45, the U.S. Embassy or Consulate will place a Machine-Readable Visa (MRV), also called a foil or sticker, in the applicant's passport. The MRV is computer-readable and contains:

- Passport number
- Date of birth
- Nationality
- Entry: M (multiple) or 01 (single), 02 (double) or other numerical limit
- Date of issue
- Expiration date

Step 4 - Clearing the INS at a U.S. Port of Entry

INS Immigration Inspectors at a U.S. port of entry have the right and responsibility to ensure that all medical reports and other required documents are in order for entry under the chosen nonimmigrant classification. They do, after all, have the final responsibility for making a determination on your eligibility for entry in your desired classification regardless of whether you have a DOS visa in your hand.

While Immigration Inspectors are not expected to second guess the work of other agencies with whom you have dealt, they must be satisfied that you have supplied all the necessary paperwork along the way. To expedite processing, you are encouraged to bring copies or originals of all documents which you have filed in previous steps.

With the exception of entries in E and K status, Canadians are not required to have obtained Department of State visas (MRVs).

In special cases, an alien may apply for and obtain a waiver of the visa and passport requirement under INA 212(d)(4)(A) without the prior concurrence of the Department of State if, either prior to the alien's embarkation abroad or upon arrival at a port of entry, the responsible District Director of the Immigration and Naturalization Service (INS) in charge of the port of entry concludes that:

- The alien is unable to present the required documents because of an unforeseen emergency, and
- The alien's claim of emergency circumstances is legitimate, and
- Approval of the waiver would be appropriate under all the attendant facts and circumstances

Ref: FR Vol. 64, No. 103, May 28, 1999; 8 USC 1104 41.2(j);22 CFR 41 and 42

Applicants are cautioned to be truthful and avoid raising suspicions as Immigration Inspectors who suspect fraud may order "Expedited Removal" which bars an alien from entering the U.S. for five years. In some INS districts, the Immigration Inspector at the port of entry must obtain permission from the district duty officer before initiating this process.

Documentation and supporting evidence includes:

- *INS forms*
  - nonimmigrant status, or
  - immigrant status
- *Passports and photographs*
  - passport valid for at least six months beyond intended stay
  - photographs 1½" square (37 mm) square showing right ear without head covering against a light background
- *Current and prior immigration status*
  - such as I-94, Arrival/Departure Record
- *Prior DOL and DOS approvals*
  - DOL Labor Condition Application or Labor Certification
  - DOS Machine-Readable Visa (MRV) in passport
- *Professional credentials*
  - such as university diploma
- *Employer's supporting documentation*
  - supporting letter confirming salary, function and source of funds
- *Proof of financial support or solvency*
  - Form I-134, Affidavit of Support from family sponsor
  - own funding

- *Civil documents, including dependents*
  - birth
  - marriage
  - divorce
  - death of spouse
- *Police clearance*
- *Medical clearance*
  - if history of medical ineligibility
  - Consular medical examination
- *Evidence that U.S. stay is temporary (intent to depart)*
  - binding family ties
  - return tickets
  - no intention to abandon residence abroad

Entry Formalities

Your I-94 or passport may be stamped for single-entry or multiple-entry depending on how a U.S. citizen is treated in similar circumstances in your home country and may differ from the terms of the visa issued by the State Department.

Citizens of Iran have only single-entry visas which are canceled on entry. However, nationals of other countries with single-entry visas may be able to visit Canada or Mexico for fewer than 30 days.

There is a fee of $6 for an I-94 although this fee is waived for some aliens such as diplomats or those entering under the Visa Waiver Pilot Program.

- When meeting an INS Immigration Inspector:
  - tell the *whole* story of what you are trying to accomplish
  - have a passport, birth certificate, I-94 in your hands
  - have all other required documents immediately available
  - a Driver's License is not acceptable proof of immigration status

An alien who makes an application for a visa or for admission into the United States is required to possess a passport that:

- Authorizes the alien to return to the home country, and
- Is valid for a minimum of six months beyond the date of the expiration of the initial period of the applicant's admission or contemplated stay in the United States, or
- Is issued by a country which the U.S. accepts as having agreed that their passports will be valid for reentry up to six months after expiring

Ref: FR Volume 63, Number 196, October 9, 1998

Grounds of Inadmissibility

There are a number of Grounds of Inadmissibility including:

- Being present in the U.S. without having been admitted or paroled

- Being in the U.S. unlawfully for more than 180 days after April 1, 1997
- Inciting terrorist activity to cause death or serious bodily harm
- Lacking a legally binding family-sponsored immigrant's affidavit of support
- Nurses failing to have a certificate from the Commission on Graduates of Foreign Nursing Schools or approved equivalent
- Intending immigrants without the required vaccinations
- Failing to attend a proceeding to determine inadmissibility
- Falsely claiming to be U.S. citizens
- Violating the new student visa terms
- Accompanying other aliens inadmissible for medical reasons
- Voting in a U.S. election
- Renouncing U.S. citizenship to avoid taxation

Ref: INS Fact Sheet, March 26, 1997

If you must enter despite your inadmissibility as a nonimmigrant, a Form I-192, Application for Advance Permission to Enter as a Nonimmigrant with the $170 filing fee plus an additional $25 for fingerprints must be filed with the District Director and approved before you may enter. Processing may take four months. Form I-601 should only be used for immigrant visa cases. Be prepared to offer such proof as:

- Fingerprint evidence
- A list of convictions and dispositions
- A letter from your employer with reasons why you must enter the U.S.
- A letter of clearance from your physician if narcotics are on your record
- Letters of reference

Counting from April 1, 1997, aliens seeking to enter the U.S. after being out of status (unlawfully present) in the U.S. from six months to a year are barred from admission for three years while those out of status for one year or more are barred for ten years.   *Ref: IIRIRA96.301*

All address changes must be reported to the INS within ten days. Either a letter or Form AR-11 may be used. Form AR-11 may be ordered online or by telephone from the INS Forms Center and is to be handed in to the local INS office.

Long-range border control plans

Looking ahead, the INS has been mandated by the Illegal Immigration and Immigrant Responsibility Act of 1996 (IIRIRA96) to phase in several changes dealing with the entry of aliens over the next few years. Some examples include:

- Introducing border crossing documents with machine-readable biometric identifiers [104]
- Introducing an automated system to match the exit and entry record of every alien [110]
- Increasing the penalties for:
  - illegal entry [105]

- alien smuggling [203]
- document fraud [211 and 212]

In keeping with this mandate, airlines have started issuing an automated I-94 card to passengers who are not U.S. citizens, Green Card holders or aliens with visas when they check in for flights to the United States. Under the new system, the card is to be given to the immigration officer at the port of entry and a new departure record card is to be generated and turned in by the alien traveler when departing the U.S.

Step 5 - Application for Employment

The rules for accepting employment vary from classification to classification. However, as a general principle, employment must be temporary and, in certain cases, it should not displace a U.S. citizen or legal permanent resident and the alien should be paid the prevailing rate for the specific type of work in the area.

Students may accept employment under strict conditions including prior approval.

To make sure that there are no misunderstandings, read the employment parameters of your chosen classification and discuss your conclusions with the DOL and/or the INS.

The IIRIRA96 and the new H-1B legislation have tightened alien employment practices in an effort to protect the U.S. worker..

Some examples include:

- Increasing the number of unlawful employment investigators [131]
- Increasing the fines for hiring illegal aliens [203]
- Establishing three pilot programs of employment eligibility confirmation [403]
- Establishing a toll-free telephone or electronic media to provide confirmation on an alien's identity and authorization to be employed [404]
- Social Security advising the INS of aliens not authorized to work [414]
- A new act in 1998 which:
  - increases the annual quota of temporary professionals for three years
  - requires major employers of H-1Bs to attempt to employ qualified U.S. workers before employing foreign workers
  - introduces a $500 filing fee, a training program for low-income students and stiffer penalties for infractions

Normally, a Form I-765, Application for Employment Authorization is submitted to the INS regional Service Center having jurisdiction over your location. In 1997, the INS began issuing Form I-766 Employment Authorization Document (EAD) cards which are meant to be more tamper proof. Form I-688A and I-688B EADs are being phased out.

Step 6 - Application for Renewal or Change of Status

Application to the INS within the United States

Aliens living in the United States as legal nonimmigrants may be able to renew their temporary status or change to another classification without leaving the United States. Usually, this is done by filing with the INS. Frequently, either Form I-539, Application to Extend/Change Nonimmigrant Status or Form I-129, Petition for a Nonimmigrant Worker is used, depending on the classification and whether the petition is on behalf of the principal alien or a dependent.

Application for renewal or change of status may be filed and the alien remain in the United States during the grace period which follows a period of admission. However, the alien may not work until approval is received.

To avoid unnecessary problems, be sure to:

- Use forms that are not out of date
- Fill out the forms correctly and completely
- Enclose the correct filing fee and documents
- Sign all papers requiring a signature
- Answer all questions, if not applicable, answer N/A
- Make a checklist and mark off each item that must be remembered
- Not conceal information or submit false information or documents
- Keep photocopies of all papers filed
- Send all mail certified, return receipt requested

INS Regional Service Centers - Where to File

Generally, an alien filing an application for an extension of status or a change to another temporary or permanent classification, should file the application with the INS regional Service Center having jurisdiction over his or her place of residence.

It should also be noted that certain types of transactions must be filed at one specific Service Center. For example, most Reentry Permits are to be filed with the Nebraska Service Center.

The following list is included for reference only. Always check the required INS address before submitting any paperwork.

Vermont Service Center

75 Lower Welden Street
Saint Albans, VT 05479-0001

(802) 527-4913

Serving: Connecticut, Delaware, District of Columbia, Maine, Maryland, Massachusetts, New Hampshire, New Jersey, New York, Pennsylvania, Puerto Rico, Rhode Island, Vermont, the Virgin Islands, Virginia, West Virginia.

Texas Service Center

4141 St. Augustine Road   7701 N. Stemmons Freeway
Dallas, TX 75227   Dallas, TX 75247
(214) 381-1423   (214) 767-7770

Serving: Alabama, Arkansas, Florida, Georgia, Kentucky, Louisiana, Mississippi, New Mexico, North Carolina, Oklahoma, South Carolina, Tennessee, Texas.

California Service Center

P.O. Box 30111
24000 Avila Road
Laguna Niguel, CA 92607-0111
(949) 831-8427

Serving: Arizona, California, Guam, Hawaii, Nevada.

Nebraska Service Center

100 Centennial Mall North
Room B-26, Lincoln, NE 68508
(402) 323-7830

Serving: All other states.

Note: With the exception of the initial NAFTA application which may be made by Canadians at a U.S. port of entry, all Mexican and Canadian TN (NAFTA) applications should be filed with the Director of the Northern Service Center.

A Nonimmigrant L or Immigrant Alien Worker petition should be mailed to the Eastern Service Center if the beneficiary will be located within the jurisdiction of either the Eastern or Southern Service Centers. Otherwise petitions should be filed with either the Western or Northern Service Centers, as defined above.

Applications for Amerasians and special immigrant juveniles should be filed at the local INS office having jurisdiction over the alien's future place of residence.

Visa Revalidation by the Department of State (DOS)

After the INS has extended your stay, your visa may need to be renewed before attempting to reenter the United States from a business or pleasure trip of more than 30 days outside the contiguous United states and Canada. Depending on how U.S. citizens are treated in your home country in similar circumstances, your original visa may have been restricted to a limited number of entries and short period of validity. If so, you need to renew your visa. As visas are a State Department document, they cannot be issued at an INS-operated port of entry. Only Canadians in E status require State Department issued visas for reentry to the U.S.

Application for visa renewal may be made at a U.S. Embassy or Consulate in your home country. Revalidations of Third-Country Nationals (TCNs) may also be made at a U.S. Consulate in Mexico or Canada by calling (900) 443-3131 for an appointment. A, G, E, H, I, L, O, P and NATO classifications may be renewed by mail by the DOS in the United States. Tourist visas and student visas may not.

It is not possible to obtain expedited processing or status reports. If you do not have time to get your visa renewal in the U.S., you should apply in person to the consular office of the country of destination.

Documentation and supporting evidence includes:

- *DOS form*
  - OF 156, Nonimmigrant Visa Application
- *Fees*
  - $45 non-refundable Machine-Readable Visa (MRV) fee
  - visa reciprocity fee equating to fees charged in similar circumstances in alien's home country
- *Passport and photographs*
  - passport valid for at least six months beyond intended stay
  - passport-size photographs for each applicant
- *Current and prior immigration status*
  - original current I-94 (no copies)
  - copy of I-171C (H's or L's) or I-797 Petition Approval Notice
- *Employer's supporting documentation*
  - detailed letter identifying:
    - the employee
    - his or her position
    - travel itinerary

When a fee is charged for visa reciprocity, include two certified checks or money orders, one for the visa application and one for the reciprocity charge. Personal checks cannot be accepted.

Further recorded information may be obtained by calling (202) 663-1213. It may be possible to speak with an officer between 2 and 4 pm, Monday to Friday.

An alien living in the United States or Canada must pay a fee for a call to a central number to obtain visa information or book a visa appointment interview with a consular officer at any of the U.S. Consulates along the U.S. border with Canada or Mexico. The system is run by a contractor in Canada and can be reached by calling:

- (900) 443-3131 to book an appointment from the U.S.
- (900) 656-2222 for operator-assisted visa information from the U.S.
- (900) 451-2778 to book an appointment from Canada
- (900) 451-6663 for operator-assisted visa information from Canada

- (900) 451-6330 for recorded visa information from Canada
- (888) 840-0032 to make an appointment (pay for service)
- (888) 611-6676 to cancel an appointment (toll-free)

Operators are available to make appointments from 7 am to 10 pm, Eastern Time, Monday to Friday.

Appointments may also be booked on the internet at http://www.nvars.com. Each appointment costs $CDN 20 charged to a major credit card.

The contractor will send the applicant the appropriate forms, instructions about what is needed at their interview and confirmation of the details of the appointment. It should only be necessary to contact a consulate for information not provided by the contractor.

At the time of writing, depending on which consulate is involved, appointments were being made between one day and two weeks or more in advance. The advance booking service is available for all of the following consulates except Matamoros. Walk-ins are no longer permitted at consulates in Canada.

Tijuana, Mexico
The U.S. Consulate-General is located at Tapachula 96, 22420 Tijuana, Baja California Norte, across the border from San Diego, California. Telephone: 52 66 81-7400.

Matamoros, Mexico
The U.S. Consulate is located at Tamaulipas Calle Primera 2002, Matamoros Mexico, across the border from Brownsville, Texas. Telephone: 52 88 12-4402. Central booking appointments are not made for this U.S. Consulate.

Ciudad Juarez, Mexico
The U.S. Consulate-General is located at Chihuahua, Avenue Lopez Mateos 924N 32000, Ciudad Juarez across the border from El Paso, Texas. No Mexican visa is necessary to go to the consulate. Telephone: 52 16 11-3000.

Vancouver, B.C., Canada
The U.S. Consulate-General is located at 1095 West Pender Street, 21st Floor, Vancouver, BC V6E 2M6. Telephone: (604) 685-4311.

Calgary, Alberta, Canada
The U.S. Consulate-General is located at 615 Macleod Trail, S.E., Room 1000, Calgary, AB T2G 4T8. Telephone: (403) 266-8962.

Toronto, Ontario, Canada
The U.S. Consulate-General is located at 360 University Avenue, Toronto, Ontario M5G 1S4. Telephone: (416) 595-1700.

Ottawa, Ontario, Canada

Visas are issued by the Consular section of the U.S. Embassy at 85 Albert Street, Suite 805, Ottawa, ON. Mailing address: 100 Wellington Street, Ottawa, ON K1P 5T1. Telephone: (613) 238-4470 ext. 300.

Montréal Québec, Canada

The U.S. Consulate is located at 1155 St-Alexandre St. Montréal, QC, H2Z 1Z2. Telephone: (514) 398-9695, extension 402.

Québec City, Québec, Canada

The U.S. Consulate-General is located at 2, Place Terrasse Dufferin, Québec, QC G1R 4T9. Telephone: (418) 692-2095 or 692-4640.

Halifax, Nova Scotia, Canada

The U.S. Consulate-General is located at 2000 Barrington Street, Suite 910, Cogswell Tower, Halifax, NS B3J 3K1. Telephone: (902) 429-2480 or 429-2485.

Approved out-of-district visas generally will be ready for pickup by specified times on the following business day.

You may also call (800) 283-4356 for a list of all (900) and (800) visa information lines.

General information is available from the American Citizen Services Consular Information Telephone Service by calling (800) 529-4410 from the United States or Canada.

When police clearance abroad is required, the processing U.S. Consulate will check names against a U.S. law enforcement data base. If further checking is required, fingerprints will be taken at the Consulate and processed by the FBI. The Consulate may waive any processing fee. Further details are contained in visa processing information sent to applicants. Information on the status of an FBI fingerprint check may be obtained by calling (304) 625-5590. INS officers work in conjunction with FBI officers.

Chapter 3

Visitor Classifications

F oreign nationals who meet the intent of the law may enter the United States as visitors for varying periods and purposes. Most, but not all visitors are required to obtain visas.

In general, visitors are those aliens who are coming to the United States:
- For a relatively short period, and
- Will not become either temporary or permanent residents

Since this chapter deals with the vacations, business trips and brief stop overs, you need to review the following criteria before deciding which option applies to your situation:
- The purpose of your trip
- The duration of your trip
- Your home country

Vacationers who will leave after a set period are easy to characterize as visitors. They have different options depending on how long they will stay and which country they are from.

People on business trips are more difficult to categorize as they may require more formal visa and status arrangements.

Aliens who are passing through the country constitute a third group. Their status depends on why they are passing through and what they plan to do while they are in the United States.

Canadians and Mexicans are visa exempt in certain circumstances.

Visitors from several other countries may also come to the United States without a visa if their country is a participant in the U.S. tourist promotion Visa Waiver Pilot Program.

VWPP

Visa Waiver Pilot Program

The Visa Waiver Pilot Program (VWPP) permits nationals from designated countries who participate in the VWPP to apply for admission to the United States for 90 days or less as nonimmigrant visitors for business or pleasure, without first obtaining a B-1/B-2 nonimmigrant visa.   *Ref: INA 217*

The Attorney General, in consultation with the Secretary of State, is authorized to establish a pilot program which waives the necessity of obtaining a visa by an alien who meets the following requirements:

- Seeking entry as a visitor for pleasure or business
- Entering for 90 days or less
- National of a pilot program country   *Ref: 9 FAM 31.2(l)*

All other entries may require the issuance of a visa.

Aliens entering under the terms of the Visa Waiver Pilot Program are called Visa Exempt. However, since they are limited to 90 days, it may be preferable to enter with a visa if there is a possibility of requesting an extension or change to another status.

The program has expired and been extended several times. In May, 2000 it had expired again and was awaiting a further extension. At that time, the INS was continuing to issue I-94Ws under special internal procedures with the CP designation. Congress was also considering making the program permanent.

Regular sub-categories are:

- WB - Visa Waiver, Business
- WT - Visa Waiver, Tourist

To qualify, a country must:

- Extend a reciprocal privilege to U.S. citizens
- Have a nonimmigrant visa refusal rate of less than 2 percent of its nationals over the previous two fiscal year period
- Have a nonimmigrant visa refusal rate of less than 2.5 percent of its nationals in either fiscal year
- Have a machine-readable passport program

In May, 2000, entry was available to the following countries:

Andorra	Iceland	Portugal **
Argentina	Ireland	San Marino
Australia	Italy	Singapore **
Austria	Japan	Slovenia
Belgium	Liechtenstein	Spain
Brunei	Luxembourg	Sweden
Denmark	Monaco	Switzerland
Finland	the Netherlands	United Kingdom*
France	New Zealand	Uruguay **
Germany	Norway	

*   United Kingdom includes only British citizens who have the unrestricted right of permanent abode in England, Scotland, Wales, Northern Ireland, the Channel Islands, and the Isle of Man.

**   Effective August 9, 1999. Added by interim rule.

Ref: 64 FR 42006

Citizens of a lesser number of countries may visit Guam for up to 15 days under the Visa Waiver Pilot Program without first obtaining a nonimmigrant visitor visa.

Admission

Single Step - Clearing the INS at a U.S. Port of Entry

A passport is necessary and, unless you are entering overland from Canada or Mexico, you may need to produce a round trip ticket when you enter.

Aliens from Visa Waiver Pilot Program countries have special rules. Airlines which carry them to the United States are required to check their passengers for eligibility to enter the United States before allowing them to board their flight. An I-94W, Arrival/Departure Record is distributed during the flight. Passengers fill out the form and have it stamped by an INS Immigration Inspector at a U.S. port of entry. The Form I-94W may be stamped Multiple Entry and a $6 fee paid.

Documentation and supporting evidence includes:
- *INS form*
  - completed and signed Form I-94W, Arrival/Departure Record
- *Fee*
  - $6
- *Passport*
  - passport valid for at least six months beyond intended stay

- *Proof of financial support or solvency*
  - proof of financial solvency
- *Special conditions*
  - be seeking entry into the U.S. for business or pleasure
  - waive the right to a hearing of exclusion or deportation
  - not be a threat to U.S. welfare, health, safety or security
  - not have failed to comply with the conditions of any previous visa waiver admission
  - not ineligible under INA
  - not change status, work or study
- *Evidence that U.S. stay is temporary (intent to depart)*
  - if entering by air or sea:
    - have a round-trip transportation ticket issued on a carrier that has a signed an agreement with the U.S. government to participate in the waiver program
    - arrive in the United States aboard such a carrier
                                           Ref: 8 CFR 217, 60 FR 15855, April 1, 1995

Canadian citizens and permanent residents living in Canada do not require B-2 tourist visas and passports to enter for up to six month periods.
                                           Ref: DOS Publication 10311, November, 1995

Mexican nationals with a border crossing identification card do not need a visa and passport when applying for admission as a temporary visitor for business or pleasure.   *Ref: DOS TL:Visa-94, 9-30-94*

B

Temporary Visitor
for Business or Pleasure

T he B classification is reserved for those who have a home in a foreign country where they will return after a short stay in the U.S. and their stay is for:
- Business - to attend meetings, buy goods, negotiate contracts, act as representative of a foreign employer
- Pleasure - to tour, visit friends or family, sightsee   *Ref: ER 806 3-8-94*

Sub-categories are:
- B-1 - Temporary Visitor for Business
- B-2 - Temporary Visitor for Pleasure
                Ref: INA 101(a)(15)(B); 9 FAM 41.12, 41.31

Visitors may be admitted for professional or commercial endeavors but not employment. Although compensation must be earned and paid from abroad, B-1 and B-2 scholars who in engage in academic activities may receive honoraria in exchange for services that benefit an academic institution provided that the student has not received honoraria from more than five institutions during the previous six months.
                Ref: ACWIA96; INS memorandum, November 30, 1999

Visa Waiver Country business visitors may be able to avoid the necessity of obtaining status in this classification.

Canadians and Mexicans also have special status. They are covered under four nonimmigrant classifications of the North American Free Trade Agreement (NAFTA) including B, Temporary Visitor for Business or Pleasure.

B-1 Visitor for Business
Aliens with B status are not permitted to accept employment during their stay in the United States.

B-2 Visitor for Pleasure
A B-2 is usually the appropriate classification when a tourist visa becomes necessary. It is used when an alien enters for activities of a recreational character including tourism, amusement, visits with friends or relatives, rest, medical treatment and activities of a fraternal, social or service nature.   *Ref: 9 FAM 41.31(2)*

If you are inviting a friend or relative to visit the United States, the INS suggests that you send a personal letter of invitation and a completed Form I-134, Affidavit of Support to the person abroad. These and personal documents which show ties to their home country should be taken to the nearest U.S. Consulate.   *Ref: ER-722*

Intending student status is permitted for aliens who enter the U.S. in B-2 status to visit schools which may be of interest. In these cases, if your B-2 is issued with the annotation "Intending Student" and, after being accepted by an accredited school, you may apply for a change of status to one of the student classifications without leaving the United States.

Medical treatment for U.S. visitors is permitted. Be prepared to produce a letter from a U.S. doctor who will undertake treatment and from a specialist in your home country confirming that treatment is not available there. Also, be prepared to prove that you have the necessary funds to pay for your treatment and living expenses.

Medical externships are permitted on B-2 visas. You may observe but may not be paid or provide any direct patient care.

Seeking employment is permitted although you may be under more scrutiny if there is any feeling that you may not leave the U.S. by the end of your period of admittance. Factors considered on whether you will be admitted include your:

- Financial support
- Intent to depart
- Commitment to remain within the terms of your admittance

Proof which may be required includes your:

- Residential lease or home ownership in your home country
- Bank statements
- Utility bills
- Employer's letter

Admission Process

Step 1 - Clearing the Department of State (DOS) Abroad

If you are not Canadian, Mexican or from a Visa Waiver country, you should generally apply for your visitor visa at the U.S. Embassy or Consulate having jurisdiction over your place of permanent residence. Although you are permitted to apply at any consular office abroad, it may be more difficult to qualify for the visa outside your country of permanent residence

Ref: DOS Publication 10311, November, 1995

Visitors for Business or Pleasure usually obtain a visa from a U.S. Consulate in their home country. The visa may be good for applications for visits over periods of up to ten years by aliens who are:

- Nationals of countries that offer a reciprocal treatment of U.S. citizens
- In possession of a valid passport
- Bona fide visitors and will continue to enter the United States only for such purpose for an indefinite period of time   *Ref: 9 FAM 41.112*

Documentation and supporting evidence includes:

- *DOS form*
  - OF 156, Nonimmigrant Visa Application
- *Fees*
  - $45 non-refundable Machine-Readable Visa (MRV) fee collected at posts which issue MRVs
  - visa reciprocity fee equating to fees charged in similar circumstances in alien's home country
- *Passport and photographs*
  - passport valid for at least six months beyond intended stay
  - two photographs 1½" square (37 mm) square showing full face without head covering, against a light background
- *Employer's supporting documentation*
  - letter confirming function, amount and source of salary
- *Special conditions*
  - classifiable as a visitor under U.S. law
  - purpose of the trip
- *Proof of financial support or solvency*
  - letters confirming your financial support, if applicable
  - letters of invitation from hosting relatives or friends
  - confirmation of participation in planned tours
- *Additional evidence*
  - classifiable as a visitor under U.S. law
  - purpose of the trip
- *Evidence that U.S. stay is temporary (intent to depart)*
  - binding family ties
  - employment abroad
  - copy of return tickets
  - no intention to abandon residence abroad

A Machine-Readable Visa (MRV) valid for entry or entries for up to ten years is placed in the applicant's passport but a visa may be placed on Form OF 232, Nonimmigrant Visa Stamp in some circumstances.

A criminal record makes an applicant inadmissible.

The Form OF 156 and any additional evidence furnished by the alien shall be retained in the consular files.   *Ref: 9 FAM 41.113*

Step 2 - *Clearing the INS at a U.S. Port of Entry*

Application for entry should be made at a U.S. port of entry no later than the expiration date on the visa.

The bearer of the visa is subject to inspection by an INS Immigration Inspector who has the authority to determine how long a visitor may stay or deny admission. To lessen this risk, a visitor should carry any evidence originally presented when the visa was issued by the consulate abroad, unless entry is based on the 90-day Visa Waiver Pilot Program.

A Visitor for Pleasure is now automatically admitted for six months as an administrative convenience. However, an Immigration Inspector has the discretion to admit for up to 12 months. It is usually wise to pay $6 for an I-94 as proof of the 12 month entry. Visitors for Business usually obtain status for a maximum of 12 months.

It is important to tell the truth about your reason for coming to avoid the risk of expedited removal which comes with an automatic five-year ban on future entry. It is acceptable to be looking for work but very important to prove that you do not intend to work, that you have a permanent residence abroad and you intend to depart the U.S. by the expiration date of your visitor status.

It is not acceptable to say that you are on vacation when your real intent is to get married. That is seen as fraudulent and carries serious consequences. On the other hand, if you suddenly have an unanticipated change of plans such as getting married, you may be able to change status without leaving the United States. However, it must be unanticipated and you should be able to prove it.

Option 1 - *Mexicans and Canadians*

Under the terms of NAFTA, both Mexican and Canadian citizens and permanent residents may apply directly at a U.S. port of entry without obtaining employment authorization and without numerical restriction provided that:

- They comply with other immigration measures applicable to temporary entry
- Their entry does not affect adversely:
  - the settlement of any labor dispute at the place of employment
  - the employment of any person involved in the labor dispute

Canadian citizens and permanent residents living in Canada do not require B visas and passports when they apply for admission as a temporary visitor for business.

Ref: DOS Publication 10311, November, 1995

Mexican nationals are now issued Form I-94, Arrival/Departure Record instead of Form I-444, Mexican Border Visitors Permit for visits up to six months. An unexpired passport, State Department Laser Visa or INS "Mica" must still be presented.

Documentation and supporting evidence includes:

- *Proof of Citizenship*
  - passport or other proof of citizenship
- *Employer's supporting evidence (B-1)*
  - how the business person will be engaged
  - description of the purpose of entry
  - the proposed business activity is international in scope
  - the business person is not seeking to enter the local market, including:
    - the primary source of remuneration for the proposed business activity is outside the territory of the United States
    - the business person's principal place of business and the actual place of accrual of profits, at least predominantly, remain outside the United States (proof is normally an oral declaration or, if required, a letter of attestation from the employer)

Ref: NAFTA Annex 1603

A Form I-797 is not issued for B status.

Option 2 - Non-NAFTA

The expiration date on the visa is the last day you may apply at a U.S. port of entry for permission to enter the United States.

The decision on whether to admit you is up to an INS Immigration Inspector who may refuse admission if something is discovered which is contrary to your declared intention.

Grounds for Exclusion include:

- Discovery of documents indicating the applicant is planning to get married and live in the United States
- Past criminal convictions
- Past immigration violations
- Certain diseases

Documentation and supporting evidence includes:

- *INS form*
  - I-94, Arrival/Departure Record
- *Fee*
  - $6
- *Passport*
  - passport valid for at least six months beyond intended stay

- *Prior DOS approval*
  - DOS Machine-Readable Visa (MRV) in passport
- *Professional credentials*
  - qualifications need not be proven
- *Evidence to support request*
  - employer's letter explaining role in project, source of salary (B-1), or
  - letter of invitation (B-2)
- *Proof of financial support or solvency*
  - Form I-134, Affidavit of Support from family or friend sponsor
  - own funding
- *Evidence that U.S. stay is temporary (intent to depart)*
  - binding family ties
  - employment abroad
  - copy of return tickets
  - no intention to abandon residence abroad

If your admission is approved, your Form I-94, Arrival/Departure Record will be validated for a maximum of twelve months in B-2, Temporary Visitor for Pleasure status or 12 months in B-,1, Temporary Visitor for Business status beginning on the date of entry. The charge for issuing the B is approximately the same as is charged to U.S. citizens in your home country.   *Ref: DOS Publication 10311, November, 1995*

A Form I-797 is not issued for B status.

An alien may request a written statement of the factual and legal reasons for denial and a copy may be sent to the alien's attorney for review.

Step 3 - Revalidation/Extension or Change of Status by the INS within the United States

You should file with the INS regional Service Center having jurisdiction over your place of residence at least 45 days before your stay expires for either:

- An extension of B status
- Change of status from another classification to B
  Ref: INS Instructions - Form I-539; DOS Publication 10311, November, 1995

It may be possible to obtain a change of status without leaving the country, depending on the circumstances. Once your extension application is filed, you remain in status until a decision is made.

Documentation and supporting evidence includes:

- *INS form*
  - I-539, Application to Extend/Change Nonimmigrant Status
  - supplement for dependents

- *Fee*
  - filing fee of $120
- *Current and prior immigration status*
  - original Form I-94, Nonimmigrant Arrival/Departure Record
- *Evidence to support request*
  - employer's detailed written explanation of why an extension is required
  - other supporting documentation to extend Visitor for Pleasure
- *Proof of financial support or solvency*
  - proof of financial support
- *Evidence that U.S. stay is temporary (intent to depart)*
  - binding family ties
  - copy of return tickets
  - firm ties to home country which you have no intention of abandoning

Pending Green Card or Labor Certification applications are not considered to be valid reasons for an extension. Otherwise, you are normally permitted to remain while an extension is being processed.

While there are no formal rules on how often an alien may enter on a B visa, it is important to maintain your permanent residence abroad.

Border Crossing Card
Mexicans and Canadians

Border Crossing Cards have been used by residents of Canada and citizens of Mexico but are now essentially only for use on the Mexican border.

Mexico   *Ref:64 FR 45162*

Mexican Combination B-1/B-2/Border Crossing Card

Mexican citizens who would be eligible to receive a B-1 or B-2 visa may now obtain a combined B-1/B-2/BCC, Form DSP-150 as a stand-alone card containing the applicant's digitized image and a machine readable biometric identifier. As of October 1, 2000 the old style I-186 or I-586 cards are not valid.

Applicants are required to appear before a Consular Officer in a U.S. Consulate in Mexico and must:

- Be a citizen of Mexico
- Be residing in Mexico
- Be Seeking to enter the U.S. as a temporary visitor for business or pleasure for periods of stay not exceeding six months
- Be eligible to receive a B-1/B-2 visa, or
- Have received a waiver of a ground of ineligibility for at least ten years

Documentation and supporting evidence includes:

- *Form*
  - *OF 156, Nonimmigrant Visa Application*
- *Fee*
  - filing fee of $45 ($13 fora child under 15 valid only until 15th birthday)
- *Evidence of Mexican citizenship and residence*
  - *Mexican passport, or*
  - Certificate of Mexican Nationality (CMN) and either:
    - an additional piece of photo identification, or
    - a valid or expired U.S. visa, BCC or B-1/B-2/BCC (not voided)
- *Photograph and fingerprints taken at the time of the application*
  - digitized photographic image
  - digitized impression of the applicant's index fingers

Canada   *Ref: 64 FR 45164*

Border Crossing Card

Canadian Border Crossing Cards (BCCs) are not available to Canadian citizens although they have been available for the use of permanent residents of Canada.

In theory, the Border Crossing Card has been valid for an indefinite number of applications for admission to the United States with no restrictions as to extensions of temporary stay or itinerary. In reality, they are now practically phased out.

The Canadian BCC was last described at 64 FR 45164, August 19, 1999 which said that a nonresident alien Canadian border crossing identification card (BCC) or the BCC portion of a Canadian B-1/B-2/BCC issued to a permanent resident of Canada, pursuant to provisions revised as of April 1, 1998, is valid until the date of expiration, if any, unless previously revoked, but not later than the date, currently October 1, 2001, on which a machine-readable biometric identifier is required in order for a BCC to be usable for entry.

Canadian Boat Landing Card

By paying a yearly fee of $16 or $32, families may file for a Form I-68, Canadian Border Boat Landing Card. This permits small boat visits of a maximum of 72 hours within 25 miles of the border shoreline with only an annual inspection. However, inspection on returning to Canada is still required.   *Ref: 8 CFR Part 235.1(e)*

Canadian Permanent Commuter s

Canadians holding Green Cards who work in the U.S. may live in Canada if they obtain Canadian Permanent Commuter status.

C–1/D

Alien in Transit/ Crew member, Sea or Air

These two visa categories may be issued separately as a C-1 or D or, alternatively, as a joint C-1/D classification.

In general terms, the D portion facilitates the entry to the United States and controls the activities of crew members of cruise ships, cargo ships and aircraft while the C-1 permits transit within the country of these and other foreign visitors.

The individual classification are:

- C-1 - Alien in Transit
- D   - Crew member, Sea or Air   *Ref: INA 101(a)(15)(C)*

Specifically, the C-1 classification is used by visitors with confirmed onward reservations who stop in the U.S. to:

- Change planes or ship
- Pass through the United States with permission to enter a third country and will leave the U.S. in a few days
- Make a short shore visit from a cruise or cargo ship

D status is for bona fide crew members of foreign ships or aircraft. This includes aliens:

- Who come to a U.S. land or water port to take on or offload cargo or passengers
- Whose work is required for the normal operation of the ship or aircraft

Admission Process

INS and Consular Officers issue the joint C-1/D Classification to accommodate crew members who must spend short periods in the United States between assignments and may have to leave from a different location than the one in which they arrived.

Each time cargo ship crew members enter a U.S. port, they are placed in C-1/D status and issued a new Form I-95, Crewman's Landing Permit, which is good for a maximum of 29 days. However, cruise ships have their entire ship inspected and new crew lists made every 90 days although the INS is advised of changes to the crew list as they occur. Crew members have no rights other than entry unless prior permission is obtained for longshore work.

Step 1 - Clearing the Department of Labor (DOL)

This step applies only to alien crew members who intend to perform longshore activities in U.S. ports. Others may skip Step 1.

The loading and unloading of vessels in U.S. ports has traditionally been performed by U.S. longshore workers. Until the passage of IMMACT90, INS had allowed alien crew members to do this kind of work because longshore work was considered to be within their scope of permitted employment. The IMMACT90 limited this practice to provide greater protection to U.S. longshore workers.

The use of alien crew members for longshore activities is governed by prevailing practice in a given U.S. port. In certain circumstances, employers are required to submit attestations to the DOL and then apply to the INS for permission to use alien crew members to perform specified longshore activities.

Before undertaking longshore work, it is advisable to determine whether longshore work is permitted under prevailing practice or the Department of Labor's Employment and Training Administration (ETA) requires an attestation. Further information should be obtained from the regional ETA office having jurisdiction over the state in which the port is located. See Appendix G for telephone numbers. Further information is available by calling (202) 219-5263.

DOL Form ETA 9033, Attestation by Employer using Alien Crew members for Longshore Activities in U.S. Ports still exists but is currently not being used. If it were to be used, it would apply only to ports in the lower 48 states where the overriding principle is that U.S. workers must not be displaced and alien crew members may only perform a particular activity of longshore work if that work were permitted by the prevailing practices in the port during the preceding 12-month period.

Ref: 60 FR.12, 1995

The process has been modified for Alaskan ports. The Coast Guard Authorization Act of 1993 amended the INA and established a new Alaska exception to the general prohibition on the performance of longshore work by alien crew members in U.S. ports.

While the Alaska exception is intended to provide a preference for hiring U.S. longshoremen over the employer's alien crew members, the prohibition does not apply where an employer has filed, with the Department of Labor, a successful attestation with accompanying documentation for the performance of specified longshore work at a particular location in the State of Alaska. The attestation process, as administered by ETA, became effective October 7, 1996. *Ref: 20 CFR, part 655, Subpart F and G*

The information collection requirements of the new Form ETA 9033-A under the Alaska exception under the prevailing practice exception were published in the Federal Register on January 19, 1995 (60 FR 3950). The ETA estimates that employers will be submitting 350 attestations per year under the Alaska exception.

Alaska is served by the ETA's Region X (ten) office in Seattle, Washington. Information on submitting an attestation may be obtained by calling (206) 553-8037.

Documentation and supporting evidence includes:

- *DOL form*
  - Form ETA 9033-A, Attestation by Employers Using Alien Crew members for Longshore Activities at Locations in the State of Alaska
- *Employer's supporting attestation*
  - the employer will:
    - make a bona fide request for help and employ qualified and available U.S. longshore workers from contract stevedoring companies and private dock operators before using alien crewmen to perform the activity specified in the attestation
    - provide notice of filing the attestation to such stevedoring companies and private dock operators, and to labor organizations recognized as exclusive bargaining representatives of U.S. longshore workers
    - not use alien crew members to perform longshore activities to influence the election of a bargaining representative for workers in the State of Alaska

Exceptions are permitted in:

- The use of an automated self-unloading conveyor belt or vacuum-actuated system unless the Administrator has determined that it is not the prevailing practice in a specific location
- The loading or unloading of hazardous cargo

Step 2 - Clearing the Department of State (DOS) Abroad

Usually the foreign vessel personnel will make arrangements for C-1/ D visa issuance. Application may be made at a U.S. Embassy or Consulate abroad.

The requirement of a personal appearance before a consular officer may be waived in the case of an aircraft crewman seeking a C-1 or D visa classification if the application is supported by a letter from the employing carrier certifying that the crewman is employed as an aircraft crewman, and the consular officer is satisfied that an appearance is not necessary.

Step 3 - *Clearing the INS at a U.S. Port of Entry*

Visitors in Transit

Only certain designated U.S. ports of entry process applications for C-1 Visitor in Transit status. Before arriving in the United States you are required to fill out a Form I-94, Arrival/Departure Record if you:

- Are a non-U.S. Citizen or Permanent Resident, and
- Are in transit to a country outside the United States, and
- You do not hold a valid U.S. visa
- Hold a common carrier ticket or other evidence of outbound travel arrangements

The bottom portion of the I-94 (Departure Record) must be kept with your passport until you leave the United States. *Ref: INA 238(d)*

Crew members

Application for crew members to enter the United States in C-1/D status is made on INS Form I-418, Passenger - Crew List. An I-95, Crewman's Landing Permit - Land or Sea is issued. Aircrews may use International Civil Aviation Organization (ICAO) or Customs Form 7507, General Declaration in lieu of Form I-418. *Ref: 9 FAM 41.42.*

Cargo crews receive an I-95 each time they come into port while the entire crew of cruise ships are inspected every three months and the cruise line reports interim crew changes.

Crew members performing longshore work

Before longshore work may be performed, the INS must be satisfied that the Department of Labor concurs.

The maximum period of admittance is 29 days. It is not renewable*Ref: INA 248*

Step 4 - *Change of Status*

An alien may not change to or from another classification. *Ref: INA 248*

Advance Parole

Aliens who are in the final stages of their application for a new permanent or temporary resident status risk being deemed to have abandoned their application if they cross the U.S. border in either direction. However, recognizing that circumstances sometimes make it necessary to enter or leave the United States during this period, a process called Advance Parole may be granted by the INS to allow short and necessary trips across U.S. borders.

As a general rule, Advance Parole may apply to either aliens who are living outside the United States and have not yet received final permission to enter or to those who are living in the United States and are upgrading their status to a working temporary classification or a legal permanent resident.

Advance Parole may be granted to:

- An alien whose case parole has been authorized by the district director because of emergent, humanitarian, personal or bona fide business considerations
- A refugee from Cuba or other asylee who is in parole or voluntary departure status
- A member of the professions or a person having exceptional ability in the sciences or arts who had been granted voluntary departure
- A lawful permanent resident who, because of emergent reasons, must embark before action can be completed on his Reentry application

Inside the United States

Except for aliens in H-1 or L-1 status and their dependents, applicants needing to leave the United States temporarily with a pending I-485 Adjustment of Status or I-539 Change of Status petition, shall file a Form I-131 petition with $95 filing fee for a Reentry Perm with the INS Nebraska Service Center. This serves as an application for an Authorization for Parole Form I-512.

Parole authorization on Form I-512 may be issued to a principal alien by the district director having jurisdiction over the place where the principal alien resides in the United States, and sent to the alien. Return of the principal alien shall be required within four months of the date of issuance of the parole authorization., except that an alien required to abroad in connection with his or her qualifying profession or occupation must return within a period not to exceed one year from the date of issuance of parole authorization, including multiple applications. The remarks block of Form I-512 sets the time which the alien may be paroled and the conditions for re-parole.

An applicant who is under exclusion, deportation or removal proceedings loses any protection derived from a pending Green Card petition by departing. However, departure from the United States before a decision is made on an application for a Reentry Permit or refugee travel document shall not affect the application.

The remarks block of Form I-512 shall show the basis for parole, by whom it was issued, whether the alien is to be paroled or re-paroled on arrival and whether it is valid for multiple applications. For a nonimmigrant, it shall also show the period of parole.

Outside the United States

An otherwise eligible applicant who is outside the United States and wishes to come to the United States to apply for benefits under section 202 of P.L. 105-100 may request parole authorization by filing for Travel Document (Form I-131) and Form I-864, Affidavit of Support with the Texas Service Center and a photocopy of the Form I-485 that will be filed on entering the United States. If the director of the Texas Service Center is satisfied that the alien will be eligible for adjustment of status and will file the application, he may issue an Authorization for Parole Form I-512 to allow the alien to be paroled into the U.S. for a period of 60 days. The alien shall have 60 days from the date of the parole to file the application for adjustment of status.

A Reentry permit shall be valid for two years and a refugee travel document shall be valid for one year. Neither may be extended. An alien who presents a valid unexpired refugee travel document, or who has been allowed to file an application for a refugee travel document, and this application has been approved, shall be examined as to his or her admissibility under the Act.

In special cases, application for Advance Parole may be made on Form I-512 to enter the United States for multiple entries for one year, that is to leave and return as often as necessary.

Admission

When applying for Advance Parole to enter the United States from abroad, you must submit the following to:

> Immigration and Naturalization Service
> Office of International Affairs and Parole
> 425 I Street N.W., Room 1203
> Washington, DC 20536

Documentation and supporting evidence includes:

- *INS forms*
  - I-512, Authorization for Parole of an Alien into the United States with:
    - details of why a U.S. visa cannot be obtained
    - details of efforts to obtain a waiver of inadmissibility

- copy of any decision or details on pending immigrant petition
- complete description of emergent reasons for, and requested duration of, parole
- I-131, Application for Travel Document with:
  - I-134, Affidavit of Support
- *Fee*
  - I-131 filing fee of $95
- *Proof of financial support or solvency*
  - statement of how medical, housing, transportation and other subsistence expense needs will be met

TWOV

Transit WithOut Visa

T ransit WithOut Visa or TWOV status (pronounced trove or twove) is reserved for travelers or air or ship crews who:

- Are transit aliens traveling without a nonimmigrant visa   *Ref: INA 238*
- Are in immediate and continuous transit through the U.S.
                                      Ref: 9 FAM 41.2(i)
- Are stopping in the United States solely for the purpose of changing to planes or ships which are headed to a remote foreign destination
- Have confirmed immediate onward reservations or crew assignments
- Do not have to be admitted to the United States

The Attorney General shall have the power to enter into contracts including bonding agreements with transportation lines to guarantee the passage through the United States in immediate and continuous passage of aliens to foreign destinations. Such aliens may not have their classification changed.   *Ref: INA 238(c)*

As aliens in this status are not admitted, they are not permitted to leave the secure area of the landing station. However, they may be left in the care of an airline or ship representative for eight hours or until their departure whichever is earlier. After the alien's departure, the carrier must complete and turn in the I-94T Departure Record to the INS.

Application Process

Application for Transit WithOut Visa (TWOV) can only be made at certain designated U.S. land and sea ports of entry.

Before arriving in the United States you are required to fill out a Form I-94T, Arrival/Departure Record - Transit WithOut Visa if you:

- Are a non-U.S. Citizen or Permanent Resident, and
- Are in transit to a country outside the United States, and
- Do not hold a valid U.S. visa, and
- Do not need to be admitted to the United States

Chapter 4

Educational Classifications

T hree classifications are available to students who wish to further their education in the United States. For the most part, students in these classifications pursue post-secondary education. New legislation in 1996 has restricted the alien student's access to public secondary educational opportunities.

The appropriate classification is determined in part by who pays and how formal is the training. Regardless of the classification selected, there are strict rules which are meant to ensure that the student's educational expectations are met with a minimum of financial and administrative distractions.

F is the most flexible student status as it enables students with financial support to take full advantage of the U.S. educational process while providing some access to career-oriented employment opportunities. The description of this classification begins on the following page.

J, the most complex student classification, permits a student with limited resources to participate in a program approved by the United States Information Agency (USIA). The program takes full advantage of financial support from the home country or the United States. J status is usually offered with the proviso that the student practice his or her new skills at home for a minimum of two years after graduation. Details are furnished beginning on page 65.

M, the least formal student status, has been established to permit vocational training, non-academic schooling or schooling in a language other than English. Details about this visa may be found beginning on page 84.

Dependents of A, E, G, H, I and L aliens may study on a full or part-time basis in the U.S.

Workers in the B-2, E-1, E-2, H-1, H-2, H-3 and L-1 classifications may pursue incidental educational activities as long as the educational activity is not the primary activity.

F

Academic Student

F status is reserved for those who will be studying an academic course at a school authorized to allow foreign students to attend. They must have a home in a foreign country to which they will return when they complete their studies.

Students may be admitted for study at the elementary level through the post-graduate and doctoral level. However, there are severe restrictions on pre-university study as explained in *Step 4 - Maintenance of Status.*

The F classification can include a spouse and unmarried children under 21 years of age. *Ref: INS ER 806 3-8-94*

Sub-categories are:
- F-1 Student (academic or language training program)
- F-2 Spouse and minor children of alien classified F-1
  Ref: 9 FAM 41.12; INA 101(a)(15)(F)

To be eligible, a student must:
- Be enrolled in an INS-accredited institution
- Be proficient in English or engaged in English language courses leading to English proficiency
- Demonstrate sufficient financial resources to complete studies without having to work
- Show that there is no intent to abandon residency in the home country
- Be studying on a full-time basis if at the undergraduate level (normally at least 12 academic hours per semester)

Students may be permitted to pursue part-time study if their foreign student advisor recommends this for academic reasons, illness or the need to improve English skills. English as a Second Language (ESL) places students at their appropriate levels; reading, writing, and speaking are practiced.

At the graduate level, the definition of full-time is left up to the school since work on a thesis or dissertation may constitute full-time work even though no credit hours are being taken.

Financial aid may not be available to international students. However, they may qualify for academic or athletic scholarships. Because of visa regulations, academic pressures and a competitive employment market, international students should not count on financing their education by part-time employment.

A dependent spouse and minor children (under age 21) who are admitted in F-2 status may study on a full-time or part-time basis, but may not receive financial aid or accept employment.

Admission Process

Step 1 - Acceptance by an INS-accredited Educational Institution

A student must be accepted by an INS-accredited institution before submitting a visa application to a U.S. Embassy or Consulate abroad.

Documentation and supporting evidence includes:
- Application for admission
- School transcripts
- Diplomas, official reports (translated into English)
- Standardized test scores - SAT or ACT
- Evidence of English proficiency, such as TOEFL
- Recent photograph

Additional supporting documentation which may be required includes:
- Application fee/tuition deposit
- Housing application and deposit
- Personal recommendations
- Health information

Upon acceptance of a student, the school issues:
- Letter of acceptance
- Form I-20 A-B/I-20 ID - Certificate of Eligibility
  (commonly known as I-20 A-B)

All students must be protected by health insurance. If you choose not to take the insurance available through the university, you should obtain adequate coverage elsewhere. Students may also need to submit proof of required immunization.

Students should also check whether the INS has implemented its planned new $95 fee which the institution would collect and forward to the INS along with the new Form I-901, Remittance of the Fee for Certain F-1 Nonimmigrants. *Ref: 64 FR 71323*

Step 2 - Clearing the Department of State (DOS) Abroad

Application is made to the visa officer at the U.S. Embassy or Consulate serving the student's home country   *Ref: 9 FAM 41.61*

Documentation and supporting evidence includes:

- *DOS form*
  - OF 156, Nonimmigrant Visa Application
- *Fees*
  - $45 non-refundable Machine-Readable Visa (MRV) fee collected at posts which issue MRVs
  - visa reciprocity fee equating to fees charged in similar circumstances in an alien's home country
- *Passport and photographs*
  - passport valid for at least six months beyond intended stay
  - one photograph 1½" (37 mm) square showing full face without head covering against a light background
- *Prior approval*
  - Form I-20 A-B, Certificate of Eligibility, issued by the university
- *Additional evidence*
  - proof of adequate English language skills
- *Proof of financial support or solvency*
  - evidence of adequate financial resources to cover expenses for full proposed period of study without work, including:
    - school financial aid
    - personal and family funds
    - government assistance
  (anticipated employment earnings may not be included as resources)
- *Evidence that U.S. stay is temporary (intent to depart U.S.)*
  - job prospects upon returning home
  - details about immediate family members back home
  - student's involvement in community organizations
  - financial ties and assets in the home country
  - why the same quality of education is not available at home

Although it is not normally required, the consul has the right to request that a student post a Maintenance of Status and Departure Bond with the local INS office.

Depending on which country a student is from, it may be necessary to apply for a multiple-entry visa to permit periodic trips back home. Whether a single-entry or multiple-entry visa is issued depends on how U.S. citizens are treated in similar circumstances in the student's home country.

Some U.S. Embassies or Consulates abroad allow a student to apply by mail.

Step 3 - Clearing the INS at a U.S. Port of Entry

A potential student may enter as a B-2 visitor to compare schools with the notation "intending student" being placed on the I-94. It is then possible to change status when enrolling.

Canadians with all necessary documentation from the school may apply directly at a port of entry. All other students apply for admission after the MRV is placed in their passport at the U.S. Embassy or Consulate.

If a student is already in the United States in another nonimmigrant status, application for change of status must be made at the INS.

As in other classifications, the INS has the obligation to reexamine all documents including proof of financial solvency submitted to, and visas obtained from, a U.S. Embassy or Consulate abroad. An INS Immigration Inspector may refuse entry if not satisfied that the documents presented meet the intent of the law under which admittance is requested.

Documentation and supporting evidence includes:

- *Prior approval*
  - Form I-20 A-B, Certificate of Eligibility, issued by the university with DOS endorsement stapled to passport
- *Additional evidence*
  - copies of evidence presented to DOS including proof of financial solvency and intent to return to home country at completion of studies

Foreign students are normally issued an I-94 Arrival/Departure Record at the port of entry. This card admits them for either Duration of Status (D/S) or for a specific period. Under D/S, and provided that they remain in good standing with their educational institution, they may stay in the United States for the entire period of enrollment in the academic program plus any period of authorized practical training and a 60-day grace period to leave the country. Students who are admitted with a specific termination date and expect to require additional time to complete their studies, must apply for an extension. See Step 5 - Option 2.

Step 4 - Maintenance of Status

A student must complete the academic program prior to the date of expiration on the I-20 A-B issued by the Designated School Official (DSO). However, a student who is eligible to return to school may take a summer vacation in the United States between semesters.

The Illegal Immigration Reform and Immigrant Responsibility Act of 1996 included several provisions which impact on foreign students and are being phased in. These include:

- Students who violate a term or condition of their F-1 status are excludable for five years   *Ref: IIRIRA96.346*
- F-1 status is not available to study for more than 12 months at a public elementary or secondary school, or in a publicly funded adult education program   *Ref: IIRIRA96.625*
- F-1 students at a private elementary or secondary school or in a language training program void their status by transferring to a publicly funded program   *Ref: IIRIRA96.625*
- A program is to be introduced to electronically collect personal and academic progress data on foreign students from approved institutions of higher education in the United States   *Ref: IIRIRA96.641*
- Collection of a fee not to exceed $100 when an alien first registers with an institution after entering the United States is being introduced
                                                                       Ref: IIRIRA96.641

Step 5 - Employment/Training

Congress has decided that since **undergraduate** foreign students need time to adjust to U.S. college life, they may not accept off-campus employment during the first academic year (nine months) even if employment is required for their degree.

Graduate students, on the other hand, may begin off-campus work immediately if employment is required for their degree. Otherwise, they must complete nine months of study before beginning employment.

The role of the Department of Labor in the foreign student employment process has been changed. The filing of DOL Form 9034 and the U.S. employers' worker recruitment process to which it was tied have been eliminated.

The level of involvement of the Immigration and Naturalization Service (INS) depends on whether the job opportunity is on-campus or off-campus and how closely it relates to the student's course of study or financial situation.

Job opportunities and the process of qualifying for them generally fall within three broad categories:

- **On-campus employment** which provides a service to students, or
- **Off-campus employment** directly related to their area of study, or
- **Other off-campus employment**, in cases of substantial unanticipated economic hardship or internship with an international organization

On-campus Employment

F-1 students may accept on-campus employment provided that the school's Designated School Official (DSO) has determined that the student is in good academic standing and is otherwise qualified. The INS is not involved in the on-campus employment qualifying process.

To meet on-campus employment rules, jobs must:

- Be 20 hours or less per week when school is in session but may be full-time when school is not in session
- Be filled traditionally by students
- Not displace U.S. residents
- Be on school premises, including on-location commercial firms which provide services for students on campus, such as a school bookstore or cafeteria, or
- Be at an off-campus location which is educationally-affiliated with the school and associated with the school's established curriculum, or
- Be related to contractually-funded research projects at post-graduate level

On-campus jobs may not:

- Be with on-site commercial firms such as a construction company building a school building which do not provide direct student services
- Be continued unless a student:
  - intends to enroll for the next regular academic year, or
  - is authorized for practical training

Off-campus Employment

Off-campus employment encompasses two options.

The first option includes practical training employment opportunities directly related to a student's area of study. The second option includes jobs which may be unrelated to a student's major area of study such as those obtained to meet an unforseen economic necessity or through an internship with an international organization.

F-1 students may accept off-campus employment provided that the schools's DSO has determined that they are in good academic standing and meet several important conditions which vary significantly according to the category of off-campus employment opportunity. If a student fails to maintain status, these employment opportunities are automatically terminated.

In most situations, before accepting off-campus employment, students must:

- Have completed at least one full academic year (nine months)
- Have the approval of their Designated School Official (DSO) (foreign student advisor)
- Be in good academic standing
- Be currently pursuing a full course of study
- Demonstrate that the employment will not interfere with their carrying a full course of study
- Accept an employment limit of 20 hours a week or less when school is in session or full-time during holiday or vacation periods

- Not displace U.S. residents

The process wherein an employer submits a formal DOL labor and wage attestation has been terminated.

Option One - Practical training related to student's major area of study

Practical training is available to F-1 students (except students in English language training programs) who have been lawfully enrolled on a full-time basis in an INS-approved college, university, conservatory or seminary for at least nine months. An eligible F-1 student may request employment authorization for practical training in a position directly related to their area of study.

There are two types of practical training available.

Curricular practical training programs

An F-1 student may be authorized, by the DSO or international student advisor, to participate in a curricular practical training program which is an integral part of an established curriculum.

Curricular practical training is defined to be alternate work/study, internship, cooperative education, or any other type of required internship or practicum which is offered by sponsoring employers through cooperative agreements with the school.

Curricular practical training employment authorization may be possible if any of the following apply:

- The job is an integral or important part of the student's curriculum
- Employment is required for the degree
- Course credit is available for the employment
- It is listed in the school's course handbook and is overseen by a faculty member
- It applies to a full-time student
- It is approved by the DSO
- It is unavailable back home

Exceptions to the one full academic year (nine months) pre-requirement are provided for students enrolled in graduate studies which require immediate participation in curricular practical training.

The student must submit a request for authorization of curricular practical training to the DSO on Form I-538, Certification by Designated School Official.

Upon certifying the request for authorization, the DSO shall:

- Send the certified Form I-538 to the INS's data processing center
- Endorse the student's I-20 ID with "full-time (or part-time) curricular practical training authorized for (name employer and location)"
- Sign and date the I-20 ID and return it to the student

A student may begin curricular practical training on receipt of the I-20 with the DSO endorsement.

A student may do a maximum of one year of curricular practical training while working toward a degree.

Optional practical training

Like curricular practical training programs, optional practical training programs require that the employment opportunity be directly related to the student's major area of study.

Unlike curricular practical training, the rules for optional practical training do not require that the job be an integral part of an established curriculum. The down side is that the application process is longer and more complex.

There is a 60 day grace period following graduation during which time students may remain in the United States and apply for optional practical training. It may take four to six weeks to get approval.

A job offer is not required but it is desirable because the clock starts ticking on the practical training time limits as soon as the EAD card is issued.

A post-graduation practical training application must be filed between 90 days prior to graduation or 30 days after. Approval ends 12 months after it begins or within 14 months of graduation, whichever comes first.

A student who returns home for five months or more and returns to a new course of studies, gets 12 more months of employment authorization.

Students who have received one year or more of full-time curricular practical training are ineligible for post-completion practical training.

The total periods of authorization for optional practical training shall not exceed a maximum of 12 months. Part-time practical training of 20 hours per week or less shall be deducted from the available practical training at one-half the full-time rate.

F-1 students must apply to the INS for authorization which terminates if the student transfers to another school.

Temporary employment for practical training may be authorized:

- During the student's annual vacation and at other times when school is not in session if the student is currently enrolled, eligible and intends to register for the next term or semester
- While school is in session, provided that practical training does not exceed 20 hours a week
- After completion of all bachelor's, master's, or doctoral degree course requirements (excluding thesis)
- Within the 14 months following the completion of the course of study

The authorization process is in two parts.

Initial request for authorization to accept practical training must be made to the Designated School Official (DSO) of the school the student is authorized to attend.

Documentation and supporting evidence includes:

- *INS form*
  - Form I-538, Certification by Designated School Official
- *Prior approval*
  - Form I-20 ID, Certificate of Eligibility

In making a recommendation for practical training, the DSO must:

- Certify on Form I-538 that the proposed employment is directly related to the student's major area of study and commensurate with the student's educational level
- Endorse and date the student's Form I-20 ID to show that practical training in the student's major field of study is recommended "full-time (or part time) with start and end dates", and
- Return the Form I-20 ID to the student
- Send the school certification on Form I-538 to the INS data processing center

The **second part** of the process requires that the student apply to the INS regional Service Center having jurisdiction over location of the school for an Employment Authorization Document (EAD) for optional practical training.

Ref: 8 CFR 274a

This step is not required for curricular practical training.

Documentation and supporting evidence includes:

- *INS form*
  - Form I-765, Application for Employment Authorization
- *Fee*
  - filing fee of $100
- *Prior DSO recommendation*
  - Form I-20 ID endorsed by the DSO within the past 30 days for full-time or part-time employment with start and end dates

The INS shall adjudicate the Form I-765 and issue an EAD on the basis of the DSO's recommendation unless the student is found otherwise ineligible.

The applicant cannot appeal a denial.   *Ref: 60 FR 21973*

Any employment authorization, whether part of an academic program, is automatically suspended upon certification by the DOL to the INS that a strike or other labor dispute is in progress in the occupation at the place of employment.

The spouse and children of an F-1 student may not accept employment.

Option Two - Non-practical training employment

F-1 students may apply for employment which does not take the form of practical training directly related to their major area of study. These employment opportunities fall within the categories of:

- Severe economic hardship
- Internship with an international organization

Severe economic hardship

If other employment opportunities are not available or are otherwise insufficient, an eligible F-1 student may request off-campus employment work authorization unrelated to his or her major area of study based upon severe economic hardship caused by unforseen circumstances beyond the student's control such as:

- Loss of financial aid or on-campus employment
- Currency fluctuations
- Inordinate tuition and living increases
- Unexpected changes in the financial condition of the student's source of support
- Other substantial and unexpected expenses

Internship with an international organization

A bona fide F-1 student who has been offered employment by a recognized international organization within the meaning of the International Organization Immunities Act (59 Stat. 669) may apply for employment authorization.

The process for obtaining employment authorization in these two categories is similar to that required for optional practical training. It is in two parts and requires the concurrence of both the DSO and INS.

Initial request for authorization to accept employment must be made to the Designated School Official (DSO) of the school the student is authorized to attend for either:

- Severe economic hardship, or
- Internship with an international organization

Documentation and supporting evidence includes:

- *INS form*
  - Form I-538, Certification by Designated School Official
- *Prior approval*
  - Form I-20 ID, Certificate of Eligibility

The DSO may recommend off-campus work for one year by certifying on the Form I-538 that the student:

- Has been in F-1 status for one full academic year

- Is in good standing and is carrying a full course of study
- Has demonstrated that acceptance of employment will not interfere with the carrying of a full course of study

In cases of severe economic hardship, the DSO must also certify that the student has demonstrated that:

- Employment is necessary due to unforseen circumstances beyond the student's control, and
- Authorized on or off-campus employment is unavailable or otherwise insufficient to meet the needs that have arisen as a result of the unforseen circumstances

The **second part** of the process requires that the student apply for an Employment Authorization Document (EAD) to the INS regional Service Center having jurisdiction over the location of the school.

Documentation and supporting evidence includes:

- *INS form*
  - Form I-765, Application for Employment Authorization
- *Fee*
  - filing fee of $100
- *Prior DSO recommendation*
  - Form I-20 ID endorsed by the DSO within the past 30 days for full-time or part-time employment with start and end dates
  - Form I-538, Certification by Designated School Official
- *Supporting documentation - severed economic hardship*
  - affidavits which further detail the unforseen economic circumstances that cause the request
  - evidence of unavailability or insufficiency of on-campus or off-campus employment opportunities in area of study
- *Supporting documentation - internship with an international organization*
  - international organization's letter of certification that the proposed employment is within the scope of its sponsorship

If employment is authorized, the adjudicating officer shall issue an endorsed EAD and notification to the student which permits off-campus employment. The employment authorization may be granted in one-year intervals up to the expected date of completion of the student's course of study. No appeal of a denial is permitted.

Off-campus employment authorization may be renewed by the INS only if the student is maintaining status and good academic standing. However, it is automatically terminated whenever the student fails to maintain status.   *Ref: Service Law Books*

Because of the economic hardship arising from the devaluation of their home currencies, the INS has temporarily eased the employment rules for students from

Indonesia, Malaysia, the Philippines, South Korea and Thailand. The 20-hour limit is lifted and the minimum course load is reduced.

Step 6 - Reinstatement/Revalidation/Extension/Change of Status

Application to the INS within the United States

A change of status to F shortly after entering in another classification is not advisable as it may circumvent the intent of the normal entry process.

An application for reinstatement, revalidation or change of status should be filed with the appropriate INS regional Service Center.

Documentation and supporting evidence includes:

- *INS form*
  - I-539, Application to Extend/Change Nonimmigrant Status
- *Fee*
  - filing fee of $120
- *Passport*
  - passport valid for at least six months beyond intended stay
- *Prior approval*
  - original Form I-20 A-B issued by the school
- *Current and prior immigration status*
  - original Form I-94, Arrival/Departure Record, or
  - Form I-102, Application for Replacement/Initial Nonimmigrant Arrival/ Departure Record, if applicable
- *Proof of financial support or solvency*
  - proof of financial support

Change of School or Program

A student in good standing academically and with the proper financial resources may transfer to another school. A new I-20 A-B must be obtained from the new school and sent to the INS with a copy to the old school.

A student who changes programs must apply for a new I-20 A-B for the new program and submit it to the Designated School Official (DSO) (or foreign student advisor) within 15 days of beginning the new program. The DSO will return pages 3 and 4 of the I-20 A-B and send pages 1 and 2 to the INS regional Service Center within 30 days. Permission to work off-campus is not affected.

No notification is required when changing majors, but still pursuing the same degree.

Out of Status Prior to Completion of Program

A student who goes out of status should submit evidence to prove that:

- The violation of status was solely due to circumstances beyond his or her control, or
- Failure to receive reinstatement would result in extreme hardship
- The student is pursuing or will pursue a full course of study at the school listed on the I-20 A-B
- The student has not engaged in unauthorized off-campus employment, or
- Any unauthorized off-campus employment was related to a scholarship, fellowship or assistantship
- A U.S. resident was not displaced
- The student is not in deportation proceedings

A student may be able to regain status by departing and reentering the United States using a valid F-1 visa and Form I-20 A-B (student copy) validated by the DSO or foreign student adviser.

Change To or From F-1

H-4s wishing to change their status to F-1 may:

- File by mail for a status change with the appropriate INS regional Service Center, or
- Apply at a U.S. Consulate in Mexico or Canada with an I-20 A-B, proof of financial support and other F-1 documents

F-1s wishing to change their status to H-1 will not go out of status if their practical training expires while an H-1 petition is pending. However, they must await receipt of the H-1 before starting work.

Students with an F-1 visa who marry a Green Card holder may remain in the United States as long as they stay in school. However their spouse should file an I-130 Green Card application with the INS.

Visa Revalidation by the Department of State (DOS)

A student who is unable to complete the program within the deadline indicated on the I-20 A-B may seek the approval of both the school's DSO or foreign student advisor and the State Department to extend their stay.

A request to extend an F-1 may be processed by the State Department in a student's home country, but not in the United States. However, renewal in Canada or Mexico is permitted. It is advisable to check whether a Canadian visitor's visa is required to enter Canada.

A request should be submitted within 30 days of the expiration of the I-20A-B and should normally be granted if a student:

- Applies on time
- Has maintained status without violation
- Can demonstrate that the extension is required because of compelling medical or academic reasons

As long as their I-94 is valid, students may reenter the United States regardless of whether their F-1 renewal is approved abroad.

Documentation and supporting evidence includes:

- *Passport*
  - passport valid for at least six months beyond intended stay
- *Prior approval*
  - valid I-20 A-B
- *School's evidence to support request*
  - letter from your department explaining why you need the extension
- *Proof of financial support or solvency*
  - proof of financial resources

It is advisable to retain the I-94 for reentry when leaving the United States for State Department processing in case your visa application is denied. It may also be used if the visa is granted.

Change of Status to H-1B After Completion of Studies - Effect of H-1B Cap

Following completion of their studies or program, F-1 nonimmigrant aliens may seek employment in H-1B status. However, since there is an annual cap on the number of H-1Bs issued in any INS Fiscal Year, petitions on behalf of F-1 aliens may not be processed for a work start date in the current INS Fiscal Year if the H-1B cap has already been reached.

A new rule implemented on June 15, 1999 permits the INS to extend the period of duration of status of certain F-1 nonimmigrant aliens who are still in status for such time as is necessary for the INS to act on the petition for a change of their status to H-1B with a work start date in the following fiscal year. Such F-1 aliens and their F-2 dependents will not be required to depart the United States to avoid going out of status and may remain in the U.S. to wait for H-1B numbers to again become available at the start of the next fiscal year beginning October 1. *Ref: Federal Register, June 15, 1999*

Employment or other activities inconsistent with the terms of their F-1 status is not permitted without INS authorization until H-1B visa numbers become available and the INS has approved the change of status for a date no earlier than October 1.

H-1B amended petitions, extensions of stay and petitions filed on behalf of an H-1B alien by a new or additional employer are not counted against the cap.

J

Exchange Visitor

J status is reserved for persons from other countries to participate in educational and cultural visitor, work, study or training exchange programs which implement the Fulbright-Hays Act of 1961. Its stated objective is:

- To mutually increase understanding between the people of the United States and the people of other countries by means of educational and cultural exchange

Sub-categories are:

- J-1 - Exchange visitor
- J-2 - Spouse and children of alien classified J-1

Ref: 9 FAM 41.12: INA 101(a)(15)(J)

Background

This act and the INA provide nonimmigrant status for a person having a residence in a foreign country which he or she has no intention of abandoning, who seeks to enter the United States temporarily, and who has been selected to participate in an Exchange Visitor Program.

Each year, some 175,000 foreign nationals enter the United States in the Exchange Visitor Program as part of the public diplomacy efforts of the United States Government designed to promote peaceful relations and mutual understanding with other countries. At the end of their program, the visitors are expected to return home within thirty days to share their experiences and new skills with their fellow citizens.

Program Operation

In October, 1999, the Foreign Affairs Reform and Restructuring Act of 1998 was implemented and as a result the exchange visitor functions of the former program administrator, the United States Information Agency (USIA) were absorbed into the Department of State. Consequently, the functions related to operation of the Exchange Visitor Program were delegated to the Under Secretary of State for Public Diplomacy and Public Affairs. The functions related to the waiver of the foreign residency requirement were delegated to the Assistant Secretary for Consular Affairs in the Waiver Review Division of the Office of Legislation, Regulation and Advisory Assistance in the Visa Office of the Bureau of Consular Affairs.

Program participants include students, medical and on-the-job trainees, teachers, professors, research scholars and international visitors coming for the purpose of travel, observation, consultation, research, training, sharing, or demonstrating specialized knowledge or skills, or participating in organized people-to-people programs.

Although many large companies participate as sponsors, J status is grouped with other educational classifications in this chapter because of its heavy educational concentration. However, as an indication of its diversity, J status may apply to the following classifications:

	22 CFR	Maximum Program
• Education		
• professors and research scholars	(514.20)	three years
• short-term scholars	(514.21)	six months
• college and university students	(514.23)	duration of status or non-degree - 24 months
• teachers	(514.24)	three years
• secondary school students	(514.25)	one year
• Other employment		
• specialists	(514.26)	one year
• alien physicians	(514.27)	seven years
• camp counselors	(514.30)	four months
• au pairs	(514.31)	one year
• Other visitors		
• trainees	(514.22)	18 months
• international visitors	(514.28)	one year
• government visitors	(514.29)	18 months
• summer student travel/work	(514.80)	four months

An estimated 100,000 Exchange Visitors are currently subject to a statutory provision of 8 USC 212(e) which requires that they return to their country of citizenship or last permanent residence for a period of two years when their exchange program is completed and their J-1 or J-2 status expires. Waivers of this requirement are possible but not necessarily easily attainable. Details follow in Step 8.

Health insurance is mandatory. Some scholarships include coverage for the J-1 visa holder. In those cases, coverage must still be purchased for the dependents. If the scholarship does not include health insurance, then the alien must find coverage.

Admission Process

Step 1 - Obtaining Approval of Programs

Program sponsors must obtain prior State Department approval.

For approval as program sponsors, U.S. educational institutions, U.S. government agencies, foreign or U.S. private organizations must submit Form IAP-37, Exchange Visitor Program Application. The form is available by calling (202) 401-9810 or writing:

> Department of State
> Program Designation
> 301 4ᵗʰ Street S.W.
> Washington, DC 20547

There is a $799 charge for the application and it must be returned to this address and include:

- The applicant's proposed exchange program activity and ability to comply
- Evidence of legal status and financial responsibility of the organization
- Accreditation, if a post-secondary institution
- Evidence of licensure if required by law
- Certification that chief executive and responsible officers are U.S. citizens

Each approved program has a responsible officer named to assist applicants with the immigration process. By way of example, several programs designed to enable au pairs to reside with U.S. families for temporary periods were approved.

Program information is available from the State Department at (202) 401-9810, or by fax at (202) 401-9809. A fax-on-demand information line is also available by calling (202) 205-8237 using the telephone on your fax machine.

Step 2 - Clearing the Approved Sponsoring Agency

In order to participate in the program, a foreign national must be accepted by one of the approximately 1,400 designated sponsoring agencies which will issue a Form IAP-66, Certificate of Eligibility for (J-1) Exchange Visitor.

Students should also check whether the INS has implemented its planned new $95 fee which the institution would collect and forward to the INS along with the new Form I-901, Remittance of the Fee for Certain J-1 Nonimmigrants. *Ref: 64 FR 71323*

Foreign medical graduates who wish to study further or train in the U.S. may want to first contact the Educational Commission for Foreign Medical Graduates (ECFMG) in Philadelphia, Pennsylvania.

Step 3 - Clearing the Department of State (DOS) Abroad

After being accepted in an approved program and receiving the Form IAP-66, Certificate of Eligibility, an alien living abroad must apply to the U.S. Embassy or to a Consulate in his or her home country   *Ref: 9 FAM 41.62*

Documentation and supporting evidence includes:

- *DOS form*
  - OF 156, Nonimmigrant Visa Application
- *Fees*
  - $45 Machine-Readable Visa (MRV) fee is waived in this classification
  - reciprocity fee equating to fees charged in similar circumstances in an alien's home country
- *Passport and photograph*
  - passport valid at least six months beyond intended stay
  - photograph - 1½" (37 mm) square showing full face without head covering against a light background
- *Prior approval*
  - Form IAP-66, Certificate of Eligibility for Student (J-1) Status
- *Additional evidence*
  - proof of sufficient scholastic preparation unless the exchange program is designed to accommodate non-English speaking participants
  - proof of adequate knowledge of English
- *Proof of financial support or solvency*
  - sufficient funds to cover all expenses while participating in the exchange program, or
  - funds provided by the sponsoring organization in the form of a scholarship or other stipend
- *Evidence that U.S. stay is temporary*
  - proof of binding ties to the home country and intent to depart the United States after completing the program

If you are taking a spouse and minor children with you, additional documentation is required.

Documentation and supporting evidence includes:

- *Passport and photograph*
  - passports of dependents
- *Civil documents*
  - proof of marriage
  - proof of parenthood of each child

If an alien is found to be an appropriate candidate and all necessary documents are in order, the consulate will place a J visa stamp in the alien's passport.

Although Canadians do not need passports or visa stamps to enter the United States, they should carry proof of citizenship.

Step 4 - Clearing the INS at a U.S. Port of Entry

An alien must apply for entry with the INS at a port of entry.

Documentation and supporting evidence includes:

- *Passport and photograph*
  - a valid passport with its valid J visa stamp
- *Prior DOS and program approval*
  - Form IAP-66, Certificate of Eligibility for Exchange Student (J-1)
  - DOS Machine-Readable Visa (MRV) in passport
- *Proof of financial support or solvency*
  - evidence of financial support

A spouse and minor children may be granted J-2 status.

The INS will issue a Form I-94 Arrival/Departure Record card and Copy 3 (pink) of the Form IAP-66. They should be kept with the passport as they represent the only proof of J-1 status.

The INS Immigration Inspector makes the determination of whether the Exchange Visitor is subject to the two-year home residency requirement. Key indicators are whether any funding of the exchange visitor's program is from either the home country or the United States. Also, if the exchange visitor's skills are on a shortage list in his or her home country, he or she will be subject to the two-year home residency requirement on page 74. It is important to understand that a total of two years must be spent in the home country, not just outside the United States. However, it may be possible to eliminate the two-year requirement by working in a third country for a home country employer such as a government agency.

An alien is usually admitted for the period of time necessary to complete the program. See page 66 for the maximum program participation period for each classification of Exchange Visitor.

Canadian citizens and landed immigrants in Canada who are British subjects or citizens of a Commonwealth country or citizens of Ireland do not need to obtain a J visa from a U.S. consular office in order to apply for admission to the United States as exchange visitors. Persons from those countries should present proof of citizenship and landed immigrant status, evidence of financial support and Form IAP-66 directly to the Immigration Inspector at a port of entry.

Step 5 - Maintenance of Status

An Exchange Visitor must complete the program for which he or she was admitted prior to the date of expiration of their status. However, a student eligible to return to school may take a summer vacation in the United States between semesters.

Sponsors must notify the State Department program administrators in writing when an Exchange Visitor has withdrawn from or completed a program 30 or more days before the ending date on his or her IAP-66, or if he has been terminated.

The Illegal Immigration Reform and Immigrant Responsibility Act of 1996 included several provisions to be implemented for foreign students including:

- A program to electronically collect personal and academic progress data on foreign students from approved designated exchange visitor programs in the United States   *Ref: IIRIRA96.641*
- Collection of a fee not to exceed $100 when an alien first registers with the institution after entering the United States   *Ref: IIRIRA96.641*

Step 6 - Employment/Training

There are several avenues available for employment and training.

Option One - Student Employment

Application for employment must be made in writing to your school's J-1 responsible officer or international student advisor who must evaluate your proposed employment in relation to your academic program and your personal situation before deciding whether employment is appropriate. If approved, employment may be permitted for up to one year at a time.

J-1 student employment is limited to 20 hours per week except during school breaks and annual vacations.

There are three types of Student Employment.

- **Scholarship, fellowship or assistantship** required employment usually occurs on campus with the school as the employer. However, it is possible to obtain work such as in a government or private research laboratory if your major professor supervises you in work that would count toward your degree.
- **On-campus** jobs unrelated to study are allowed for work in which the school is not the employer and the work is unrelated to the study program.
- **Off-campus** jobs are permitted in cases of serious, urgent, and unforseen economic circumstances that have arisen since your arrival in the U.S.

Option Two - Academic Training

Academic Training is the name used for certain types of study-related employment. It offers a variety of employment situations to supplement an academic program both during and after completion of the study program.

Academic training is divided into training **before completion of your program of study** and **after completion of your program of study**.

Before completion of your program of study

You may interrupt study to work full-time while you are writing a thesis. The limit is 18 months or the time that you have been a full-time student, whichever is shorter, unless the employment is a degree requirement.

After completion of your program of study

You will be eligible for academic training if you submit a written offer of appropriate employment within 30 days after the end of your program. The limit is 18 months or the time that you were a full-time student, whichever is shorter minus any previous academic training.

After receiving a doctorate, you become eligible for any postdoctural training minus any academic training prior to receipt of the doctorate.

Academic Training allows part-time work when classes are in session and full-time during vacation periods and other times such as when a thesis is being written.

To be eligible for employment:

- Your primary purpose must be study rather than academic training
- You must be in good academic standing at the school on your Form IAP-66
- The proposed job must be directly related to your major field of study
- You must maintain permission to remain in the United States throughout your training
- You must maintain health insurance for yourself and your dependents throughout your academic training

Employment may be authorized for the length of time necessary to complete the goals and objectives of the training, provided that:

- The amount of time is approved by both the academic dean or advisor and the responsible officer
- The employment does not exceed the period of:
  - the full course of study or 18 months, whichever is shorter, or
  - 36 months in the case of a Ph.D.
- Any Academic Training after completion of the program must be reduced by any prior periods of Academic Training
- Any Academic Training after completion of the program involves paid employment
- A written job offer is presented to the Responsible Officer within 30 days of the completion of the program

If Employment Authorization is not obtained before leaving the country, reentry may be difficult.

J-1 students in non-degree programs are also eligible for Academic Training.

To qualify, it is necessary to:
- Obtain a written offer from your prospective employer including:
  - your job title
  - brief description of the goals and objectives of your job
  - dates and location of employment
  - number of hours per week
  - the name and address of your training supervisor
- Have your academic advisor write a letter recommending your academic training to your J-1 Responsible Officer setting forth:
  - the goals and objectives of the specific training program
  - a detailed description of the training program
  - how the training program relates to the major field of study
  - why it is an integral or critical part of the academic program
  - adviser's approval of the length of time necessary to complete the goals and objectives of the training
- If in agreement, your J-1 responsible officer must write you a letter of approval
- The Responsible Officer must issue a new IAP-66 for a maximum of 18 months of post-doctoral training at a time

A maximum of 36 months of practical training is permitted including all periods before and after completion of your program.

Option Three - All Other Employment Options

As listed in the introduction to this J Exchange Visitor section, there are several options for a person who wishes to enter the United States temporarily to gain job experience. These range from the graduate medical student and professor to the au pair and camp counselor. Each has its own rules and restrictions on employment.

J Status U.S. jobs may be arranged for a fee through placement organizations which have the authority to issue Form IAP-66 to allow a student, recent graduate, or young professional to obtain temporary J-1 status. The following internet addresses are offered without recommendation as a service to those who may wish to consider the use of a placement agency.

AIESEC: http://www.us.aiesec.org/index.asp
Association for International Practical Training: http://www.aipt.org/index.html
CDS International: http://www.cdsintl.org/cdsctpinusaprogram.html
Institute of International Education: http://www.iie.org

Spousal Employment

A spouse may work on a J-2 visa during the J-1's stay after submitting an application and receiving permission from the INS regional Service Center. The process takes about four weeks.

A J-1 student should take the most recent Form IAP-66 and a new IAP-66 will be issued for the spouse.

Documentation and supporting evidence includes:

- *INS form*
  - I-765, Application for Employment Authorization
- *Fee*
  - filing fee of $100
- *Photographs*
  - two photographs
- *Prior program approval*
  - Form IAP-66
- *Current and prior immigration status*
  - copy of Form I-94 of principal alien and dependent
- *Dependent's evidence to support request*
  - letter explaining why employment is desired and that it is not necessary to support J-1 spouse
- *Additional evidence*
  - letter from Foreign Student Advisor confirming that student is enrolled and making satisfactory progress toward graduation
- *Proof of financial support or solvency*
  - source and amount of principal alien's financial support of spouse evidence that job income is not required to support the J-1

Step 7 - Change of Programs

If a student decides to change schools before graduation and before the J-1 expires the action you take depends on whether your I-94 shows a specific expiration date or Duration of Status (D/S). A $198 payment to the State Department is required.

If your I-94 shows Duration of Status or D/S, there are three parts to the process.

Part One - Preparing the Form

- Fill out and sign the white page of the Form IAP-66

Part Two - Release to Another Program

- Have your present J-1 Responsible Officer complete and sign the lower right-hand corner of all three copies of your IAP-66 form to release you to the second school's sponsorship

Part Three - Notifying the INS

- Take Form IAP-66 to the second school's International Office which will:
  - mail the yellow copy to the INS
  - return the pink copy to you

If your I-94 shows a specific expiration date, you must mail your application to the INS regional Service Center having jurisdiction over your new school.

Documentation and supporting evidence includes:

- *INS form*
  - I-539, Application to Extend/Change Nonimmigrant Status
- *Fee*
  - filing fee of $120
- *Prior approval*
  - both sides of the white page of Form IAP-66
- *Current and prior immigration status*
  - copies of prior Forms IAP-66
  - copies of front and back of I-94 Arrival/Departure Record cards of principal alien and J-2 dependents

Work for the new school cannot begin until the documents are received from INS.

Step 8 - The Two-year Home Residency Requirement (HRR)

Option 1 - Serving the Two-year HRR

As previously noted, the INS makes a determination of who is subject to the two-year HRR when they first obtain J status. This is to ensure that designated Exchange Visitor Program participants share with their countrymen the knowledge, experience and impressions gained during their sojourn in the U.S.

Ref: 9 FAM 41.53; INA 101(a)(15)(H); 8 USC 212(e)

Exchange Visitors are currently subject to the two-year return home requirement (HRR) if they:

- Receive U.S. or foreign government financing for any part of their studies or training in the U.S.
- Are engaged in studies or trained in a field deemed of importance to their home government and such field is on the "skills list" maintained by the program administrator in consultation with foreign governments
- Entered the U.S. to pursue graduate medical education or training

An alien is subject to the two-year HRR unless evidence is produced to demonstrate that all of the following terms have been met:

- A preliminary decision has been made by the immigration officer on the initial Form IAP-66 stating that the alien is not subject to the HRR (see the bottom left corner of the IAP-66 Form and the visa stamp in the passport)
- The J-1 participation was not funded in whole or in part, directly or indirectly, for the purpose of exchange, by either the home government or the U.S. government

- The skills on the alien's training program as described on the IAP-66 are not on the home country's list of urgently needed skills (per the U.S. government's Exchange Visitor Skills List)
- The J-1 did not participate in a graduate medical education or training program
- The J-2 is not the dependent of an Exchange Visitor subject to the HRR

If an alien is subject to the two-year HRR:
- Visits to the United States are permitted while serving the HRR but the time in the U.S. should be subtracted from the two-year residence time
- Time spent residing in a third country does not meet the intent of the two-year HRR
- Working for a home country employer such as the government in a third country may not meet the intent of the two-year HRR
- It is not possible to change status to permanent resident or nonimmigrant H-1 or L status until evidence is submitted that the two-year HRR has been waived or served   *Ref: 9 FAM 40.202*

It is advisable to provide documentary proof of having resided and worked in the home country for a full two years to satisfy the HRR.

Option 2 - Waiver of the Two-year HRR

Applicants should be aware that waivers are not liberally granted, although the law allows an application every six months.

The State Department's Waiver Review Division makes recommendations to the INS on waivers of the two-year HRR.

Applicants may obtain general information through a fax-on-demand system by calling (202) 647-3000. The Public Inquiries Division may be reached at (202) 663-1225.

On March 17, 1997, the USIA amended its skills list of experts lacking in a particular country. J-1s studying in a field covered by the list may not change to any other classification before serving the 2-year HRR or obtaining a waiver.

Ref: HR, January 16, 1997, pages 2448 - 2516

An Exchange Visitor may seek a waiver of the two-year HRR based on:
- A no objection statement from the visitor's home country
- A request by an interested United States Government agency
- A request by a state on behalf of an exchange visitor who has pursued graduate medical education or training in the U.S.
- A reasonable fear of persecution if returning to his or her home country
- Exceptional hardship to the visitor's U.S. citizen spouse or child

When considering a request for a waiver, be aware that:

- It is not necessary to have a job waiting in the United States in order to apply for a waiver
- An alien who has been granted a waiver of the HRR, becomes subject to the two-year HRR rule all over again by renewing the J-1
- The refund of HRR funds such as college grants does not constitute grounds for a waiver
- Because of the complexity of this process, it may be advisable to consult the International Student office for assistance

To request a waiver of the Foreign Resident requirement of the INA under section 212(e), you must submit your application to:

- The office of the INS having jurisdiction over your place of residence if residing in the United States, or
- The office of the INS having jurisdiction over the place of last residence in the United States if residing abroad

Documentation and supporting evidence includes:

- *INS form*
  - I-612, Application for Waiver of the Foreign Residency Requirement
- *Fee*
  - INS filing fee of $170
  - Exchange Visitor filing fee of $136 (Payable to Department of State)
- *Current and prior immigration status*
  - I-94 Arrival/Departure Record if applying in U.S.
- *Additional evidence*
  - documentary evidence relating to exceptional hardship or persecution
- *Civil documents*
  - proof of birth if spouse or child is a U.S. citizen by U.S. birth, or
  - proof of U.S. citizenship of foreign-born spouse or child such as:
    - marriage
    - marriage termination
    - birth certificate
    - statement of dates, ports, means of all U.S. arrivals and departures by spouse and child, or
    - Certificate of Naturalization of spouse or child (if occurred within 90 days of filing Form I-612)

Before requesting other status changes in the Exchange Visitor program, applicants should determine whether proposed additional fees have been implemented.

The State Department operates a service offering status reports on HRR waiver applications by calling (202) 663-1600 or by email usvisa@state.gov. Waiver correspondence should be addressed to:

CA/VO/L/W
Department of State
SA-1, Room L603
2401 E Street, N.W.
Washington, DC 20522-0106

With an overall 1997 success rate of 91 percent, five alternative approaches may be followed to obtain a waiver of the Home Residency Requirement. These include:

Alternative 1 - NORI - No Obligation to Return

This is a "no-objection" statement and issued by the home government, usually through their consulate. In 1997, 68 percent of the 5,752 waiver applications fell within this alternative. The process should be started six months before the J status expires. The NORI is an important aspect of the waiver process but other supporting documentation may also be needed.

Since the NORI is issued routinely by most European countries, it is of limited value. On the other hand, Indian citizens have found this to be a successful approach.

The NORI process includes:

- Obtaining the NORI application forms from the home country's consulate
- Completing the forms in quadruplicate, having them notarized and returned to the consulate
- The consulate endorsing and returning the forms to the alien to obtain a NORI statement or clearance from three home country agencies such as:
  - local passport office
  - state government
  - federal Department of Education
  - Ministry of Health (physicians)
  - police
  - tax authorities
- Each agency sending a NORI statement to the alien and to the country's consulate in the United States for forwarding to their embassy in the U.S.
- The embassy sending a NORI statement to the program administrator
- The program administrator making a recommendation and forwarding it to the INS
- The INS issuing the final waiver

One cannot appeal a denial to an application for a waiver based on a "no objection" statement.

Alternative 2 - Interested Government Agency

An Interested Government Agency (IGA) such as NASA, the CIA, Departments of Commerce, Health or Defense which wants to hire a J-1 alien subject to the two-year HRR to do security-related, research or other work must file for a waiver of the two-year HRR. 15 percent of all waiver applications fell within this alternative in 1997.

Submissions must be accompanied by strong and convincing supporting documentation to demonstrate such evidence as:

- Their research or other work will lead to the development of a product or technology which will give the United States a market or technological edge

The Interested Government Agency (IGA) petition process includes the:

- IGA examining the case and deciding whether to apply to the program administrator for a waiver
- Alien completing and submitting an Exchange Visitor Program Data Sheet
- Program administrator forwarding its recommendation directly to the alien's local INS office
- INS sending the applicant a Form I-797C Notice of Action acknowledging receipt of the recommendation and advising that it takes 30-60 days to process the case
- INS sending the final letter to the applicant (INS usually accepts a waiver recommendation)

An employer may write a supporting letter which makes the alien the beneficiary of a petition with an interested U.S. government agency. The Interested Government Agency may then act as sponsor for a waiver. However, letters to the program administrator or Congressional Representatives only serve to delay the process.

A university must demonstrate through extensive documentation that the U.S. would get a significant edge in terms of contributions to the education field generally or to the successful completion of a project which is of great interest to the Department of Education.

This process may take four to six months once all necessary papers are submitted to the Interested Government Agency. Application is made via Registered Mail, Return Receipt Requested to:

> Department of State
> GC/V Waiver Review Division
> Room 734
> 301 4th Street S.W.
> Washington, DC 20547

Include 5-digit case number on check

The Department of Housing and Urban Development (HUD) announced that it will not process waiver recommendations for physicians subject to the J-1 two-year HRR.   *Ref: HUD, December 13, 1996*

Alternative 3 - Conrad Amendment - State 20 Program

The Conrad Amendment State 20 Waivers for Foreign Medical Graduates enables each participating state to obtain a waiver of the two-year HRR in order to bring in 20 physicians to areas with a shortage of physicians. The program has been extended to 2002.

Ref: IIRIRA96.622

Almost 10 percent of 1997 waiver requests were on behalf of Foreign Medical Graduates (FMGs) who entered the U.S. for graduate medical education or training and were subject to the two-year home-country physical presence requirement (HRR).

Currently, the Department of Agriculture and the Appalachian Regional Commission act as an interested government agency on behalf of foreign medical graduates seeking a waiver of their two-year HRR. If approved, doctors provide primary medical care to Americans living in a health professional shortage area without adequate access to medical care and where there are few doctors such as in a rural area or inner city However, only 20 waivers may be allowed for each state each year, hence the name Conrad 20 Program.

Ref: P.L. 103-416

Applications must come from each state's designated Department of Health in the form of a letter to the program administrator stating that it is in the public interest that the alien physician remain in the United States together with a completed data sheet. The physicians must demonstrate a bona fide offer of full-time employment at a health facility designated by the Secretary of Health and Human Services as having a shortage of health care professionals and present a signed contract in which the physician agrees to practice medicine for at least three years. The state body should confirm that it intends to renew the contract after the initial three-year period.

Ref: 22 CFR 514.44 (e)

Required documentation
- A three-year employment contract of at least 40 hours per week of primary medical care in a designated primary care Health Professional Shortage Area ("HPSA") or designated Medically Underserved Area ("MUA") or psychiatric care in a designated Mental Health Professional Shortage Area ("MHPSA").
- Two written statements must be included:
  - the facility is located in a designated HPSA, MHPSA, or MUA and the facility provides medical care to Medicaid or Medicare eligible and indigent uninsured patients
  - the medical graduate does not have a pending interested state or federal request awaiting approval and will not request that another agency pursue a request on his or her behalf

Alternative 4 -Fear of Persecution
Less than one percent of all requests for waivers were based on fear of persecution on account of race, religion or political opinion if the visitor were to return to his or her home country.

After Form I-612 is filed, if the INS makes a preliminary finding of probable persecution, the file is forwarded to the State Department's Bureau of Democracy, Human Rights and Labor. This determination is relied on heavily.

Extreme hardship to a U.S. citizen or permanent resident, spouse or child may constitute grounds for a waiver. Economic hardship or relocation are not necessarily sufficient.

Qualifying residents of the People's Republic of China may take advantage of a blanket waiver.

Alternative 5 - Exceptional Hardship

Six percent of all waiver applications were based on exceptional hardship to a U.S. citizen or legal permanent resident spouse and/or children.

The process is initiated by filing Form I-612 with the INS which forwards the file to the Waiver Review Division if it determines exceptional hardship. If U.S. Government funding was expended on the Exchange Visitor, the opinion of the funding agency is sought. It is then the responsibility of the Waiver Review Division to weigh the relative merits of the program, policy and foreign relations considerations against the exceptional hardship which would befall the U.S. citizen or legal permanent resident and/or children if the two-year HRR were enforced. Decisions are made on a case-by-case basis. Considerations include:

- The amount and source of funding
- General home country conditions
- The absence of any objection
- The spouse and/or child's a chronic medical condition
- The spouse and/or child's safety in the home country
- The existence of a child custody order
- Military service which would prevent the spouse from accompanying
- Applicant's marital status and children

Requests for further information on waivers should be directed to (202) 401-9800.

Step 9 - Reinstatement/Revalidation/Extension or Change of Status

Application to the Department of State in the United States

When requesting a reinstatement or extension, the State Department must be satisfied that you do not intend to abandon the Exchange Visitor Program.

If your I-94 Arrival/Departure Record shows Duration of Status or D/S instead of a specific expiration date, you may extend your IAP-66 in the United States.

After confirming the necessity for your reinstatement or extension, your J-1 responsible officer will take your IAP-66 and mail the yellow copy to the program administrator and return the pink copy to you. A $198 DOS fee applies.

Application to the INS within the United States

Regardless of the instructions on the Form I-539, if your I-94 Arrival/ Departure Record shows a specific IAP-66 expiration date instead of Duration of Status or D/S, you must mail your extension application directly to the INS regional Service Center having jurisdiction over your place of residence at least 45 days before your stay expires.

Documentation and supporting evidence includes:

- *INS form*
  - I-539, Application to Extend/Change Nonimmigrant Status
- *Fees*
  - filing fee of $120
- *Current and prior immigration status*
  - original IAP-66 issued by your program sponsor

Retain the copy of the IAP-66 designated for the J-1.

A request for a waiver of the two-year HRR would lead the State Department and sponsor to believe that the alien intends to abandon the exchange program. Hence, any request for an extension of J-1 status might not be successful.

If your application is approved, you will be mailed an approval notice which should be kept with your Form I-94 and your copy of your IAP-66. These documents together demonstrate your status.

Visa Revalidation by the Department of State (DOS)

Your permission to stay in the United States ends on the date shown on your Form I-94, Arrival/Departure Record card. However, if your card is marked Duration of Status or D/S you may stay until 30 days after the date on Item 3 of your IAP-66.

To extend your permission to stay in the United States, you must:

- Contact your J-1 Responsible Officer at least three months before the expiration date on your IAP-66
- Be making satisfactory academic progress and have adequate funding, or
- Have completed your program of study and want to participate in an academic program, or
- Be participating in an authorized academic training program and need an extension to finish the program (within the established time limits)

Leaving and Reentering the United States

If you leave and reenter the country using your new IAP-66, this will extend your permission to stay. This is not an option if your are in Canada, Mexico or the Caribbean for periods of fewer than 30 days as the INS Inspector may not record your reentry and thus "turn on" your new IAP-66.

If you leave North America you will need a valid J-1 visa stamp in your passport. If yours has expired, you will need to apply for a new one at a U.S. Embassy or Consulate abroad.

Documentation and supporting evidence includes:

- *DOS form*
  - OF 156, Nonimmigrant Visa Application
- *Fees*
  - $45 non-refundable Machine-Readable Visa (MRV) fee collected at posts which issue MRVs
  - visa reciprocity fee equating to fees charged in similar circumstances in an alien's home country
- *Passport and photograph*
  - passport valid for at least six months beyond intended stay
  - photograph - 1½" (37 mm) square showing full face without head covering against a light background
- *Prior approval*
  - Form IAP-66
- *Additional evidence*
  - dependents' passports
- *Proof of financial support or solvency*
  - proof of funding and support
- *Civil documents*
  - proof of marriage and parenthood

Application to the INS for Change of Status to J within the United States

If you and your dependents are filing for a change to J status, you must mail your application to the INS regional Service Center having jurisdiction over your location.

Documentation and supporting evidence includes:

- *INS form*
  - I-539, Application to Extend/Change Nonimmigrant Status
- *Fee*
  - filing fee of $120
- *Prior approval*
  - Form IAP-66, Certificate of Eligibility for (J-1) Exchange Visitor
  - original I-94, Arrival/Departure Record for principal alien and dependents (if none available, file Form I-102, Application for I-94)

Retain your copy of the IAP-66. The INS issues a Form I-797, Notice of Approval which serves as evidence of the change of status.

Application to the INS for Change of Status from J within the United States

A petition for change in status to H-1 or Green Card may be made as soon as a favorable recommendation is received on the request for a waiver of the two-year HRR. It is not necessary to wait for the final waiver from INS. This is advisable as the LCA or Labor Certification processes take a long time in many states.

An applicant may apply for H-1B or permanent residency while serving the HRR. If approved, the visa can be issued the day the two years are up. This is particularly advisable for those who can get permanent visas without Labor Certification such as on the basis of family preference. You can apply at a U.S. Embassy or Consulate in your home country.

It is possible to accept a tenure track university position on the basis of completing the first 18 months on a J-1 visa as practical training, then return home for two years before returning to the United States. An applicant must ensure that:

- The employer is willing to keep the position open for two years and sponsor the alien for an H-1 visa and a return to the United States, or
- If a waiver of the HRR has been applied for, and there is a reasonable assurance that it will be issued, the employer can sponsor for an H-1 visa

A J-1 Exchange Visitor subject to the foreign residency requirement who has not received a waiver is not eligible to change status to H-1B or L.

A J-1 Exchange Visitor whose status was for the purpose of receiving graduate medical training is ineligible for change of status unless a waiver is obtained under the Conrad 20 Program.

Change of Status to H-1B After Completion of Studies - Effect of H-1B Cap

Following completion of their studies or program, J-1 nonimmigrant aliens may seek employment in H-1B status provided that they are not subject to the HRR. However, since there is an annual cap on the number of H-1Bs issued in any INS Fiscal Year, petitions on behalf of J-1 aliens may not be processed for a work start date in the current INS Fiscal Year if the H-1B cap has already been reached.

A new rule implemented on June 15, 1999 permits the INS to extend the period of duration of status of certain J-1 nonimmigrant aliens who are still in status for such time as is necessary for the INS to act on the petition for a change of their status to H-1B with a work start date in the following fiscal year. Employment or other activities inconsistent with the terms of their J-1 status is not permitted without INS authorization until H-1B visa numbers become available and the INS has approved the change of status for a date no earlier than October 1.

J-1 aliens and their J-2 dependents will not be required to depart the United States to avoid going out of status and may remain in the U.S. to wait for H-1B numbers to again become available at the start of the next fiscal year, October 1.

Ref: Federal Register, June 15, 1999

M

Vocational or Non-Academic Student

Mstatus is reserved for "those who will be studying at a vocational or other non-academic school and who have a home in a foreign country to which they will return after they complete their studies.

This classification can include a spouse or unmarried children under the age of 21." *Ref: INS ER 806 3-8-94*

Although the M is for less formal academic studies, it has many of the same prerequisites and limitations which apply to the F. An alien is admitted initially for a maximum of one year with extensions possible if the study extends longer.

An M-1 student may not change status to an H classification if the training received as an M-1 helped him or her qualify for H status. However, transfer to another school during the first six months and change of status to F-1 is permitted.

Sub-categories are:
- M-1 - Vocational Student or Other Recognized Nonacademic Student
- M-2 - Spouse and children of alien classified M-1
    Ref: 9 FAM 41.12; INA 101(a)(15)(M)

Admission Process

Step 1 - Acceptance by an Accredited Institution

The application process is similar to that for the F-1.

A student must be accepted by an INS-accredited institution before submitting a visa application to a U.S. Embassy or Consulate abroad.

Documents required by the institution include:
- Application for admission
- Diplomas, official reports (translated into English)
- School transcripts
- Recent photograph
- Evidence of English proficiency, such as TOEFL

Additional documentation which may be required includes:
- Application fee/Tuition deposit
- Housing application and deposit
- Personal recommendations
- Health information

Upon acceptance, the school issues:
- Letter of acceptance
- Form I-20 M-N/I-20 ID - Certificate of Eligibility (commonly known as I-20 M-N)

All students must be protected by health insurance. If they choose not to take the insurance available through the school, they should find adequate coverage elsewhere. Students may also need to submit proof of required immunization.

Students should also check whether the INS has implemented its planned new $95 fee which the institution would collect and forward to the INS along with the new Form I-901, Remittance of the Fee for Certain M-1 Nonimmigrants. *Ref: 64 FR 71323*

Step 2 - Clearing the Initial Application

Option 1 - By the INS in the United States

A student who is already in the United States with legal immigration status, may make application at the local INS office having jurisdiction over the area where the institution is located.

Documentation and supporting evidence includes:
- *INS form*
  - I-539, Application to Extend/Change Nonimmigrant Status
- *Fee*
  - filing fee of $120
- *Passport*
  - passport valid for at least six months beyond intended stay
- *Prior approval*
  - Form I-20 M-N - Certificate of Eligibility for Nonimmigrant (M-1) from school
- *Proof of financial support or solvency*
  - proof that the applicant has sufficient funds to pay school-related expenses and to support himself or herself during the program

Option 2 - By the Department of State (DOS) Abroad

Application must be made to a U.S. Embassy or Consulate abroad

Ref: 9 FAM 41.61

Documentation and supporting evidence includes:

- *DOS form*
  - OF 156, Nonimmigrant Visa Application
- *Fees*
  - $45 non-refundable Machine-Readable Visa (MRV) fee collected at posts which issue MRVs
  - visa reciprocity fee equating to fees charged in similar circumstances in an alien's home country
- *Passport and photographs*
  - passport valid for at least six months beyond intended stay
  - two passport photographs
- *Prior approval*
  - Form I-20 M-N - Certificate of Eligibility for Nonimmigrant (M-1) issued by the school
- *Alien's evidence to support request*
  - proof of adequate English language skills
- *Proof of financial support or solvency*
  - evidence of adequate financial resources to cover expenses for the full program including:
    - school financial aid
    - personal and family funds
    - government assistance
- *Evidence that U.S. stay is temporary (intent to depart U.S.)*
  - bona fide evidence that the student intends to return home

Step 3 - Clearing the INS at a U.S. Port of Entry

Students who are already in the United States may omit this step if their I-20 M-N petition has been granted at their local INS office.

Documentation and supporting evidence includes:

- *Passport*
  - passport valid for at least six months beyond date of entry (citizens of Canada exempt)
- *Prior approval*
  - Form I-20 M-N
- *Additional evidence*
  - copies of all documentation previously submitted to the U.S. consulate abroad
- *Proof of financial support or solvency*
  - evidence of financial support for full term

The Immigration Inspector should:
- Issue and date a Form I-94 to the student
- Send Form I-20 M-N to the INS for processing
- Admit an eligible spouse and minor children in M-2 status

The Immigration Inspector will issue an I-94 Arrival/Departure Record card to each family member entering the U.S. in M-2 status. Employment is not permitted.

Documentation and supporting evidence includes:
- *Passport*
  - passport valid for at least six months beyond date of entry
- *Prior approval*
  - the principal alien's Form I-20 M-N
- *Proof of financial support or solvency*
  - evidence of financial support

The INS should send Form I-20 M-N to the sponsoring school.

Step 4 - Maintenance of Status

A student must complete the vocational or non-academic program prior to the date of expiration of status. However, a student who is eligible to return to school may take a summer vacation in the United States between semesters.

The Illegal Immigration Reform and Immigrant Responsibility Act of 1996 included several provisions which impact on foreign students including:

- A program to electronically collect personal and academic progress data on foreign students from approved institutions　　*Ref: IIRIRA96.641*

- Collection of a fee not to exceed $100 when an alien first registers with the institution after entering the United States　　*Ref: IIRIRA96.641*

Step 5 - Employment Authorization by the INS

Part-time employment is permitted on campus but off-campus employment is restricted to practical training required for the certificate or degree and the permission of the INS must be obtained. Students may apply for paid practical training upon completion of their program.

The maximum time for training is one month for each four months of full-time study to a maximum of six months plus 30 days to depart the country.

Obtaining work authorization is a three-part process.

Part One - Designated School Official

Certification of the school's Designated School Official (DSO) is required.

Documentation and supporting evidence includes:

- *INS form*
  - I-538, Certification by Designated School Official
- *Fee*
  - filing fee of $70
- *Current and prior immigration status*
  - Form I-20 M-N

Part Two - School Submission to the INS

The school submits the Form I-538 to the INS to certify that employment is directly related to the student's field of study.

Part three - Application to the INS

The student applies in person to the local INS for an Employment Authorization Document (EAD).

Documentation and supporting evidence includes:

- *Form*
  - I-765, Application for Employment Authorization
- *Fee*
  - filing fee of $100
- *Required approval*
  - Form I-20 M-N endorsed for practical training by DSO

The INS issues the student:

- Authorizing Form I-766
- Endorsed Form I-20 M-N

Employment without authorization makes an alien subject to deportation.

Step 6 - Change of School by the INS Within the United States

Students may change school within the first six months of enrollment by filing with the INS office having jurisdiction over the first school.

Documentation and supporting evidence includes:

- *INS form*
  - I-539, Application to Extend/Change Nonimmigrant Status
- *Fees*
  - filing fee of $120
- *Prior approval*
  - Form I-20 M-N from the new school
- *Current and prior immigration status*
  - Student's old Form I-20 M-N

- *Additional evidence*
  - Forms I-94 for student and family

A student must wait 60 days before starting at the new school. The Visa will be extended.

Step 7 - Revalidation/Extension

Application to the INS within the United States

An M-1 student must not go out of status. An M-1 student is considered to be legally in the United States as long as he or she has met and continues to meet all the requirements for maintaining status.

To extend their stay, M-1 students should apply to the INS office having jurisdiction over their school not less than 15 or more than 60 days before their stay expires.

Documentation and supporting evidence includes:

- *INS form*
  - I-539, Application to Extend/Change Nonimmigrant Status
- *Fee*
  - filing fee of $120
- *Prior approval*
  - new Form I-20 M-N, if applicable
- *Current and prior immigration status*
  - student's old Form I-20 M-N
- *Additional evidence*
  - Form I-94 of dependents, if any

The student should not send his or her Form I-94 or passport to the INS.

Visa Revalidation by the Department of State Abroad

The State Department does not do M visa renewals in the United States. However, renewals can be done at a U.S. Embassy or Consulate abroad by filing the same documents as required in the initial entry.

Chapter 5

Business Professionals

Several visa options are available to business professionals wishing to work in the United States on a temporary basis. Some classifications permit a stay of several years.

Chapter 5 focuses on four of the less restrictive classifications which permit the entry of business entrepreneurs, transferees and trainees as well as professionals who benefit from the NAFTA agreement. Included are:

- E   Treaty Trader or Investor
- H   Professional, Temporary Worker or Trainee
- L   Intracompany Transferee
- TN   Treaty NAFTA - Professional

In selecting the most appropriate classification you should consider:

- The length and purpose of your proposed stay
- Your future immigration plans
- Your professional credentials and experience
- The availability of U.S. workers with similar qualifications, and
- The willingness of U.S. employers to undertake a potentially complex, expensive and protracted visa application process

Depending on the length of the U.S. stay or other circumstances, Mexican and Canadian applicants may be able to enter the United States on business for short periods without obtaining a formal visa. (See Chapter 1).

See also Chapters 6, 7 and 8 which describe classifications with more restrictive or specialized entry criteria.

E

Treaty Trader or Investor

E status is available only to an alien who is a national of a country which has a treaty of commerce and navigation with the United States. These treaties are sometimes called friendship treaties or bilateral investment treaties.

To qualify, an alien must be coming to carry on substantial trade in goods or services principally between their home country and the United States.

Sub-categories are:

- E-1 Treaty trader, spouse and children
    - the person represents a company which will carry on trade with the United States [the U.S. office must do a substantial amount of its business (trade) with the person's country], or
- E-2 Treaty investor, spouse and children
    - the person is directing and developing a business in which they have invested a substantial amount of capital.
    Ref: INS ER 806 3-8-94; INA 101(a)(15)(E)(i),(ii); 9 FAM 41.12

While there are not firm financial guidelines on the amount of investment required, $100,000 is often used as a benchmark.

E status should not be confused with Employment-Based immigrant (Green Card) status which provides for aliens willing to invest between $500,000 and one million dollars in a U.S. enterprise. This is described in Part III of Book 1.

To qualify for Treaty Trader (E-1) status in the United States:

- You must:
    - be a national of your treaty country
    - have the same nationality as your trading firm
    - be employed in a supervisory or executive capacity, or
    - possess highly specialized skills essential to the efficient operation of the firm
- Your trading firm must:
    - have a volume of international trade of goods, services and technology which is sizeable and continuing and more than 50 percent of the trade must be between the United States and your home country

- produce evidence of substantial trade supported by three or more of the following:
  - bills of lading
  - customs receipts
  - letters of credit
  - insurance papers documenting commodities imported
  - carrier inventories
  - trade brochures
  - sales contracts

To qualify for Treaty Investor (E-2) status in the United States:

- You must:
  - be a national of your treaty country
  - be coming to the United States to develop and direct the operation
  - have control of the funds and the investment must be at risk
  - in a partnership, submit copies of partnership agreements with a statement of proportionate ownership
- Your investment must:
  - be a new or pre-existing active U.S. business
  - be substantial enough to ensure the successful operation of the enterprise
  - be a real operating enterprise, not speculative and not idle (uncommitted funds do not count)
  - have a significant impact in the United States and may not be marginal, generating only a living for the investor and family
  - not have loans secured with the assets of the enterprise
  - be supported by:
    - articles of incorporation
    - payments for the rental of business premises or office equipment
    - business licenses
    - stock certificates
    - office inventories
    - insurance appraisals
    - advertising invoices
    - annual reports
    - net worth statements from certified professional accountants
    - business bank accounts for routine operations and escrow

Both categories are available to Canadians and Mexicans under the terms of NAFTA.   *Ref: DOS Publication 10074, August, 1995*

Admission Process

Step 1 - Clearing the Department of State (DOS) Abroad

The consular officer must be satisfied that the alien qualifies under the provisions of INA 101(a)(15)(E).   *Ref: 9 FAM 41.51*

If you are living outside the United States, the employer is not required to file an INS petition in order to apply for an original E-1 or E-2.
Ref: INS Instructions - Form I-129

The State Department advises that visa applicants should generally apply at the U.S. Embassy or Consulate having jurisdiction over their place of permanent residence although they may also apply in a third country.
Ref: DOS Publication 10074, August 1995

Few of the Canadian and Mexican border posts handle E cases. Although Canadian nationals all require an E visa, the U.S. Consulate in Toronto is the only Consulate in Canada which processes E visa applications for Canadian Citizens and Landed Immigrants of Canada as well.   *Ref: 9 FAM 41.2(m)*

The U.S. Consulate in Ciudad Juarez only accepts cases from residents of Chihuahua and those with a business enterprise in New Mexico or West Texas. The U.S. Consulate in Tijuana will not accept applications for E visas from persons not legally resident in Mexico.

The DOS also advises that none of the participating posts will accept applications from TCN E Visa applicants who are not resident in their consular districts.
Ref: DOS Publication - TCN Present in United States

Documentation and supporting evidence includes:
- *DOS form*
  - OF 156, Nonimmigrant Visa Application
- *Fees*
  - $45 non-refundable Machine-Readable Visa (MRV) fee collected at posts which issue MRVs
  - visa reciprocity fee equating to fees charged in similar circumstances in alien's home country
- *Passports and photographs*
  - passport valid for at least six months beyond intended stay
  - photographs 1½" square (37 mm) square showing full face without head covering against a light background
- *Current and prior immigration status*
  - I-94, Arrival/Departure Record, as an example

- *Professional credentials*
  - university diploma(s)
  - supporting documentation
- *Evidence to support request*
  - very detailed explanatory letter from the company
  - forms required by the consular officer to ensure that the enterprise meets the requirements of the law
- *Proof of financial support or solvency:*
  - extensive documentation to demonstrate financial solvency such as a letter from the bank
  - employer's supporting letter confirming salary, function and source of funds
- *Medical clearance*
  - if history of medical ineligibility
- *Evidence that U.S. stay is temporary (intent to depart)*
  - binding family ties
  - copy of return tickets
  - no intention to abandon residence abroad

The charge for issuing the E-1 or E-2 is approximately the same as the fee charged to U.S. citizens in your home country.

Ref: DOS Publication 10311, November, 1995

Step 2 - Clearing the INS at a U.S. Port of Entry

Option 1 - NAFTA Only

- Under the terms of NAFTA, citizens of Canada and Mexico may apply directly at a U.S. port of entry without obtaining employment authorization and without numerical restriction provided that they:
  - have established all necessary documentation and obtained a visa at a U.S. Embassy or Consulate serving their home country
  - carry on substantial trade in goods or services principally between their home country and the United States
  - establish, develop, administer or provide advice or key technical services to the operation of an investment to which a substantial amount of capital is committed
  - act in a capacity that is supervisory, executive or involves essential skills   *Ref: NAFTA Annex 1603*

Option 2 - Non-NAFTA

The expiration date on the visa issued by the consular officer abroad is the last day you may apply at a U.S. port of entry for permission to enter the United States.

The decision on whether to admit is up to the INS Immigration Inspector. If admission is approved, the officer will validate your Form I-94, Arrival/Departure Record and note the length of stay permitted.

Documentation and supporting evidence includes:

- *Prior DOS approval*
  - DOS Machine-Readable Visa (MRV) in passport
- *Evidence to support request*
  - employer's letter confirming function, amount and source of salary
  - details of how enterprise qualifies for E status
- *Evidence that U.S. stay is temporary (intent to depart)*
  - binding family ties
  - copy of return tickets
  - no intention to abandon residence abroad

The E-1 or E-2 is valid for a maximum of 12 months from the date of entry.

Aliens with E-1 or E-2 status may bring a spouse and unmarried children under 21 years of age but the dependents may not accept employment.

Holders of E visas may reside in the United States as long as they continue to maintain their status with the enterprise. *Ref: DOS Publication 10074, August 1995*

Step 3 - Revalidation/Extension or Change of Status

Application to the INS within the United States

The **Principal Alien** must apply between 60 days before or one year after expiration. The alien is permitted to remain while the extension is being processed.

The employer of the principal alien should file with the INS regional Service Center in Texas or California depending on the location of the enterprise for either:

- An extension of E status, or
- A change to E status from another classification   *Ref: INS- Form I-129*

The decision to grant or deny a request for extension of stay is made solely by the INS. The INS issues a Form I-797, Notice of Approval which serves as evidence of the extension or change of status.

Documentation and supporting evidence for the principal alien includes:

- *INS forms*
  - Form I-129, Petition for a Nonimmigrant Worker
  - E Classification Supplement page
  - Form I-126, Report of Status by Treaty Trader or Investor
  Fees
  - I-129 filing fee of $110

- *Passports and photographs*
  - passport valid for at least six months beyond intended stay and containing the present visa for the same classification (may be in a previous passport)
  - photographs 1½" square (37 mm) square showing right ear without head covering against a light background
- *Current and prior immigration status*
  - copy of Form I-94, Arrival/Departure Record
- *Professional credentials*
  - evidence of the applicant's special knowledge, skills, training, education
- *Employer's supporting documentation*
  - letter from the petitioner explaining the reasons for the change of status
- *Proof of financial support or solvency*
  - substantial trade in the case of an E-1 petition
  - substantial investment in the case of an E-2 petition
  - the unavailability of U.S. workers in the case of a non-executive/managerial employee
  - ownership and nationality such as:
    - lists of investors with their nationalities
    - stock certificates
    - certificates of ownership issued by a foreign embassy
  - supporting letter confirming salary, function and source of funds
- *Civil documents to confirm relationship with accompanying dependents*
  - birth
  - marriage
  - divorce
  - death of spouse
- *Medical clearance*
  - if history of medical ineligibility
- *Evidence that U.S. stay is temporary (intent to depart)*
  - binding family ties
  - return tickets
  - no intention to abandon residence abroad

Dependents

Dependents of principal E status aliens should file with the INS regional Service Center having jurisdiction over their state to change or extend their status. They may study on a full or part-time basis.

Documentation and supporting evidence for E-1 and E-2 dependents includes:

- *INS form*
  - Form I-539, Application to Extend/Change Nonimmigrant Status

- *Fees*
  - filing fee of $120
- *Passports and photographs*
  - passport valid for at least six months beyond intended stay and containing the present visa for the same classification (may be in a previous passport)
  - photographs 1½" square (37 mm) square showing right ear without head covering against a light background
- *Current and prior immigration status*
  - copy of Form I-94, Arrival/Departure Record
- *Professional credentials*
  - evidence of the applicant's special knowledge, skills, training, education
- *Employer's supporting documentation*
  - letter from the petitioner explaining the reasons for change of status
- *Principal alien's supporting documentation*
  - the petition filed for the principal alien or evidence that it is pending
  - a copy of the principal alien's Form I-94, Arrival/Departure Record or approval notice showing status granted
- *Proof of financial support or solvency*
  - supporting documentation from principal alien
- *Civil documents to confirm relationship with principal alien*
  - birth
  - marriage
  - divorce
  - death of spouse
- *Evidence that U.S. stay is temporary (intent to depart)*
  - binding family ties
  - copy of return tickets
  - no intention to abandon residence abroad

Dependents of E aliens may study on a full or part-time basis in the U.S.

Visa Revalidation by the Department of State (DOS)

After the INS has extended your stay, your visa may need to be renewed before attempting to reenter the United States after a business trip abroad. Depending on how U.S. citizens are treated in your home country in similar circumstances, your original visa may have been issued with restrictions on the number of entries into the United States and its period of validity, perhaps six months or a year.

Application for visa renewal may be made at a U.S. Embassy or Consulate in your home country. Revalidations may also be made at a U.S. Consulate in Mexico or Canada by calling (900) 443-3131 for an appointment.

As a service to aliens in a few classifications such as E, the Department of State renews E visas by mail in the United States.

It is not possible to obtain expedited processing or status reports. If you do not have time to get your visa renewal in the U.S., you should apply in person to the consular office of the country of destination.

As a service to aliens in a few classifications such as E, the Department of State renews visas by mail in the U.S., if time permits. Full information on revalidations is available from the State Department website at http://travel.state.gov/revals.html. You may download the required Form OF 156 there.

Documentation and supporting evidence includes:

- *DOS form*
  - OF 156, Nonimmigrant Visa Application
- *Fees*
  - $45 non-refundable Machine-Readable Visa (MRV) fee
  - visa reciprocity fee equating to fees charged in similar circumstances in alien's home country
- *Passport and photographs*
  - passport valid for at least six months with previous visa
  - passport-size photographs for each applicant
- *Current and prior immigration status*
  - original current I-94 (no copies), or
  - I-797 Petition Approval Notice
- *Employer's supporting documentation*
  - financial statement, income tax and W-2 forms (E-2) 10 or fewer staff
  - detailed and signed letter on letterhead identifying:
    - the employee
    - his or her position
    - travel itinerary

When a fee is charged for visa reciprocity, include two certified checks or money orders, one for the visa application and one for the reciprocity charge. Personal checks cannot be accepted.

Applications should be sent in a padded envelope with a stamped padded envelope enclosed for return mailing. If return by courier is requested, an air bill is required. Processing may take six to eight weeks. Call (202) 663-1213 for further information.

Completed applications may be sent by mail to:

> U.S. Department of State/Visa
> P.O. Box 952099
> St. Louis, MO 63195-2099

Completed applications may also be sent by courier to:

> U.S. Department of State/Visa (Box 2099)
> 1005 Convention Plaza
> St. Louis, MO 63101-1200

H

Professional, Temporary Worker or Trainee

H status meets a broad spectrum of employment, training and residency needs ranging from the experienced professional to the trainee. It is reserved only for "those who are coming to the United States to work in a temporary job." *Ref: ER 806 3-8-94*

Sub-categories are:
- H-1B Professionals or other skilled workers
  - specialty occupations and fashion models
- H-1C Nurses in Health Professional Shortage areas
  - registered professional nurses (formerly H-1A)
- H-2A Temporary services for general labor - Agricultural Services
- H-2B Temporary services for general labor - Non-agricultural Services
  - skills in short supply
  - seasonal services unavailable in the United States
- H-3 Occupational Trainee/Special Education Visitor
  - H-3 Trainee
    - in an established formal occupational training program
    - program not available in the home country
    - skills to be used outside the United States
  - H-3 Special Education Exchange Visitor
    - participant in structured special education exchange visitor program providing practical training and experience in the education of children with physical, mental or emotional disabilities
- H-4 Dependents
  - H-4 Spouse and unmarried children under 21 of principal alien classified H-1, H-2, or H-3   *Ref: 9 FAM 41.12/53; INA 101(a)(15)(H)*

An H-1B nonimmigrant may be admitted for up to three years initially, extendable for another two to seven years depending on the sub-category.

After the expiration of the full six-year H-1B term including extensions, aliens must remain outside the U.S. for one year before returning for a new period as an H-1B. However, entry in a status other than H, L or permanent resident is possible.

A fully qualified alien may enter with spouse and unmarried children. Although dependents may not accept employment, they may do volunteer work with public service organizations such as the American Red Cross without compensation.

With the exception of aliens in H-1 and L status, nonimmigrants living in the U.S. risk losing their status when they apply for a Green Card. The doctrine of dual intent provisions of the INA permits aliens with nonimmigrant H-1 and L status to simultaneously seek permanent resident or immigrant status without jeopardizing their nonimmigrant status. The dual intent doctrine does not apply to aliens with TN - NAFTA status as some think. The L and TN processes are discussed later.

The requirement that an H-1 nonimmigrant have a residence in a foreign country which he or she has no intention of abandoning was removed, effective October 1, 1991, by Section 205(e) of IMMACT90.   *Ref: P.L. 101-649*

A new approach
When the annual quota of 65,000 H-1B entries ran out four and a half months before the end of the 1998 fiscal year, Congress, industry and the public were forced to reconsider the old rules which have permitted the temporary entry of business professionals like the most frequent H-1B entrants: therapists, computer-related workers, college and university faculty, physicians, surgeons, auditors and accountants.

In 1998, Congress passed a short-term H-1B compromise, the American Competitiveness and Workforce Improvement Act of 1998 (ACWIA) which was included in the Omnibus Budget Bill, signed by the President on October 21, 1998. An additional $500 fee and increased annual quota were added through Fiscal Year 2001 and the requirement for a newly revised Form I-129W was added on March 30, 2000. Amendments shall sunset, cease to be effective, on September 30, 2001.

The new legislation does not change the fact that qualifying for H-1 or H-2 status is a multi-step process which requires the cooperation of the federal Departments of Justice, State and Labor to collectively establish the eligibility of a temporary worker for admission. H-3 and H-4 aliens do not require Department of Labor clearance. ACWIA was intended to change the process for some multi-H-1B employers.

Temporary annual quotas
As a result of the shortage of H-1B "numbers" in 1998, new legislation increased the Fiscal Year quotas temporarily. The H-1B quota for aliens classified as H-1B nonimmigrants, excluding those involved in Department of Defense research and development projects or coproduction projects, may not exceed:

- 115,000 in Fiscal Year 1999
- 115,000 in Fiscal Year 2000
- 107,500 in Fiscal Year 2001
- 65,000 in each succeeding Fiscal Year   *Ref: ACWIA.411 (a)*

When the Fiscal Year 2000 quota ran out in the spring of 2000, it only served to increase efforts in Congress to draft legislation which would raise the annual limits.

The annual caps do not apply to sequential or concurrent employment, extensions or amended petitions.   *Ref: INA 214(g)(A)*

Temporary supplementary fee

Under section 414, the Attorney General shall impose an additional fee of $500 for each petition filed from December 1, 1998 to October 1, 2001 on behalf of all H-1B nonimmigrants unless employed by nonprofit or institutions of higher education for:

- An initial grant of H-1B status
- An extension of stay
- A change of employer

Fees are to be deposited into an H-1B nonimmigrant petitioner account and used for scholarships for low-income math, engineering, and computer science students and job training of U.S. workers who are citizens, Green Card holders or refugees according to a precise formula. Applications for grants must be mailed to the U.S. Department of Labor, Employment and Training Administration. Information is available at http://www.doleta.gov and 65 FR 16658.

Exempt H-1B nonimmigrant

A new classification of exempt H-1B nonimmgrant was created and aliens who qualify are not counted against the annual H-1B quota during the longer of the six-month period beginning on the date of enactment of ACWIA98 or the period between the date of enactment of ACWIA98 and the date final regulations are issued. Exempt H-1B nonimmigrants are those who:

- Receive wages (including cash bonuses and similar compensation) at an annual rate equal to at least $60,000, or
- Have attained a master's or higher degree (or its equivalent) in a specialty related to the intended employment   *Ref: ACWIA.412 (b) (3) (B)*

H-1B-dependent employers

Although the rules remain basically unchanged for employers with a relatively small share of H-1B nonimmigrants in their workforce, the new law requires the INS to establish new more restrictive rules for employers with a higher proportion of their workforce employed as H-1B nonimmigrants. Since the ACWIA is still being phased in, it is important to check with the INS to ensure that petitions meet current rules.

H-1B-dependent employers are so defined if they have:

- 25 or fewer full-time equivalent employees in the U.S. of whom more than seven are H-1B nonimmigrants, or
- From 26 to 50 full-time equivalent employees in the U.S. of whom more than 12 are H-1B nonimmigrants, or
- At least 51 full-time equivalent employees in the U.S. of whom at least 15 percent are H-1B nonimmigrants   *Ref: ACWIA.412 (b) (3) (A)*

Admission Process

As noted earlier, three federal agencies are involved in the process which leads to H-1 or H-2 nonimmigrant classifications.

Step 1 - Blanket Application

Aliens who will apply for their visas at the same consulate or, if they do not need visas, will enter at the same port of entry and may be included in one petition filed by the employer or agent in the following classifications if the dates of employment are the same and they are also:

- H-1B   members of the same entertainment group or athletic team and accompanying aliens, or
- H-2A/B   on the same labor certification performing the same duties, or
- H-3   receiving the same training

Step 2 - Qualifying - Entry Criteria

The necessary qualifications vary according to the sub-category.

H-1B - Aliens in Specialty Occupations and as Fashion Models

The petitioner (employer) must establish that the position is a specialty occupation and that the beneficiary (alien worker) meets H-1B qualifications.

To qualify in an H-1B specialty occupation, one of the following criteria must be met:

- The beneficiary:
  - holds the required U.S. baccalaureate or higher degree from an accredited college or university, or
  - holds a foreign degree determined to be equivalent
  - holds a degree common to the industry in parallel positions which the employer normally requires for the position
  - holds an unrestricted state license, registration or certification
  - has equivalent education, training and experience plus recognized expertise through progressively responsible positions
  - the nature of the duties are so specialized, complex or unique that the knowledge required to perform the duties is usually associated with a baccalaureate or higher degree

The beneficiary may also be required to demonstrate:

- Theoretical, practical application of a body of highly specialized knowledge
- Membership in a professional organization
- The source of awards including the reputation, size, standing and membership requirements of the awarding organization

H-1C - Registered Nurses

A new classification for registered nurses was created in the Nursing Relief for Disadvantaged Areas Act of 1999 and implemented on April 19, 2000. This classification is designed to allow the entry of registered nurses to deliver health care to underserved or health professional shortage areas.   *Ref:INA 101(a)(15)(H)(i)(c); 65 FR 20903*

The unique features of the H-1C include:

- Admission for up to three years
- The classification will end in four years, unless extended by Congress
- A limit of 500 visas per year
- A limit of 50 visas to any state
- Eligible hospitals must have at least:
  - 190 acute care beds
  - 35 percent of patients on Medicare
  - 28 percent on Medicaid

H-2A - Temporary Agricultural Service Workers - U.S. Workers are Not Available

This category covers alien workers who are needed to perform agricultural labor or services of a temporary or seasonal nature.

H-2B - Other Temporary Workers - U.S. Workers are Not Available

This is a broad category to cover aliens in non-agricultural occupations such as sports instructors and minor league professional athletes, instrumental musicians, stable attendants, crab meat and fish roe workers, and housekeeping cleaners. Others may be unskilled. H-2B temporary workers must be needed to meet a specific project of not more than one year with a defined end. Portions of the annual allotment of 60,000 H-2B visas may also be used for the planned temporary Q-2 classification.

Step 3 - Clearing the Department of Labor

Step 3 applies only to H-1 and H-2 candidates who must first obtain a job offer and Department of Labor (DOL) approval before an INS petition may be filed. If you are applying for H-3 or H-4 status, go directly to Step 4.

More than one alien may be requested on an application if they are:

- To do the same work on the same terms and conditions
- In the same occupation
- In the same area(s) of employment during the same period

The Department of Labor - Employment and Training Administration may be contacted for information at:

> Division of Alien Labor Certification
> 200 Constitution Avenue, N.W., Room N4456
> Washington, DC 20210
> (202) 219-5263

Special rules for H-1B-dependent employers

Although the American Competitiveness and Workforce Improvement Act of 1998 basically left the old H-1B process in place for employers with a limited H-1B workforce, it has established more stringent rules for employers with a larger share of H-1B nonimmigrants in their full-time workforce. On an application submitted between the date the final H-1B regulations are implemented by the INS and October 1, 2001, H-1B-dependent employers must attest that they:

- Did not displace a U.S. worker in the same or essentially equivalent job
- Will not place the nonimmigrant with another employer at the other employer's worksite(s) unless the duties were not previously performed by a displaced U.S. worker within 90 days of the placing of the nonimmigrant
- Have accepted liability if the other employer displaces a U.S. worker
- Have taken good faith steps to recruit in the U.S.
- Have offered the job to any equally or better qualified U.S. applicant
- Have used relevant legitimate normal and customary selection criteria in a non-discriminatory manner   *Ref: ACWIA.212 (n) (1)*

Some teeth are added in the legislation under section 212 (n) (2) (C), in which H-1B-dependent employers face new rule changes and penalties, after notice and opportunity for a hearing if:

- The Secretary of Labor finds a failure or a substantial failure to meet a condition, or a misrepresentation of fact, the Attorney General may:
  - impose a maximum $1,000 penalty , and
  - not approve H-1B petitions for that employer for at least one year
- The Secretary finds a wilful failure to meet a condition or wilful misrepresentation of material fact in an application:
  - a civil penalty of up to $5,000 per violation may be imposed, and
  - the Attorney General shall not approve that employer's H-1B petitions for at least two years
- The Secretary finds a failure to meet a condition or a wilful misrepresentation of material fact resulting in the displacement of a U.S. worker within 90 days of the filing of any visa petition and if the placing employer knew or had reason to know of the displacement:
  - a monetary penalty not exceeding $35,000 may be imposed, and
  - the Attorney General shall not approve H-1B petitions for three years
- It is also a violation for an employer to:
  - discriminate against an employee or former employee who cooperates or seeks to cooperate in the investigation of a possible violation
  - require that an H-1B nonimmigrant pay a penalty for ceasing employment prior to a mutually agreed date
  - require that an H-1B nonimmigrant reimburse the employer for any part of the fee for the petition; a maximum $1,000 monetary penalty may be imposed and the amount paid returned to the nonimmigrant

- place an H-1B nonimmigrant designated as a full or part-time employee in nonproductive status or to fail to pay the nonimmigrant full wages due to a decision by the employer or due to the nonimmigrant's lack of a permit or license (this clause does not apply to non-work-related factors such as the nonimmigrant's voluntary request for an absence or inability to work)
- fail to offer benefits and eligibility for benefits to an H-1B nonimmigrant on the same basis and criteria as offered to U.S. workers

Arbitration process

In an effort to ensure equitable treatment, the new legislation has established a detailed arbitration process with several key elements including:

- The Attorney General shall establish an arbitration process for complaints concerning an employer's failure or misrepresentation
- The Attorney General may request the Federal Mediation and Conciliation Service to appoint an arbitrator to initiate binding arbitration proceedings
- If the arbitrator concludes that there is a failure or misrepresentation, the Attorney General may impose administrative remedies up to $5,000 per violation and not approve petitions for up to two years
- An employer on probation may be subject to random investigations for a period of five years after a wilful failure to meet a condition or wilful misrepresentation of material fact
- Such actions may only be set aside in a U.S. Court of Appeals

Non-H-1B-dependent employers

Employers of H-1 candidates must submit a Labor Condition Application (LCA) with the regional office of the Employment and Training Administration (ETA) of the DOL serving the area where the alien will be employed no more than six months before the start of employment. An LCA application may also be downloaded from the internet at http://edc.dws.state.ut.us/Faxback.htm. The completed and signed form may be faxed to the appropriate DOL office and approval may be faxed back in as little as one minute.

A determination whether to certify is made by the ETA regional Certifying Officer. The LCA must be valid for the period of time requested to a maximum of three years employment. It may not extend outside the dates on the LCA. A subsequent three-year renewal may be made to a maximum stay of three years. Nurses are limited to a total of five years.   *Ref: 59 FR.243, 1994*

A U.S. health care provider may file for nurses under H-1B status although a new H-1C classification has been implemented for nurses in health shortage areas.

If the H-1B nonimmigrant agrees, an employer that is a school or other educational institution may pay an annual salary in disbursements over fewer than 12 months to the H-1B nonimmigrant in accordance with an established salary practice which applies equally to U.S. workers in the same occupational classification.

Documentation and supporting evidence includes:
- *DOL form*
  - Form ETA 9035, Labor Condition Application
- *Employee's professional credentials*
  - Bachelor's degree in a narrowly defined subject area, or
  - an Associate degree plus three years of equivalent experience for each required year of schooling in a narrowly defined subject area may be sufficient
- *Employer's evidence to support request - Attestation on Form ETA 9035*
  - job data - question 7
    - three-digit occupational group code from Dictionary of Occupational Titles (DOT) (see Appendix E)
  - wage statement - question 8 (a)
    - required wage will be paid for the entire period of employment
    - the greater of the actual or prevailing wage will be paid
    - wage sources in order of priority:
      - SESA determination
      - independent authoritative source
      - another legitimate source of wage information
  - working conditions statement - question 8 (b)
    - hiring of the alien will not adversely affect the working conditions of similarly employed workers in the area
  - no strike or lockout statement - question 8 (c)
    - there is currently no strike or lockout in a labor dispute in the occupational classification at the place of employment
  - labor condition statement - question 8 (d)
    - if there is no bargaining representative, posted notice of filing a total of 10 days
- *Additional evidence - registered professional nurses only*
  - the nurse:
    - has received appropriate nursing education in the United States or Canada or has a full and unrestricted license to practice
    - pending a final ruling on IIRIRA96.343, the INS and DOS have agreed to waive the certification requirement   *Ref: INS10/14/98*
    - is fully qualified, eligible and will practice as a registered nurse in the place of intended employment
  - the employer will:
    - comply with any limitations which the laws in the state place on the nurse's services
- *Additional evidence - foreign physicians performing direct patient care*
  - the physician must have:
    - a license or authorization required by the state of employment

- a full and unrestricted license to practice medicine in a foreign country, or
- graduated from a medical school in the U.S. or a foreign country
- completed a medical residency in the U.S. (see exception below)
  - the employer must confirm that:
    - it is a nonprofit educational or research institution or agency and if the physician will teach or conduct research, or
    - the foreign doctor has passed the Federation Licensing Examination (FLEX) or an equivalent accepted by the U.S. Department of Health and Human Services and is:
      - competent in spoken and written English, or
      - a graduate of a medical school accredited by the U.S. Department of Education

Canadian physicians

Since the U.S. Department of Education has accredited all U.S. and Canadian medical schools, Canadians are not usually required to have completed a medical residency in the United States. Nevertheless, they must still have passed the FLEX, NBME, or USMLE licensing examinations. To date, no foreign medical examinations have been accepted as equivalent to the FLEX.

Mechanisms for enforcement

The DOL does not require proof that the employer has been unable to find qualified U.S. workers unless the employer is H-1B-dependent. Although the job does not have to be advertised outside the company:

- The employer:
  - must post a labor attestation at the work site to indicate the presence of an H employee
  - must pay the greater of the actual or prevailing rate
- Co-workers:
  - should report alleged H status violations to the Department of Labor
- DOL:
  - may initiate independent investigations

H-1C - Registered Nurses
To qualify:
- The nurse must:
  - have been educated in the U.S. , or
  - have a full unrestricted license to practice nursing in the country where the nursing education was obtained
  - have a full unrestricted license in the state of employment, or
  - have passed the appropriate examination
  - be fully qualified and authorized to work as a registered nurse in the place of intended employment

- The employer must attest that:
  - the facility meets the required definition of facility
  - employment will not affect the wages and working conditions of other nurses
  - the alien will be paid the wage rate of other similarly employed nurses
  - it is taking steps to recruit and retain U.S. nurses
  - there is no strike or lockout in progress
  - notice of filing has been provided to the union, if any, or to staff
  - it will not employee more than 33 percent of its RNs as H-1Cs
  - will not assign the H-1C to other than its worksites

H-2A - Temporary Agricultural Service Workers

An employer who anticipates a shortage of H-2A U.S. workers needed to perform agricultural labor or services of a temporary or seasonal nature may apply for temporary alien agriculture labor certification to the Regional Administrator (RA) in whose region the intended employment is located.   *Ref: INA 101(a)(15)(H)(ii)(a)*

The petition for an H-2A may be filed by the employer or the employer's agent or U.S. agriculture producers as a joint employer on the Labor Certification.

The application must be filed no less than 60 calendar days before the first date of need. The state and employer begin to recruit U.S. workers. Job order initiates a search of potential interstate and intrastate sources of U.S. workers.

The Regional Administrator (RA) makes a determination to grant or deny by 20 calendar days before the date of need. Labor Certification is granted only for enough H-2A workers to fill the employer's job opportunities for which U.S. workers are not available.   *Ref: 57 FR.181, 1992*

Documentation and supporting evidence includes:

- *DOL form*
  - Form ETA 750, Part A, Application for Alien Employment Certification
- *Fees*
  - $100 for Labor Certification
  - $10 for each job opportunity
  - $1,000 maximum (employer or joint employer association)
  - payable within 30 calendar days of granting Labor Certification
- *Employer's evidence to support request*
  - total number of workers anticipated employing
  - copy of job offer
  - compliance
    - with DOL Occupational Safety and Health standards
    - with Federal, state and local employment-related laws and regulations
    - agreement to abide by assurances

- U.S. workers
  - offered no fewer benefits, wages and working conditions
  - provide employment to any qualified eligible U.S. worker applying before 50 percent of foreign worker's work contract has elapsed
  - documentation of any positive efforts to recruit U.S. workers
- labor relations
  - job not vacant because the former incumbent on strike or locked out
  - no retaliation against any person initiating complaint

H-2B - Other Temporary Workers - U.S. Workers are Not Available
The employer's need for services must be one of:

- One-time occurrence
- Seasonal need
- Peakload need
- Intermittent need

As a general rule, the period of the employer's need must be one year or less, although there may be extraordinary circumstances where the need may be for longer than one year. The Labor Certification application may be filed for up to, but not exceeding 12 months. If there are unforseen circumstances where the employer's need exceeds one year, a new certification is required for each period beyond one year to a three year maximum.

Applications for certification shall be filed with the State Employment Security Agency (SESA) serving the area of employment between 60 and 120 days before the Labor Certification is needed. The SESA will prepare a job order and place it into the regular ES system for ten days. Walk-in applicants and those in SESA files will be referred to the employer.

The employer must advertise the job opportunity for three days in the most appropriate general circulation newspaper, professional, trade or ethnic publication to attract U.S. workers before aliens may be considered.

The SESA office will forward the application to the appropriate Regional Administrator, Employment and Training Administration (ETA).

The regional Certifying Officer shall determine whether to grant the temporary Labor Certification based on:

- Availability of U.S. workers for the temporary employment
- Whether the employment of the alien will adversely affect wages and working conditions of similarly employed U.S. workers
- Whether the job opportunity contains restrictions which preclude consideration of U.S. workers   *Ref: 20 CFR 655.3*

The Certifying Officer who makes a temporary Labor Certification determination sends the employer the certified application containing the official temporary Labor

Certification stamp and other documents including the Temporary Determination Form. These documents should all be submitted to the INS.

In 1995, only 2,398 visas were issued.

Documentation and supporting evidence includes:

- *DOL form*
  - Form ETA 750, Part A, Application for Alien Employment Certification
- *Employer's evidence to support request*
  - documentation of any efforts to recruit U.S. workers
  - statement explaining:
    - why the job opportunity is temporary
    - why the need meets the standard of:
      - a one-time occurrence
      - a seasonal or peakload need
      - an intermittent need
- *Aerospace engineer documentation*
  - SESA job order
  - employer's blind ad in a newspaper or engineering publication
  - offer of reemployment to laid-off engineers
  - identification of alien engineer's work location
  - employee's contract
  - all certification job orders in interstate and intrastate clearance
- *Construction worker documentation*
  - union representatives contacted to determine availability of U.S. workers when ten or more workers in the same occupation requested
  - within six months
- *Boilermaker documentation*
  - in emergency situations, boilermaker applications must be sent directly to National Office of the U.S. Department of Labor, Washington
  - in nonemergency situations, applications are processed like all H-2s

H-3 - Temporary Trainee
H-3 - Special Education Exchange Visitor
Department of Labor attestation is not required.

H-4 - Spouse and Minor Children
Department of Labor attestation is not required but the working spouse must complete the admission process before the spouse and minor children may be admitted.

Step 4 - Clearing the INS - Initial Petition

After receiving Department of Labor approval, the employer may file a petition with the INS regional Service Center having jurisdiction over the state in which the alien will be working. If approved, the INS issues a Form I-797, Notice of Approval which the DOS requires.

In December, 1999, the four INS Service Centers briefly stopped processing H-1Bs so that they could do an audit on the number of cases being processed and to bring the Service Centers in line. It is expected that these periodic holds could continue.

Physicians may be admitted in H-1B status if their entry is primarily to teach or conduct research at or for a public nonprofit public educational or research institution or agency in which no patient care will be performed except that which is incidental to the teaching or research. However, doctors may also be admitted for direct patient care on a case by case basis on the approval of the appropriate INS regional Service Center. In such cases, the physician must have a state license or authorization and a full degree.   *Ref: INS Northern Service Center*

A second simultaneous H-1B petition may be filed while the first is still in force. A spouse and minor children are processed with the principal alien as H-4s.

Documentation and supporting evidence includes:

- *INS forms*
  - Form I-129, Petition for a Nonimmigrant Worker
  - H Classification Supplement page which confirms:
    - that the job is new to the alien
    - the job description, proposed duties and location
    - details about the business
    - details about the alien and his or her qualifications
    - agreement to the terms of the LCA and return transportation if the alien is dismissed early
    - compensation at the average current wage for the job in the area
    - the dates of employment   *Ref: INS ER-721 EFC*
  - Form I-129W, Date Collection and Filing Fee Exemption
    (Complete Part B if claiming exemption)   *Ref: ACWIA*
- *Fees*
  - Form I-129 filing fee of $110
  - H-1B filing fee of $500 (except exempt organization) **one $610 check**
- *Prior DOL approval*
  - copy of Form ETA 9035, Notice of Acceptance from the Department of Labor
- *Employer's evidence to support request*
  - letter describing the job and sponsorship in detail
  - contract describing who controls the alien's work and whether he or she controls the work of others
  - company's annual report
  - agreement to pay the alien's return fare home

- evidence of nonprofit organization status if claiming $500 fee exemption
- *Employee's professional credentials*
  - work experience, résumé, diplomas, professional memberships and qualifications, as applicable

The employer must be prepared to make available the additional documentation filed with the Department of Labor as noted previously. Also, submit the following additional documentation to the INS for **H-1B Registered Professional Nurses** and **practicing physicians**:

- Letter from health care facility to the Department of Labor containing:
  - statement that employment will be as a registered nurse or physician
  - proof of the alien's professional credentials

The petitioner must submit additional documentation for **H-3 Temporary Trainees** including:

- Written description which details:
  - duration of the different phases of training including classroom work
  - the professional instructors who will provide the training
  - the reading and course work required during the training
  - why the training is not available at home
  - the job the alien will occupy at home at the end of the training period

The petitioner must submit additional documentation for **H-3 Special Education Exchange Visitors:**

- Written description of the training program
- Written description of the facility's professional staff
- Written description of the alien's participation in the training program
- Evidence that the alien is nearing completion of a baccalaureate degree or higher, or has extensive prior training and experience in teaching children with physical, mental or emotional disabilities

Upon approval, the INS will:

- Issue a Form I-797C Notice of Action approval to the petitioner with the bottom portion being Form I-94 to be cut off and retained by the worker
- Cable the notice of approval to the American consulate if the alien will be processed abroad for a visa
- Grant approval for an initial three-year period

After receiving INS approval, the petitioner should forward the approval notice to the alien so that he or she may make a visa application at a U.S. Embassy or Consulate abroad. It should take a few weeks to get the H-1B Visa after the LCA is approved by the Department of Labor. However, you may not begin work until the employer has all necessary approvals.

An employer who believes that a visa was denied as the result of an error in law, may file a request for reconsideration with the regional INS office. Filing does not authorize employment.

Step 5 - Clearing the Department of State (DOS) Abroad

In order to finalize visa proceedings, the first time an H visa is issued, it usually means a trip to a U.S. Embassy or Consulate in your home country or in a third country such as Canada or Mexico.

After INS approval is received by the alien and the consular officer, the alien should make an appointment for State Department processing at a U.S. Embassy or Consulate abroad where you will file documents according to the requirements of the requested classification. If you qualify, you will be issued a visa to be presented at a U.S. port of entry. Canadians do not require visas.

Former J Exchange Visitors who are subject to the two-year Home Residency requirement are ineligible to apply for H visas.   *Ref: 9 FAM 41.53*

At the Consulate, be prepared for the consular officer's questions about your residence at home, your job and employer, your financial situation and your future immigration plans. Be truthful and try to focus your answers on the questions asked.

Since it is the consular officer's responsibility to evaluate an applicant's credentials, take all your evidence to your interview. According to one senior consular officer, a credentials evaluation agency's report is just another piece of paper.

The visa issued by the State Department is presented at the a U.S. port of entry. A single-entry visa generally allows an alien to make a trip of less than 30 days to Canada and Mexico. However, visas of Iranians are canceled on entry.

Some H-1 visas issued abroad do not permit unlimited entry to the U.S. but application may be made to permit multiple-entry at U.S. Consulates near the Canadian or Mexican borders.

H-1B - Aliens in Specialty Occupations and as Fashion Models

Documentation and supporting evidence includes:
- *DOS form*
  - OF 156, Nonimmigrant Visa Application
- *Fees*
  - $45 non-refundable Machine-Readable Visa (MRV) fee collected at posts which issue MRVs
  - visa reciprocity fee equating to fees charged in similar circumstances in alien's home country

- *Passport and photographs*
  - passport valid for at least six months beyond intended stay
  - passport-sized photographs for each applicant regardless of age if including dependents on application
- *Prior INS and DOL approvals*
  - certified copy of employer's petition Form ETA 9035, Labor Condition Application (LCA) including copy of DOL certification
  - original Form I-797, Notice of Approval for each applicant
- *Current and prior immigration status*
  - I-94, Arrival/Departure Record when the United States was last entered, if applicable
  - previous visa, if applicable (may be in a previous passport)
- *Professional credentials*
  - university degree and/or other professional certification (including nurse's nursing diploma)
- *Employer's evidence to support request*
  - letter from employer giving such information as job title, salary, date of joining company
  - letter from your immediate supervisor confirming the need to travel abroad on company business if multiple-entry visa is required
  - copies of all documents filed with the INS by employer
  - forms required to ensure that the enterprise meets legal requirements
- *Additional evidence*
  - certified copies of all your documentation if your spouse and children are applying separately
- *Proof of financial support or solvency*
  - extensive documentation to demonstrate the alien's financial solvency such as a letter from the bank
- *Evidence that U.S. stay is temporary (intent to depart)*
  - binding family ties
  - copy of return tickets
  - no intention to abandon residence abroad
- *Payment by bank check or money order*

MRV and reciprocity visa fees require separate payment made payable to "Department of State"   *Ref: DOS instructions, January 3, 1995*

H-2A - Temporary Agricultural Service Workers
H-2B - Other Temporary Workers - U.S. Workers are Not Available

The process for obtaining a visa is similar to the H-1. However, evidence is required of DOL approval of ETA, Part A and professional credentials in keeping with the requirements of the job.

H-3 - Temporary Trainee
H-3 - Special Education Exchange Visitor
The process for obtaining a visa is similar to the H-1 without DOL approval and detailed professional qualifications.

Only 50 children per year with physical, mental or emotional handicaps will be permitted H-3 Special Education status. Maximum duration is 18 months.

H-4 - Spouse and Minor Children
Processing is with the principal alien.

Third Country Visa Processing in Canada and Mexico.
Should you choose to have your visa processed at a Canadian or Mexican consulate, it is now necessary to make an appointment in advance and at your expense by calling a central appointment 900 number or by booking online on the internet at http://www.nvars.com. 900 service operators are available between 9 am and 10 pm Eastern Time to make appointments at any participating U.S. Consulate in Canada or Mexico. Appointments are currently running two to three weeks in advance. Delays in getting through to operators have been widely reported.

The key telephone numbers are:

- From the United States:
  - To make an appointment: (900) 443-3131, or
    (888) 840-0032 (payment required)
  - General visa information: (900) 656-2222
  - To speak with a visa officer: (202) 663-1225 (during business hours)
    (202) 663-1213

- From Canada:
  - To make an appointment: (900) 451-2778
  - General visa information: (900) 451-6330
  - To speak with an operator: (900) 451-6663

You may cancel an appointment by calling (888) 611-6676 (have passport handy).

The contractor will send the appropriate forms, detailed instructions about the interview and will confirm the appointment. The contractor may also advise if certain types of applicants may encounter difficulties when they apply for their visas.

U.S. Consulates for obtaining H-1Bs are located in Ciudad Juarez, Tijuana and Matamoros, Mexico and in Halifax, Québec City, Montréal, Ottawa, Toronto, Calgary and Vancouver, Canada.

Step 6 - Clearing the INS at a U.S. Port of Entry

After being cleared at a Consulate abroad, the last step is to bring all papers to a U.S. port of entry and have the passport stamped as a legal nonimmigrant.

A person may enter the U.S. up to ten days prior to their start date to find accommodation and carry out other startup activities in their new location.

Canadians not already in status in the U.S. may apply directly to a U.S. port of entry after receiving Department of Labor Approval and INS approval of the initial petition. Canadians may also live in Canada and commute to work in the United States while in H-1B status.

Documentation and supporting evidence includes:
- *Passport*
  - passport valid for at least six months beyond intended period of stay
- *Prior INS / DOL / DOS approvals*
  - INS I-797, Notice of Approval
  - DOL Labor Condition Application or Labor Certification
  - DOS Machine-Readable Visa (MRV) in passport
- *Current and prior immigration status*
  - such as I-94
- *Professional credentials*
  - copies of documents filed with DOS and DOL
- *Evidence to support request*
  - employer's letter confirming function
- *Proof of financial support or solvency*
  - employer's letter confirming amount and source of salary and period of employment
- *Evidence that U.S. stay is temporary (intent to depart)*
  - all except H-1
  - no intention to abandon residence abroad (H-2, H-3, H-4)

As previously noted, the INA permits an H-1 to have the dual intent of remaining in the United States with a pending Green card application while maintaining temporary H-1 status. Therefore, it is not necessary to demonstrate that you will at all times maintain a foreign residence during your temporary stay in the United States and consequently, there is no longer a presumption of immigrant intent to overcome for the H-1 visa applicant.   *Ref: INA 214; 8 USC 1184*

However, the rules are quite different for an alien in H-2 or H-3 status.

A spouse or minor child holding an H-4 visa is not permitted to engage in any type of employment in the U.S. To do so is a violation of their immigration status, and could result in deportation and/or denial of future visas, including a Green Card.

Six years is the total cumulative time most aliens are allowed to remain in H status. However, there are exceptions:

- Nurses may remain a total of five years
- Aliens working on a U.S. Department of Defense administered cooperative research and development project may remain a total of 10 years
- Temporary workers performing agricultural or other services unavailable in the United States may remain a total of three years
- Special education exchange visitors may remain a total of 18 months
- Trainees in an established occupational training program may remain a total of two years

An employee who resigns or is fired has 30 days to leave the country unless he or she has legal status in another classification. If the employee is fired, the employer must pay the employee's fare back to his or her country of residence.

Canadian musicians and accompanying crews, who have an engagement within 50 miles of the U.S.-Canadian border may apply directly to a port of entry for admission in H-2 classification for up to 30 days. Application must be made to the appropriate regional Service Center if the engagement is more than 50 miles from the border or longer than 30 days. Certification by the Department of Labor is not required.

Step 7 - Revalidation/Extension or Change of Status

H-1B renewals, amendments, change of employer or additional jobs do not count against the H-1B annual quota.

An alien has 30 days of grace to depart the United States after the expiration of an initial H-1B. An I-129 renewal petition must be filed within ten days of the end of the first H-1B and the beneficiary must be in valid nonimmigrant status both when the petition is filed and on the date on which the requested change becomes effective. The alien is not permitted to work until the new petition is effective. The approval of a permanent Labor Certification, or the filing of a preference petition by an alien in H-2 or H-3 status shall be reason by itself to deny the alien's extension of stay.

Changes of status from F-1 and J-1 to H-1B can be processed as long as the effective date of the H-1B falls within the lawful duration of status which includes the grace period.

When it is not possible to bridge the gap between the end of the first status and the start of the new status for reasons beyond the applicant's control, like in 1998 and 1999 when the H-1B cap was exceeded before the end of the fiscal year, it may be possible to obtain B-2 visitor status. The INS says that in such circumstances, the pending H-1B application will not undermine eligibility for visitor status.

H-1 and H-2 candidates must first obtain Department of Labor approval before an INS petition may be filed.

Applications for H-2A extensions of up to 2 weeks are made to the INS while extensions for longer periods are made to the Department of Labor. DOL extensions are not normally permitted if the total work period including past periods and requested extension exceed 12 months or if a short term extension has been granted by the INS. Extensions for longer periods not to exceed three years may be granted by the DOL only in extraordinary circumstances.

Department of Labor clearance

Labor clearance applies only to aliens in H-1 or H-2 status. If you are applying for H-3 or H-4 status, go directly to Application to the INS within the United States.

H-1B - Aliens in Specialty Occupations and as Fashion Models

As in the case of the initial petition, the employer must file for a Labor Condition Application (LCA) renewal with the regional office of the Department of Labor before an H-1B revalidation may be filed. The LCA renewal must be valid for the period of time requested on the INS petition to a maximum of three additional years or a total of six years. Nurses are limited to a total of five years.

Documentation and supporting evidence includes:

- *DOL form*
  - Form ETA 9035, Labor Condition Application
- *Employer's attestation to support request*
  - it has offered the prevailing wage for the type of work in the geographical area as proven by:
    - salary data from the state's Department of Labor, or
    - an independent wage analysis by the company, or
    - a relevant industry wage survey
  - employment of the H-1B will not adversely affect the working conditions of workers similarly employed in the area of intended employment
  - there is not a strike, lockout or work stoppage in the occupation in which the H-1B will be employed at the place of employment
  - a copy of the labor attestation will be provided to all H-1Bs affected
  - notice of filing has been provided to the bargaining agent, if any
  - if no bargaining agent, a notice has been posted for 10 consecutive working days in two locations, including the actual work site if other than the main location, to advise other employees that it is filing for a Labor Condition Application for a prospective H-1B employee
- *Employee's professional credentials*
  - Bachelor's degree in a narrowly defined subject area, or
  - an Associate degree plus three years of equivalent experience for each required year of schooling in a narrowly defined subject area may be sufficient

H-2A - Temporary Agricultural Service Workers
H-2B - Other Temporary Workers - U.S. Workers are Not Available

The employer must file Form ETA 750, Part A with the local office of the State Employment Service to request temporary Labor Certification.

The petition for an H-2A may be filed by the employer or the employer's agent or an association of the U.S. agriculture producers named as a joint employer on the Labor Certification.

The State Employment Service will instruct the prospective employer on what steps must be taken (such as newspaper or trade magazine ads) to attract U.S. workers before aliens may be considered. If it is satisfied, the DOL will issue certification.

Application to the INS within the United States

Aliens in all classifications must apply to the INS regional Service Center having jurisdiction over their place of residence. To avoid going out of status, an application must be submitted before the grace period expires after graduation (60 days for F-1s and 30 days for J-1s). Applicants may remain in the United States during this waiting period but may not work until the H-1 is received.

Aliens who are not from a country participating in the Visa Waiver Program may submit an application for renewal between 45 days and four months prior to expiration, to the INS regional Service Center having jurisdiction over their place of residence.

As previously noted, H-2A extensions of up to two weeks may be filed directly with the INS without DOL approval.

Documentation and supporting evidence includes:

- *INS forms*
  - Form I-129, Petition for Nonimmigrant Worker
  - H Classification Supplement page
  - Form I-129W, Petition for Nonimmigrant Worker Filing Fee Exemption (if claiming exempt organization status)
- *Fees*
  - filing fee of $110
  - H-1B filing fee of $500 (except exempt organizations) **one $610 check**
- *Current and prior immigration status*
  - copy of Form I-94 Arrival/Departure Record
- *Prior DOL approval*
  - current copy of the Department Of Labor's:
    - certified Labor Condition Application ETA 9035 (H-1), or
    - Labor Certification ETA 750 (H-2A), or
    - blanket DOL team certification letter
    - required supporting documentation

- *Employer's evidence to support request*
  - letter from petitioner explaining the reasons for the extension
  - proof of financial support
  - evidence of nonprofit organization status if claiming $500 filing fee exemption

The INS issues a Form I-797, Notice of Approval which serves as evidence of the extension or change of status.

Dependents

Family members should file Form I-539 for an extension with the INS regional Service Center having jurisdiction over their state.

An H-4 spouse may request permission to convert from H-4 to H-1 and obtain permission to work after obtaining a job offer, and an LCA.

Documentation and supporting evidence includes:

- *INS form*
  - Form I-539, Application to Extend/Change Nonimmigrant Status
- *Fee*
  - filing fee of $120 for the dependent
- *Prior INS approval*
  - Original I-797 form (spouse's H-1B working permit)
- *Passports and photographs*
  - passport valid for at least six months beyond intended stay
  - passport photographs
- *Principal alien's evidence of support*
  - letter from H-1 spouse supporting the visa application
  - notarized copy of first five pages of H-1 spouse's passport (including the current visa)
- *Employer's evidence of support*
  - letter confirming function, amount and source of salary and period of employment of principal alien
- *Proof of financial support or solvency*
  - bank statement with proof of funds to support H-4 spouse
  - recent paychecks
- *Civil documents*
  - notarized copy of marriage certificate and translation
  - wedding photographs and a wedding invitation

The papers sent for the H-4 are valid for at least two months. Dependents of H aliens may study on a full or part-time basis in the U.S.

Visa Revalidation by the Department of State (DOS)

After INS has extended your stay, your visa may need to be renewed before attempting to reenter the United States after business or personal travel abroad. Depending on how U.S. citizens are treated in your home country in similar circumstances, your original visa may have been issued with restrictions on the number of entries into the United States and its period of validity, perhaps six months or a year.

Application for visa renewal may be made at a U.S. Embassy or Consulate in your home country. Although Canadians do not need visas, others may seek revalidations at a U.S. Consulate in Mexico or Canada by calling (900) 443-3131 for an appointment.

As a service to aliens in a few classifications such as H, the Department of State renews visas by mail in the U.S., if time permits. Full information on revalidations is available from the State Department website at http://travel.state.gov/revals.html. You may download the required Form OF 156 there.

It is not possible to obtain expedited processing or status reports. If you do not have time to get your visa renewal in the U.S., you should apply in person to the consular office of the country of destination.

Documentation and supporting evidence includes:

- *DOS form*
  - OF 156, Nonimmigrant Visa Application
- *Fees*
  - $45 non-refundable Machine-Readable Visa (MRV) fee
  - visa reciprocity fee equating to fees charged in similar circumstances in alien's home country
- *Passport and photographs*
  - passport valid for at least six months beyond intended stay
  - passport-size photographs for each applicant
- *Current and prior immigration status*
  - original current I-94 (no copies)
  - copy of I-171C (H's or L's) or I-797 Petition Approval Notice
- *Employer's supporting documentation*
  - detailed letter identifying:
    - the employee
    - his or her position
    - travel itinerary

When a fee is charged for visa reciprocity, include two certified checks or money orders, one for the visa application and one for the reciprocity charge. Personal checks cannot be accepted.

Applications sent through the U.S. Postal Service should be mailed in a padded envelope with a stamped padded envelope enclosed for return mailing. An airbill is required for return by courier. Processing may take from six to eight weeks.

Completed applications may be sent by mail to:

> U.S. Department of State/Visa
> P.O. Box 952099
> St. Louis, MO 63195-2099

Completed applications may also be sent by courier to:

> U.S. Department of State/Visa (Box 2099)
> 1005 Convention Plaza
> St. Louis, MO 63101-1200

Recorded information may be obtained by calling (202) 663-1213. It is possible to speak with an officer Monday to Friday. The fax number is (202) 663-1608.

Step 8 - Retaining H Status

H-1 Visa Holders must:

- Obtain another H-1 visa to work at a second full or part-time job
- Obtain a new H-1 visa if changing employers (no stamp needed)

H-1 Visa Holders may not:

- Establish a company which sponsors themselves
- Work as a contractor or on a free-lance basis
- Sponsor parents
- Always get their I-94 back when the INS approves a petition
- Be placed on absence without pay
- Remain in the United States for more than 30 days after termination of employment if they have no other legal status
- Reenter the U.S. as an H-1B for a year after completing six years in H-1B status

The Employer should:

- File an explanatory letter when the employee is promoted, provided that the jobs are similar (legal counsel may again be advisable)
- File an explanatory letter with the INS when the company changes ownership if there is no change in the employee's status and the successor company undertakes all rights, liabilities, assets and privileges of the previous owner (legal counsel may be advisable)

An INS interim rule effective July 1, 1999 has eliminated the requirement for H-1B nonimmigrants and their dependent family members to obtain Advance Parole prior to traveling outside the U.S. while they have an Adjustment of Status pending.

L

Intra-Company Transferee

Lstatus is designed to facilitate the temporary intra-company transfer of the management, executive and specialized skills of foreign nationals to the United States. It also allows a spouse and unmarried children under the age of 21 to accompany the transferee.

The classifications include:

- L-1 Intra-company transferee
  - This status permits the temporary employment of executive, managerial and specialized personnel continuing their employment with an international firm or corporation
  - L-1A - Manager/Executive "managing an essential function"
  - L-1B - Aliens with specialized knowledge
- L-2 Spouse and children of L-1 alien

Ref: 9 FAM 41.12; INS ER 806 3-8-94

To be eligible, a foreign national must:

- Have been employed abroad by an international company for at least one continuous year within the three years immediately prior to the date of the application for admission
- Be seeking temporary admission to be employed by a parent/branch/ affiliate/subsidiary of that foreign employer
- Be employed in a managerial or executive capacity, or in a position requiring specialized knowledge

Ref: INA 101(a)(15)(L)

Although it was originally targeted toward large U.S. multi-national corporations, the L-1 allows the entry of executives or managers of foreign companies with as few as four full-time employees abroad. Visas are valid for up to seven years and allow the alien to work for a newly formed U.S. branch office of the foreign company. Those corporate transferee visas do not require an initial U.S. investment, other than incorporating the U.S. subsidiary, and arranging adequate office space.

While this classification is open to qualified aliens world-wide, it is specifically identified as available to Canadians and Mexicans under the terms of NAFTA.

Ref: DOS Publication 10074, August 1995; NAFTA Annex 1603

The approval of a permanent Labor Certification or the filing of a preference petition shall not be the basis for denying an L petition, a request to extend an L petition or the alien's application for admission, change of status or extension of stay. The alien may legitimately come to the United States as a nonimmigrant under the L classification and depart voluntarily at the end of his or her authorized stay, and at the same time, lawfully have the dual intent of seeking to become a permanent resident of the United States.

It may be possible for Multi-national Business Executives or manager and executive Priority Worker Transferees to adjust their status to immigrant after the U.S. company has operated for at least one year and the importance of their role can be demonstrated.

Admission Process

Step 1 - Filing the Blanket Petition

A Form I-129S blanket L petition must be filed with the appropriate INS regional Service Center by a U.S. employer who will be the single representative between the INS and the qualifying organizations. It simplifies the process of filing for a number of L-1 workers in the future. Visa exempt beneficiaries must file abroad.

This process is available for L-1A Managers and Executives who will be managing an essential function.

This process is also available for L-1B specialized knowledge professionals who:
- Will be employed in positions requiring the theoretical and practical application of a body of highly specialized knowledge
- Will fully perform the occupation, and
- Require completion of a specific course of education culminating in a baccalaureate degree in a specific occupational specialty

After receiving approval of a blanket petition, the employer may file for individual employees to enter as an L-1A Manager/Executive or L-1B specialized knowledge professional under the blanket petition.

Step 2 - Initial Petition

Option 1 - Clearing the INS in the United States - Non-NAFTA applicants

Existing U.S. Offices
The U.S. subsidiary of the alien's company must file an application on Form I-129 with the appropriate INS regional Service Center for a determination of whether the alien is eligible for the L classification and the petitioner is a qualifying organization.

This includes proof of the existence of a subsidiary in the country where the alien currently lives.

Documentation and supporting evidence includes:

- *INS form*
  - I-129, Petition for a Nonimmigrant Worker with:
  - L Classification Supplement page
- *Fee*
  - filing fee of $110
- *Employee's evidence to support request*
  - proof of professional job-related credentials, degrees and/or certification
  - at least one continuous year of full time employment abroad within the three years preceding the filing of the petition
  - the prior year of employment abroad was in a position that was managerial, executive, or involved specialized knowledge
  - prior education, training, and employment qualifies the alien to perform the intended services in the United States
- *Employer's evidence to support request*
  - the employing organization is qualified as defined in 8 CFR 214.2(1)(1)(ii)(G)
  - extensive tax documents to confirm ownership and control
  - extensive job description
  - the alien will be employed in an executive, managerial, or specialized knowledge capacity

If filing under a blanket petition, the application must be accompanied by:

- A copy of the approval notice of the blanket petition
- A letter from the alien's employer detailing:
  - dates of employment
  - job duties
  - qualifications
  - previous three years salary

If entering as a specialized knowledge professional:

- A copy of a U.S. degree or foreign equivalent, or
- Evidence establishing that the beneficiary's education and experience is the equivalent of a U.S. degree

Legal assistance is not absolutely necessary although many companies hire an attorney.

New U.S. Offices

If a beneficiary is coming to be employed as an executive or manager in a new U.S. office, the petitioner shall submit evidence that:

- Sufficient physical premises exist
- The beneficiary meets the one continuous year in the last three year requirement
- The beneficiary will be employed in an executive or managerial authority over the new operation
- Within one year the operation will support an executive or managerial position with the following evidence:
  - the scope, structure and goals of the entity
  - the size of the U.S. investment and the ability to remunerate the beneficiary and commence doing business in the United States
  - organizational structure of the foreign entity

If the beneficiary is coming to be employed in a specialized knowledge capacity in a new office in the United States, the petitioner shall submit evidence that:

- Sufficient physical premises exist
- The business entity in the United States is or will be a qualifying organization
- The petitioner has the financial ability to remunerate the beneficiary and to commence doing business in the United States

Option 2 - Clearing the Department of State (DOS) Abroad - Non-NAFTA Applicants

The consular officer must be satisfied that the alien qualifies under INA 101(a)(15)(L).   *Ref: 9 FAM 41.54*

Visa interviews are necessary and must be scheduled by calling the 900 toll appointment number. It may take up to three weeks to get an appointment.

All applicants including minor children must appear for the interview. Although interviews will be in English, outside translators may be used in certain situations.

Depending on the consulate, the visa may be ready for pickup the working day following the interview.

Documentation and supporting evidence includes:

- *DOS form*
  - OF 156, Nonimmigrant Visa Application
- *Fees*
  - $45 non-refundable Machine-Readable Visas (MRV) fee collected at posts which issue MRVs (NAFTA nationals from Canada and Mexico are exempt from this fee)

- visa reciprocity fee equating to fees charged in similar circumstances in alien's home country
- *Passport*
  - passport valid for at least six months beyond intended stay
- *Current immigration status*
  - evidence of immigration status in the country in which the Consulate is located
- *Prior immigration status*
  - passports, visas, I-20, I-797, I-94, Employment Authorization Document
- *Prior INS approvals*
  - the original I-797 Notice of Approval petition and a copy of either:
    - the I-129 that was filed on their behalf with the INS, or
    - the approved petition, Form I-129 on file at the consulate
- *Employee's evidence to support request*
  - evidence of previous employment with the subsidiary company in the home country or abroad
- *Employer's evidence to support request*
  - proof that the employer abroad still exists

Ref: DOS Calgary Appointment Letter

Step 3 - Clearing the INS at a U.S. Port of Entry

Option 1 - Non-NAFTA

An alien may be admitted for full-time or part-time work and paid through either the overseas parent or the U.S. subsidiary. It may be useful to check which method of payment is more beneficial for tax purposes.

L-2 visas may be obtained for the spouse and minor children allowing them to enter the U.S. with the principal alien. Unless they qualify on their own for a work visa, they cannot work but may attend school and/or participate in voluntary organizations.

An L-1 petition may be approved initially for managers and executives for up to three years, with the possibility of two-year extensions to a total of seven years. L-2 employees with specialized knowledge may be approved for three years and extended to a total of five years.

In the case of a new enterprise in the United States, the L-1 will be limited to one year initially with extensions depending on whether the new business is successful.

Documentation and supporting evidence includes:

- *Passport*
  - passport valid for at least six months beyond intended stay

- *Prior INS and DOS approvals*
  - Form I-129, Petition for a Nonimmigrant Worker
  - Form I-797, INS Notice of Approval
  - DOS Machine-Readable Visa (MRV) in passport
- *Evidence to support request*
  - copies of employer's evidence to DOS
  - copies of employee's evidence to DOS
- *Evidence that U.S. stay is temporary (intent to depart)*
  - no intention to abandon residence abroad

Option 2 - NAFTA Only

Under the terms of NAFTA, citizens of Canada and Mexico may apply directly at a U.S. port of entry without obtaining employment authorization and without numerical restriction provided that they comply with other immigration measures applicable to temporary entry.   *Ref: NAFTA Annex 1603*

Documentation and supporting evidence includes:

- *INS form*
  - I-129, Certificate of Eligibility
- *Fee*
  - filing fee of $110

The INS Immigration Inspector will:

- Issue Form I-94, Arrival/Departure Record
- Stamp passport
- Send the application to the appropriate INS regional Service Center

The Service Center will:

- Assign a number
- Issue a Form I-797

The $45 MRV charge per applicant is waived for Canadians and Mexicans in accordance with the NAFTA agreement.

Step 4 - Revalidation/Extension or Change of Status

Application to the INS within the United States

Any alien legally in status seeking a change of status to L-1 must apply before their grace period expires to avoid going out of status. They may remain in the United States during this waiting period but may not work until their L-1 is received.

Aliens who are not from a country participating in the Visa Waiver Program may submit an application for L-1A and L-1B renewal between 45 days and four months to the INS regional Service Center having jurisdiction over their place of residence.

Applications are to be filed by mail at the INS regional Service Center having jurisdiction over their place of residence.

Documentation and supporting evidence for the principal alien includes:

- *INS form*
    - I-129, Petition for Nonimmigrant Worker with:
        - L Classification Supplement page
- *Fees*
    - filing fee of $110
- *Current and prior immigration status*
    - copy of Form I-94 Arrival/Departure Record
- *Employer's evidence to support request*
    - letter explaining the reasons for the extension
- *Proof of financial support or solvency*
    - financial proof

Dependents of L aliens must file for their extension or change of status with the INS regional Service Center having jurisdiction over their state.

Documentation and supporting evidence for dependents includes:

- *INS form*
    - I-539, Application to Extend/Change Nonimmigrant Status
- *Fees*
    - $120 for the dependent

The INS issues Form I-797, Notice of Approval which serves as evidence of the extension or change of status.

Dependents may study on a full or part-time basis in the United States.

Visa Revalidation by the Department of State (DOS)

After the INS has extended your stay, your visa may need to be renewed before attempting to reenter the United States after travel abroad for business or pleasure. Depending on how U.S. citizens are treated in your home country in similar circumstances, your original visa may have been issued with restrictions on the number of entries into the United States and its period of validity, perhaps six months or a year.

Application for visa renewal may be made at a U.S. Embassy or Consulate in your home country. Revalidations may also be made at a U.S. Consulate in Mexico or Canada by calling (900) 443-3131 for an appointment.

As a service to aliens in a few classifications such as L, the Department of State renews L visas by mail in the United States.

It is not possible to obtain expedited processing or status reports. If you do not have time to get your visa renewal in the U.S., you should apply in person to the consular office of the country of destination.

As a service to aliens in a few classifications such as L, the Department of State renews visas by mail in the U.S., if time permits. Full information on revalidations is available from the State Department website at http://travel.state.gov/revals.html. You may download the required Form OF 156 there.

Documentation and supporting evidence includes:

- *DOS form*
  - OF 156, Nonimmigrant Visa Application
- *Fees*
  - $45 non-refundable Machine-Readable Visa (MRV) fee
  - visa reciprocity fee equating to fees charged in similar circumstances in alien's home country
- *Passport and photographs*
  - passport valid for at least six months beyond intended stay
  - passport-size photographs for each applicant
- *Current and prior immigration status*
  - original current I-94 (no copies)
  - copy of I-171C (H's or L's) or I-797 Petition Approval Notice
- *Employer's supporting documentation*
  - detailed letter identifying:
    - the employee
    - his or her position
    - travel itinerary

When a fee is charged for visa reciprocity, include two certified checks or money orders, one for the visa application and one for the reciprocity charge. Personal checks cannot be accepted.

Applications sent through the U.S. Postal Service should be mailed in a padded envelope with a stamped padded envelope enclosed for return mailing. If return by courier is requested, an air bill is required. Processing may take six to eight weeks. You may call (202) 663-1213 for more information.

Completed applications may be sent by mail to:

U.S. Department of State/Visa
P.O. Box 952099
St. Louis, MO 63195-2099

Completed applications may also be sent by courier to:

> U.S. Department of State/Visa (Box 2099)
> 1005 Convention Plaza
> St. Louis, MO 63101-1200

Step 5 - Retaining L Status

You may remain in the U.S. after the expiration date of the original visa until the end of your 30 day grace period but may not work until the renewal is received.

The total period of a temporary stay for an executive or manager is seven years and for specialized knowledge personnel the maximum stay is five years including all time spent in H status.

After these limits are reached, the alien must reside and be physically present outside the United States for at least one year before being readmitted in H or L status. However, entry in another visa status such as F-1 is permitted.

Dependents of L aliens may study on a full or part-time basis in the U.S.

Loss of Status

An alien whose original visa expires before an application for renewal is filed, becomes out of status and must file for renewal outside the country within 120 days of expiration.

Aliens who lose their L-1 status also lose the right to work and remain in the United States. However, you may remain in the U.S. after the expiration date of the original visa until the end of your grace period but may not work until the renewal is received.

If a petition for a different visa is denied while you still are working with a valid L-1, the denial does not affect any extension petition for the current L-1, if it can still be extended.

If either the U.S. or foreign side of the company ceases to operate, the L-1 visa automatically becomes void and the work permit terminated.

L-1 nonimmigrants and their dependent family members no longer risk loss of status when they travel abroad while they have an Adjustment of Status pending. An INS interim rule effective July 1, 1999 has eliminated the requirement to obtain Advance Parole.

TN

Treaty NAFTA Professional

TN status is reserved for business professional citizens of Canada and Mexico to enter the United States temporarily under the terms of the North American Free Trade Agreement (NAFTA) to practice one of the professions listed in the NAFTA Agreement in Appendix 1603.D.1 of Chapter 16.

Legal residents who are not citizens of Canada and Mexico and physicians working in clinical or primary care do not qualify.   *Ref: INS ER 806 3-8-94*

NAFTA classifications include:
- B-1   - Visitor for Business
- E-1/E-2 - Treaty Trader or Investor
- L-1   - Intracompany Transferee
- TN   - Business Professional

TN sub-categories include:
- TN   - Treaty NAFTA - Professional
- TN-1   - Canadian citizen
- TN-2   - Mexican citizen
- TD   - Trade Dependent - Spouse or minor child of NAFTA Professional
          Ref: INA 214(e)(2); 9 FAM 41.12; NAFTA Annex 1603

A TD spouse and children under 21 may attend school full or part time without a separate student visa. The TD spouse is not permitted to work but may apply for a temporary working visa, study or do volunteer work or, if living in a border community, commute to work in Canada or Mexico.

While TNs are issued a year at a time, they may be renewed indefinitely. The only advantage in converting to H-1 status with its absolute limits is that you may have a Green Card application pending at the same time as you hold temporary status. Dual intent is only permitted in H-1 and L status, not TN.

A job may be full-time or part-time.

Canada and Mexico permit the entry of U.S. workers on the same basis as Canadian and Mexican workers entering the U.S. under the terms of NAFTA and Canadians do not require Labor Certification.

However, Section D of Annex 1603 of NAFTA permits the United States to establish an annual numerical limit of 5,500 Mexican Trade Professionals for a transition period of up to 10 years.

The $45 Machine-Readable Visa (MRV) fee is waived in this classification.

Admission Process

Step 1 - Qualifying - List of NAFTA Professions

NAFTA Professionals

Profession	Minimum Education Requirements And Alternative Credentials
General	
Accountant	Baccalaureate or Licenciatura Degree; or C.P.A., C.A., C.G.A. or C.M.A.
Architect	Baccalaureate or Licenciatura Degree; or state/provincial license
Computer Systems Analyst	Baccalaureate or Licenciatura Degree; or Post-Secondary Diploma or Post-Secondary Certificate, and three years experience
Disaster Relief Insurance Claims Adjuster (claims adjuster employed by an insurance company located in the territory of a Party, or an independent claims adjuster)	Baccalaureate or Licenciatura Degree, and successful completion of training in the appropriate areas of insurance adjustment pertaining to disaster relief claims; or three years experience in claims adjustment and successful completion of training in the appropriate areas of insurance adjustment pertaining to disaster relief claims
Economist	Baccalaureate or Licenciatura Degree
Engineer	Baccalaureate or Licenciatura Degree; or state/provincial license
Forester	Baccalaureate or Licenciatura Degree; or state/provincial license
Graphic Designer	Baccalaureate or Licenciatura Degree; or Post-Secondary Diploma or Post-Secondary Certificate, and three years experience

Hotel Manager	Baccalaureate or Licenciatura Degree in hotel/restaurant management; or Post-Secondary Diploma or Post-Secondary Certificate in hotel/restaurant management and three years experience in hotel/restaurant management
Industrial Designer	Baccalaureate or Licenciatura Degree; or Post-Secondary Diploma or Post-Secondary Certificate, and three years experience Interior Designer Baccalaureate or Licenciatura Degree; or Post-Secondary Diploma or Post-Secondary Certificate, and three years experience
Land Surveyor	Baccalaureate or Licenciatura Degree; or state/provincial/federal license
Landscape Architect	Baccalaureate or Licenciatura Degree
Lawyer (including Notary in the Province of Quebec)	LL.B., J.D. , LL.L., B.C.L. or Licenciatura Degree (five years); or membership in a state/provincial bar
Librarian	M.L.S. or B.L.S. (for which another Baccalaureate or Licenciatura Degree was a prerequisite)
Management Consultant	Baccalaureate or Licenciatura Degree; or equivalent professional experience as established by statement or professional credential attesting to five years experience as a management consultant, or five years experience in a field of specialty related to the consulting agreement
Mathematician (including statistician)	Baccalaureate or Licenciatura Degree
Range Manager/ Range Conservationalist	Baccalaureate or Licenciatura Degree
Research Assistant (working in a post-secondary educational institution)	Baccalaureate or Licenciatura Degree
Scientific Technician/ Technologist	Possession of (a) theoretical knowledge of any of the following disciplines: agricultural sciences, astronomy, biology, chemistry, engineering, forestry, geology, geophysics, meteorology or physics; and (b) the ability to solve practical problems in any of those disciplines, or the ability to apply principles of any of those disciplines to basic or applied research
Social Worker	Baccalaureate or Licenciatura Degree
Sylviculturist (including Forestry Specialist)	Baccalaureate or Licenciatura Degree

Technical Publications Writer	Baccalaureate or Licenciatura Degree; or Post-Secondary Diploma or Post-Secondary Certificate, and three years experience
Urban Planner (including Geographer)	Baccalaureate or Licenciatura Degree
Vocational Counsellor	Baccalaureate or Licenciatura Degree

Medical/Allied Professional

Dentist	D.D.S., D.M.D., Doctor en Odontologia or Doctor en Cirugia Dental; or state/provincial license
Dietitian	Baccalaureate or Licenciatura Degree; or state/provincial license
Medical Laboratory Technologist (Canada)/ Medical Technologist (Mexico and the United States)	Baccalaureate or Licenciatura Degree; or Post-Secondary Diploma or Post-Secondary Certificate, and three years experience
Nutritionist	Baccalaureate or Licenciatura Degree
Occupational Therapist	Baccalaureate or Licenciatura Degree; or state/provincial license
Pharmacist	Baccalaureate or Licenciatura Degree; or state/ provincial license
Physician (teaching or research only)	M.D. or Doctor en Medicina; or state/provincial license
Physiotherapist/ Physical Therapist	Baccalaureate or Licenciatura Degree; or state/provincial license
Psychologist	State/provincial license; or Licenciatura Degree
Recreational Therapist	Baccalaureate or Licenciatura Degree
Registered Nurse	State/provincial license; or Licenciatura Degree
Veterinarian	D.V.M., D.M.V. or Doctor en Veterinaria; or state/provincial license

Scientist

Agriculturist (including Agronomist)	Baccalaureate or Licenciatura Degree
Animal Breeder	Baccalaureate or Licenciatura Degree
Animal Scientist	Baccalaureate or Licenciatura Degree
Apiculturist	Baccalaureate or Licenciatura Degree

Astronomer	Baccalaureate or Licenciatura Degree
Biochemist	Baccalaureate or Licenciatura Degree
Biologist	Baccalaureate or Licenciatura Degree
Chemist	Baccalaureate or Licenciatura Degree
Dairy Scientist	Baccalaureate or Licenciatura Degree
Entomologist	Baccalaureate or Licenciatura Degree
Epidemiologist	Baccalaureate or Licenciatura Degree
Geneticist	Baccalaureate or Licenciatura Degree
Geologist	Baccalaureate or Licenciatura Degree
Geochemist	Baccalaureate or Licenciatura Degree
Geophysicist (including Oceanographer in Mexico and the United States)	Baccalaureate or Licenciatura Degree
Horticulturist	Baccalaureate or Licenciatura Degree
Meteorologist	Baccalaureate or Licenciatura Degree
Pharmacologist	Baccalaureate or Licenciatura Degree
Physicist (including Oceanographer in Canada)	Baccalaureate or Licenciatura Degree
Plant Breeder	Baccalaureate or Licenciatura Degree
Poultry Scientist	Baccalaureate or Licenciatura Degree
Soil Scientist	Baccalaureate or Licenciatura Degree
Zoologist	Baccalaureate or Licenciatura Degree

Teacher

College	Baccalaureate or Licenciatura Degree
Seminary	Baccalaureate or Licenciatura Degree
University	Baccalaureate or Licenciatura Degree

Ref: NAFTA Appendix 1603.D.1

As noted above, not all NAFTA professions require at least a bachelor's degree. Some require as little as two years of post-secondary education and work experience.

Step 2 - Clearing The Department of Labor - Mexicans Only

NAFTA includes a provision that permits a country to require a business person seeking temporary entry to obtain a visa or its equivalent prior to entry. This provision applies to Mexican nationals.   *Ref: NAFTA Annex 1603*

The employer must submit evidence that a Form ETA 9035 has been filed with the Department of Labor for all NAFTA Appendix 1603.D.1 professionals.

Step 3 - Clearing the INS Before Entry - Mexicans Only

After clearing the Department of Labor, Mexican citizens applying for their initial TN classification must file an application with the Director of the Northern Service Center between 45 days and four months before the proposed employment will begin.

Documentation and supporting evidence includes:

- *INS form*
  - Form I-129, Petition for a Nonimmigrant Worker
- *Fee*
  - filing fee of $110
- *Passport or proof of citizenship*
  - proof of Mexican citizenship
- *Employer's evidence to support request*
  - list of job duties
  - evidence that job applicant meets the educational/experience requirements
- *Employee's evidence to support request*
  - evidence to satisfy all licensure requirements
  - certification of labor condition application or labor attestation
- *Additional evidence*
  - confirmation that the job is on the NAFTA list
- *Evidence that U.S. stay is temporary*
  - evidence to confirm a foreign residence with no intent to abandon

The INS issues a Form I-797, Notice of Approval which must be presented on entry.   *Ref: INA 214(e)*

Step 4 - Clearing the Department of State Abroad - Mexicans Only

The consular officer must have received an approved petition from the INS according classification as a NAFTA Professional and be satisfied that the alien is so classifiable and that the proposed stay is temporary with a reasonable finite end and the alien will depart.   *Ref: 9 FAM 41.59*

Step 5 - Clearing the INS at a U.S. Port of Entry

Canadians are not required to file Form I-129. They may make their initial application at a U.S. port of entry.

The TN is applied for at a Class A port of entry or at a U.S. airport handling foreign traffic or at a foreign airport which handles preflight and preclearance formalities. Immigration lawyers sometimes are retained to assist their TN clients on entry.

The Free Trade Officer has the right to ask such questions or take action to verify the applicant's records. As in other NAFTA classifications and in the spirit of the Department of Labor clearance proceedings, employment authorization may be refused to an alien whose entry might adversely affect:

- Settlement of any labor dispute that is in progress at the employment site
- Employment of any person who is involved in the dispute

If TN status is refused, it is the responsibility of the INS to inform the alien and his or her government of the reasons for refusal.

Documentation and supporting evidence includes:

- *INS forms*
  - no TN application form
  - I-194 - principal alien and dependents
- *Fees*
  - $50 entry fee (principal alien only)
  - $6   I-94 fee for principal alien and each dependent
- *Passport*
  - passport valid for at least six months beyond intended stay , or
  - proof of citizenship
- *Prior INS and DOS approvals*
  - Form I-797, Notice of Approval
  - DOS Machine-Readable Visa (MRV) in passport, if required
  - I-94, if previously held
- *Professional credentials*
  - Professional diploma and license, as applicable
  - credentials evaluation
- *Employee's evidence to support request*
  - proof that the applicant meets the education and experience requirements of the job category
  - (transcript may be required)
- *Employer's evidence to support request*
  - signed employment contract with prospective employer including:
    - job description which demonstrates that the job falls within a NAFTA classification
    - salary
    - temporary status
    - time frame - one year limit
- *Proof of financial support or solvency*
  - financial proof

A dependent spouse who is not a Mexican or Canadian citizen enters as a TD but follows the process as though entering as an H-4. This requires:

- A nonimmigrant visa
- Evidence of the TN's application approval
- Form I-94, Arrival/Departure Record with validity date

Step 6 - Revalidation/Extension or Change of Status

Application to the INS within the United States

Canadian and Mexican citizens may file to renew their TN status by mail with the Director of the INS Nebraska Service Center between 45 days and four months before the extension of stay is required. TNs may also be renewed at the border.

Documentation and supporting evidence for principal alien includes:

- *INS form*
  - I-129, Petition for a Nonimmigrant Worker
- *Fee*
  - filing fee of $110

A **dependent** spouse and minor children who are physically present in the United States and requesting an extension of stay or a change of nonimmigrant classification to TD should file Form I-539 with the Director of the Northern Service Center.

Documentation and supporting evidence for dependents requesting an extension or change to TD status includes:

- *INS form*
  - I-539, Application to Extend/Change Nonimmigrant Status
- *Fee*
  - filing fee of $120
- *Current and prior immigration status*
  - Form I-129 of the TN Professional

If an alien is not applying for an extension of stay as a TD at the same time that the TN professional is applying for an extension, or is applying for a change of nonimmigrant status to TD after the TN nonimmigrant obtains status, the alien must present a copy of the TN's Form I-94, Nonimmigrant Arrival/Departure Record, to establish that the TN is maintaining valid nonimmigrant status.

The INS issues a Form I-797, Notice of Approval which serves as evidence of change of status.

When duties are amended, the alien may apply for another TN at the border or list the new duties in an extension application by mail.

Chapter 6

Extraordinary/Internationally-Recognized Persons

There are two classifications which closely parallel permanent resident criteria.

O and P classifications are reserved for persons who are nationally or internationally recognized in their field.

O status is available to "extraordinary" applicants. To qualify they must have:

- Extraordinary ability in the fields of sciences, arts, education, business or athletics, or
- Extraordinary achievement in the motion picture or television industry

P status is available to "outstanding" applicants. To qualify, they must be:

- Internationally-recognized athletes and entertainers
- Seen as "outstanding" for a "sustained and substantial period of time"

O

Aliens of Extraordinary Ability
in the Sciences, Arts, Education, Business, Athletics

This new classification was created in the Immigration and Nationality Act of 1990 and moved from H-1B to enable an employer to petition to classify an alien as a nonimmigrant worker who may enter the United States temporarily to perform services or labor as an O-1.

This classification is reserved for "those who have extraordinary ability in the sciences, arts, education, business and athletics as demonstrated by sustained national or international acclaim, whose entry the Attorney General believes will substantially benefit the United States.

This classification can also include those accompanying and assisting the alien as well as a spouse and unmarried children under the age of 21."

Ref: 9 FAM 41.12; INS ER 806 3-8-94

Sub-categories are:
- O-1 - Aliens with extraordinary ability in sciences, arts, education, business or athletics
- O-2 - Accompanying alien to assist alien in athletic or artistic performance
- O-3 - Spouse or child of O-1 or O-2   *Ref: INA 101(a)(15)(O)(i),(ii),(iii)*

Applicants in the fields of sciences, arts, education, business or athletics must be able to prove their "extraordinary ability" by:
- Meeting very high standards
- Having a level of expertise attained by a person who is one of a small percentage and who has risen to the top of their field
- Having extensive documentation of sustained national or international acclaim

Applicants in motion pictures and television must be able to prove a demonstrated record of "extraordinary achievement" by demonstrating distinction.

Accompanying aliens may be admitted in O-2 status to assist in the artistic or athletic performance of the O-1 alien. However, if their entry is to support a motion picture or television alien, they must:

- Have the necessary skills and experience with the alien, and
- Have a longstanding or pre-existing relationship with the alien
- Be performing a role which is essential to the successful completion of the production, if it is taking place both inside and outside the United States

As in most other categories, the INA requires that aliens admitted in O status maintain a foreign residence to which they intend to return.

Admission Process

Step 1 - Establishing Eligibility

Aliens in the Sciences, Arts, Education, Business or Athletics

Aliens with extraordinary ability in the sciences, arts, education, business, or athletics require:

- A consultation from a labor organization or peer group representing their area of occupational specialization containing:
- A description of their ability and achievements in the field
- A description of the duties to be performed
- A determination of whether the position requires the services of an O-1, alien of extraordinary ability

The standards for determining "Extraordinary Ability" are very detailed and include:

Receipt of a major international award
- Three of the following pieces of documented evidence:
  - national or international prizes or awards
  - involvement in the field of outstanding achievement
  - major publication of material about the alien and his or her work
  - panelist or judge of work of others in alien's specialty field
  - contribution of scholarly work or contributions in specialty field
  - authorship of professionally published scholarly articles
  - employment in organizations with distinctive reputations
                              Ref: Code of Federal Regulations

Aliens in the Motion Picture or Television Industries

Aliens of extraordinary achievement in the motion picture or television industries require:

- A consultation report from an appropriate union representing their occupational peers, and

- A consultation report from a management organization in their area of expertise containing:
  - a description of their ability and achievements
  - a description of the duties to be performed
- A determination of whether the position requires an O-1 alien of "extraordinary achievement or extraordinary ability in the arts" such as:
  - recipient or nominee for prestigious international awards such as an Emmy, Grammy or Directors Guild award
    OR
  - three of the following pieces of documented evidence:
    - performance as a lead in productions with a distinguished reputation
    - nationally or internationally published recognition
    - performance as a lead or in a starring role for organizations with a distinguished reputation
    - published record of major box office success, standing in the field, research, product development and occupational achievements
    - significant recognition for achievements from acknowledged leaders in the field
    - record of commanding a high salary in relation to others in the field, or
    - other comparable evidence

Step 2 - Clearing the INS in the United States - Initial Petition

A U.S. employer or foreign employer may file with the appropriate INS regional Service Center in the United States.

Documentation and supporting evidence includes:

- *INS forms*
  - I-129, Petition for a Nonimmigrant Worker
  - O and P Classifications Supplement page
- *Fees*
  - filing fee is $110
- *Prior INS approvals*
  - written consultation with a peer group
- *Employee's evidence to support request*
  - the alien has received a major, internationally recognized award, such as a Nobel Prize or copies of evidence of at least three of the following:
    - receipt of nationally or internationally recognized prizes or awards for excellence in the field of endeavor

- membership in associations in the field which require outstanding achievements as judged by recognized international experts
- published material in professional or major trade publications or newspapers about the alien and his work in the field
- participation on a panel or individually as a judge of the work of others in the field or an allied field
- original scientific or scholarly research contributions of major significance in the field
- authorship of scholarly articles in the field in professional journals or other major media, or
- evidence the alien commands a high salary or other high remuneration for services

- *Employer's evidence to support request*
  - copy of the contract with the alien or the terms of an oral agreement
  - copies of evidence the services to be performed are:
    - a specific scientific or educational project, conference, convention, lecture, or exhibit sponsored by scientific or educational organizations or establishments, or
    - consist of a specific business project that requires an extraordinary executive, manager, or highly technical person due to the complexity of the project

The law requires that the INS consult with union and management groups in the motion picture and television industries prior to deciding on whether to issue a visa. The union or peer group response to the INS must be provided within 15 days. Only after it is received may the applicant file the formal visa application.

The petition may not be filed more than four months before the employment is to begin and should be filed at least 45 days before the employment will begin.

The INS reserves the right to request that the applicant provide more information or appear for an interview.

The INS issues a Form I-797, Notice of Approval which must be submitted to the DOS.

Step 3 - Clearing the Department of State (DOS) Abroad

After receiving notice of approval from the INS, applicants should normally apply at the U.S. Embassy or Consulate having jurisdiction over their place of permanent residence. Although visa applicants may apply at any U.S. consular office abroad, it may be more difficult to qualify for the visa outside the country of permanent residence.

Documentation and supporting evidence includes:
- *DOS form*
  - OF 156, Nonimmigrant Visa Application
- *Fees*
  - $45 non-refundable Machine-Readable Visa (MRV) fee collected at posts which issue MRVs
  - visa reciprocity fee equating to fees charged in similar circumstances in alien's home country
- *Passport and photograph*
  - passport valid for at least six months beyond intended stay
  - one full face photograph 1½" (37 mm) square
- *Prior INS approval*
  - I-797, Notice of Approval
- *Evidence that U.S. stay is temporary (intent to depart)*
  - no intention to abandon residence abroad

Issue of a visa does not guarantee entry to the United States. That decision rests with the INS Immigration Inspector at a port of entry.

Step 4 - Clearing the INS at a U.S. Port of Entry

Form I-129 may be submitted by mail or at some U.S. ports of entry when entering the country. As a mail application to an INS regional Service Center may take as much as two months, you should select an entry point which admits O applicants.

Documentation and supporting evidence includes:
- *INS form*
  - I-129, Petition for a Nonimmigrant Worker
- *Fee*
  - filing fee of $110 (when applying at the border)
- *Prior DOS approval*
  - DOS Machine-Readable Visa (MRV) in passport

O-2 applicants must:
- Have a long-time professional relationship with the O-1 alien
- Skills which cannot be readily replaced, and
- Demonstrate that they have a foreign residence which they have no intention of abandoning

There is a three-year limit on the initial entry.

Step 5 - *Revalidation/Extension or Change of Status*

Application to the INS within the United States

A petition requesting an extension of stay or change to O status may be filed with the INS regional Service Center having jurisdiction over your location.

Ref: INS recorded information service

Documentation and supporting evidence for principal alien includes:

- *INS form*
  - I-539, Application to Extend/Change Nonimmigrant Status
  - O and P Classifications Supplement page
- *Fees*
  - principal alien:
    - filing fee of $120
  - dependents:
    - filing fee of $120:
- *Passport*
  - passport valid for at least six months beyond intended stay
- *Current and prior immigration status*
  - copy of Form I-94, Nonimmigrant Arrival/Departure Record
- *Employer's evidence to support request*
  - letter from the petitioner explaining the reasons for the extension
- *Proof of financial support or solvency*
  - financial proof

Where there has been a change in the circumstances of employment, you must also submit the evidence required for a new petition.

The INS issues a Form I-797, Notice of Approval which serves as evidence of an extension or change of status.

Visa Revalidation by the Department of State (DOS)

After INS has extended your stay, your visa may need to be renewed before attempting to reenter the United States after travel abroad for business or pleasure. Depending on how U.S. citizens are treated in your home country in similar circumstances, your original visa may have been issued with restrictions on the number of entries into the United States and its period of validity, perhaps six months or a year.

Application for visa renewal may be made at a U.S. Embassy or Consulate in your home country. Revalidations may also be made at a U.S. Consulate in Mexico or Canada by calling (900) 443-3131 for an appointment.

As a service to aliens in a few classifications such as O, the Department of State renews O visas by mail in the United States.

As it is not possible to obtain expedited processing or status reports, you should apply in person to the consular office of the country of destination if you do not have time to get your visa renewal in the U.S.

If time permits, and as a service to aliens in a few classifications such as O, the Department of State renews visas by mail in the U.S. Full information on revalidations is available from the State Department website at http://travel.state.gov/revals.html. You may download the required Form OF 156 there.

Documentation and supporting evidence includes:

- *DOS form*
  - OF 156, Nonimmigrant Visa Application
- *Fees*
  - $45 non-refundable Machine-Readable Visa (MRV) fee
  - visa reciprocity fee equating to fees charged in similar circumstances in alien's home country
- *Passport and photographs*
  - passport valid for at least six months beyond intended stay
  - passport-size photographs for each applicant
- *Current and prior immigration status*
  - original current I-94 (no copies)
  - copy of I-171C (H's or L's) or I-797 Petition Approval Notice
- *Employer's supporting documentation*
  - detailed letter identifying:
    - the employee
    - his or her position
    - travel itinerary

When a fee is charged for visa reciprocity, include two certified checks or money orders for the visa application and the reciprocity charge. No personal checks.

Applications sent through the U.S. Postal Service should be mailed in a padded envelope with a stamped padded envelope enclosed for return mailing. If return by courier is requested, an air bill is required. Processing may take from six to eight weeks. Further recorded information may be obtained by calling (202) 663-1213.

Completed applications may be sent by mail to:

> U.S. Department of State/Visa
> P.O. Box 952099
> St. Louis, MO 63195-2099

Completed applications may also be sent by courier to:

> U.S. Department of State/Visa (Box 2099)
> 1005 Convention Plaza
> St. Louis, MO 63101-1200

P

Internationally-Recognized Athlete and Entertainer

This new classification was created in the Immigration and Nationality Act of 1990 and moved from H-1B.

This classification is for the use of athletes and entertainers who have achieved international recognition. It allows for the temporary admission of entertainment groups, individual or team athletes and accompanying individuals to permit performance in a specific event.

This is reserved for "those recognized at the international level, entering under a reciprocal exchange program or entering in a culturally unique program. This classification can also include a spouse and unmarried children under the age of 21.
Ref: INS ER 806 3-8-94

Sub-categories are:
- P-1- Internationally recognized athlete or member of internationally recognized entertainment group
- P-2 - Artist or entertainer in a reciprocal exchange program
- P-3 - Artist or entertainer in a culturally unique program
- P-4 - Spouse or child of P-1, P-2 or P-3
Ref: INA 101(a)(15)(P)(I),(ii),(iii),(iv)

The P-1 classification is divided into three separate categories:
- Internationally-recognized individual athletes
- Internationally-recognized athletic teams
- Internationally-recognized entertainment groups

An annual ceiling of 25,000 visas is proposed for P-1 and P-3 visas.

Admission Process

Step 1 - Establishing Eligibility

Individual athletes must demonstrate "international recognition" by coming to the United States with an international reputation to participate in a competition which also has a distinguished reputation.

A whole team to be admitted must show evidence that it has achieved international recognition in its sport.

A P-1 petition for an athlete requires:

- A tendered contract with a team in a U.S. league or in an individual sport based on international recognition in that sport, and
- Two of the following pieces of documented evidence:
  - previous participation in a major U.S. sports league
  - previous participation in international competition with a national team
  - previous participation in a U.S. intercollegiate competition
  - statement from league or governing body official detailing how the alien or his or her team is internationally recognized
  - statement from media or sports expert detailing how the alien or his
  - or her team is internationally recognized
  - international ranking of the team or individual
  - significant honor or award in the sport

A P-1 petition for a group of entertainers requires:

- Evidence of performing together for at least one year
- A listing of all members and their date of joining the group
- Evidence of international standing such as nomination for awards or prizes, or by three of the following pieces of documented evidence of:
  - past and future performances in events with a distinguished reputation
  - international recognition and acclaim for outstanding achievement
  - past and future performances for organizations with a distinguished reputation
  - major critically acclaimed successes
  - significant recognition from organizations, critics, experts or government agencies
  - high salaries or remuneration

A P-1 classification may be accorded to an entertainment group who perform as a group but not to an individual to perform apart from his or her group. Except for circus members, 75 percent of the members must have been an integral part of the group for at least a year.

Exceptions may be made in cases where there was limited access to news media or special geographical considerations existed.

A P-2 classification may be accorded to individuals and groups of artists and entertainers participating in a temporary reciprocal exchange program between foreign and U.S.-based organizations.

A P-3 classification may be accorded to artists and entertainers who perform under a program that is culturally unique.

Step 2 - Clearing the INS in the United States - Initial Petition

Form I-129 is for an employer to petition for aliens to come to the United States temporarily to perform services or labor as a P-1, P-2.

For P-3 nonimmigrant workers, a petition is always required for both an initial visa or entry for new or concurrent employment, and any extension or change of status.

Documentation and supporting evidence includes:

- *INS form*
  - I-129, Petition for a Nonimmigrant Worker
- *Fee*
  - filing fee of $110

A U.S. employer may file to classify an alien in a P-2 classification if:

- They are members of the same group (accompanying aliens must be filed for on a separate petition)
- They will accompany the same P-2 alien or group for the same period of time, in the same occupation, and in the same location(s)

P-2 alien coming temporarily to perform as an artist or entertainer, individually or as part of a group, under a reciprocal exchange program between an organization in the United States and an organization in another country

The petition must be filed by the sponsoring organization or employer in the United States with:

- Written consultation with an appropriate labor organization
- A copy of the formal reciprocal exchange agreement between the U.S. organization(s) sponsoring the aliens, and the organization(s) in a foreign country which will receive the U.S. artists or entertainers
- A statement from the sponsoring organization describing the reciprocal exchange, including the name of the receiving organization abroad, length of their stay, activities in which they will be engaged and the terms and conditions of their employment
- Copies of evidence the aliens and the U.S. artists or entertainers are experienced artists with comparable skills and that the terms and conditions of employment are similar

P-2 support personnel

Accompanying support personnel are highly skilled aliens coming temporarily as an essential and integral part of the competition or performance of a P-2, or because they perform support services which cannot be readily performed by a U.S. worker and which are essential to the successful performance or services by the P-2. The aliens must each also have significant prior work experience with the P-2 alien.

The petition must be filed in conjunction with the employment of a P-2 alien with:

- Written consultation with a labor organization in the skill in which the alien will be involved
- A statement describing the alien's prior and current essentiality, critical skills and experience with the P-2
- Statements or affidavits from persons with first hand knowledge that the alien has had substantial experience performing the critical skills and essential support services for the P-2
- A copy of any written contract with the alien or a summary of the terms of the oral agreement under which the alien will be employed

Step 3 - Clearing the Department of State (DOS) Abroad

After receiving notice of approval of their petition from the INS, applicants should normally apply at the American Embassy or Consulate having jurisdiction over their place of permanent residence. Although visa applicants may apply at any U.S. consular office abroad, it may be more difficult to qualify for the visa outside the country of permanent residence.   *Ref: 9 FAM 41.56*

Documentation and supporting evidence includes:

- *DOS form*
  - OF 156, Nonimmigrant Visa Application
- *Fees*
  - $45 non-refundable Machine-Readable Visa (MRV) fee collected at posts which issue MRVs
  - visa reciprocity fee equating to fees charged in similar circumstances in alien's home country
- *Passport and photograph*
  - passport valid for at least six months beyond intended stay
  - one full face photograph 1½" square (37 mm) square
- *Prior INS approval*
  - Form I-797, Notice of Approval
- *Evidence to support request*
  - purpose of trip
- *Evidence that U.S. stay is temporary (intent to depart)*
  - no intention to abandon residence abroad

Issue of a visa does not guarantee entry to the United States. That decision rests with the INS Immigration Inspector at a port of entry.

Step 4 - Clearing the INS at a U.S. Port of Entry

Form I-129 may be submitted by mail or at some U.S. ports of entry when entering the country. As a mail application to an INS regional Service Center may take as much as two months, you should select an entry point which admits applicants.

Documentation and supporting evidence includes:
- *INS forms*
  - I-129, Petition for a Nonimmigrant Worker when applying at the border
  - O and P Classifications Supplement page
- *Fee*
  - filing fee of $110
- *Passport*
  - passport valid for at least six months beyond intended stay
- *Prior DOS approval*
  - DOS Machine-Readable Visa (MRV) in passport
- *Current and prior immigration status*
  - copy of Form I-94, Nonimmigrant Arrival/Departure Record
- *Additional evidence*
  - peer group
  - labor organization
- *Employer's evidence to support request*
- *Evidence that U.S. stay is temporary (intent to depart)*
  - no intention to abandon residence abroad

Maximum Duration of Stay:
- Individual P-1 athletes: up to 10 years based on the trend of signing long-term contracts
- Teams: one year
- P-2 and P-3: the time involved in the event or events to a maximum of one year
- P-4: same length of time as the principal alien

Step 5 - Revalidation/Extension or Change of Status

Application to the INS within the United States

A petition requesting an extension of stay or change to P status may be filed by mail with the INS regional Service Center having jurisdiction over your place of residence.   *Ref: INS recorded information service*

Documentation and supporting evidence by the principal alien includes:
- *INS form*
  - I-129, Application to Extend/Change Nonimmigrant Status with:
    - O and P Classifications Supplement page
- *Fees*
  - filing fee of $110
- *Passport*
  - passport valid for at least six months beyond intended stay

- *Current and prior immigration status*
  - copy of Form I-94, Nonimmigrant Arrival/Departure Record
- *Employer's evidence to support request*
  - letter from the petitioner explaining the reasons for the extension

Where there has been a change in the circumstances of employment, the evidence required for a new petition must be submitted.

Dependents should file Form I-539 to apply for a change of status or extension of stay with the appropriate INS regional Service Center.

Documentation and supporting evidence by dependents includes:

- *INS form*
  - I-539, Application to Extend/Change Nonimmigrant Status
- *Fees*
  - filing fee of $120

The INS issues a Form I-797, Notice of Approval which serves as evidence of the extension or change of status.

Visa Revalidation by the Department of State (DOS)

After INS has extended your stay, your visa may need to be renewed before attempting to reenter the United States after travel abroad for business or pleasure. Depending on how U.S. citizens are treated in your home country in similar circumstances, your original visa may have been issued with restrictions on the number of entries into the United States and its period of validity, perhaps six months or a year.

Application for visa renewal may be made at a U.S. Embassy or Consulate in your home country. Revalidations may also be made at a U.S. Consulate in Mexico or Canada by calling (900) 443-3131 for an appointment.

As a service to aliens in a few classifications such as O, the Department of State renews O visas by mail in the United States.

As it is not possible to obtain expedited processing or status reports, you should apply in person to the consular office of the country of destination if you do not have time to get your visa renewal in the U.S.

As a service to aliens in a few classifications such as P, the Department of State renews visas by mail in the U.S., if time permits. Full information on revalidations is available from the State Department website at http://travel.state.gov/revals.html. You may download the required Form OF 156 there.

Documentation and supporting evidence includes:

- *DOS form*
  - OF 156, Nonimmigrant Visa Application

- *Fees*
  - $45 non-refundable Machine-Readable Visa (MRV) fee
  - visa reciprocity fee equating to fees charged in similar circumstances in alien's home country
- *Passport and photographs*
  - passport valid for at least six months beyond intended stay
  - passport-size photographs for each applicant
- *Current and prior immigration status*
  - original current I-94 (no copies)
  - copy of I-797 Approval Notice
- *Employer's supporting documentation*
  - detailed letter identifying:
    - the employee
    - his or her position
    - travel itinerary

When a fee is charged for visa reciprocity, include two certified checks or money orders, one for the visa application and one for the reciprocity charge. Personal checks cannot be accepted.

Applications sent through the U.S. Postal Service should be mailed in a padded envelope with a stamped padded envelope enclosed for return mailing. If return by courier is requested, an air bill is required. Processing may take from six to eight weeks. Further recorded information may be obtained by calling (202) 663-1213.

Completed applications may be sent by mail to:

U.S. Department of State/Visa
P.O. Box 952099
St. Louis, MO 63195-2099

Completed applications may also be sent by courier to:

U.S. Department of State/Visa (Box 2099)
1005 Convention Plaza
St. Louis, MO 63101-1200

Chapter 7

Special Purpose Classifications

Several classifications are available for the use of aliens with specialized qualifications and visa needs.

The available categories include:

- I - Foreign Information Media Representative
- K - Marriage to U.S. Citizen
- Q - International and Irish Peace Process Cultural Exchange Programs
- R - Religious Worker
- S - Alien Witness and Informant
- - Other Status (Humanitarian Parole, Retirement Visa)

I

Foreign Information Media Representative

I status is accorded, upon a basis of reciprocity, to an alien who is a bona fide representative of foreign press, radio, film, or other foreign information media, who seeks to enter the United states solely to engage in such vocation, and the spouse and children of such a representative if accompanying or following to join.

Classification is:

- I - Representative of Foreign Information Media, Spouse and Minor Child
  Ref: INA 101(a)(15)(I)

Dependents of I aliens may study on a full or part-time basis in the U.S.

Admission Process

Step 1 - Clearing the Department of State (DOS) Abroad

Application should be made to the U.S. Embassy or Consulate in your home country. Canadians are visa exempt.

Documentation and supporting evidence includes:

- *DOS form*
  - OF 156, Nonimmigrant Visa Application
- *Fees*
  - $45 non-refundable Machine-Readable Visa (MRV) fee collected at posts which issue MRVs
  - visa reciprocity fee equating to fees charged in similar circumstances in alien's home country
- *Passport and photograph*
  - passport valid for at least six months beyond intended stay
  - two passport size photographs
- *Employer's evidence to support request*
  - comprehensive letter on company letterhead which:
    - is signed by the company's responsible officer
    - describes your job and your business in detail

- justifies the need for the visa
- identifies you
- names your dependents, if any

Any changes to the visa page necessitate the issuance of a different visa.

A separate check must be submitted if there is a visa reciprocity fee. Very few visas are issued in this classification.

Step 2 - Clearing the INS at a U.S. Port of Entry

The admission of an alien of the class defined in INA 101(a)(15)(I) constitutes an agreement by the alien not to change the information medium or his or her employer until he or she obtains permission to do so from the district director having jurisdiction over his or her residence. An alien classified as an information media nonimmigrant may be authorized admission for the duration of employment.   *Ref: 8 CFR 214.(i)*

Documentation and supporting evidence includes:
- *Prior DOS approval*
  - DOS Machine-Readable Visa (MRV)

The Machine-Readable Visa issued by the State Department abroad is subject to electronic verification by the INS at U.S. ports of entry where a Form I-94 is issued.

I visa holders are admitted to the U.S. for the duration of their assignment.

Step 3 - Revalidation/Extension

Visa Revalidation by the Department of State (DOS)

I visas are among a limited list of classifications which permit revalidation without leaving the United States. Journalists who need to renew their I visas may call the State Department for information at (202) 663-3111 between 11:00 am and 12:00 noon daily, Eastern Time.

Full information on revalidations is available from the State Department website at http://travel.state.gov/revals.html and you may download the required Form OF 156.

Completed applications may be sent by mail to:

    U.S. Department of State/Visa
    P.O. Box 952099
    St. Louis, MO 63195-2099

Completed applications may also be sent by courier to:

    U.S. Department of State/Visa (Box 2099)
    1005 Convention Plaza
    St. Louis, MO 63101-1200

Applications may be dropped in a mail slot at 526 N.W. 23rd Street in Washington or delivered in person between 11 am and 12 noon, Monday through Friday. A self-addressed, stamped or pre-paid envelope is required for the return of passports.

Application may also be made at a U.S. Consulate along the Canadian or Mexican border. Appointments must be made in advance by calling the State Department's 900 service at (900) 443-3131 from the United States. Proof of immigration status in those countries may be required.

Documentation and supporting evidence includes:

- *DOS form*
  - OF 156, Nonimmigrant Visa Application
- *Fees*
  - $45 non-refundable Machine-Readable Visa (MRV) fee
  - visa reciprocity fee equating to fees charged in similar circumstances in alien's home country
- *Passport and photographs*
  - passport valid for at least six months and containing the present visa for the same classification (may be in a previous passport)
  - photographs 1½" inches (37 mm) square for each applicant regardless of age if including dependents in application
- *Current and prior immigration status*
  - original Form I-94 issued by the INS when last entered the U.S., or, if expired, valid Form I-797, Notice of Approval for each applicant
- *Prior INS approvals*
  - a valid employment petition Form I-797 showing:
    - applicant's current employer and
    - INS-approved extension of temporary stay
- *Employer's evidence to support request*
  - comprehensive letter on company letterhead which:
    - is addressed to the Visa Office, Department of State
    - is signed by the company's responsible officer
    - describes the job and business in detail
    - justifies the need for the visa
    - identifies you and names your dependents, if any
- *Additional evidence*
  - certified copies of all the principal alien's documentation if spouse and children are applying separately
  - proof of your relationship to accompanying dependents
- *Proof of financial support or solvency*
  - arrangements to cover U.S. expenses
- *Evidence that U.S. stay is temporary (intent to depart)*
  - proof of intention to depart after completion of assignment
  - no intention to abandon residence abroad

K

Marriage to U.S. Citizen

T his chapter deals only with the marriage of aliens to U.S. citizens, not Green Card holders. Described is the processing of the K visa which allows a U.S. citizen to sponsor a foreign national fiancé(e) to enter the U.S., obtain work authorization, marry within 90 days and apply for a conditional Green Card. Also described is the process by which a U.S. spouse may petition for a conditional Green Card for a foreign spouse living abroad or in the U.S. in temporary legal status.

Green Card holders petitioning for the entry of a foreign spouse are bound by different rules which involve a waiting period of several years. See Chapter 9, Family-Sponsored Preferences on page 216 for details.

Pre-marriage sub-categories are:
- K-1 - Fiancé(e) of United States Citizen
- K-2 -Minor Unmarried Child(ren) of Alien Classified K-1

Ref: INA 101(a)(15)(K)

Post-marriage sub-category is:
- Unlimited Family-Sponsored - Immediate Relative   *Ref: INA 101(a)(16)*

Sponsors should be aware that a new binding Form I-864, **Affidavit of Support**, has been introduced to ensure that an intending immigrant has adequate means of financial support and is not likely to become a public charge. The financial obligation remains in place until the sponsored immigrant becomes a U.S. citizen, is credited with 40 qualifying quarters of work, departs the U.S. permanently or dies.

The sponsor's household income must equal or exceed 125 percent of the Federal Poverty Line, adjusted annually, for the sponsor's household size which includes the sponsor and all other persons who are related and living with the sponsor as well as previously sponsored immigrants and the intending immigrant and dependents. The Federal Poverty Line is adjusted each year. See http://aspe.hhs.gov/poverty.

In 2000, a U.S. citizen living alone sponsoring an alien spouse with no dependents would be required to prove an individual annual income of at least $14,062.50 if living in the 48 contiguous states or the District of Columbia, more elsewhere.

Qualified co-sponsors and the sponsored immigrant may also file Form I-864A when their income will be used to determine the sponsor's ability to support a spouse and any accompanying minor unmarried children.   *Ref: INA 213A*

It should be noted that a second less financially-constraining affidavit, Form I-134, must also be filed when petitioning for an alien fiancé(e).

Admission Process

Step 1 - Clearing the INS in the U.S. - Initial Petition

Option 1 - Before Marriage in the U.S. - Fiancé(e) living abroad

A U.S. citizen who plans to have a U.S. wedding to an alien living abroad should file with the INS regional Service Center having jurisdiction over his or her place of residence before the alien's entry. Notice of INS approval is sent to a U.S. Embassy or Consulate serving the alien's home country within about 30 to 90 days. The INS approval is valid for four months and may be revalidated by a consular officer.

The U.S. citizen fiancé(e) sends Form I-134, Affidavit of Support to the alien fiancé(e) for presentation at the consulate.

Documentation and supporting evidence includes:

- *INS forms*
  - I-129F, Petition for Alien Fiancé(e)
  - Form G-325A, Biographic Information for the petitioner and fiancé(e)
- *Fee*
  - filing fee of $95
- *Proof of birth of U.S. citizen*
  - U.S. birth certificate
  - Certificate of Naturalization or Citizenship
  - Form FS-240 Report of Birth Abroad of a U.S. Citizen
  - unexpired U.S. passport
- *Photographs*
  - 3/4 frontal color photograph of each person showing right ear
- *Evidence to support request*
  - proof of consent if required because of age
- *Civil documents*
  - copy of divorce or death certificate from previous marriage(s)
  - copy of birth certificate or passport
  - proof of name changes

If documents are unavailable, it may be possible to substitute:

- Church, school or census record
- Affidavits

The petition is subject to denial if the alien applicant:

- Has a communicable disease or a dangerous physical or mental disorder

- Is a drug addict
- Has committed serious criminal acts
- Has entered the United States illegally
- Is ineligible for citizenship

Option 2 - *Spouse living abroad*

If your alien spouse is living abroad, a petition for entry may be filed at the INS regional Service Center having jurisdiction over the place of residence of the U.S. citizen. Application for minor unmarried children may also be made. The spouse of a U.S. citizen is not subject to immigrant visa waiting periods, only processing delays. If both the U.S. citizen and alien spouse are living abroad, see Step 2, Option 2.

Documentation and supporting evidence includes:

- *INS forms*
  - I-130, Petition for Alien Relative
  - G-325A, Biographic Information for the petitioner and spouse
- *Fees*
  - I-130 filing fee of $110
- *Passport*
  - passport valid for at least six months beyond intended entry
- *Civil documents*
  - marriage certificate
  - proof of termination of previous marriage(s)
- *Photograph*
  - one 3/4 frontal color photograph of both husband and wife taken within 30 days

The U.S. citizen sponsor will be notified later by the Department of State when to submit a Form I-864 to guarantee financial support.

Step 2 - *Clearing Abroad*

Option 1 - *Before Marriage - After INS Approval - By the Department of State (DOS)*

A visa is required of an alien who is classified under INA 101(a)(15)(K). After receiving notification of the approval of the initial petition from the INS, the U.S. Consulate will send the alien fiancé(e) a packet explaining the documents to be collected and submitted and the process to be followed.   *Ref: 9 FAM 41.2(k)*

The alien fiancé(e) must submit originals wherever possible including documents filed with the INS.

Documentation and supporting evidence includes:

- *DOS forms*
  - OF 156, Nonimmigrant Visa Application

- G-325A, Biographic Information from the petitioner and fiancé(e)
- *Fees*
  - $45 non-refundable Machine-Readable Visa (MRV) fee collected at posts which issue MRVs
  - visa reciprocity fee equating to fees charged in similar circumstances in alien's home country
- *Passport and photographs*
  - passport valid for at least six months beyond intended entry
  - photographs
- *Prior INS approval*
  - I-129F Petition for Alien Fiancé(e).
- *Proof of financial support or solvency*
  - Form I-134, Affidavit of Support received from U.S. citizen
  - letters from the U.S. citizen's employer and bank
- *Civil documents*
  - birth certificate
  - divorce or death certificate from previous marriage(s)
- *Police clearance*
  - certificate from all residences since alien's 16th birthday
- *Medical clearance*
  - results of medical exam, chest x-ray and blood test by a DOS doctor
- *Additional evidence*
  - evidence of valid relationship with the U.S. petitioner
  - both persons are legally willing and able to marry in the U.S.
  - both persons have met in person during the past two years unless the Attorney General waives the requirement

The alien fiancé(e) must be interviewed by a consular officer. If approved, a K visa, good for six months, is issued for presentation at a U.S. port of entry. The nonrenewable visa is valid only for 90 days from the date of entry to the United States.

Option 2 - After Marriage - By the Department of State (DOS) or the INS Abroad

If your wedding takes place abroad, most U.S. Embassies or Consulates or INS offices abroad will allow you to file all documents abroad:

- If you are both present there, and
- If the consulate is acting for the INS
- Regardless of whether the citizen resides in the consular district

Documentation and supporting evidence includes:

- *INS forms*
  - I-130, Petition for Alien Relative
  - G-325A, Biographic Information from the petitioner and spouse

- *Fee*
  - I-130 filing fee of $110
- *Passport*
  - passport valid for at least six months beyond intended entry
- *Civil documents*
  - marriage certificate
  - proof of termination of previous marriage(s)
- *Proof of financial support*
  - Form I-864, Affidavit of Support
- *Photograph*
  - one 3/4 frontal color photograph of both husband and wife taken within 30 days
- *Police clearance*

Step 3 - Clearing the INS at a U.S. Port of Entry

Option 1 - Before Marriage in the United States

Following K-1 consular approval abroad, the alien fiancé(e) must apply to an INS Immigration Inspector for entry at a U.S. port of entry. A work permit good for 90 days may be obtained at this time. Then, a Social Security number should be applied for at the local Social Security Office as soon as possible.

An alien fiancé(e) living abroad and entering as a K-1 may neither begin the K process at a port of entry nor change to another classification after entry.

Ref: INA 248

Option 2 - After Marriage Abroad

If married more than two years, the alien spouse applies for entry at a U.S. port of entry as an IR1, immediate relative. However, if the wedding was within the two years prior to entry, the status is CR1, conditional relative which requires the removal of the conditional status by filing another petition within two years of entry.

The spouse of a U.S. citizen is not subject to immigrant visa waiting periods, only processing delays. It may be advisable to file an application for employment authorization when entering.

If your wedding took place abroad, it has not been possible since February, 1998 to be paroled in or to file all documents at a port of entry. However, an alien spouse may sometimes be allowed to enter in B-2 status at the discretion of the Immigration Inspector. In such a case, the initial petition as described in Step 1, Option 1 should be filed in the U.S. for processing at a U.S. consulate abroad.

Documentation and supporting evidence includes:

- *INS form*
  - I-765, Application for Employment Authorization

- *Fee*
  - I-765 filing fee of $100
- *Prior approvals*
  - INS and DOS approvals

Step 4 - Adjustment of Status by the INS in the United States

If you have both been living legally in the United States, as soon as possible after your marriage, you should both go to the local INS office to file a petition to adjust status to Permanent Resident or Green Card holder. A minor unmarried child admitted with the alien spouse may also apply based on the parent's adjustment application.

It may be possible for an alien in B-2 status who marries in the U.S. to adjust status by filing Form I-512, Authorization for Parole of an Alien into the United States, at a local INS office in the U.S. if there was no preconceived intent to marry when he or she entered.

No K visa is required if the couple is married and legally in the United States.

Documentation and supporting evidence includes:

- *INS forms*
  - I-130, Petition for Alien Relative
  - I-485, Adjustment of Status
  - I-765, Application for Employment Authorization
  - G-325A, Biographic Information for the petitioner and spouse
- *Fees*
  - I-130 filing fee of $110
  - I-485 filing fee of $220 ($160 for dependents under 14)
  - I-765 filing fee of $100
  - fingerprinting fee of $25
- *Passport and photograph*
  - passport valid for at least six months
  - two 3/4 frontal photographs - maximum size 2" square
- *Current and prior immigration status*
  - copy of Form I-94
- *Proof of financial support or solvency*
  - Form I-864, Affidavit of Support
  - employment letter
- *Civil documents*
  - marriage certificate
  - proof of termination of previous marriage(s)
  - birth certificate
- *Police clearance*

Step 5 - Green Card Interview

You should be called in for your Green Card interview within six months.

At the interview, it is normal to expect questions which confirm the details of your relationship with, and knowledge of, the background of your spouse. It may be useful to produce photographs or letters you have written to each other. The examiner must be sure that you:

- Agree that all information in the application is accurate, or
- Correct your petition to reflect actual facts
- Have lawful immigration status in the United States
- Have any necessary proof of financial support
- Resolve any last minute doubts about whether:
  - your marriage was entered into as a "sham" to help the alien spouse evade U.S. immigration laws
  - you have been living together since getting married, or
  - you have valid reasons for not living together

The Marriage Fraud Act of 1986 provides for fines up to $250,000, five years imprisonment of both parties and deportation of the alien if a fraudulent marriage is used as a means to obtain a Green Card.

Documentation and supporting evidence includes:

- *Passport and photographs*
  - passport valid for at least six months
  - four color photographs
- *Civil documents*
  - proof of the joint relationship
  - two certified copies of birth certificate
  - two copies of the marriage certificate
  - proof of termination of previous marriage(s)
- *Proof of financial support or solvency*
  - Form I-864, Affidavit of Support
  - other proof that the alien will not become a public charge:
    - income, property, and investment information
    - loans and expenses
    - latest tax return
    - statement from employer about salary
    - statement from bank officer about accounts
- *Police clearance*
  - police certificate(s) in duplicate, certifying no criminal record

At the Green Card interview, the alien spouse should receive conditional approval good for two years and have the passport stamped to allow international travel until the actual Green Card arrives by mail. Adjustment should be made the same day.

If you are unable to satisfy the examiner that you are legally *In Status* in the United States, it is no longer possible to pay a $1,000 fine to adjust status in the U.S.

If your case is "closed" (approved), the examiner will place a temporary I-551 Green Card stamp in your passport and you will have conditional Green Card status which must be confirmed in two years.

If your case is "continued" because of something missing or incomplete, you must turn in all required additional documentation to the office where the interview was held. If you do not receive written notification of the decision in the mail, you or your attorney may need to follow up with the INS.

Step 6 - Removal of Conditional Status

90 days before the second anniversary of the date of the granting of the Green Card, it is necessary to apply to have the conditional status removed.

A petition should be filed at the INS regional Service Center having jurisdiction over your place of residence.

Documentation and supporting evidence includes:

- *INS form*
  - I-751, Petition to Remove the Conditions on Residence
- *Fee*
  - filing fee of $125
- *Passport and photograph*
  - passport valid for at least six months
  - new photograph
- *Current immigration status*
  - I-551, Permanent Resident Card
- *Evidence to support request*
  - copies of documents indicating that your marriage was entered into in good faith and not to avoid U.S. immigration laws
  - sworn or affirmed affidavits by at least two people who have personal knowledge of your continuing marriage and relationship
  - lease or mortgage contracts showing joint tenancy
- *Proof of financial support or solvency*
  - financial records showing joint ownership of assets
- *Civil documents*
  - birth certificate(s) of child(ren) born to the marriage

If you choose to not file, you will lose your Green Card on the second anniversary of the date on which you were granted status. However, if you are out of the United States at the time of your second anniversary, you must file within 90 days of your return.

Q-1/Q-2

International Cultural Exchange Program Participant (Q-1) and Irish Peace Process Cultural and Training Program Participant (Q-2/3)

Q status has been temporarily divided into two parts to permit participation in two special programs.

Sub-categories are:

- Q-1 - Participant in an International Cultural Exchange Program
- Q-2 - Participation in Irish Peace Process Cultural and Training Program
- Q-3 - Dependent of Irish Peace Process Cultural and Training Participant
  Ref: INA 101(a)(15)(Q)(i), (ii) and (iii); P.L. 105-319

Q-1 - Participant in an International Cultural Exchange Program

Q-1 status is for "an exchange visa permitting 15 months admission to participate in designated international cultural exchange programs."
Ref: INS ER 806 3-8-94; 9 FAM 41.12

The Q-1 classification was added to the Immigration and Nationality Act in 1990 to:

- Enhance the knowledge and appreciation of different world cultures by the American people by:
  - taking place in a school, museum, business or other establishment
  - exposing the public to the history and traditions of a foreign culture
  - being part of a structured program
  - providing practical training and employment
  - allowing employers such as Disney to bring foreign nationals to the United States for temporary periods to work in places such as Epcot Center in Florida

The prospective Exchange Visitor must be at least 18 years old and able to effectively communicate about his or her home country. But, it is not necessary that the Exchange Visitor derive any cultural benefit from exposure to the American people.

Q-2 - Participant in Irish Peace Process Cultural and Training Program

The Q-2 classification was added temporarily to the Immigration and Nationality Act in 1998 by incorporating the Irish Peace Process Cultural and Training Program Act of 1998. It was signed into law on October 30, 1998 and was created to:

- Promote cross-community and cross-border initiatives to build grassroots support for long-term peaceful coexistence
- Develop job skills and conflict resolution abilities in a diverse, cooperative, peaceful, and prosperous environment   *Ref: H.R. 4293*

Participation is limited to aliens:

- Who are 35 years of age or younger who wish to enter the United States with their spouse and children for a period not to exceed 36 months
- From disadvantaged areas of the six counties of Northern Ireland and the counties of Louth, Monaghan, Cavan, Leitrim, Sligo and Donegal in the Republic of Ireland suffering from sectarian violence and structural unemployment, and
- Who can return to their homes better able to contribute toward economic regeneration and the Irish peace process

The interim rule became effective on March 17, 2000. It is subject to repeal on October 1, 2005.   *Ref: 65 FR 14764 and 65 FR 14774*

Admission Process

Step 1 - Clearing the INS in the United States - Initial Petition

Either a U.S. employer or a foreign employer may submit a petition which must be filed with the appropriate INS regional Service Center. A foreign employer's petition must be signed by a senior member of U.S. management who has worked for the organization for the prior year.

Documentation and supporting evidence includes:

- *INS forms*
  - I-129, Petition for a Nonimmigrant Worker
  - Q & R Classifications Supplement page
- *Fee*
  - filing fee of $110
- *Evidence to support request*
  - evidence that an established cultural exchange program exists and is being maintained
  - a qualified employee has been designated and will act as program administrator and INS liaison
  - the company has been conducting business in the United States for at least two years

- the company will offer the same wages and working conditions as are provided to similarly employed U.S. workers
    - the company employs at least five full-time U.S. workers
- *Proof of financial support or solvency*
    - the ability to remunerate participants
- *Additional evidence*
    - the employment or training takes place in a public setting where the alien's culture may be shared with the American people
    - the American people will derive an obvious cultural benefit
    - the cultural component is designed to give an overview of the alien's home country

The INS issues Form I-797, Notice of Approval to the employer or agent. It is subject to approval by the DOS.

Q-2/3 admission is limited to not more than 4,000 aliens including spouses and minor children in each of three consecutive program years. Each admission will reduce by one the number of H-2B nonimmigrants allowed in a given year. The INS is responsible for employment authorization, monitoring status and reporting to Congress.

Step 2 - Clearing the Department of State (DOS) Abroad

After receiving INS notice of approval, applicants should normally apply at the American Embassy or Consulate having jurisdiction over their place of permanent residence. Although visa applicants may apply at any U.S. consular office abroad, it may be more difficult to qualify for the visa outside the country of permanent residence.

The State Department is responsible for Q-2 and Q-3 program administration, design, policies, procedures and coordination with U.S., Irish and Northern Ireland government agencies. The designated Program Administrator, Logicon, Inc. may be contacted for details of the employer approval process by calling (877) 925-7484 or on the internet at http://www.WalshVisa.net. Q-2 and Q-3 applicants must apply at either the U.S. Embassy in Dublin or the U.S. Consulate in Belfast.

Documentation and supporting evidence includes:

- *DOS form*
    - OF 156, Nonimmigrant Visa Application
    - prior written certification from the Program Administrator (Q-2/3)
- *Fees*
    - $45 non-refundable Machine-Readable Visa (MRV) fee collected at posts which issue MRVs
    - visa reciprocity fee equating to fees charged in similar circumstances in alien's home country
- *Passport and photograph*
    - passport valid for at least six months beyond intended stay
    - one full face photograph 1½" square

- *Prior INS approval*
  - Form I-797, Notice of Approval
- *Evidence that U.S. stay is temporary (intent to return)*
  - proof of binding ties to a residence outside the United States which you have no intention of abandoning

Issue of a visa does not guarantee entry to the United States.

Step 3 - Clearing the INS at a U.S. Port of Entry

The INS Immigration Inspector has the authority to deny admission or determine the period for which the alien is authorized to remain in the United States to a maximum of 15 months for Q-1 and 36 months for Q-2 and Q-3.

The spouse or unmarried minor children of a Q-2 may be admitted as Q-3s. While there is no such provision for Q-1s, their dependents may request admission in B-2 Visitor status or any other classification for which they qualify.

An accompanying or following spouse and children may enter in Q-3 status.

Documentation and supporting evidence includes:

- *Prior approvals*
  - DOS Machine-Readable Visa (MRV) in passport
  - written certification from the Program Administrator (Q-2/3)

The INS Immigration Inspector will validate a Form I-94 Arrival/Departure Record as proof of status. This will serve as employment authorization.

Step 4 - Revalidation/Extension or Change of Status

Application to the INS within the United States

If the alien has been in Q-1 status for 18 months, revalidation is not permitted unless the alien has resided outside the United States for the immediate prior year.

A petition requesting an extension of stay may be filed for a Q employee by mail with the INS regional Service Center having jurisdiction over your location.

The stay of Q-2 and Q-3 aliens may not be extended beyond a total of 36 months including the original authorized period of stay.

Documentation and supporting evidence for principal alien includes:

- *INS form*
  - I-129, Application to Extend/Change Nonimmigrant Status
- *Fees*
  - filing fee of $110
- *Passport*
  - passport valid for at least six months beyond intended stay

- *Current and prior immigration status*
  - a copy of the Form I-94, Nonimmigrant Arrival/Departure Record
- *Employer's evidence to support request*
  - letter explaining the reasons for the extension

Dependents should file for an extension of stay with the INS regional Service Center having jurisdiction over their place of residence.

Documentation and supporting evidence for dependents includes:

- *INS form*
  - I-539, Application to Extend/Change Nonimmigrant Status
- *Fees*
  - filing fee of $120
- *Evidence to support request*
  - copies of current documentation of principal alien

All checks and money orders must be drawn on banks or other financial institutions in the United States and must be payable in U.S. dollars.

Where there has been a change in the circumstances of employment, you must also submit the evidence required for a new petition.

The INS issues Form I-797 Notice of Approval which serves as evidence of the extension or change of status.

Visa Revalidation by the Department of State (DOS)

After INS has extended your stay, your visa may need to be renewed before attempting to reenter the United States after travel abroad for business or pleasure. Depending on how U.S. citizens are treated in your home country, your visa may be issued with restrictions on the number of entries into the U.S. and its period of validity.

Aliens may apply for a change of status or extension of Q status at a U.S. Consulate in Mexico or Canada by calling for an appointment on the State Department 900 telephone appointment service. Q revalidations are not processed in the U.S.

Documentation and supporting evidence includes:

- *DOS form*
  - OF 156, Nonimmigrant Visa Application
- *Prior INS approval*
  - an original Form I-797
  - approved I-129 petition
- *Fees*
  - filing fee of $110
- *Professional credentials*
- *Evidence that U.S. stay is temporary (intent to depart U.S.)*
  - no intention to abandon residence abroad

R

Alien in a Religious Occupation

Rstatus includes ministers of religion, professional religious workers, and other members of religious denominations having a bona fide nonprofit religious organization in the United States.

R status is for those who have been a member of a religious denomination for the preceding two years and plan to carry on the activities of a religious worker.

Ref: INS ER 806 3-8-94

Sub-categories are:

- R-1 - Alien in a Religious Occupation
- R-2 - Spouse or Child of R-1   *Ref: INA 101(a)(15)(R)(I),(ii)*

Initial admission for the religious worker, spouse and children under 21 is for three years with an extension of stay to a maximum of five years.

Ref: Northern Service Center

The spouse and minor children of religious workers are eligible for R-2 classification visas which are valid for study but not employment.

Religious workers classifications fall into three categories:

- Professional capacity
  - occupations for which a baccalaureate degree or foreign equivalent is required
- Religious occupation
  - an activity relating to a traditional religious function such as:
  - liturgical worker
  - religious instructor
  - religious counselor
  - cantor
  - catechists
  - worker in religious hospital or religious health care facility
  - missionary
  - religious translator
  - religious broadcaster

- Religious vocation
  - a calling to religious life evidenced by the demonstration of commitment practiced in the religious denomination, like taking vows
  - nuns
  - monks
  - religious brothers and sisters

To qualify, it is necessary to come solely to work for a specified period of time:
- As a minister of that denomination
- In a professional capacity for that organization
- In a religious vocation or occupation for the organization or its nonprofit affiliate

The term "minister" means a recognized religious individual authorized to conduct religious worship and to perform other religious duties. There must be a reasonable connection between the activities performed and the religious calling of the minister. This does not apply to lay preachers not authorized to perform the duties of a minister.

Affiliation between the religious worker and the religious denomination means not only an organization which is closely associated with the religious denomination but also tax-exempt.

Admission Process

Step 1 - Clearing the Department of State (DOS) Abroad

Since no INS petition is required, you may apply at a consulate or a port of entry, if visa exempt.

If not visa exempt, aliens may apply for the R-1 visa at the U.S. Embassy or Consulate having jurisdiction over their place of foreign residence or at any other U.S. consular office abroad.   *Ref: 9 FAM 41.58*

Documentation and supporting evidence includes:
- *DOS form*
  - OF 156, Nonimmigrant Visa Application
- *Fees*
  - $45 non-refundable Machine-Readable Visa (MRV) fee collected at posts which issue MRVs
  - visa reciprocity fee equating to fees charged in similar circumstances in alien's home country
  - visa filing fee may be waived by Secretary of State for alien engaged in charitable activities

- *Passport and photograph*
  - passport valid for at least six months beyond intended stay
  - one passport photograph for each applicant 16 years of age and older,
    - 1½" square, full face against a light background
- *Professional credentials*
  - if the applicant is a minister, he or she is authorized to conduct religious worship for that denomination and the duties are described in detail, or
  - if the applicant is a religious professional, he or she has at least a baccalaureate degree or equivalent, and that such a degree is required for entry into the religious profession, or
  - if the applicant is to work in a nonprofessional vocation or occupation, he or she is qualified if the type of work to be done relates to a traditional religious function
- *Employer's evidence to support request*
  - letter from an authorized official of the specific unit of the employing organization certifying:
    - if the applicant's religious membership was maintained, in whole or in part, outside the United States, the foreign and United states religious organizations belong to the same religious denomination
    - immediately prior to the application for the R visa, the alien has been a member of the religious denomination for at least two years
    - the name and location of the specific organizational unit of the religious denomination or affiliate for which the applicant will be providing services
    - if the alien is to work for an organization which is affiliated with a religious denomination, a description of the nature of the relationship between the two organizations
- *Proof of financial support or solvency*
  - letter from an authorized official of the specific unit of the employing organization certifying the arrangements for remuneration, including the amount and source of salary, other types of compensation such as food and housing, and any other benefits of a monetary value, and a statement whether such remuneration shall be in exchange for services rendered
  - evidence of the religious organization's assets and methods of operation
  - the organization's papers of incorporation under applicable state law
  - proof of tax-exempt status or eligibility for tax-exempt status
- *Evidence that U.S. stay is temporary (intent to depart U.S.)*
  - no requirement that applicants for R visas have a residence abroad which they have no intention of abandoning, but
  - must intend to depart the United States at the end of lawful status

Ref: DOS, August 1995

Step 2 - Clearing the INS at a U.S. Port of Entry

Aliens may apply directly at a port of entry, if visa exempt.

If a visa is issued, it does not guarantee entry into the United States because the INS has the authority to deny admission or determine the period for which the alien is authorized to remain in the United States.

Religious workers may be admitted to the United States for an initial period of three years with extensions to a maximum stay of five years.

Documentation and supporting evidence includes:

- *Passport*
    - passport valid for at least six months beyond date of entry
- *Prior DOS approval*
    - DOS Machine-Readable Visa (MRV) in passport
- *Employer's evidence to support request*
    - letter from the authorizing official of the organization which will employ the alien, confirming:
        - that the foreign and United States religious organizations belong to the same religious denomination
        - that immediately prior to the application for the nonimmigrant visa or application for admission, the alien had the required two years of membership in the religious denomination
        - how the alien's religious work qualifies
        - details of the proposed employment
- *Proof of financial support or solvency*
    - particulars of the remuneration for services to be rendered by the alien with the amount and source of any salary including:
        - housing
        - food
        - clothing
        - any other benefits to which monetary value may be affixed
        - a copy of the tax-exempt certificate showing the religious organization which will employ the alien is:
            - a bona fide nonprofit, religious organization in the United States exempt from taxation in accordance with section 501(c)(3) of the Internal Revenue Code of 1986

The INS Immigration Inspector will validate a Form I-94 Arrival/Departure Record to denote the length of stay permitted.

Applicants should be prepared to return directly to their home country if the INS refuses entry to the United States.

Step 3 - Renewal/Extension or Change of Status

Application to the INS within the United States

Those who wish to stay beyond the time permitted on their Form I-94 must file with the appropriate INS regional Service Center. The decision on whether to grant the request is made solely by the INS.

Documentation and supporting evidence includes:

- *INS forms*
  - I-129, Petition for Nonimmigrant Worker
  - Q & R Classifications Supplement page
- *Fees*
  - filing fee of $110
- *Passport*
  - passport valid for at least six months beyond intended stay
- *Current and prior immigration status*
  - I-94, Arrival/Departure Record
- *Professional credentials*
  - proof of membership in the religious organization
- *Employee's evidence to support request*
  - evidence of qualifications for employment
  - employment letter indicating the nature, duration and remuneration of employment
- *Additional evidence*
  - proof of the organization's tax-exempt status
- *Proof of financial support or solvency*
  - several recent pay stubs
  - financial proof that you will not become a public charge
- *Evidence that U.S. stay is temporary (intent to depart U.S.)*
  - proof of intent to depart the U.S. upon completion of assignment

Dependents should file for an extension of stay with the INS regional Service Center having jurisdiction over their place of residence.

Documentation and supporting evidence for dependents includes:

- *INS form*
  - I-539, Application to Extend/Change Nonimmigrant Status
- Fees
  - filing fee of $120
- *Evidence to support request*
  - copies of current documentation of principal alien

Visa Revalidation by the Department of State (DOS)

After INS has extended your stay, your visa may need to be renewed before attempting to reenter the United States after travel abroad. Depending on how U.S. citizens are treated in your home country in similar circumstances, your original visa may have been issued with restrictions on the number of entries into the United States and its period of validity, perhaps six months or a year.

Aliens in the United States may apply for an extension of their R status or for a change of status to R at a U.S. Consulate in Mexico or Canada.

An appointment must be made via the State Department's 900 service.

Depending on the consulate involved, the visa will be issued the same day or the following business day.

Documentation and supporting evidence includes:

- *Form*
  - OF 156, Nonimmigrant Visa Application
- *Fee*
  - $45 non-refundable Machine-Readable Visa (MRV) fee collected at posts which issue MRVs.
- *Passport*
  - passport valid for at least six months beyond intended stay
- *Prior INS approval*
  - copy of I-129 petition
  - original Form I-797
- *Employee's evidence to support request*
  - evidence of qualifications for employment
  - proof of membership in the religious organization
- *Employer's evidence to support request*
  - proof of the organization's tax-exempt status
  - employment letter indicating the nature, duration and remuneration of employment
- *Proof of financial support or solvency*
  - several recent pay stubs
- *Evidence that U.S. stay is temporary (intent to depart U.S.)*
  - proof of intent to depart upon completion of assignment

S

Alien Witness and Informant

The Violent Crime Control and Law Enforcement Act of 1994 created a new immigrant visa classification by adding section 101(a)(15)(S) to the INA. It was further amended by the Illegal Immigration and Immigrant Responsibility Act of 1996, and, is scheduled to end in 2000, unless extended.

Sub-categories are:
- S-5 - Certain Aliens Supplying Critical Information Relating to a Criminal Organization or Enterprise (referred to as S-1 under 9 FAM 41.83)
- S-6 - Certain Aliens Supplying Critical Information Relating to Terrorism (referred to as S-2 under 9 FAM 41.83)
- S-7 - Qualified family members
  Ref: INA 101(a)(15)(S)(i),(ii); INA 214(j);8 CFR214

S-5 status provides for the admission of an alien determined by the Attorney General to possess critical reliable information concerning a criminal organization or enterprise. The alien must be willing to provide that information to federal and/or state authorities, and the Attorney General must determine that his/her presence is essential to the success of an authorized criminal investigation or prosecution. 200 visas per fiscal year are available in this classification. *Ref: INA 101(a)(15)(S)(i); IIRIRA96.621*

S-6 status provides for nonimmigrant visas for aliens whom the Secretary of State and the Attorney General jointly determine to possess critical reliable information about a terrorist organization, enterprise or operation, and who are willing to provide or have provided such information to federal law enforcement authorities, or a federal court, and who will be or have been placed in danger as the result of providing such information. They must also be eligible for an award under section 36(a) of the State Department's Basic Authorities Act of 1956. Pursuant to the IIRIRA96, INA 214(j) is amended to make no more than 50 visas available in this classification per fiscal year. *Ref: INA 101(a)(15)(s)(ii); IIRIRA96.621*

S-7 derivative status is available to accompanying or following spouse, married and unmarried sons and daughters, and parents of S-5 or S-6 aliens.

Admission Process

Step 1 - S-5 - Certification by the Attorney General

The INS certifies on behalf of the Attorney General that the alien is accorded this classification under subsection (S)(i).

Step 1 - S-6 - Certification by the Secretary of State and the Attorney General

Acting on behalf of the Assistant Secretary of State for Consular Affairs, the Visa Office will certify to the Attorney General the alien's eligibility for classification under subsection (S)(ii).

Step 2 - Clearing the INS - Initial Petition

The petitioner is the requesting law enforcement agency. When determinations of entitlement to visa status under either section (S)(i) or (S)(ii) are completed, the INS on behalf of the Attorney General, certifies such to the Visa Office which then communicates with the relevant consular post. Financial proof is required.

Step 3 - Clearing the Department of State (DOS) Abroad

The consular officer will process the visa application pursuant to guidance and instruction provided by the Department of State Visa Office. A visa may be authorized for the period necessary pursuant to the Attorney General's certification, but for a period not to exceed the three-year statutory limit.   *Ref: 9 FAM 41.83*

Step 4 - Clearing the INS at a U.S. Port of Entry

Documentation and supporting evidence includes:

- *Passport*
  - passport valid for at least six months beyond intended stay
- *Prior DOS approval*
  - DOS Machine-Readable Visa (MRV) in passport
- *Additional evidence*
  - copies of such documentation as required by the Attorney General and Secretary of State
- *Evidence that U.S. stay is temporary (intent to depart U.S.)*
  - evidence of intent to depart

Step 5 - Adjustment of Status

Principal aliens and their dependents may not change status but may be permitted to adjust to permanent status if the principal alien's information substantially contributed to the successful disposition of a criminal investigation or resulted in the prevention of terrorism or the apprehension of a terrorist. Application is filed on Form I-854 with adjustment of status on Form I-485.

Other Status

Humanitarian Parole

Humanitarian Parole is an exclusion from the rules. It is exercised very rarely in the discretion of the Regional INS Director in cases where an alien is ineligible for any kind of visa in the U.S. Strong documentation is needed and it may be granted for a one-year period.

Retirement Visa

There is no provision for granting visas for either temporary or permanent retirement status even though an alien can prove self-sufficiency.

There is also no formal prohibition against staying six months, leaving the country and reentering. It is possible to extend status while in the U.S.

While an alien is not limited to 180 days in the U.S. per year, it will still be necessary to maintain enough links to the home country to call it home.

Alternatives include the E-1 Treaty Trader and E-2 Treaty Investor categories which enable the alien to enter the United States to engage in trade with the home country or invest in the United States.

There may be hope on the horizon for retirees. A bill in the House of Representatives has been seeking for some time to amend IIRIRA96 and ultimately the INA to permit designated aliens who are at least 55 years of age to obtain four-year nonimmigrant visitor visas which would be renewable for an unlimited number of additional four-year periods. At the time of writing, the bill had been referred to a subcommittee of the house judiciary committee. If enacted, retirees would still be required to maintain a residence abroad.

Chapter 8

Foreign Government and Organization Representative

 S everal classifications are used by officials, families and staff of foreign governments and international organizations including:.

- A - Senior Government Official
  - ambassador
  - diplomat
  - consular officer
  - family
  - staff
- C-2 Alien in Transit to United Nations and C-3 Foreign Government Official
  - official
  - family
  - staff
  - personal employee in transit
- G - Government Representative to International Organization
  - principal government representative
  - other representative
  - representative of nonrecognized or nonmember government
  - international organization representative or employee
  - family
  - staff
- N - International Organization Family Member
  - unmarried son or daughter of a current or former international organization officer or employee
  - surviving spouse of a deceased international organization officer
  - retired international organization officer or employee

- immigrant spouse of a retired international organization officer or employee
- NATO Representative of Member State
  - principal permanent representative
  - senior NATO executives
  - other representatives
  - official clerical staff
  - other NATO officials
  - NATO experts
  - accompanying civilians
  - family
  - staff

A

Senior Government Official

Astatus is a very formal classification for the use of representatives of foreign governments. It is reserved for "ambassadors, public ministers, diplomats or consular officers assigned to represent a country to the United States". Family, servants or attendants, and their immediate families are also included. *Ref: INS ER 806 3-8-94*

Sub-categories are:
- A-1 - Ambassador, Public Minister, Career Diplomat or Consular Officer, or Immediate Family
- A-2 - Other Foreign Government Official or Employee, or Immediate Family (on the basis of reciprocity)
- A-3 - Attendant, Servant, or Personal Employee of A-1 and A-2 Classes or Immediate Family (on the basis of reciprocity)
        Ref: INA 101(a)(15)(A)(I),(ii),(iii); 9 FAM 41.12, 41.21, 41.22

The Department of State (DOS) and the Immigration and Naturalization Service (INS) have the joint responsibility for the adjudication of applications relating to A nonimmigrants.

Admission Process

Step 1 - Clearing the Department of State (DOS) Abroad

The sponsoring agency usually handles the processing of these visas and related matters.

Applications for entry in this classification may be made at a U.S. Embassy or Consulate abroad. Consular officials may not require the use of Optional Form 156. Canadians do not have to go to the U.S. Embassy or Consulate.

Documentation and supporting evidence includes:
- *DOS and INS forms*
  - OF 156 Nonimmigrant Visa Application, or
  - I-566, Inter-Agency Record of Individual Requesting Change/ Adjustment or Dependent Employment Authorization

- *Fee*
  - $45 Machine-Readable Visa (MRV) fee is waived in this classification
- *Passport and photograph*
  - passport valid for at least six months beyond intended stay
  - one recent passport-sized photograph
- *Third Country immigration status*
  - evidence of current immigration status in third country if applying as third-country national (TCN)
- *Current and prior immigration status*
  - (expired) documents relating to previous U.S. visits:
  - passports with visas
  - Forms I-20, I-797, I-94 cards, Employment Authorization Documents
- *Employer's evidence to support request*
  - original letter from the employing embassy/mission/international organization describing:
  - nature of your work
  - length of your intended stay in the United States
- *Civil documents*
  - proof of relationship of dependents applying for derivative visa status
  - marriage certificate
  - birth certificate(s)
  - adoption papers

Step 2 - Clearing the INS at a U.S. Port of Entry

Entry is granted by the INS based on the approval of the DOS.

Documentation and supporting evidence includes:

- *Prior DOS approval*
  - DOS Machine-Readable Visa (MRV) in passport

Step 3 - Extension/Change of Status in the United States

An extension or change from another nonimmigrant status to A-1 or A-2 is a two-part process. Except for A-3 applicants, it is necessary to first file with the State Department through your diplomatic mission or international organization. Then, your application is to be filed with the INS.

Part One - DOS:

Documentation and supporting evidence includes:

- *INS and DOS forms*
  - I-566, Inter-Agency Record of Individual Requesting Change/Adjustment or Dependent Employment Authorization
  - DS-394, Notification of Foreign Government Related Employment Status, or
  - DS-1497, Notification of Appointment of Foreign Diplomatic Officer

- *Current and prior immigration status*
  - I-94, Arrival/Departure Record

Part Two - INS:

After you receive your I-566 with a favorable endorsement from the DOS, submit your application to the INS office having jurisdiction over your place of residence.

File for A-3 status, file directly with the appropriate INS regional Service Center.

If you are a permanent resident who wishes to be employed in an A occupation while retaining your permanent resident status, contact the INS office having jurisdiction over your place of residence for procedures under INA 247(b).

Documentation and supporting evidence includes:

- *INS forms*
  - I-539 Application to Extend/Change Nonimmigrant Status
  - I-407, Abandonment by Alien of Status as Lawful Permanent Resident
- *Fee*
  - I-539 filing fee of $120
- *Prior DOS approval*
  - original Form I-566 certified by the State Department with favorable DOS endorsement recommending that the request be granted
- *Current and prior immigration status*
  - I-94 Arrival/Departure Record (nonimmigrant)
  - I-551 (Green Card) (immigrant)
  - Additional evidence
  - A-3 applicants only:
    - copy of employer's Form I-94 or approval notice demonstrating G status
    - original letter from employer describing your duties and stating that he/she intends to personally employ you
    - original Form I-566, certified by the DOS indicating your employer's continuing accredited diplomatic status

The INS issues a Form I-797, Notice of Approval, as evidence of change of status

Visa Revalidation by the Department of State

After INS has extended your stay, your visa may need to be renewed before attempting to reenter the United States after travel abroad. Depending on how U.S. citizens are treated in your home country in similar circumstances, your original visa may have been issued with restrictions on the number of entries into the United States and its period of validity.

As a service to aliens in a few classifications such as A, the Department of State processes A visa renewals in the United States. Forms may be requested by writing:

> Department of State
> Visa Office
> Room L703
> 2401 E Street N.W.
> Washington, DC 20522-0106

Documentation and supporting evidence includes:

- *DOS form*
  - OF 156, Nonimmigrant Visa Application
- *Fee*
  - Machine-Readable Visa (MRV) fee is waived
- *Passport and photographs*
  - passport valid for at least six months beyond intended stay
  - passport-size photographs for each applicant
- *Current and prior immigration status*
  - original current I-94 (no copies)
- *Employer's supporting documentation*
  - detailed letter identifying:
    - the employee
    - his or her position
    - travel itinerary

Your completed application should be mailed to:

> Department of State
> Visa Office
> Room L703
> 2401 E Street N.W.
> Washington, DC 20522-0106

Step 4 - Application for Dependent Employment Authorization

The process for obtaining employment authorization as an A dependent was modified in 1998.

Part One - DOS:

In all cases, the employment authorization application process must start with the alien's diplomatic mission or international organization submitting an application to the State Department, Office of Protocol. The DOS will process the application and forward it directly to the INS Nebraska Service Center.

Documentation and supporting evidence includes:

- *INS form*
  - I-566 Inter-Agency Record of Individual Requesting Change/ Adjustment or Dependent Employment Authorization

- *Passport*
  - passport valid for at least six months beyond intended stay
- *Additional evidence*
  - diplomatic note requesting employment authorization
  - employer's offer of employment (when required under the terms of de facto arrangements (statement must identify the dependent by name, describe the position and salary offered, detail the duties, and verify that the dependent possesses the necessary qualifications)
  - completed Form I-765 signed by the applicant
  - no filing fee or fingerprints required
  - two color photographs with the name of the applicant and mission on the back of each
  - clear photocopy of applicant's photograph from passport, MRV, DOS identification document or other acceptable identity document issued by the sending state or U.S. government
  - copy of Form I-94 Arrival/Departure Record - front and back

If requesting an extension or reapplying for an EAD, photocopies of IRS tax returns for previous years that the dependent worked must be provided. The Nebraska Service Center will direct concerns regarding the sufficiency of an application to the embassy or international organization in the address block of the I-765.

Ref: 8 CFR 214.2(a) (6) and 214.2(g) (6)

Part Two - INS:

Applications related to employment authorization for the dependents of A nonimmigrants should be filed with the Nebraska Service Center.

Step 5 - Change to Other Status by the DOS and INS in the U.S.

To change from A status to either another nonimmigrant or immigrant status, you must first file Form I-566, Inter-Agency Record of Individual Requesting Change/Adjustment or Dependent Employment Authorization with the State Department.

After clearing the DOS, check the application process for the classification of your choice as detailed elsewhere in this book.

C-2/C-3

Alien in Transit to United Nations (C-2) and Foreign Government Official (C-3)

The following sub-categories are for foreign government representatives and aliens coming to the United Nations, their families and staff.

- C-2 - Alien in Transit to United Nations Headquarters District under 11.(3), (4), or (5) of Headquarters Agreement with the United Nations

- C-3 - Foreign Government Official, Immediate Family, Attendant, Servant, or Personal Employee in Transit
  Ref: INA 101(a)(15)(C)(ii),(iii); 9 FAM 41.12, 41.23

Admission Process

Step 1 - Clearing the Department of State (DOS) Abroad

Applications for entry in this classification may be made at a U.S. Embassy or Consulate abroad. While the Form OF 156 is used, some consular officials do not require its use.

Aliens in transit to the United Nations who are issued a C-2 visa are subject to travel restrictions imposed by the Attorney General.   *Ref: 9 FAM 41.71*

The processing of these visas and related matters is usually handled directly by the sponsoring agency.

The $45 Machine-Readable Visa (MRV) fee is waived in this classification.

Step 2 - Clearing the INS at a U.S. Port of Entry

Entry is granted by the INS based on the approval of the State Department.

Documentation and supporting evidence includes:
- *Prior DOS approval*
  - DOS Machine-Readable Visa (MRV) in passport

G

Government Representative to International Organization

G status is reserved for "those who are accredited by their government to represent it to an international organization such as the United Nations, World Bank or Red Cross. This classification can include staff, a spouse, unmarried children under the age of 21 and servants and attendants.   *Ref: INS ER 806 3-8-94*

Sub-categories are:

- G-1 - Principal Resident Representative of Recognized Foreign Member Government to International Organization, Staff or Immediate Family

- G-2 - Other Representative of Recognized Foreign Member Government to International Organization, or Immediate Family

- G-3 - Representative of Nonrecognized or Nonmember Foreign Government to International Organization, or Immediate Family

- G-4 - International Organization Officer or Employee, or Immediate Family

- G-5-Attendant, servant, or   personal employee of G-1 through G-1 or immediate family   *Ref: INA 101(a)(15)(G);9 FAM 41.12, 41.21, 41.24*

The Department of State (DOS) and the Immigration and Naturalization Service (INS) have the joint responsibility for the adjudication of applications.

Admission Process

Step 1 - Clearing the Department of State (DOS) Abroad

The sponsoring agency usually handles the processing of these visas and related matters.

Applications for entry in this classification may be made at a U.S. Embassy or Consulate abroad.

Documentation and supporting evidence includes:
- *DOS forms*
  - OF 156 Nonimmigrant Visa Application, or
  - I-566, Inter-Agency Record of Individual Requesting Change/Adjustment or Dependent Employment Authorization
- *Fee*
  - $45 Machine-Readable Visa (MRV) fee is waived in this classification
- *Passport and photograph*
  - passport valid for six months beyond intended stay
  - one recent passport-sized photograph
- *Third Country immigration status*
  - evidence of current immigration status in third country if applying as third-country national (TCN)
- *Current and prior immigration status*
  - (expired) documents relating to previous U.S. visits:
    - passports with visas
    - Forms I-20, I-797, I-94 cards, Employment Authorization Documents
- *Employer's evidence to support request*
  - original letter from the employing international organization describing:
    - nature of your work
    - length of your intended stay in the United States
- *Additional evidence*
  - "Howe Letter" from U.N. or similar G-4 visa request letter from other qualifying organizations such as the World Bank
  - employment contract (G-5 applicants) describing:
    - nature of your work
    - length of your intended stay in the United States
- *Civil documents*
  - proof of relationship of dependents applying for derivative visa status
  - marriage certificate
  - birth certificate(s)
  - adoption papers

A "Howe Letter" is named after the former Chief (latterly Bonner) of the Transportation Division of the United Nations who issues letters of request for G-4 visas. Letters are to be sent to the consular section prior to your scheduled appointment.

Step 2 - Clearing the INS at a U.S. Port of Entry

Entry is granted by the INS based on the approval of the State Department.

The Machine-Readable Visa is subject to electronic verification by the INS at U.S. ports of entry.

Documentation and supporting evidence includes:

- *Prior DOS approval*
  - DOS Machine-Readable Visa (MRV) in passport

Step 3 - Extension/Change of Status in the United States

An extension or change from another nonimmigrant status to G is a two-part process. Except for G-5 applicants, it is necessary to first file with the State Department through your international organization. Then, your application is to be filed with the INS.

Part One - DOS:

Documentation and supporting evidence includes:

- *DOS forms*
  - I-566, Inter-Agency Record of Individual Requesting Change/Adjustment or Dependent Employment Authorization
  - if applying to be the principal alien:
    - DS-394, Notification of Foreign Government Related Employment Status, or
    - DS-1497, Notification of Appointment of Foreign Diplomatic Officer
- *Current and prior immigration status*
  - I-94, Arrival/Departure Record

Part Two - INS:

After you receive your I-566 with a favorable endorsement from the DOS, submit your application to the INS office having jurisdiction over your place of residence.

If filing for G-5 status, file directly with the appropriate INS Service Center.

If you are a permanent resident who wishes to be employed in a G occupation while retaining your permanent resident status, contact the INS office having jurisdiction over your place of residence for procedures under INA 247(b).

Documentation and supporting evidence includes:

- *INS forms*
  - I-539 Application to Extend/Change Nonimmigrant Status
  - I-407, Abandonment by Alien of Status as Lawful Permanent Resident, (Green Card holders only)
  - original Form I-566 certified by the State Department with favorable DOS endorsement recommending that the request be granted
- *Fee*
  - I-539 filing fee of $120

- *Current and prior immigration status*
  - I-94 Arrival/Departure Record (nonimmigrant)
  - I-551 Green Card (immigrant)
  - Prior DOS approval
- *Employer's evidence to support request - G-5 only*
  - copy of employer's Form I-94 or approval notice demonstrating G status
  - original letter from employer describing your duties and stating that he/she intends to personally employ you

The INS issues a Form I-797, Notice of Approval, which serves as evidence of the change of status.

Visa Revalidation by the Department of State

After INS has extended your stay, your visa may need to be renewed before attempting to reenter the United States after travel abroad. Depending on how U.S. citizens are treated in your home country in similar circumstances, your original visa may have been issued with restrictions on the number of entries into the United States and its period of validity.

As a service to aliens in a few classifications such as A, the Department of State processes A visa renewals in the United States. Forms may be requested by writing:

Department of State
Visa Office
Room L703
2401 E Street N.W.
Washington, DC 20522-0106

Documentation and supporting evidence includes:

- *DOS form*
  - OF 156, Nonimmigrant Visa Application
- *Fee*
  - Machine-Readable Visa (MRV) fee is waived
- *Passport and photographs*
  - passport valid for at least six months beyond intended stay
  - passport-size photographs for each applicant
- *Current and prior immigration status*
  - original current I-94 (no copies)
- *Employer's supporting documentation*
  - detailed letter identifying:
    - the employee
    - his or her position
    - travel itinerary

Your completed application should be mailed to:

> Department of State
> Visa Office
> Room L703
> 2401 E Street N.W.
> Washington, DC 20522-0106

Step 4 - Application for Dependent Employment Authorization

The process for obtaining employment authorization as a G dependent was modified in 1998.

In all cases, the employment authorization application process must start with the alien's international organization submitting an application to the State Department, Office of Protocol, or the United States Mission to the United Nations (USUN) for foreign UN dependents.

The DOS or USUN will process the application and forward it to directly to the INS Nebraska Service Center.

Part One - DOS or USUN:

Part one involves the initial submission to the State Department or USUN.

Documentation and supporting evidence includes:

- *DOS form*
  - I-566 Inter-Agency Record of Individual Requesting Change/Adjustment or Dependent Employment Authorization
- *Passport*
  - passport valid for at least six months beyond intended stay
- *Additional evidence*
  - diplomatic note requesting employment authorization
  - employer's offer of employment (when required under the terms of de facto arrangements (statement must identify the dependent by name, describe the position and salary offered, detail the duties, and verify that the dependent possesses the necessary qualifications)
  - completed Form I-765 signed by the applicant
  - no filing fee or fingerprints required
  - two color photographs with the name of the applicant and mission on the back of each
  - clear photocopy of applicant's photograph from passport, MRV, DOS identification document or other acceptable identity document issued by the sending state or U.S. government
  - copy of Form I-94 Arrival/Departure Record - front and back

If requesting an extension or reapplying for an EAD, photocopies of IRS tax returns for previous years that the dependent worked must be provided. The Nebraska Service Center will direct concerns regarding the sufficiency of an application to the embassy or international organization in the address block of the I-765.

Ref: 8 CFR 214.2(a) (6) and 214.2(g) (6)

Part Two - INS:

Applications related to employment authorization should be filed with the Nebraska Service Center.

Step 5 - Change to Other Status by the DOS and INS in the United States

To change from G status to either another nonimmigrant or immigrant status, you must first file Form I-566, Inter-Agency Record of Individual Requesting Change/Adjustment or Dependent Employment Authorization with the State Department.

After clearing the DOS, check the application process for the classification of your choice as detailed elsewhere in this book.

N

International Organization Family Member

N status is reserved for "the parent, child or sibling of an alien granted SK-3 special immigrant status under INA Section 101(a)(27)(I) and generally relates to officers or employees of international organizations." It may be available to retired officers and employees previously accorded G-4 status

Ref: INS ER 806 3-8-94

Sub-categories are:

- N-8 - parent of an alien accorded the status of special immigrant under INA 101(a)(27)(I)(I) if and while the alien is a child
- N-9 - child of parent or alien accorded the status of special immigrant under INA 101(a)(27)(I)(ii),(iii),(iv)

Ref: INA 101(a)(15)(N)(I),(ii); 9 FAM 41.82

The classification includes:

- An unmarried son or daughter of a current or former international organization officer or employee
- A surviving spouse of a deceased international organization officer
- A retired international organization officer or employee
- An immigrant spouse of a retired international organization officer or employee   *Ref: INA 101(a)(27)(I)((I),(ii),(iii),(iv)*

Admission Process

Step 1 - Clearing the Department of State (DOS) Abroad

The sponsoring agency usually handles the processing of these visas and related matters.

Applications for entry in this classification may be made at a U.S. Embassy or Consulate serving your home country.

Documentation and supporting evidence includes:
- *DOS Form*
  - OF 156, Nonimmigrant Visa Application
- *Fees*
  - $45 non-refundable Machine-Readable Visa (MRV) fee collected at posts which issue MRVs
  - visa reciprocity fee equating to fees charged in similar circumstances in alien's home country
- *Passport and photographs*
  - passport valid for at least six months beyond intended stay
  - two passport size photographs
- *Employer's evidence to support request*
  - comprehensive letter from the principal alien's employer on company letterhead which:
    - is signed by the company's responsible officer
    - describes your job and your business in detail
    - justifies the need for the visa
    - identifies you
    - names your dependents

Upon receipt of satisfactory documentation, the consulate abroad will issue a Machine-Readable Visa. If a visa reciprocity fee is charged, you must submit a separate check.

Step 2 - Clearing the INS at a U.S. Port of Entry

Very few visas are issued in this classification.

The Machine-Readable Visa issued by the State Department abroad is subject to electronic verification by the INS at U.S. ports of entry.

Documentation and supporting evidence includes:
- *Prior DOS approval*
  - DOS Machine-Readable Visa (MRV) in passport

N visa holders are admitted to the United States for the duration of their assignment.

A Form I-94 is issued by the INS at a port of entry.

NATO
Representative of Member State

Ostatus is reserved for representatives and staff of member states to NATO. Sub categories are:

- *NATO-1* - Principal Permanent Representative of Member State to NATO (including any Subsidiary Bodies) Resident in United States and Resident Official Staff Members, Secretary General, Assistant Secretary General, and Executive Secretary of NATO, and other Permanent NATO Officials of Similar Rank, or members of Immediate Family
  Ref: Article 12, 5 UST 1094 and Article 20, 5 UST 1098

- *NATO-2* - Other Representatives of Member State to NATO (including any Subsidiary Bodies) including its Advisors and Technical Experts of Delegations, Members of Immediate Family, Dependents of Member of a Force Entering in Accordance with the Status-of-Forces Agreement or in Accordance with Provisions of the Protocol on status of International Military Headquarters and Members of Such a Force if Issued Visas
  Ref: Article 13, 5 UST 1094 and Article 1, 4 UST 1794

- *NATO-3* - Official Clerical Staff Accompanying Representative of Member State to NATO (including any Subsidiary Bodies) or Members of Immediate Family
  Ref: Article 14, 5 UST 1096

- *NATO-4* - Official of NATO (Other than Classifiable as NATO-1 or Members of Immediate Family
  Ref: Article 18, 5 UST 1098

- *NATO-5* - Expert, Other than NATO Officials Classifiable as NATO-4, employed in Missions on Behalf of NATO, and their dependents
  Ref: Article 21, 5 UST 1100

- *NATO-6* - Member of a Civilian Component Accompanying a Force Entering in Accordance with Provisions of the NATO Status-of-Forces Agreement, Member of a Civilian Component Attached to or Employed by an Allied Headquarters Under the Protocol on Status of International Military Headquarters Set Up Pursuant to the North Atlantic Treaty and their Dependents   *Ref: Article 1, 4 UST 1794; Article 3, 5 UST 877*

- *NATO-7* - Attendant, Servant, or Personal Employee of NATO-1 through NATO-6 Classes or Members of Immediate Family
  Ref: Article 12-20 5 UST 1094-1098; 9 FAM 41.21, 41.25

Admission Process

Step 1 - Clearing the Department of State (DOS) Abroad

Visas in this classification are arranged by the home government directly with their official diplomatic contacts. The $45 Machine-Readable Visa (MRV) fee is waived.

Ref: 5 UST 1094-1098

Step 2 - Clearing the INS at a U.S. Port of Entry

Entry is granted by the INS based on the approval of the DOS.

Documentation and supporting evidence includes:

- *Prior DOS approval*
  - DOS Machine-Readable Visa (MRV) in passport

Step 3- Extension/Change of Status

Visa Revalidation by the Department of State

Your visa may need to be renewed before attempting to reenter the United States after travel abroad. Depending on how U.S. citizens are treated in your home country in similar circumstances, your original visa may have been issued with restrictions on the number of entries into the United States and its period of validity.

As a service to aliens in the NATO classification, the Department of State processes NATO visa renewals in the United States. Forms may be requested by writing:

Department of State
Visa Office
Room L703
2401 E Street N.W.
Washington, DC 20522-0106

Documentation and supporting evidence includes:

- *DOS form*
  - OF 156, Nonimmigrant Visa Application
- *Fee*
  - Machine-Readable Visa (MRV) fee is waived
- *Passport and photographs*
  - passport valid for at least six months beyond intended stay
  - passport-size photographs for each applicant
- *Current and prior immigration status*
  - original current I-94 (no copies)

- *Employer's supporting documentation*
  - detailed letter identifying:
    - the employee
    - his or her position
    - travel itinerary

Your completed application should be mailed to:

Department of State
Visa Office
Room L703
2401 E Street N.W.
Washington, DC 20522-0106

Step 4 - Application for Dependent Employment Authorization

The process for obtaining employment authorization asa NATO dependent was modified in 1998.

In all cases, the employment authorization application process must start with the alien's diplomatic mission submitting an application to NATO's Supreme Allied Commander, Atlantic (SACLANT).

Part One - SACLANT

Part one involves the initial submission to SACLANT.

Documentation and supporting evidence includes:

- *INS form*
  - I-566 Inter-Agency Record of Individual Requesting Change/Adjustment or Dependent Employment Authorization
  - Form I-765 signed by the applicant
- *Passport*
  - passport valid for at least six months beyond intended stay
- *Additional evidence*
  - diplomatic note requesting employment authorization
  - employer's offer of employment (when required under the terms of de facto arrangements (statement must identify the dependent by name, describe the position and salary offered, detail the duties, and verify that the dependent possesses the necessary qualifications)
  - no filing fee or fingerprints required
  - two color photographs with the name of the applicant and mission on the back of each
  - clear photocopy of applicant's photograph from passport, MRV, DOS identification document or other acceptable identity document issued by the sending state or U.S. government
  - copy of Form I-94 Arrival/Departure Record - front and back

If requesting an extension or reapplying for an EAD, photocopies of IRS tax returns for previous years that the dependent worked must be provided. The Nebraska Service Center will direct concerns regarding the sufficiency of an application to the embassy or international organization in the address block of the I-765.

Ref: 8 CFR 214.2(a) (6) and 214.2(g) (6)

Part Two - INS

Applications related to employment authorization for the dependents of NATO nonimmigrants should be filed with the INS Nebraska Service Center.

Part III

Green Cards

Green Card holders are also known as legal permanent residents, immigrants and landed immigrants. The real name of the Green Card is Permanent Resident Card (formerly Alien Registration Receipt Card) or Form I-551. To reduce document fraud and help employers and government agencies identify valid cards, the INS has started production of a new plastic state-of-the-art tamper-resistant Green Card like a credit card at its Service Centers and a production facility in Corbin, Kentucky. The high-tech security features on the front of the card include digital photograph and fingerprint images and a hologram depicting the Statue of Liberty. The laser-etched optical memory strip on the reverse side cannot be altered and must be read by a special INS card reader. It contains the cardholder's photograph, signature, date of birth, fingerprint, name and registration number.

Although a Green Card must be renewed every ten years, it offers its holder the privilege of living and working in the United States in what is supposed to be an unrelinquished permanent U.S. residence. While a Green Card makes available many of the benefits enjoyed by U.S. citizens, it also comes with important responsibilities such as good conduct.

An alien who is ineligible for citizenship shall be ineligible for a Green Card. However, those who receive a Green Card may apply for U.S. citizenship after five years in most cases or in three years if married to a U.S. citizen.   *Ref: 9 FAM 40.81*

A nonimmigrant A or G is not eligible to obtain an immigrant visa until executing a written waiver of all rights, privileges, exemptions and immunities which accrue from their immigration status.   *Ref: 9 FAM 40.203*

Entry Criteria

The process of obtaining a Green Card may seem long and frustrating, yet it is actually both thorough and fair. Your chance of success depends on:
- Your qualifications or family relationship
- The parameters of your chosen classification
- The supply of available qualified U.S. workers in your function
- Whether there are other special conditions which influence entry

How Part III is Divided

Part III provides a detailed introduction to the Green Card. Its four chapters offer a step-by-step explanation of each of the main options for obtaining a Green Card.

Chapter 7-Family-Sponsored Preferences
- Four preference options

Chapter 8-Employment-Based Preferences
- Five preference options

Chapter 9-Diversity (DV) Lottery
- Annual worldwide lottery for citizens of underserved countries

Chapter 10-Refugees/Asylees
- Aliens with a well-founded fear of persecution

Overview

The number of permanent visas issued each year is controlled by Congress and their distribution depends on a number of variables.

Unlimited Immigrants obtain permanent residence without numerical limitation and are not counted against the annual quotas. These include:
- Immediate relatives of a U.S. citizen 21 or over
  (spouse, minor children and parents)
- Returning residents - previous U.S. lawful residents returning after more than a year abroad
- Immigrant applying for reacquisition of U.S. citizenship
- Refugees and asylees
- Foreigners in the Amnesty Legalization Program (LULAC)
- Foreigners granted suspension of deportation or registry
- Children born to a permanent resident during a temporary visit abroad
- An unspecified number of visas for qualified aliens

Limited immigrants are subject to certain transitional laws and limited to 675,000 persons per year from Fiscal Year 1995 to 1997. These include:
- Family-Sponsored: no fewer than 226,000 nor more than 480,000 immigrant visas per year
- Employment-Based - 140,000 immigrant visas yearly   *Ref: INA 201*
- Diversity (Green Card) Lottery - 50,000 immigrant visa numbers annually

In 1997, the **per-country limit** for preference immigrants from independent countries was set at 7 percent or 25,620 and 2 percent or 7,320 for dependent areas. Mexico led all countries of birth with 146,865.*Ref: INS Annual Report, January 1999*

In **Fiscal Year 1997:**
- Admissions were down 13 percent to 798,378
- 535,771 family-sponsored
- 90,607 employment based (140,000)
- 49,374 Diversity program
- 112,158 refugees and asylees converting to legal permanent resident
- 10,468 others *Ref: INS Annual Report, Legal Immigration, January 1999*

The INS attributes the decrease to an increase in the backlog of adjustment of status applications, not to a decline in the demand to immigrate.

The top countries of birth were, in order, Mexico, the Philippines, China, Vietnam and India. California was the leading intended state of residence, followed by New York, Florida, Texas and New Jersey.

The three largest occupational groups were:
- Professional, specialty and technical
- Service occupations
- Executive, administrative and managerial

Admission Process

The following chapters detail the different requirements and processes associated with obtaining a Green Card.

All roads to a Green Card require that the would-be immigrant meet certain criteria and have a reason for coming which is consistent with the spirit and the letter of the Immigration and Nationality Act.

As previously noted, permanent residency is granted generally as a result of:
- A family member filing a petition, or
- A (future) employer filing a petition, or
- Being selected in an annual immigration lottery drawing, or
- Having been granted asylum or refugee status

Often, applicants are living and working or studying in the United States on the basis of a nonimmigrant visa when they are processed for their Green Card. For them, an adjustment of status to immigrant at a U.S. INS office is necessary. Others, living outside the United States, will deal with a U.S. Embassy or Consulate abroad.

Step 1 - Labor Certification

Second (EB2) and Third Preference (EB3) Employment-Based classifications require an employer to file for Labor Certification, In those cases, the Department of Labor must be convinced that there is a need to admit an alien to carry out a job for which there are no qualified U.S. citizens or residents available. It should be noted that a Second Preference waiver is possible.

In Fiscal Year 1995, the occupations which received the most Labor Certification approvals were foreign food specialty cook, software engineer, programmer analyst, college or university faculty member, systems analyst and cook.

Step 2 - Clearing the INS in the United States - Initial Petition

Many J-1 Exchange Visitors must either obtain a waiver or serve the two-year Home Residency Requirement before they may file for an adjustment of status. Also, inadmissible aliens should file Form I-601, Application for Waiver of Grounds of Excludability with $170 to the appropriate Service Center or U.S. Consulate.

An applicant's family or (future) employer may file a petition with the INS in the United States on behalf of an alien living in the U.S. or abroad.

The date on which a Green Card petition is filed is known as the Priority Date which shall be the date the properly completed and signed petition is accepted for filing in the first step of the process. Priority Dates have the most impact on Family-Sponsored applicants and EB3 Other Workers.   *Ref: 8 CFR 204.5 (d)*

All immigrant visa applicants are processed in the order of their Priority Date within their classification. Depending on the classification and qualifications involved, the process could take anywhere from a few weeks to several years. This is especially true for natives of India and China who hold more than half of the H-1Bs. Adjustment is thus slower for them and for the many applicants from Mexico and the Philippines.

Due to the uncertainty of how long processing may take, the INS now requires that a $25 fingerprinting fee be submitted with the petition instead of the fingerprint card, Form FD-258 for all in-U.S. Adjustment of Status cases. The applicant will be advised when and where to have fingerprints taken. The fee is not submitted if processing will be at a U.S. Consulate abroad.

After approval, a Form I-797, Notice of Approval is sent to the petitioner.

The State Department's National Visa Center at Portsmouth, New Hampshire is notified and holds all approved immigrant visa petitions until the alien's priority date is about to become current and the alien is advised.

A spouse and child not otherwise entitled to an immigrant status and the immediate issuance of a visa are entitled to the same status and the same order of consideration if accompanying or following to join their spouse or parent.
Ref: INA 203(d)

Family-Sponsored Petitions
INS Form I-130, Petition for Alien Relative is filed by the U.S. resident family member at the local INS office along with an $110 filing fee and documentation.

There are four preference categories:

- First (F1), Second (F2), Third (F3) and Fourth (F4) Preference

Which preference is appropriate is determined by:

- The citizenship of the petitioner
- The relationship, age and civil status of the beneficiary

Employment-Based Petitions

One of three INS forms is filed at the INS regional Service Center having jurisdiction over the location concerned.

INS Form I-140, Immigrant Petition for Alien Worker is generally filed by the employer along with a $115 filing fee for the following preference categories:

- First (EB1), Second (EB2) and Third (EB3) Preference

INS Form I-360, Application for Amerasian, Widow(er) or Special Immigrant is filed along with an $110 filing fee for the following preference category:

- Fourth (EB4) Preference

INS Form I-526, Immigrant Petition by Alien Entrepreneur is filed along with a $350 filing fee for the following preference category:

- Fifth (EB5) Preference

Which preference is appropriate is determined by:

- The nature of the employment
- The professional qualifications of the beneficiary
- The special status of the beneficiary
- The status of a multi-national enterprise

Diversity (DV) Lottery

The annual worldwide lottery is carried out by the State Department for citizens of underserved countries. No INS or DOS Form is involved in the initial application.

Refugees/Asylees

INS Form I-589, Application for Asylum and Withholding of Deportation may be filed for asylee status by an alien with a well-founded fear of persecution at a U.S. port of entry or at a local INS office in the U.S. Form I-590, Registration for Classification as Refugee may be filed by an alien who holds a similar well-founded fear of persecution at an INS office or U.S. Consulate or Embassy abroad.

Step 3 - Processing

All family-sponsored applications and those employment-based applications from employers with family ties to the alien require a Form I-864 Affidavit of Support. INS information is at http://www.ins.usdoj.gov/graphics/formsfee/forms/index.htm and State Department is available at http://travel.state.gov/i864gen.html.

As noted in Step 2, all INS-approved immigrant visas are retained by the State Department's National Visa Center until they are within a year of being current and a visa number becoming available. At that time they are forwarded to the appropriate U.S. Embassy or Consulate abroad for adjudication by a consular officer and the applicant or attorney is sent a Packet 3 which may also be downloaded from the internet at http://travel.state.gov/nvc.html. If the applicant is adjusting status in the U.S., the appropriate INS office is notified. To ensure notification, it is very important that the National Visa Center be advised of any change of address. Their address is:

> National Visa Center
> 32 Rochester Avenue
> Portsmouth, New Hampshire, 03801-2909.

Changes of address may also be faxed to (603) 334-0759.

A 24-hour automated visa system is operated to provide status of case information by calling (603) 334-0700.

Regardless of whether you take Step 3 by applying for an INS adjustment of status in the U.S. or for an immigrant visa at a U.S. Embassy or Consulate abroad, you cannot be processed until your Priority Date, the date of filing your approved petition is current and a visa number is immediately available. In other words, your Priority Date must be earlier than the State Department visa cut-off date for your classification.
Ref: INA 245

To check on whether your Priority Date has become current, you may call the State Department's 24-hour recorded message service which provides Priority Dates (cut-off dates) for the following month. This service is updated in the middle of each month and may be reached by calling (202) 663-1541. Priority Dates are also available via the internet at: http://travel.state.gov/visa_bulletin.html.

Waiting list records of individual visa applicants entitled to an immigrant classification and their priority dates are maintained at posts which will issue the visa.
Ref: 9 FAM 42.52

Option 1 - Adjustment of Status by the INS in the United States

Aliens living in the United States, normally go through the formality of adjusting status to permanent resident via the INS in the United States. Family-sponsored and Diversity Lottery petitions are filed at local INS offices while the rest are filed at Service Centers. But once a bar has kicked in, it is too late for a waiver.

After the initial petition is approved and you are advised that a visa number is immediately available, the next step is to file an application for permanent resident status on Form I-485 with the director having jurisdiction over the applicant's place of residence. A separate application shall be filed by each applicant. File Form I-485 with $220 filing fee and concurrently with the I-130 and its $110 filing fee and Form I-765 and its $100 filing fee along with $25 for fingerprinting.

An alien who has been the beneficiary of approved Labor Certifications and I-140s from two different companies may use the earlier priority when filing an I-485, Adjustment of Status if the first employer has not withdrawn the earlier petition.

Ref: 8 CFR 204.5 (e)

If the application for adjustment of status is approved, the director shall record the lawful admission of the applicant as of the date of approval. The applicant shall be notified of the decision and, if the application is denied, of the reasons therefor. INS advises that the historical denial rate is seven percent. No appeal of the denial may be made but the alien may renew his or her application.

An applicant for adjustment of status shall be required to have a medical examination by a designated civil surgeon unless medically examined in connection with entry in K Fiance(e) status.

For family-sponsored applicants, the interview may not be waived.

If you have overstayed your temporary status and are still physically present in the United States, you are *Out of Status*, may no longer pay a $1,000 fine and should be processed in your own country. This is because of the termination of INA 245(i) which had allowed in-U.S. Green Card processing after payment of the penalty. However, Out of Status aliens may be able to petition for adjustment in the United States if they have anchor relatives and extreme hardship is involved.

The processing of Adjustment of Status cases at the four INS regional Service Centers was temporarily suspended in 1998 due to a computer problem dealing with the delivery of fingerprints to the Federal Bureau of Investigation (FBI) and Central Intelligence Agency (CIA). However, processing was resumed in December, 1999.

Advance Parole

If you live in the United States, you are placed under a travel embargo:

- After your Priority Date has become current, and
- You have filed a Form I-485 for Adjustment of Status, and
- Before your final Green Card processing

At this time, the departure of an applicant who is not under exclusion, deportation, or removal proceedings shall be deemed an abandonment of his or her application constituting grounds for termination, unless the applicant was previously granted Advance Parole by the INS for such absence and inspected upon returning.

If you must leave and reenter the country prior to your final Green Card processing for emergent, business, personal or humanitarian reasons, you should obtain a Form I-512 by filing Form I-131 with the $95 filing fee and an additional $25 for fingerprinting at the appropriate INS office or Application Support Center (ASC).

Form I-512 may be issued to:

- A member of the professions or a person having exceptional ability in the sciences or arts who had been granted voluntary departure

- A person who holds valid refugee or asylee status
- An alien who seeks to depart temporarily for any emergent bona fide business, personal or humanitarian reason
- A lawful permanent resident who, because of emergent reasons, must embark before action can be completed on his reentry application

As a word of warning, aliens subject to deportation waive their rights to a deportation hearing and risk being placed in exclusion if they obtain Advance Parole and leave the country before their deportation case is resolved.

Parole authorization on Form I-512 may be issued to a principal alien by the district director having jurisdiction over the place where the principal alien resides in the United States, and sent to the alien. The multi-page Advance Parole Form I-512 is stamped and issued before departing.

However, departure from the United States before a decision is made on an application for a refugee travel document shall not affect the application.

Form I-512 may be issued valid for multiple applications for parole into the United States, generally for an alien who, for business purposes, frequently departs the United States.

The remarks block of Form I-512 sets forth the time which the alien may be paroled and the conditions for re-parole. If it is marked for multiple applications, generally to a principal alien who, for business purposes, frequently departs the United States, it will be stamped at the port of entry with the arrival date and returned to the alien for future use.

Return of the principal alien shall be required within four months of the date of issuance of the parole authorization., except that the return of an alien who will be abroad in connection with his qualifying profession or occupation shall be required within the time needed for such purpose, not to exceed one year from the date of issuance of parole authorization.

On returning, all copies of the form are stamped with a parole stamp and retained by the traveler except one copy which is sent to the traveler's A file."

An otherwise eligible applicant who is outside the United States and wishes to come to the United States to apply for benefits under section 202 of P.L. 105-100 may request parole authorization by filing for Travel Document (Form I-131) with the Texas Service Center and a photocopy of the Form I-485 that will be filed on entering the United States. If the director of the Texas Service Center is satisfied that the alien will be eligible for adjustment of status and will file the application, he may issue an Authorization for Parole Form I-512 to allow the alien to be paroled into the U.S. for a period of 60 days. The alien shall have 60 days from the date of the parole to file the application for adjustment of status.

Interviews

The INS is moving toward the processing of most Employment-Based adjustment of status cases on an "interview waiver" basis.

When an interview is held, its purpose is to ensure that:
- You agree that all information in the application is correct, or
- You correct your petition to reflect actual facts
- The examiner can resolve any last minute questions or doubts such as:
  - proof of receipt of the salary offered
  - evidence of financial support or lawful employment authorization
  - you have lawful immigration status in the United States

If you are unable to satisfy the examiner that you are legally *In Status* you must meet the following conditions in order to remain and adjust status in the United States:
- A relative or employer must have filed a petition making you eligible for an immigrant visa
- An immigrant visa must be immediately available
- If you have not maintained lawful status, you may no longer pay a $1,000 fine and must be processed in your home country.

If your case is "closed", the examiner will place a temporary Green Card stamp in your passport. However, if your case is "continued", you will be required to submit all missing and necessary documentation to the office where the interview was held within 12 weeks or the case is automatically denied. Written notification of the decision is sent by mail.

An alien residing in the U.S. may not be required to produce a passport.

Option 2 - By the Department of State (DOS) Abroad

Aliens who are documentarily qualified, that is who report that they have obtained all the documents specified by the consular officer to meet the requirements of INA 222(b) may apply formally for an immigrant visa.   *Ref: 9 FAM 40.1(g)*

The permanent resident application of aliens (beneficiaries) living outside the United States, normally is processed by a consular officer at a U.S. Embassy or Consulate in their home country or in a third country such as Canada or Mexico.

You may speak with a Visa Information Officer Monday through Friday by calling (202) 663-1225 between 8:30 am and 5:00 pm, Eastern Time, or (202) 663-1213 between 2:00 pm and 4:00 pm Eastern Time.

An alien will normally be sent a "Packet III" which advises which documents will need to be presented. Later, the alien will be sent a "Packet IV" from the National Visa Center to confirm the visa interview appointment and advise that a medical and fingerprinting is necessary.

Fingerprints are no longer taken routinely at a consulate in immigrant visa cases because the congressionally-mandated pilot fingerprint program lapsed in 1997. The State Department Visa Office advises that fingerprints are only taken at the option of a consular officer if a criminal record comes up in the name and the identity of the applicant cannot be verified any other way.

Applicants from countries listed in FAM where police clearance is not available do not submit police records. However, applicants must provide police records from other countries where they have lived if those records can be obtained.

Panel physicians who conduct medical examinations are required to verify that new vaccination requirements have been met or that it is inappropriate for the applicant to receive vaccinations for one or more of: mumps, measles, rubella, polio, tetanus and diphtheria toxoids, pertussis, influenza, influenzae type b (Hib), hepatitis B, varicella, and pneumococcal.

Applicants being processed in Canada are advised that only the Consulate-General in Montreal currently processes immigrant visas.

Most consular interviews are brief, routine and in two separate interviews on the same day. The first interview is performed by a document checker who makes certain that an alien has all necessary documents and all information on the forms is correct.

The second interview with a U.S. Foreign Service Officer or consular officer generally occurs shortly afterward. The applicant is placed under oath and swears that all information submitted is correct. The Officer may ask additional questions and must be satisfied that the alien has met the requirements of the requested status.

Be honest. It may be easier to explain a previous problem which you have made a matter of record than to have the consular officer suspect you are trying to cover up something. Have available evidence of the disposition of any case before a judge or jury including original or certified copies of law enforcement agency or court record of arrests, charges, indictments, convictions, fines, imprisonment, release, pardons etc.

Documentation and supporting evidence includes:

- *Fees*
  - visa processing fee of $260
  - visa issuance fee of $65
  - proposed $50 Affidavit of Support review fee
- *Police clearance*
  - copy of police certificate(s)
  - certified copy of prison records
- *Additional evidence*
  - certified copy of military records
  - other documents the consul considers necessary
- *Civil documents*
  - documents establishing relationship of spouse and children to alien
  - records of birth

- *Medical clearance*
  - examination by approved physician
  - seriology and x-ray tests   *Ref: 9 FAM 42.66*

Passports are not required of:
- Certain relatives of U.S. citizens
- Returning residents
- Certain relatives of legal permanent residents
- Stateless persons
- Nationals of communist countries
- Alien members of U.S. Armed Forces

Visas are not required of:
- Alien members of U.S. Armed Forces
- Aliens entering from Guam, Puerto Rico or the U.S. Virgin Islands
- Child born after the issue of parent(s)' visa
- American Indians born in Canada   *Ref: 9 FAM 42.1*

Successful applicants must return later to pick up their immigrant visa and a sealed envelope of all relevant documents to be carried to the U.S. port of entry.

Step 4 - Clearing the INS at a U. S. Port of Entry

An alien living and processed in the United States skips this step.

Applicants must bring their visa and documents issued by the U.S. Embassy or Consulate abroad to a port of entry within six months. An INS Immigration Inspector has the right and responsibility to re-check all documentation and decide whether to grant permanent residency and admit the applicant.   *Ref: IIRIRA96.631*

Applicants will be required to complete Form I-89 which provides a copy of their signature and fingerprint. Documentation includes Green Card information, medical and other records. Fingerprints for police clearance are not taken at a port of entry. The applicant must also have a valid passport and agree to keep it valid.

Under INA 289, American Indians born in Canada who possess at least 50 percent American Indian blood may apply for a Green Card and enter by completing Form I-181 at a port of entry. Required documentation for indian, métis and inuit candidates includes a long form birth certificate, a letter from the band council establishing blood quantity and a government status card. Spouses with less than 50 percent American Indian blood do not qualify. A preliminary visit or call to the port of entry is advised.

Step 5 - Obtaining and Retaining Your Green Card

Until recently, all Green Cards have come from Arlington, Texas, Now, the distribution is shifted to the INS regional Service Centers, the Cards may take up to a year to arrive and are good for ten years. If there is a delay, an inquiry may be filed on

Form G-731 which is available from the INS or you may call the responsible INS Service Center to inquire about the status of your card.

To avoid the risk of losing your Green Card, you should:

- "Continuously manifest an intention to reside permanently in the United States"
- Maintain your U.S. principal residence
- Report any change of address to the INS within 10 days
- Maintain U.S. bank accounts
- Register with the INS within 10 days of turning 14
- Register with Selective Service within 30 days of turning 18 (males only)
- File a U.S. resident tax return on worldwide income and pay all taxes owed

You should not:

- Be involved in illegal activities such as drug use
- Have criminal convictions
- Falsify documents
- Be a security risk
- Be a public charge   *Ref: INA 241(a)*
- Leave your Green Card job too soon after starting

Your Green Card allows you to apply for:

- Any U.S. job not requiring U.S. citizenship
- Sponsorship of a spouse and unmarried children under 21 for Green Card
- Naturalization after five years (three years for spouses of U.S. citizens)
- Social Security retirement or disability benefits
- In-state university tuition after a qualifying period
- Scholarships and student loans
- Government-sponsored financial aid for education
- Some welfare, Medicaid and unemployment and some Supplemental Security Income (SSI) benefits

Obtaining a Replacement Green Card

You should apply in person at your local INS office to replace a lost, stolen, erroneous or expired Green Card.

I-151 Green Cards issued before 1979 expired on March 20, 1996 and must be replaced. Consequently, you may experience difficulties when trying to enter a foreign country with an I-151. Also I-551 Green Cards issued since 1989 must be replaced after ten years. The INS has started issuing temporary revalidation stickers to Green Card holders when they submit their renewal application.

The INS Immigration Inspector at a U.S. port of entry may clip the bottom right corner of your I-151 and give you either:

- A Form I-90, Application to Replace Alien Registration, or

- If naturalization has been applied for, an information packet including a notice on naturalization that will be signed and stamped by the INS Immigration Inspector, or
- A temporary I-551 ADIT (Alien Documentation Identification Telecommunication) stamp in your passport or on your I-94

To replace your I-151 Green Card, you should file an application at your local INS office. You will be required to complete Form I-89, Data Collection Form including the signature and fingerprint blocks. Processing could take up to a year.

Documentation and supporting evidence includes:

- *INS form*
  - I-90, Application to Replace Permanent Resident Card
- *Fee*
  - filing fee of $110
    (a waiver to appear is available to infirm or non-ambulatory applicants)
- *Photographs*
  - two identical 2" square color photographs in 3/4 frontal profile showing the right ear
- *Prior approval*
  - original I-151 Permanent Resident Card
  - in special circumstances, an INS office may issue a temporary Green Card made from half of a Form I-94 plus a photograph and fingerprint.

If you plan to travel, you may need to file a Form I-131 for a Reentry Permit because of delays in producing replacement cards.

Absences from the United States

Each time you leave the country:

- Carry your Green Card with you to show the INS on entering the U.S.
- Keep good records of the dates and reasons for all foreign trips for a future naturalization application and interview
- Reenter legally at a port of entry

If you try to enter the U.S. with your Green Card and are suspected of not actually living in the U.S., the INS may place you in exclusion proceedings, a first step in the cancellation of your Green Card. The guidance of competent counsel is advised.

IIRIRA96.110 mandated the Attorney General to implement an automated entry and exit control system to record the exit of every alien and match it to the record of the alien's arrival in the United States but the program was delayed until March, 2000.In the meantime, INS instituted a test program at ten U.S. airports and ten land ports to determine the admissibility of travelers.

A Green Card holder shall not be considered as seeking admission unless he/she:

- Has abandoned or relinquished that status

- Has been absent more than 180 days (see up to 180 days following)
- Has engaged in illegal activity after leaving the United States
- Has departed the United States under legal process
- Has committed an offence identified as criminal and related grounds
- Is attempting to enter at a time or place other than as designated by immigration officers or has not been admitted after inspection

Ref: AERIER

The rules vary depending on the length of time you are out of the United States. However, don't expect to be able to visit the United States once a year and retain your Green Card status. The INS advises not to adopt living patterns such as two months in the U.S. and four months outside which indicate that the U.S. is not your permanent and primary residence. Also expect closer scrutiny if you do not have the economic standards to match your traveling patterns.

Up to 180 Days

Green Card holders shall not be considered as seeking admission unless they have been absent for a continuous period in excess of 180 days.   *Ref: AERIER*

As a Green Card holder, you may be away from the United States for up to six months but should be able to demonstrate that you have not abandoned your U.S. residence. Up to 180 days, the burden of proof is on the INS to prove that you have abandoned your U.S. residency.

To avoid difficulties, some of the top immigration attorneys recommend keeping trips abroad to a maximum of four months.

The Green Card travel limit does not apply to the spouse or children of a member of the U.S. armed forces or a civilian employee of the U.S. government stationed abroad.

Ref: DOS Pub. 20520, June, 1995

Between Six Months and Two Years

After an absence of six months or more, the burden of proof is on you to prove that you have not abandoned your U.S. residency.

If you are planning to be away from the United States for between six months and two years, and have not been outside the U.S. for more than four of the last five years, it is best to apply to the INS for a Reentry Permit on Form I-131 with $95 filing fee at least 30 days before leaving the United States. The permit is good for two years. While it is not renewable, it may be used for multiple reentries. It is also possible to obtain an additional reentry permit after returning to the United States upon presentation of proof of your intent to maintain your permanent U.S. residency. Even though the Reentry Permit demonstrates your intention of not abandoning your permanent resident status, it does not absolutely ensure retention of your Green Card. As noted earlier, Form I-131 is also used for Advance Parole.   *Ref: 8 USC 1203(c)*

There is a special provision for aliens who are employees of the U.S. government and international organizations who, for business reasons, are required to remain outside the United States for over a year. They may be able to have their time outside the country counted toward the naturalization U.S. residency requirement.

Aliens working abroad should submit Form N-470, Application to Preserve Residence for Naturalization Purposes with its $80 fee if:

- They have been a legal permanent resident for at least a year
- They intend to apply for U.S. citizenship

Over Two Years

Should you be unable to return to the United States within six months as a Green Card holder or within two years with a Reentry Permit, you may apply for a special Immigrant Returning Resident (SB-1) visa at your nearest U.S. Embassy or Consulate abroad at least three months in advance. Be prepared to offer convincing evidence why your extended absence is necessary. The SB-1 is issued at the discretion of the consular officer based on proof that:

- You were a lawful permanent resident when you departed the U.S.
- You intended to return to the U.S. when you departed and maintain this intent
- You are returning from a temporary visit abroad
- If your stay was protracted, it was caused by reasons beyond your control for which you were not responsible
- You are eligible for the immigrant visa in all other respects

If an SB-1 visa cannot be obtained, it may be necessary to apply for a nonimmigrant visa.   *Ref: INA 101(a)(27)(A); DOS Pub. 20520, June, 1995*

The Attorney General may exercise authority under INA 212(c) to grant relief from certain grounds of ineligibility for certain returning aliens.   *Ref: 9 FAM 42.22*

Being away for two years means that you are treated as a non-resident for tax purposes which also impacts on your naturalization waiting period.

Permanent Commuter

A resident alien who holds an I-151 Green Card may live in a residence outside the United States such as in Canada and commute to work in the U.S. Similarly, a commuter I-151 may be held by a Green Card holder who lives outside the U.S. and commutes to work in the U.S. In both situations, it is necessary to carry formal documentation which must be renewed every six months with the INS.

Final thoughts about the Green Card process

All address changes must be reported to the INS within ten days. Either a letter or Form AR-11 may be used. Form AR-11 is available online or by telephone from the INS Forms Center and is to be handed in to the local INS office.

Don't be discouraged if you get caught by rule changes or administrative snafus during the processing of your Green card application.

Chapter 9

Family-Sponsored Preferences

Green Cards are available, in limited numbers, to qualified relatives of U.S. citizens or permanent residents based on a quota system established by Congress.

Family-sponsored immigration has two basic categories: unlimited and limited.

Unlimited family-sponsored Green Cards are available to immediate relatives of U.S. citizens and returning residents.

There are four Family-Sponsored Preference categories. Each has its own unique criteria and waiting period. The determination of which preference category is appropriate depends entirely on the relationship of the U.S. petitioner to the beneficiary and the immigration status of the beneficiary.

Preference Categories	Annual Numbers Available	Additional Numbers	Eligibility and Waiting Period
Unlimited Family-Sponsored			
Immediate Relatives of U.S. Citizens	Unlimited	No limit	Spouse, widow(er), unmarried children under 21 of U.S. citizen, parent of U.S. citizen 21 or older Priority Date - Current
Returning Residents	Unlimited	No limit	Lawful Permanent Residents returning after temporary visit abroad of more than one year Priority Date - Current
Limited Family-Based			
First (F1):	23,400	Unused Fourth Preference numbers	Unmarried Sons and Daughters of U.S. Citizens Waiting Period - 1 ¼years

Second (F2):	114,200	Unused First Preference numbers	Spouses and Children, and Unmarried Sons and Daughters of Permanent Residents
(F2A):	77% of Second Preference limitation		Spouses and Children, of Permanent Residents Waiting period - four ¼ years
(F2B):	23% of Second Preference limitation		Unmarried Sons and Daughters, 21 years of age or older, of Permanent Residents Waiting Period - seven years
Third (F3):	23,400	Unused First and Second Preference numbers	Married Sons and Daughters of U.S. Citizens Waiting Period - four ¼years
Fourth (F4):	65,000	Unused first three Preference numbers	Brothers and Sisters of Adult U.S. Citizens Waiting period - 11 years (Philippi nes - 20 years) *Ref: INA 203*

Relatives of U.S. citizens are not counted in quotas.

The world-wide Fiscal Year 1996 limit for Family-Sponsored Preference (family reunification) immigrants is set at 311,819 and determined in accordance with INA 201. The new Fiscal Year begins in October.   *Ref: DOS Visa Bulletin, September, 1996*

Entry Criteria

Sponsorship by U.S. Citizens

A U.S. citizen may sponsor:

- Sons and daughters
- Spouse
- Brothers and sisters
- Parents

Sponsorship by Permanent Residents

A Green Card holder may only sponsor:

- Spouse and unmarried children
- Second or subsequent spouse if:

- five years have elapsed since obtaining a Green Card through a previous spouse, or
- it can be proven that the prior marriage was not entered into to evade any immigration law, or
- the prior marriage was terminated by the death of the former spouse
- If they do not depend on public benefits

Spouse
Nonimmigrant spouses of Green Card holders:

- Qualify under Family-Based category 2A with its almost five year backlog
- May not automatically be allowed to remain in the United States
- May not work unless authorized under existing nonimmigrant status
- May independently seek a nonimmigrant H-1 or L visa as permitted by Dual Intent (spouse may remain and work in the United States while waiting for a Green Card)

Dependents - Change of Sub-Category
Dependents automatically move to a slower-moving classification if:

- They applied on the basis of single status but are married when their Green Card becomes available
- An unmarried child turns 21 while waiting for a Green Card

Adjustment of Nonimmigrant Status
Since all nonimmigrant classifications except H-1 and L require that the alien intend to leave the United States at the expiration of their status, it is difficult to justify maintaining nonimmigrant status while a Green Card application is pending.

Admission Process

Step 1 - Clearing the INS in the United States - Initial Petition

A citizen or permanent resident of the United States, 21 years of age or older, may file Form I-130, Petition for Alien Relative, to establish the relationship and eligibility of certain alien relatives who wish to immigrate to the United States. An alien who is ineligible to become a citizen is also ineligible for a Green Card. *Ref: INA 212(a)(8)(A)*

Documentation and supporting evidence includes:

- *INS form*
  - I-130, Petition for Alien Relative
- *Fee*
  - filing fee of $110
- *Passport and photographs*
  - passport valid for at least six months
  - 2" square color photograph of each family member taken within 30 days

- *Current immigration status of petitioner*
  - Form I-551, Permanent Resident Card (Form I-551), or
  - Certificate of Naturalization (Form N-550)
- *Civil documents*
  - birth certificate of petitioner, or
  - Form FS-240, Report of Birth Abroad of a United States Citizen or birth certificate for each alien relative
  - marriage certificate
  - documents ending marriages
  - possible substitutes include church, school or census records or affidavits
- *Additional evidence*
  - G-325A, Biographical Information for each alien relative
    (not necessary to repeat information on I-130)

As previously noted, it may also be possible to file Forms I-485 and I-765 with Form I-130 at the local INS office. The alien would be interviewed locally and could begin work immediately if approval would make a visa number immediately available. Otherwise filing is at the appropriate INS regional Service Center.

American citizens residing in Canada who wish to apply for Green Cards for their family members must submit their I-130 petitions to the INS Nebraska Service Center.

Step 2 - Processing

Option 1 - Adjustment of Status by the INS in the United States

After an initial petition is approved by the INS and an immigrant visa is immediately available, it may be possible for a legal nonimmigrant beneficiary residing in the U.S. to adjust status to permanent resident without leaving the country if you:

- Are filing an application with a complete relative, special immigrant juvenile or special immigrant military petition which, if approved, would make an immigrant visa number immediately available
- Were granted asylum or refugee status and are eligible for adjustment
- Are eligible based on Cuban citizenship or nationality
- Have continuously resided in the U.S. since 1972
- Have maintained legal status
- Are the widow(er) of a deceased U.S. service member and had been married for at least two years

A beneficiary should file with the local INS office having jurisdiction over his or her place of residence. If you move, your file stays with this office.

Aliens living in the United States who have not maintained lawful status may no longer pay a $1,000 fine or be processed in a third country such as Canada or Mexico. They must be processed in their home country.

Adjustment to permanent resident is not permitted where prohibited by the terms of the status under which you entered the U.S. as a nonimmigrant.

Documentation and supporting evidence includes:

- *INS forms*
  - I-485, Application to Register Permanent Residence or Adjust Status
  - I-765, Application for Employment Authorization (if required)
  - G-325A, Biographic Information Sheet
- *Fees*
  - I-485 filing fee of $220 if the applicant is 14 years of age or over
  - I-485 filing fee of $160 if the applicant is under 14 years of age
  - I-765 filing fee of $100
- *Passport and photographs*
  - passport valid for six months beyond intended approval date
  - two identical color photographs taken within last 30 days:
    - maximum 2" square
    - unmounted, printed on thin paper
    - glossy, unretouched
    - 3/4 frontal showing right ear and head bare
    - A number or name printed lightly in pencil on back
- *Prior approval*
  - copy of approval notice that a visa number is immediately available
- *Current and prior immigration status*
  - copy of I-94, Arrival/Departure Record, or
  - other evidence of status
- *Additional evidence*
  - supporting documents for special categories, if applicable:
    - copy of K-2 Fiancé(e) approval notice and marriage certificate
    - letter or Form I-94 showing date of approval of asylum status
    - proof of continuous residence since 1972
    - proof of Cuban citizenship or nationality
    - proof of being spouse or child of another adjustment applicant
    - other proof of eligibility
- *Proof of financial support or solvency*
  - Form I-864, Affidavit of Support
- *Civil documents*
  - copy of birth certificate
  - marriage certificate
- *Police clearance*
- *Medical clearance*
  - medical examination report on Form I-693 unless:
  - continuous resident since 1972, or
  - had official nonimmigrant medical examination during past 12 months

After filing an I-765 Application for Employment Authorization, a Form I-766 (EAD) will be issued to permit the alien to work temporarily while waiting for the Green Card Interview. Some INS offices will give permission to work as soon as the I-485 Adjustment of Status is filed. Others will not give permission until the Green Card interview is held several months later. For those working on an H-1B, it is important to seek an extension to avoid going out of status.

Dependents

A spouse and minor children may qualify to adjust status to permanent resident in the United States as long as:

- The relationship with the principal alien existed when the Green Card application was made
- The fiancé(e) entered the U.S. in K status and was married within 90 days
- They are in status in the United States
- They are not subject to the two-year HRR requirement of a J-1 or J-2
- They are processed with the principal alien

While dependents of a U.S. citizen are not subject to the immigrant visa limit and do not have to wait for a visa number, they may still have to wait for a Priority Date.

Option 2 - By the Department of State (DOS) Abroad

Once a visa number is immediately available and your petition is approved by the INS in the United States, it will usually be referred to a U.S. Embassy or Consulate in your home country for processing, if you are not living in the United States.

Under urgent circumstances, Consulates may exercise "consular discretion" and assist people by doing work that they have the emergency authority to do. They have been known to expedite the process to enable a minor child approaching his 21st birthday to be processed and cross the border with his family before his birthday.

Police Clearance

A critical step in the process involves having your police record checked to the satisfaction of the U.S. consulate. The pilot fingerprinting program at U.S. Consulates abroad ended on May 1, 1998. However, Consulates do a law enforcement data base name search and if your name matches the name of a person with a criminal record, you may be fingerprinted to confirm your identity and ensure the FBI clears you of any felony record before proceeding with your application. This may take several weeks.

Medical Examination

Also, before the final Green Card interview by a consular official, all applicants must pass a physical examination, tuberculin (TB) skin test (2 years and older) and serologic (blood) test (15 years and older) by physicians designated by the U.S. government in your home country. All medical work is carried out at your expense. You will be given your results on Form I-693 to be carried in a sealed envelope to your final interview at the U.S. Embassy or Consulate.

Consular Interview

Your interview will be not be scheduled with a consular officer until you have received police and medical clearance.

Documentation and supporting evidence includes:

- *DOS, INS and IRS forms*
  - State Department Packets III & IV, including:
    - Optional Form 168
    - Optional Form 230
      - Part I (Biographic Data) and
      - Part II (Sworn Statement)
    - Form I-864, Affidavit of Support
    - IRS Form 9003, Additional Questions to be Completed by All Applicants for Permanent Residence in the United States
- *Fees*
  - visa processing fee of $260
  - visa issuance fee of $65
  - proposed $50 Affidavit of Support review fee
- *Passport and photographs*
  - passport valid for six months beyond intended date of entry into U.S.
  - two identical 1½" (37 mm) square color photographs for each person
- *Current and prior immigration status*
  - copy of Form I-94, if in status in the United States
- *Prior approval*
  - approval notice that a visa number is immediately available
- *Employer's evidence to support request*
  - employment letter, if applicable
- *Civil documents*
  - marriage certificate
  - original of all civil documents required to prove relationship with the Family-Based petitioner
  - certified copy of birth certificates for each applicant–long form
  - divorce decree or death certificate of spouse, if applicable
- *Proof of financial support or solvency*
  - evidence of financial support, including, as required:
    - Form I-864, Affidavit of Support
    - evidence of your own assets
    - tax returns
    - bank records
  - proof that the alien will not become a public charge*Ref: 9 FAM 40.41*

A 1999 INS memorandum identified those benefits a person may accept without being a public charge. They include Medicaid, Children's Health Insurance Program, prenatal care, free and low cost clinical care, food programs, housing assistance and job training. However, receipt of cash welfare will be considered.

- *Police clearance*
  - certificate from all countries where the applicant has resided for six months or more including:
    - all arrests and reason for each
    - disposition of each case
    - court and prison records
    - military record, if applicable
- *Medical clearance*
  - Form I-693
- *Additional evidence*
  - certified translation of all documents not in English

The National Visa Center has begun mailing out Form I-864 to the petitioner who must forward it to the prospective immigrant. However, if the alien is being processed by Ciudad Juarez, Manilla or Santo Domingo, the I-864 has to be returned to the National Visa Center for review.

The scheduling of a Green Card interview does not guarantee the issuance of a visa. Applicants are advised not to give up jobs, dispose of property or make travel arrangements until a visa is actually issued.

Spouses and families cannot work in the U.S. while consular processing is pending abroad. In contrast, spouses may be able to get employment authorization immediately upon application when the principal alien is eligible for final adjustment in the United States.

Step 3 - Clearing the INS at a U.S. Port of Entry

All documentation received from the U.S. Embassy or Consulate abroad must be turned over to the INS Immigration Inspector at a port of entry.

In line with its responsibility to make a final determination on eligibility for entry, the INS may examine any documentation presented by an immigrant in other steps.

While awaiting Green Card processing, the spouse of a Green Card holder who has not been admitted for temporary or permanent residence may be able to obtain permission to visit the U.S. spouse for short visits but should be prepared to provide convincing proof of intent to depart at the end of the approved stay.

If the spouse, sons and daughters of a legal permanent resident are admitted on a conditional basis for two years, the Attorney General shall provide for notice to the spouse, son or daughter with the requirements to have the conditional status removed. The legal permanent resident and spouse or alien son or daughter must jointly submit a petition to the Attorney General for removal of their conditional status. The Attorney General's failure to provide notice shall not affect the enforcement of this section.

Ref:INA 216; 8 USC 1186a

Chapter 10

Employment-Based Preferences

Green Cards are available, in limited numbers, to qualified alien workers based on a quota system established by Congress. Each of the five Employment-Based Preference categories has its own unique criteria which is explored in the sections which follow.

Preference Categories	Annual Numbers Available	Additional Numbers	Eligibility and Waiting Period
First (EB1):	40,040 (28.6% of 140,000)	Unused Fourth and Fifth Preference Numbers	Priority Workers Waiting Period - Current
Second (EB2): *Labor Certification Required*	40,040 (28.6% of 140,000)	Unused First Preference Numbers	Professionals holding Advanced Degrees or Persons of Exceptional Ability or whose Services are Sought by U.S. Employers Waiting Period - Current
Third (EB3): *Labor Certification Required*	40,040 (28.6% of 140,000)	Unused First and Second Preference Numbers	Skilled Workers, Professionals and Other Workers Waiting Period - Current (Other Workers -6½years)
Fourth (EB4):	9,940 (7.1% of 140,000)		Certain Special Immigrants Waiting Period - Current
Fourth (EB4):			Certain Religious Ministers, Professionals and Other Religious Workers- Waiting Period - two years

Fifth (EB5):	9,940 (7.1% of 140,000)	Employment Creation (Investors) Waiting Period - Current
Fifth (EB5):	9,940 includes not less than 3,000 in targeted rural or high-unemployment areas and 300 in regional centers	Employment Creation (Investors in Targeted Employment Areas) Waiting Period - Current *Ref: INA 203*

There may be longer waiting periods for applicants chargeable to India, Mexico and the Philippines.

Entry Criteria

Currently, the number of Employment-Based Preference visas is set at an annual minimum of 140,000. The new Fiscal Year begins in October.   *Ref: INA 201*

The determination of which preference category is appropriate depends on:
- The qualifications of the beneficiary
- The needs of the employer
- The parameters of the job
- The available skills in the local job market's employment pool

Admission Process

Step 1 - Clearing the Job Offer in the United States

In most Employment-Based cases, the prospective U.S. employer must furnish a written job offer stating that the alien will be employed in the United States within the parameters of the chosen Preference category.

Step 2 - Labor Certification

Applicants for First, Fourth and Fifth Preferences skip this step. Second and Third Preference immigrant aliens must meet stringent Department of Labor criteria and they combine this step with Step 3
    Ref: ETA Instructions, Alien Employment Certification, 1980; INA 212(a)(5).

Role of the Department of Labor (DOL)

Any alien who seeks admission or status as an immigrant for the purpose of permanent employment under either Second or Third Preference Employment-Based shall be excluded unless the Secretary of Labor has first certified to the Secretary of State and to the Attorney General that:

- There are not sufficient U.S. workers who are able, willing, qualified and available at the time of application for a visa and admission into the United States and at the place where the alien is to perform the work, and
- The employment of the alien will not adversely affect the wages and working conditions of U.S. workers similarly employed.

Ref: INA 212(a)(5)(A)

Role of the Employer

The DOL requires that employers of nonimmigrant aliens follow a precise program for obtaining Labor Certification.

The employer must:

- Participate in a good faith recruitment
- Not make the job requirements too restrictive or tailored to the alien
- Test the local labor market for qualified and available U.S. workers
- Offer working conditions and wages which are realistic and appropriate for the job
- Review all applicants and be unable to find a qualified U.S. worker willing to take the job
- Demonstrate that the prospective alien employee meets the stated education, training or experience requirements of the job

Ref: 20 CFR 656

There are three ways to clear the Labor Certification process in Second and Third Preference applications. The type of occupation and the circumstances surrounding the application help determine which of the options is applicable.

Option 1 - Labor Certification by the INS

The INS is mandated to process the Labor Certification applications of:
- Schedule A, Groups I and II, occupations for which there are not sufficient U.S. workers
- Sheepherders (may also be processed for Labor Certification by the State Department abroad)   *Ref: 20 CFR 656*

An alien in the U.S. who is in status and qualified in one of these occupational groups, may apply to an INS District Office for Labor Certification. A sheepherder application may also be filed with a U.S. Embassy or Consulate abroad. The application is granted or denied by the INS in the United States or the consular office where the application is filed.

Schedule A occupations

Schedule A is a list of occupations for which the Director, United States Employment Service has determined that there *are not* sufficient U.S. workers who are able, willing, qualified and available and that the wages and working conditions of U.S. workers similarly employed will not be adversely affected by the employment of aliens in such occupations.

The Schedule A list is comprised of two groups of precertified occupations (Group I and Group II) which are subject to revision from time to time, based on U.S. labor market conditions.   *Ref: 20 CFR 656.10 and 656.22*

Group I includes Physical Therapists and Professional Nurses.

Group II includes Aliens (except Aliens in the Performing Arts) of exceptional ability in the sciences or arts, including college and university teachers of exceptional ability who have been practicing their science or art during the year prior to application and who intend to practice the same art in the United States.   *Ref: 20 CFR 656.22.*

Sheepherders
Sheepherders must have been employed in that capacity for at least 33 of the past 36 months in the United States.   *Ref: 20 CFR 656.21(b)*

Option 2 - **Labor Certification by the Department of Labor**
The DOL processes the Labor Certification applications of:
- Occupations designated for special handling
- Schedule B occupations for which there are sufficient U.S. workers

Occupations designated for special handling
This is a truncated category which includes:
- College or university teacher
- An alien represented to have exceptional ability in the performing arts
  Ref: 20 CFR 656.20

Schedule B occupations
Schedule B is a list of 49 occupations for which the Director, United States Employment Service has determined that sufficient U.S. workers *are* able, willing, qualified and available and that the wages and working conditions of U.S. workers similarly employed *will be* adversely affected by the employment of such aliens.
Ref: 20 CFR 656.11

An employer may apply to the Department of Labor for Schedule B Labor Certification on behalf of an alien. The application is granted or denied by the Department of Labor.

If the DOL does not approve an application for Labor Certification:
- A further application may not be submitted for six months
- An appeal may be filed

Labor Certification processing times vary widely, depending on where the employing company is located. It could take up to three years in some areas.

If an alien changes location or receives another job offer before the approval of the application to adjust status, a new Labor Certification process must be started.

Ref: TL:VISA-48, 10-1-91

Option 3 - National Interest Waiver

In Second Preference cases only, it is possible to obtain a National Interest Waiver from the Attorney General and thus avoid the Labor Certification process. If successful, it is not necessary to obtain Labor Certification or have a job waiting.

Step 3 - Clearing the INS in the United States - Initial Application

In the case of applications for permanent residency based on Second and Third Preference one of the foregoing three options must be successfully completed before an application for Second or Third Preference permanent residency may be processed.

Petitions for Schedule A occupations, sheepherders and National Interest Waivers, are filed with the INS, not the DOL, simultaneously with the petition described in this step. The petition should be filed with the INS regional Service Center having jurisdiction over the place where the alien will be employed. Applications for sheepherders may be filed with the INS or DOS abroad.

The INS forms which are required depend on which of the following preferences is being sought.

First (EB1), Second (EB2), and Third (EB3) Preference
- INS Form I-140, Immigrant Petition for Alien Worker
- Filing fee of $115

Fourth (EB4) Preference
- INS Form I-360, Application for Amerasian, Widow(er) or Special Immigrant
- Filing fee of $110

Fifth (EB5) Preference
- INS Form I-526, Immigrant Petition by Alien Entrepreneur
- Filing fee of $350

In some cases, it may be necessary to provide the INS with a credentials evaluation to establish the U.S. equivalent to your foreign degree. A random sampling of evaluators is provided in Appendix D.

Dependents - Derivative Status

The minor child or spouse of an Employment-Based immigrant is entitled to derivative status corresponding to the classification and priority date of the beneficiary of the petition provided that the beneficiary is:
- On a valid visa, if applying in the United States
- Included in the principal alien's petition

- Married before the filing of the I-485, Application to Register Permanent Residence or Adjust Status
- Accompanying or following to join the principal applicant
- Not subject to the two-year HRR requirement of a J-1 or J-2

Ref: TL:VISA-54, 2-28-92

An Employment-Based Green Card applicant who marries after filing a Green Card petition must add the spouse to the petition before the Green Card interview. Otherwise, the spouse will have to wait, currently four years, for entry as a Family-Sponsored Second Preference applicant.

Spouses who are in the U.S. in legal nonimmigrant status may:

- Not automatically be allowed to remain in the United States
- Not work merely because they are on the waiting list for a Green Card
- Independently seek a nonimmigrant H-1 or L visa as permitted under the terms of Dual Intent to permit them to remain and work in the United States while waiting for a Green Card

Step 4 - Processing

Option 1 - Adjustment of Status by the INS in the United States

Once an immigrant visa number is immediately available based on the approval of your petition, final processing may be carried out by the INS in the U.S., if you are living in the United States. Therefore, to adjust from a nonimmigrant category to permanent resident status, you should file with the local INS office having jurisdiction over your place of residence.

Aliens living in the United States who have not maintained lawful status may no longer pay a $1,000 fee and must be processed in their home country.

Documentation and supporting evidence includes:

- *INS forms*
  - I-485, Application to Register Permanent Residence or Adjust Status
  - I-765, Application for Employment Authorization (if required)
- *Fees*
  - I-485 filing fee of $220 if the applicant is 14 years of age or over
  - I-485 filing fee of $160 if the applicant is under 14 years of age
  - I-765 filing fee of $100 (if required)
  - fingerprinting fee of $25
- *Passport and photographs*
  - passport valid for six months beyond intended date of entry
  - two identical 1½" (37 mm) square color photographs - 3/4 angle showing right ear

- *Prior approval*
  - copy of notice of approval of immigrant petition making visa number immediately available
- *Current and prior immigration status*
  - copy of Form I-94, if applicable
- *Proof of financial support or solvency*
  - Form I-864 Affidavit of Support (if relative/relative's entity filed petition)
  - evidence of your own assets
- *Civil documents*
  - birth Certificate of principal alien and dependents - long form
  - marriage certificate, if applicable
- *Police clearance*
- *Employer's evidence to support request*
  - employment letter

Since the law requires that all temporary residents except those in H-1 and L status intend to leave the United States at the end of the period for which they have been admitted, it is difficult to justify maintaining U.S. residency if a Green Card application is pending.

Option 2 - By the Department of State (DOS) Abroad

Once a visa number is immediately available and your petition is approved by the INS in the United States, it will usually be referred to a U.S. Embassy or Consulate in your home country for processing by a consular officer, if you are not living in the United States.   *Ref: INA 203(b)*

Consular officers shall not readjudicate the petition filed with the INS, but rather shall review the petition to determine whether:

- The supporting evidence is consistent with the approval
- There was any misrepresentation of a material fact, and
- The alien meets the requirements of the employment offered, if applicable   *Ref: TL:VISA-54, 2-28-92*

An immigrant visa may not be issued to Second and Third Preference applicants until the consular officer is in receipt of Labor Certification by the Secretary of Labor.
Ref: INA 203(b), 212(a)(5)(A); TL:VISA-54; 2-28-92

Regardless of whether they are named in the petition, the child or spouse of an Employment-Based immigrant is entitled to a derivative status corresponding to the classification and priority date of the beneficiary of the petition.
Ref: INA 203(d); TL:VISA-54; 2-28-92

Medical Examination

Before the final Green Card interview by a consular official, all applicants must pass a physical examination, tuberculin (TB) skin test (2 years and older) and serologic (blood) test (15 years and older) by physicians designated by the U.S. government in your home country. All medical work is carried out at the applicant's expense. You will be given your results on Form I-693 to be carried in a sealed envelope to your final interview at the U.S. Embassy or Consulate.

Consular Interview

Your interview will be not be scheduled with a consular officer until you have received police and medical clearance.

If the Employment-Based Green Card interview is not waived, questions may focus on whether your employment status remains exactly the same as at the time the application was submitted and about the accuracy of statements on your application. The interview may be very short.

The scheduling of a Green Card interview does not guarantee the issuance of a visa. Applicants are advised to not give up jobs, dispose of property or make travel arrangements until a visa is actually issued.

Documentation and supporting evidence includes:

- *DOS forms*
  - State Department Packet III & IV including:
    - Optional Form 230 Parts I and II
    - G-325A - Biographic information Sheet
- *Fees*
  - visa processing fee of $260
  - visa issuance fee of $65
  - proposed $50 Affidavit of Support review fee (if I-864 required)
- *Passport and photographs*
  - passport valid for at least six months beyond intended date of entry
  - two identical 1½" (37 mm) square color photographs - 3/4 angle showing right ear
- *Prior approval*
  - copy of notice of approval of immigrant petition making visa number immediately available
- *Current and prior immigration status*
  - copy of Form I-94, if applicable
- *Proof of financial support or solvency*
  - evidence of support
  - Form I-864, Affidavit of Support(if relative/relative's entity filed petition)
  - notarized offer of employment
  - evidence of your own assets
- *Civil documents*
  - birth Certificate of principal alien and dependents - long form
- *Police clearance*
  - proof of police clearance

- *Medical clearance*
  - Form I-693, proof of medical clearance

The beneficiary is given a sealed package of documents to carry and give the INS Immigration Inspector at a port of entry.

Step 5 - Clearing the INS at a U.S. Port of Entry

The issuance of a visa does not guarantee entry into the United States as the INS Immigration Inspector reviews all documentation before making a final determination of whether an alien meets the intent of the law.

Step 6 - Retaining Your Green Card

There is no prescribed time which you must remain with the employer who sponsored you for your Green Card. However, remember that you obtained your Green Card based on your acceptance of a specific "permanent" position. By leaving that position too soon, the INS could consider your application to be fraudulent.

It is advisable to seek the opinion of competent counsel before considering an early job change.

Employment-Based First Preference (EB1)

Priority Workers
Aliens with Extraordinary Ability, Outstanding Professors and Researchers, Certain Multinational Executives and Managers

T his is the elite of the Employment-Based Preferences. It does not require Labor Certification and, in some circumstances, does not require a job offer. However, in all cases, it requires extensive and conclusive proof that an alien is deserving.

Sub-categories are:

First Preference (EB1)	Priority workers

A Aliens with Extraordinary Ability (EB11)
B Outstanding Professors and Researchers (EB12)
C Certain Multinational Executives and Managers (EB13)
Ref: INA 203(b),in part; TL:VISA-55, 3-13-92

Entry Criteria

A) Aliens of Extraordinary Ability in the Sciences, Arts, Education, Business, and Athletics (EB11)

The alien applicant must:

- Have extraordinary ability in the sciences, arts, education, business or athletics, demonstrated by sustained national or international acclaim
- Be coming to work in the area of extraordinary ability

8 CFR section 204.5(h)(2) defines "extraordinary ability" as"a level of expertise indicating that the individual is one of that small percentage who have risen to the top of the field of endeavor". *Ref: TL:VISA-54, 2-28-92*

B) Outstanding Professors/Researchers (EB12)

The alien applicant must:
- Have at least three years of experience in teaching or research in the academic area
- Be in a tenured or tenure-track position at a university or institution of higher education to teach in the academic area, or
- Be in a comparable position at a university or institution of higher education to teach in the academic area, or
- Be in a comparable position to conduct research for a private employer which employs at least three persons in full-time research activities and have has achieved documented accomplishments in an academic field
- Have the required written offer of employment
- Have achieved documented accomplishments in the academic field
- Be recognized internationally as outstanding in the specific academic area

C) Certain Multinational Executives and Managers (EB13)

The alien applicant must:
- Have been employed for at least one year in the three years preceding the filing of this petition by a firm or corporation or other legal entity
- Seek to enter the United States to continue to render services to the same employer or to a subsidiary or affiliate in a capacity that is managerial or executive
- Have been employed for one of last three years by a firm or corporation
- Not be coming to open a new office (one year minimum requirement)

Admission Process

Step 1 - Clearing the Job Offer in the United States

A) Aliens of Extraordinary Ability (EB11)
- Requires evidence of either pre-arranged U.S. employment, or
- Seeks to continue work in the area of extraordinary ability
- May file a petition with the INS on their own behalf

Ref: TL:VISA-54, 2-28-92

B) Outstanding Professors and Researchers (EB12)
- The prospective U.S. employer must furnish in writing:
  - a job offer stating that the alien will be:
    - employed in the United States
    - in a teaching or research capacity in the academic area
  - a clear description of the duties to be performed

Ref: TL:VISA-54; 2-28-92

C) Certain Multinational Executives and Managers (EB13)

- The prospective U.S. employer must furnish in writing:
  - a job offer stating that the alien will be:
  - employed in the United States
  - in a managerial or executive capacity
  - a clear description of the duties to be performed

Ref: TL:VISA-54; 2-28-92

Step 2 - Clearing the INS in the United States - Initial Petition

While any person, including the beneficiary, may file a First Preference A petition, only a U.S. employer may file a First Preference B or C petition.

A Form I-140, Immigrant Petition for Alien Worker, must be filed with the INS regional Service Center having jurisdiction over the place where the alien will be employed as a First Preference alien who qualifies under INA 203(b)(1) under in one of the following three sub-categories:

- A Aliens with Extraordinary Ability
- B Outstanding Professors and Researchers
- C Certain Multinational Executives and Managers

Ref: INA 203(b),in part; TL:VISA-55, 3-13-92

Whether or not named in the petition, the child or spouse is entitled to a derivative status corresponding to the classification and priority date of the beneficiary of the petition. *Ref: 9 FAM 42.32*

Documentation and supporting evidence includes:

- *INS form*
  - I-140, Immigrant Petition for Alien Worker
- *Fee*
  - I-140 filing fee of $115
  - fingerprinting fee of $25
- *Civil documents*
  - no birth certificate is required
    (as you are not relying on a family connection)
- *Employer's evidence*
  - all necessary supporting documentation as required in First Preference B and C employment letters
- *Proof of financial support or solvency*
  - all necessary proof of financial support
  - Form I-864, Affidavit of Support(if relative/relative's entity filed petition)

- *Professional criteria*
  - all necessary professional qualifying evidence, as required, on the following pages under A, B or C

The INS must approve I-140 petitions of aliens for First Preference *Priority Workers* Employment-Based status in the following sub-categories:

A) Aliens of Extraordinary Ability in the Sciences, Arts, Education, Business, and Athletics (EB11)   *Ref: INA 203(b)(1)(A)*

Any person may file on behalf of an alien applying for First Preference A. No offer of employment or Labor Certification is required.

The alien must:

- Have achievements recognized through extensive documentation
- Include with the petition convincing evidence that he or she is coming to continue work in the area of expertise such as:
  - letter(s) from prospective employer(s)
  - evidence of prearranged commitments, such as contracts, or
  - a statement from the beneficiary detailing plans for continuing work in the United States   *Ref: TL:VISA-54, 2-28-92*

Additional supporting evidence includes:

- One-time achievement such as a major, internationally-recognized award, or prize, or
- at least three of:
  - receipt of lesser nationally or internationally recognized prizes or awards for excellence in the field of endeavor
  - membership in associations in the field which require outstanding achievements as judged by recognized national or international experts
  - published material about the alien in professional or major trade publications or other major media
  - participation on a panel as a judge of the work of others in the field or an allied field
  - original scientific, scholarly, artistic, athletic or business-related contributions of major significance in the field
  - authorship of scholarly books or articles in the field, in professional or major scholarly journals or trade publications with international circulation or other major media
  - display of the alien's work at artistic exhibitions or showcases
  - evidence that the alien has performed in a leading or critical role for organizations or establishments that have a distinguished reputation
  - evidence that the alien has commanded a high salary or other high remuneration for services, or

- evidence of commercial successes in the commercial arts, as shown by box office receipts, cassette, compact disc, or video sales

If the above standards do not readily apply to the alien's occupation, comparable evidence may be submitted to establish eligibility.

B) Outstanding Professors/Researchers (EB12)   *Ref: INA 203(b)(1)(B)*

A U.S. employer who wishes to employ an outstanding professor or researcher in First Preference B must file this petition.

The alien applicant must:

- Be recognized internationally as outstanding in the specific academic area and have submitted at least two of the following pieces of evidence:
  - major international prizes or awards for outstanding achievement
  - membership in associations in the academic field requiring outstanding achievements of their members
  - published material in professional publications written by others about the alien's work
  - participation as the judge of the work of others in the same or allied academic field
  - evidence of original scientific or scholarly research contributions, or authorship of scholarly books or articles with international circulation in the academic field
  - display of work in exhibitions or showcases
  - leading or critical role for organizations with a distinguished reputation
  - high salary or remuneration in relation to others in the field
    Ref: 8 CFR 204.5(h)(3); TL:VISA-54; 2-28-92

Initial evidence should be submitted of at least two of the following:

- Receipt of major prizes for outstanding achievement in the academic field
- Membership in associations in the academic field, which require outstanding achievements of their members
- Published material in professional publications written by others about the alien's work in the academic field
- Participation on a panel, or individually, as the judge of the work of others in the same or an allied academic field
- Original scientific or scholarly research contributions to the academic field
- Authorship of scholarly books or articles, in scholarly journals with international circulation, in the academic field

If the above standards do not readily apply, the petitioner may submit comparable evidence to establish eligibility.

A university or other institution of higher education must provide:

- A letter indicating its intention to employ the beneficiary in a tenured or tenure-track position as a teacher or in a permanent position as a researcher in the academic field, or

A private employer must provide:

- A letter indicating its intention to employ the beneficiary in a permanent research position in the academic field, and
- Evidence it employs at least three full-time researchers and has achieved documented accomplishments in the field

C) Certain Multinational Executives and Managers (EB13)

Ref: INA 203(b)(1)(C)

A U.S. employer who wishes to employ Multinational Executives and Managers First Preference C must file this petition with a statement on behalf of an alien in First Preference C class to demonstrate that:

- If the alien is outside the United States, he or she has been employed outside the United States for at least one year in the past three years   in a managerial or executive capacity by a firm or corporation or other legal entity, or by its affiliate or subsidiary, or
- If the alien is already in the United States working for the same employer, or a subsidiary or affiliate of the firm or corporation or other legal entity, by which the alien was employer abroad, he or she was employed by the entity abroad in a managerial or executive capacity for at least one year in the three years preceding his or her entry as a nonimmigrant:
- The prospective employer in the United States is the same employer or a subsidiary or affiliate of the firm or corporation or other legal entity by which the alien was employed abroad
- The prospective U.S. employer has been doing business for at least one year, and
- The alien is to be employed in the United States in a managerial or executive capacity and describing the duties to be performed

Executive capacity

If entering in an "executive capacity", an alien must:

- Direct the management of an organization or major component
- Establish the goals and policies of the organization, component or function
- Exercise wide latitude in discretionary decision-making
- Receive only general supervision or direction from higher level executives, the board of directors, or stockholders of the organization

Managerial capacity

If entering in a "managerial capacity" primarily, an alien must:

- Manage the organization, or its department, subdivision, function, or component
- Supervise and control the work of other supervisory, professional, or managerial employees, or
- Manage an essential function within the organization, or its department or subdivision
- Have the authority to hire and fire directly supervised employees or recommend those as well as other personnel actions (such as promotion and leave authorization) or
- Function at a senior level within the organization hierarchy with respect to the function managed if no other employee is directly supervised
- Exercise discretion over the day-to-day operations of the activity or function for which the employee has authority

Supervisory capacity

A first-line supervisor is not considered to be acting in a managerial capacity merely by virtue of supervisory responsibilities unless the employees supervised are professional. *INA 101(a)(44)(A); TL:VISA-54; 2-28-92*

Multinational

To qualify as "multinational", the qualifying entity, or its affiliate or subsidiary must conduct business in two or more countries, one of which is the United States.

Subsidiary

A qualifying "subsidiary" is a firm, corporation, or other legal entity of which a parent owns:

- Directly or indirectly, 50 percent of a 50-50 joint venture and has equal control and veto power over the entity, or
- Directly or indirectly, less than half of the entity, but in fact controls the entity   *Ref: INA 101(a)(44)(C) and 203(d); 9 FAM 42.31*

Step 3 - Processing

Option 1 - Adjustment of Status by the INS in the United States

If you have maintained lawful status in the United States and have been notified that a visa number is immediately eligible, you may apply to adjust status to permanent resident by filing with the local INS office having jurisdiction over the place where the alien will be employed.

Aliens living in the United States who have not maintained lawful status may no longer pay a $1,000 fine and must be processed in their home country.

Documentation and supporting evidence includes:

- *INS forms*
  - I-485, Application to Register Permanent Residence or Adjust Status
  - I-765, Application for Employment Authorization (if required)
- *Fees*
  - I-485 filing fee of $220 if the applicant is 14 years of age or over
  - I-485 filing fee of $160 if the applicant is under 14 years of age
  - I-765 filing fee of $100 (if required)
  - fingerprinting fee of $25
- *Passport and photographs*
  - passport valid for six months beyond intended date of entry
  - two identical 1½" (37 mm) square color photographs - 3/4 angle showing right ear
- *Prior approval*
  - copy of approved Notice for immigrant petition making visa number immediately available
- *Current and prior immigration status*
  - copy of Form I-94, if applicable
- *Proof of financial support or solvency*
  - Form I-864, Affidavit of Support(if relative/relatives's entity filed petition)
  - evidence of your own assets
- *Civil documents*
  - birth Certificate of principal alien and dependents - long form
  - marriage certificate, if applicable
- *Police clearance*
- *Employer's evidence to support request*
  - employment letter

Option 2 - By the Department of State (DOS) Abroad

An applicant may be processed as an Employment-Based First Preference immigrant at a U.S. Embassy or Consulate abroad after receiving notification that the consular office has received an INS Petition approved in accordance with INA 204 and a visa number is immediately available.

The consular officer must be satisfied that the alien is within one of the classes described in INA 203(b)(1).   *Ref: INA 203(b)(1); 9 FAM 42.32*

Documentation and supporting evidence includes:

- *DOS forms*
  - State Department Packet III & IV including:
    - Optional Form-230 Parts I and II
    - G-325A - Biographic information Sheet

- *Fees*
    - visa processing fee of $260
    - visa issuance fee of $65
    - proposed $50 Affidavit of Support review fee (if I-864 required)
- *Passport and photographs*
    - passport valid for at least six months beyond intended date of entry
    - two identical 1½" (37 mm) square color photographs - 3/4 angle showing right ear
- *Prior approval*
    - copy of approved Notice for immigrant petition making visa number immediately available
- *Current and prior immigration status*
    - copy of Form I-94, if applicable
- *Proof of financial support or solvency*
    - notarized offer of employment
    - evidence of your own assets
    - Form I-864, Affidavit of Support (if relative/relative's entity filed petition)
- *Civil documents*
    - birth Certificate of principal alien and dependents - long form
- *Police clearance*
    - proof of police clearance
- *Medical clearance*
    - Form I-693, proof of medical clearance

If the consular officer is satisfied with the evidence presented, an alien will receive a First Preference Employment-Based visa.

Step 4 - Clearing the INS at a U.S. Port of Entry

The INS has the final authority to review the documents presented for compliance and make a decision on whether to admit the alien.

Employment-Based

Second Preference (EB2)

Professionals Holding Advanced Degrees, Aliens of Exceptional Ability, National Interest Waivers

&

Third Preference (EB3)

Skilled Workers, Professionals, Other Workers

Only some Second (EB2) and all Third (EB3) Employment-Based Preferences require permanent Labor Certification. Since these two Preference categories, the Labor Certification processes, and the agencies which administer them are so interrelated, the two Preference categories are presented together in this section for the sake of clarity.

Second Preference sub-categories are:

Second Preference (EB2):	Professional Holding Advanced Degrees, or
	Persons of Exceptional Ability in the Arts, Sciences or Business who will substantially benefit the national economy, cultural or educational interests, or
	National Interest Waivers

Third Preference sub-categories are:

Third Preference (EB3):	Skilled Workers with at least two years of specialized training for which qualified workers are not available in the U.S.
	Members of Professions with a Baccalaureate Degree
	Other Unskilled Workers to perform labor for which qualified workers are not available in the United States (Only 10,000 visas are available)

Ref: INA 203(b)(3)

Entry Criteria - Second Preference (EB2)

In order to qualify for Second Preference status, you must meet the entry criteria and offer supporting evidence in one of the following three sub-categories:

A) Members of the professions holding advanced degrees or their equivalent

Advanced degree means:

- Any U.S. academic or professional degree, or foreign equivalent degree above that of baccalaureate

The conference committee report (H.R. Rep. No. 101-955) states that a bachelor degree plus five years of progressive experience in the professions should be considered as the equivalent of a master's degree.

B) Aliens of exceptional ability in the sciences, arts, or business who will substantially benefit prospectively the national economy, cultural or educational interests, or welfare of the United States

Exceptional ability means:

- A degree of expertise significantly above that ordinarily encountered
- Something more than what is usual and requires some rare or unusual talent or skill, or extraordinary ability in a calling which requires that talent or skill
- Status in a field wherein contemporaries recognize exceptional individual ability

The possession of a college or university degree, diploma, certificate or similar award or certification shall not by itself be considered sufficient evidence of such exceptional ability.

C) National Interest Waiver

National Interest means:

- Exceptional ability or as a member of the professions holding an advanced degree and,
  - the alien's past record and the prospective national benefit outweigh the national interest of the Labor Certification process
- The alien seeks employment in an area of substantial intrinsic merit
- The proposed benefit will be national in scope
- Exemption from the job offer and labor certification by Attorney General would be in the national interest
- The national interest would be adversely affected if waiver denied

A finding by the Board of Immigration Appeals in 1998 helped to further define the criteria for a National Interest Waiver (NIW) as follows:

- An individual alien cannot establish the importance of a field or the urgency of an issue as a benefit to the national interest simply by working in the field or seeking an undiscovered solution
- A shortage of workers does not constitute grounds for a NIW

The National Interest Waiver expects unique knowledge, abilities or experience which will be of significant benefit to the U.S. and the field.

Many successful cases hold masters or doctoral degrees, require exceptional ability and may require a license and professional membership. They may also reflect a higher degree and salary than most in the field and at least ten years experience and significant contribution to the field.

In late 1999, President Clinton signed into law H.R. 441, a major health care immigration bill, under which a National Interest Waiver may be granted to an alien physician who agrees to work in an area designated by the Department of Health and Human Services as having a shortage of doctors or at a health care facility run by the Department of Veteran Affairs. However, Green Card processing may not be completed until the physician has worked for an aggregate of five years in the designated shortage area. This period does not include time spent as a J-1.

Qualification is possible by doing residency as an H-1B holder or if a Federal agency or State department of public health has previously determined that the physician's work is in the public interest and has obtained a waiver of the J-1 home residency requirement.

Entry Criteria - Third Preference (EB3)

In order to apply for Third Preference (EB3) status, you must meet the entry criteria and offer supporting evidence in one of the following three sub-categories.

A) Skilled Workers

Skilled Workers are those persons:

- Capable of performing skilled labor, requiring at least two years training or experience
- For whom relevant post-secondary education may be considered as training for the purposes of this provision
- Whose job is not of a temporary or seasonal nature and there are no qualified workers available in the United States *Ref: TL:VISA-54, 2-28-92*

B) Professionals

Professionals are those persons who hold baccalaureate degrees and are members of a profession.

Profession includes but is not limited to:

- Architects
- Engineers
- Lawyers
- Physicians and surgeons
- Teachers in elementary or secondary schools, colleges, academies, or seminaries

An occupation may generally be considered to be a profession if the attainment of a baccalaureate degree is usually the minimum requirement for entry into that occupation.   *Ref: INA 101(a)(32)*

C) Other Workers

Other workers are qualified aliens capable, at the time of petitioning, of performing unskilled labor:

- Requiring less than two years training
- Not of a temporary or seasonal nature
- For which there are no qualified workers available in the United States

Due to the annual limit of 10,000 "Other Workers" visas, there is a large backlog. *Ref: TL:VISA-54, 2-28-92*

Admission Process

Step 1 - Clearing the Job Offer in the United States

Except in National Interest Waiver cases, the prospective U.S. employer must furnish a written job offer which establishes that the alien will be employed in the U.S. within the chosen Preference sub-category. Labor Certification must also be cleared.

Step 2 - *Labor Certification or National Interest Waiver*

National Interest Waivers, like First Preference EB1s, do not require either Labor Certification or a job offer. Both are faster than classifications which require labor clearance and both allow the applicant to sponsor himself or herself.

Other than National Interest Waiver cases, all U.S. jobs which fall within Second (EB2) or Third (EB3) Employment-Based Preferences must satisfy the Labor Certification requirement before an I-140, Immigrant Petition for Alien Worker may be processed. National Interest Waiver applicants go directly to Step 3.

Labor Certification, or Alien Employment Certification as it is also known, is a finding by the U.S. Department of Labor (DOL) that:

- There are not sufficient U.S. workers who are able, willing, qualified and available at the time of the application
- Employment of the alien will not adversely affect the wages and working conditions of U.S. workers similarly employed   *Ref: 20 CFR 656.1*

Labor Certification clearance may take one of three forms:

- Option 1 - a formal filing with the INS to meet Department of Labor criteria
- Option 2 - a formal filing with the Department of Labor for:
  - a waiver of its standards to permit the entry of an alien where sufficient qualified U.S. workers are available (Schedule B), or
  - occupations designated for special handling
- Option 3 - a waiver of Labor Certification by the Attorney General in the national interest

Although the supporting documentation varies within these three options, the following is required of all labor certification applications.

Documentation and supporting evidence required:

- *DOL forms*
  - ETA 750A, Application for Alien Employment Certification
  - ETA 750B, Statement of Qualifications of Alien
  - G-28, if represented by an attorney
- *Fee*
  - no DOL filing fee
- *Additional evidence - by employer*
  - full description of the job
  - funds available to pay the alien
  - wage offered and paid equals or exceeds the prevailing wage for the occupation in the geographical area
  - wage is not based on commissions, bonuses or other incentives
  - employer can place the alien on the payroll immediately on entrance into the U.S.

- job opportunity does not involve unlawful discrimination
- job opportunity does not relate to a strike, lockout or labor dispute
- terms are not contrary to Federal, State or local law
- job is open to any qualified U.S. worker
- notice of filing provided to bargaining representative or if none, posted 10 consecutive days in a conspicuous place at the location of employment   *Ref: 20 CFR 656.20*
- *Additional evidence - by alien applicant*
  - offer of employment
  - alien's signed statement of qualification for the occupational group
  - any necessary supporting documentation
- *Additional evidence - physicians and surgeons*
  - passed Part I and II of the National Board of Medical Examiners Examination (NMBMEE), or
  - passed Educational Commission for Foreign Medical Graduates (ECFMG), or
  - practiced in the U.S. in 1978, or
  - graduated from a school of medicine accredited by the Secretary of Education

After the initial petition is approved, applications for permanent residency for the applicants and their families may be filed and permission for work authorization may be received within two months. Approval of residency may take several months longer.

Forms may be downloaded from http://edc.dws.state.ut.us/forms.htm.

Option 1 - Labor Certification by the INS

The INS handles the Labor Certification petitions of aliens in Schedule A and sheepherders in accordance with Department of Labor standards. Applications are submitted to the INS in Step 3 together with Form I-140, Immigrant Petition for Alien Worker. Sheepherders have the option of filing their Labor Certification application with a U.S. Embassy or Consulate abroad before submitting their Form I-140.

Schedule A occupations

Schedule A is the Department of Labor's list of precertified occupations in short supply which will not adversely affect the employment of U.S. workers.

Schedule A is divided into two groups.

- Group I consists of:
  - Physical Therapists, and
  - Professional Nurses
- Group II consists of:
  - aliens of exceptional ability in the sciences or arts, including college and university teachers of exceptional ability who have been practicing

their science or art during the year prior to application and who intend to practice the same art in the U.S.   *Ref: 20 CFR 656.10*

- *Additional evidence - Schedule A*
    - alien's work experience in the last 12 months and intended U.S. work which will require exceptional ability
    - alien has exceptional ability in the sciences or arts
    - copy and details of at least one advertisement in an appropriate national publication
    - unions unable to refer equally qualified U.S. workers, if applicable
- *Additional evidence - Schedule A - Group I Physical Therapists*
    - certification of professional qualifications and English competency by designated organization
- *Additional evidence - Schedule A - Group I Professional Nurses*
    - certification of professional qualifications and English competency by designated organization (Commission of Graduates of Foreign Nursing Schools (CGFNS)
- *Additional evidence - Schedule A - Group II aliens of exceptional ability in the sciences or arts*
    - documentary evidence testifying to the widespread acclaim and international recognition accorded to the alien by recognized experts in the field
    - documentation showing that the alien's work in that field during the past year did, and the alien's intended work in the U.S. will, require exceptional ability
    - documentation from at least two of the following seven groups within the field for which certification is sought:
        - internationally-recognized prizes or awards for excellence
        - membership in international associations
        - published material in professional publications about the alien
        - participation on a panel or as a judge of the work of others
        - original scientific or scholarly research contributions of major significance
        - authorship of published scientific or scholarly articles
        - display of the alien's work at artistic exhibitions in more than one country

An Immigration Officer shall:

- Determine whether the employer and alien have met the applicable requirements
- Review the application, and
- Determine whether the alien is qualified for and intends to pursue the Schedule A occupation

Although the Immigration Officer may request an advisory opinion from the U.S. Employment Service, the Schedule A determination of the INS is conclusive and final.

The Immigration Officer shall forward a copy of the Form ETA 750 to the DOL Director without attachments. At this point, the INS Form I-140 may be processed.
Ref: 20 CFR 656.22

Health Care Workers

Section 343 of the Illegal Immigration Reform and Immigrant Responsibility Act of 1996 (IIRIRA96) created a new ground of inadmissibilty which requires that aliens seeking to be admitted for permanent residence or adjust their status in a category involving a health care occupation must first obtain a certificate issued by a specified independent credentialing organization that verifies their education, training, licensing, experience and English competency are comparable to American health care workers. Applicants from Canada (except Quebec), Australia, New Zealand, Ireland, the United Kingdom and the U.S. are exempt from the English competency requirement.

The provision applies to nurses, physical therapists, occupational therapists, speech language pathologists, medical technologists, medical technicians, and physical assistants. Initially, only petitions from occupational therapists and nurses had designated independent credentialing organizations and, hence were being processed. The credentialing organization for occupational therapists was designated as the National Board for Certification in Occupational Therapy (NBCOT). Petitions for other health care occupations were being held in abeyance until final regulations could be developed and implemented.
Ref: INA 212(a)(5)(C)

Sheepherders

An employer shall apply for a Labor Certification to employ an alien who has been employed legally as a nonimmigrant sheepherder for at least 33 of the preceding 36 months.
Ref: 20 CFR 656.21(b)

Petitions for aliens who have been employed as sheepherders for at least 33 of the previous 36 months are filed in Step 3 with either the INS in the U.S. or at a U.S. Embassy or Consulate abroad together with Form I-140, Petition for Alien Worker.

The determination of the Immigration or Consular Officer shall be conclusive and final. They shall forward a copy of the Form ETA 750 to the DOL Director without attachments. At this point the Form I-140 may be processed
Ref: 20 CFR 656.21a

Option 2 - Labor Certification by the Department of Labor

State employment and U.S. Department of Labor offices carry the responsibility for the certification of three groups:

- Occupations designated for special handling
- Schedule B occupations
- Applicants for Reduction in Recruitment (RIR)

Occupations designated for special handling

The DOL has determined that special labor market tests and an abbreviated process are appropriate for occupations which have been designated for special handling. These are:

- College and university teacher
- Alien represented to be of exceptional ability in the performing arts

Ref: 20 CFR 656.20

College or university teacher

An employer shall apply for a Labor Certification to employ an alien as a college or university teacher or an alien represented to be of exceptional ability by filing Form ETA 750, Application for Employment Certification with the local Employment Service office serving the area where the alien proposes to be employed.

The employer must submit clear documentation to show:

- The alien was selected for the job opportunity in a competitive recruitment
- The alien was found to be more qualified than any U.S. worker applicant
- Additional evidence
  - signed statement of details of the recruiting process
  - number of applicants
  - reasons why the alien is more qualified
  - copy of at least one job advertisement in a national professional journal
  - all other recruitment sources utilized
  - attestation of the alien's educational or professional qualifications and academic achievements

Application is made within 18 months after the selection is made.

Alien represented to be of exceptional ability in the performing arts

If the application is for an alien represented to have exceptional ability in the performing arts, the employer shall the following evidence:

- The alien's work experience during the past 12 months
- The alien's intended work in the U.S. will require exceptional ability
- Additional evidence
  - documents attesting to the alien's widespread acclaim and international recognition
  - receipt of internationally recognized prizes or awards for excellence
  - published material by or about the alien
  - documentary evidence of earnings commensurate with the claimed level of ability
  - playbills and starbills
  - documents attesting to the outstanding reputations of establishments in which the alien has performed or will perform

- Repertory companies, ballet troupes, orchestras where the alien has performed in a leading or starring capacity
- One advertisement placed in a national publication appropriate to the alien's occupation

Filing is with the local Employment Service office.

The local Employment Service office, upon receipt of an application for a college or university teacher or alien represented to have exceptional ability in the performing arts shall:

- Stamp the application and make sure it is complete
- Calculate the prevailing wage for the job opportunity, and
- Advise the employer to increase the amount offered if the wages offered are below the prevailing wage   *Ref: 20 CFR 656.21*

The local Employment Service office shall transmit a file containing the application, the local officer's prevailing wage findings and any other information it determines is appropriate to the State Employment Service Agency (SESA) office or to the Certifying Officer if so directed by SESA.

The SESA office which receives an application may add appropriate data or comments and transmit the application promptly to the appropriate Certifying Officer for final approval.

Upon receipt of final approval, Form I-140 may be filed with the INS.

Reduction in Recruitment (RIR)

The Certifying Officer may reduce the employer's recruitment efforts if the employer satisfactorily documents that the employer has adequately tested the labor market with no success at least at the prevailing wage and working conditions. No reduction may be granted for job offers involving occupations listed on Schedule B.

To request a reduction in recruitment efforts, the employer shall file a written request along with the Application for Alien Employment Certification form at the appropriate local Job Service office. The request shall contain:

- Documentary evidence that within the immediately preceding six months the employer has made good faith efforts to recruit U.S. workers for the job opportunity, at least at the prevailing wage and working conditions through sources normal to the occupation, and
- Any other information that the employer believes will support the contention that further recruitment will be unsuccessful

Upon receipt, the local office shall date stamp the request and application form and shall review and process the application without requiring:

- The local office to prepare and process an Employment Service job order
- The employer to place an advertisement for the job opportunity in a newspaper of general circulation or professional, trade or ethnic publication

- The employer to provide the local office with a written report of the results of the employer's post-application recruitment efforts during the normal 30-day recruitment period

After reviewing and processing the application, the local office (and the State Employment Service office) shall process the application to the Employment Service agency's state office if not successful or to the regional Certifying Officer, if successful.

The Certifying Officer shall review the documentation submitted by the employer and the comments of the local office and shall notify the employer and the local or state Employment Service office of whether the recruitment efforts may be reduced partially or completely or the application is denied.

Unless the Certifying Officer decides to reduce completely the recruitment efforts, the application shall be returned to the local or state office so that the employer may recruit workers to the extent required in the Certifying Officer's decision.

Ref: 20 CFR 656.21(i)

Schedule B occupations

Schedule B occupations are Third Preference (EB3) for which the Department of Labor (DOL) has determined that there generally are sufficient U.S. workers who are able, willing, qualified and available. Wages and working conditions of U.S. workers similarly employed will generally be adversely affected by the employment in the U.S. of aliens in Schedule B occupations.

Regarding schedule B occupations, the DOL says:

- Little or no education or experience is required
- Employees can be trained quickly to perform satisfactorily
- Jobs are characterized by relatively low wages, long and irregular hours, poor working conditions and excessive turnover
- Employment of aliens has failed to resolve employment problems
- Aliens often quickly move to other jobs after getting Green Cards

The 49 occupations on the Schedule B list range from Assemblers to Yard Workers. Their job descriptions contain such words as repetitive, routine, service, assist, pack, type, maintain and so on.

An employer or his or her agent or attorney may petition the regional Certifying Officer for the geographic area in which the job opportunity is located for a Schedule B waiver pursuant to 20 CFR 656.23.

- *Additional Schedule B evidence*
  - written request for a Schedule B waiver
  - blind three-day job ad placed in a local newspaper or in technical/academic journals
  - English translation of documents in foreign language

- local job service office had job order on file 30 calendar days and unable to obtain a qualified U.S. worker
- carried out State Employment Service Agency's (SESA) recruitment instructions
- additional documentation submitted to the DOL:
  - newspaper ad and job posting sent to the DOL
  - results of its recruitment with names and résumés
  - justification for the selection of an alien applicant
  - employer has attempted to recruit U.S. workers prior to filing the application for certification
  - reasonable good faith efforts to recruit U.S. workers without success through the Employment Service System or normal labor referral and recruitment sources (listed)
  - job requirements described as normally required for the job in the U.S. and not duly restrictive
  - advertisements and other recruitment efforts have been and continue to be unsuccessful
  - job requirements are the minimum and workers have not been previously hired for similar jobs with less training and experience

The process calls for the petition to be submitted to the local State Employment Service Agency (SESA) office serving the geographic area of intended employment. The state office:

- Sends names and résumés of any applications it receives to employer
- Forwards the application to the Certifying Officer at the regional DOL office

After 30 days, the regional Certifying Officer either grants a waiver and issues a Labor Certification or issues a Notice of Findings, a formal request for further documentation. If the additional documentation is not satisfactory, the waiver is denied.

The regional Certifying Officer may refer either Schedule A or B cases to the national Certifying Officer for determination. The employer and the alien will be notified, in writing, when a determination is made on their application.

Upon receipt of a notice of approval, Form I-140, Immigrant Petition for Alien Worker may be filed with the INS in Step 3.

Option 3 - National Interest Waiver (NIW)

The Attorney General may deem it to be in the national interest to waive the requirement that an alien's services in the sciences, arts, professions, or business be sought by an employer in the United States. Applicants who can prove that their work will be in the national interest of the United States receive a waiver from the Labor Certification.

To qualify, an applicant must demonstrate "exceptional ability in the sciences, arts, or business and will substantially benefit prospectively the national economy, cultural or educational interests, or welfare of the United States."

As the employer does not have to apply, there is no prevailing wage requirement. However, applicants still must prove that they have the necessary personal financial resources to sustain themselves and will not be a financial burden on society.

Third Preference (EB3) NIWwaivers are not available.

A greater number of approved cases are in the areas of health and energy-related research, demonstrated extraordinary ability or previous national interest work.

Applicants may file their own petitions which should be concise and well-focused.

To apply for an exemption from the requirement of a job offer, and thus of a Labor Certification, you must file with an INS Service Center for a National Interest Waiver. This process combines Steps 2 and 3.

Documentation and supporting evidence includes:

- *INS and DOL forms*
  - INS Form I-140, Immigrant Petition for Alien Worker
  - DOL Form ETA 750B, Statement of Qualifications of Alien (in duplicate)
  - G-28, if represented by an attorney
- *Fees*
  - I-140 filing fee of $115
  - fingerprinting fee of $25
- *Evidence of financial support*
  - proof of alien's financial solvency (National Interest Waiver cases)
  - an offer of employment as evidence of financial support
  - proof of the employer's financial solvency
- *Additional evidence - alien*
  - evidence to support your claim that such exemption would be in the national interest   *Ref: INS Northern Service Center*
  - the significance of the program or activity to the economy, defense, environment or labor conditions
  - written substantiation of how your participation would benefit the national interest from:
    - an interested U.S. government agency
    - clients
    - recognized national experts in the field
    - other distinguished scientists/professors/researchers in the field
  - your academic credentials
  - a Ph.D in your field, or a B.S. or M.S if the case is strong
  - what have you already accomplished in the field

- prizes/achievements in field of expertise
- articles published in journals
- presentations at conferences
- membership in professional societies
- membership on committees in field of expertise
- the consequences if you are unable to begin or continue to participate

Step 3 - Clearing the INS in the United States - Initial Petition

Any U.S. employer may file an I-140, Immigrant Petition for Alien Worker, with the INS regional Service Center having jurisdiction over the place where the alien will be employed for classification as Employment-Based Second or Third Preference.
Ref: INA 203(b)(2); TL:VISA-54,; 2-28-92

In cases involving Schedule A occupations and sheepherders, the formal request for Labor Certification described in Step 2 is submitted to the INS along with the Form I-140 petition and all necessary supporting documentation required in this step.

In cases involving Schedule B occupations and expeditious handling, Labor Certification must be obtained before an Employment-Based Third Preference petition can be filed with the INS.

Whether or not named in the petition, the child or spouse is entitled to a derivative status corresponding to the classification and priority date of the beneficiary of the petition.
Ref: 9 FAM 42.32

Employment-Based Documentation and supporting evidence includes:

- *INS forms*
  - I-140, Immigrant Petition for Alien Worker, or
- *DOL forms (Schedule A and sheepherders only)*
  - ETA 750, Part A, Application for Alien Employment Certification
  - ETA 750, Part B, Statement of Qualifications of Alien
- *Fees*
  - INS Form I-140 filing fee of $115
  - fingerprinting fee of $25
  - no DOL filing fee
- *Civil documents*
  - no birth certificate is required
    (as you are not relying on a family connection)
- *Employer's evidence to support request*
  - all necessary supporting employment letters
  - all supporting Step 2 documentation
- *Proof of financial support or solvency*
  - all necessary proof of financial support
  - Form I-864, Affidavit of Support (if relative's entity filed petition)

- *Professional credentials*
  - all necessary professional evidence, as required

Additional documentation is required for the following categories:

A) Member of the professions holding an advanced degree

Evidence to establish an alien as a member of the professions holding an advanced degree should be in the form of the following:

- An official academic record showing possession of an advanced degree (or foreign equivalent), or
- An official academic record showing possession of a baccalaureate degree (or foreign equivalent) and a letter from current or former employer(s) showing at least five years of progressive post-baccalaureate experience in the specialty
- If the above standards do not readily apply the petitioner may submit comparable evidence to establish the beneficiary's eligibility

Although the INS will not evaluate the equivalence of education and experience to a doctorate, if a doctorate (or a foreign equivalent degree) is normally required by the specialty, the alien must possess such a degree.   *Ref: TL:VISA-54; 2-28-92*

B) Aliens of exceptional ability in the sciences, arts, or business who will substantially benefit prospectively the national economy, cultural or educational interests, or welfare of the United States

To establish evidence of exceptional ability, the petition must be accompanied by at least three of the following:

- An official academic record showing a degree, diploma, certificate, or similar award from a college, university, school, or other institution of learning relating to the area of exceptional ability
- Letter(s) from current or former employer(s) showing evidence of at least ten years of full-time experience in the occupation
- A license to practice the profession or certification for a particular profession or occupation
- Evidence that the alien has commanded a salary, or other remuneration for services, which demonstrates exceptional ability
- Evidence of membership in professional associations, or
- Evidence of recognition for achievements and significant contributions to the industry or field by peers, governmental entities, or professional or business organizations

C) National Interest Waiver by the Attorney General

A Form I-140, Immigrant Petition for Alien Worker for an Employment-Based Second Preference National Interest Waiver may be filed by the alien without Labor

Certification or job offer with the INS regional Service Center having jurisdiction over the place where the alien will be employed for classification as.

Ref: INA 203(b)(2); TL:VISA-54,; 2-28-92

Although "national interest" is not defined, some of the factors which have been deemed as being in the U.S. national interest include:

- Improving the U.S. economy
- Creating employment opportunities
- Improving the wages and working conditions of U.S. workers
- Improving the education and training programs for U.S. children and underqualified workers
- Improving health care
- Providing affordable housing for the young, old and poorer U.S. residents
- Improving the environment, making productive use of natural resources
- Research skills would exceed others in the field
- Improving cultural awareness and diversity through artistic endeavors and significant scientific contributions
- A request from an interested U.S. government agency and/or companies benefitting from research or work   *Ref: INS Administrative Appeals Unit*

Form I-797 Notice of Action serves as INS action on these cases. Mere receipt of Labor Certification does not change an alien's status.

Step 4 - Processing

Aliens living in the United States who have not maintained lawful status may no longer pay a $1,000 fine and must be processed in their home country. If your nonimmigrant grace period has expired while you have been in the United States, you must wait for your Green Card outside the United States even if you have obtained Labor Certification. However, if you are close enough to getting a Green Card to file for adjustment of status, it may be possible to obtain a work permit based on your pending adjustment of status.

Aliens in valid H-1B status when their Form I-485 and Form I-765, Application for Employment Authorization (EAD) are filed may remain but not work until their EAD is received.

Option 1 - Adjustment of Status by the INS in the United States

If you have maintained lawful status in the United States and you are immediately eligible, you may apply to adjust status from a nonimmigrant classification to permanent resident status by filing with the INS office having jurisdiction over your place of residence.

After receipt of Form I-797C Notice of Action and approval of the petition, an applicant may file Form I-485, Adjustment of Status.

Documentation and supporting evidence includes:

- *INS forms*
  - I-485, Application to Register Permanent Residence or Adjust Status
  - I-765, Application for Employment Authorization (if required)
- *Fees*
  - I-485 filing fee of $220 if the applicant is 14 years of age or over
  - I-485 filing fee of $160 if the applicant is under 14 years of age
  - I-765 filing fee of $100 (if required)
  - fingerprinting fee of $25
- *Passport and photographs*
  - passport valid for six months beyond intended date of entry
  - two identical 1½" (37 mm) square color photographs - 3/4 angle showing right ear
- *Prior approval*
  - copy of approved Notice for immigrant petition making visa number immediately available
- *Current and prior immigration status*
  - copy of Form I-94, if applicable
- *Proof of financial support or solvency*
  - Form I-864, Affidavit of Support (if relative's entity filed petition)
  - evidence of your own assets
- *Civil documents*
  - birth Certificate of principal alien and dependents - long form
  - marriage certificate, if applicable
- *Police clearance*
- *Employer's evidence to support request*
  - employment letter

Option 2 - By the Department of State (DOS) Abroad

An applicant may be processed at a U.S. Embassy or Consulate abroad after receiving notification that a visa number is immediately available.

The consular officer shall not issue an immigrant visa to any Second or Third Preference Employment-Based immigrant until receiving:

- From the INS, a Petition for Immigrant Worker approved in accordance with INA 204, or official notification of such an approval
- From the Department of Labor, an approved petition accompanied by a Labor Certification   *Ref: TL:VISA-54; 2-28-92*

Documentation and supporting evidence includes:

- *DOS forms*
  - State Department Packet III & IV including:
    - Optional Form 230 Parts I and II
    - G-325A - Biographic information Sheet
- *Fees*
  - visa processing fee of $260
  - visa issuance fee of $65
  - proposed $50 Affidavit of Support review fee (if I-864 required)
- *Passport and photographs*
  - passport valid for at least six months beyond intended date of entry
  - two identical 1½" (37 mm) square color photographs - 3/4 angle showing right ear
- *Prior approval*
  - copy of approved Notice for immigrant petition making visa number immediately available
- *Current and prior immigration status*
  - copy of Form I-94, if applicable
- *Proof of financial support or solvency*
  - notarized offer of employment
  - evidence of your own assets or support
  - Form I-864, Affidavit of Support (if relative's entity filed petition)
- *Civil documents*
  - birth Certificate of principal alien and dependents - long form
- *Police clearance*
  - proof of police clearance
- *Medical clearance*
  - Form I-693, proof of medical clearance

If the consular officer is satisfied with the evidence presented, the alien will receive a Second or Third Preference Employment-Based visa, as appropriate.

Step 5 - Clearing the INS at a U.S. Port of Entry

The INS has the final authority to review the documents presented for compliance and make a decision on whether to admit an alien.

Employment-Based Fourth Preference (EB4)

Special Immigrants
Amerasians, Widow(er)s, Religious Workers, Employees of U.S. Consulate in Hong Kong, Juveniles Under Court Protection

Applicants for Fourth Preference Employment-Based status are a diverse group assembled in this category and exempt from Department of Labor (DOL) Certification.

Sub-categories are:

Fourth Preference (EB4):　　Special Immigrants

A Amerasians (AM2)
B Widow(er)s (IW1)
C Religious Workers such as Ministers (SD1)
D Employees of the U.S. Consulate in Hong Kong (SEH)
E Juveniles under Court Protection (SL1)

Entry Criteria

In order to apply for Fourth Preference status, you must qualify in one of the following five sub-categories:

A) Amerasian

An "Amerasian" is an alien:

- Who has not remarried and was born in Korea, Vietnam, Laos, Kampuchea, or Thailand after December 31, 1950 and before October 22, 1982, and
- Who was fathered by a U.S. citizen

B) Widow(er)

A "widow(er)" is an alien:

- Who was married for at least two years to a U.S. citizen who is now deceased, and

- Who had been a U.S. citizen for at least 2 years at the time of death, and:
- Whose citizen spouse's death was less than two years ago
- Who was not legally separated from the citizen spouse at the time of death
- Who has not remarried

C) Religious Worker

A "religious worker" is an alien:

- Who has been a member of a religious denomination which has a bona fide nonprofit, religious organization in the United States, and
- Who has been carrying on the vocational, professional work, or other work described below, continuously for the past two years, and
- Who seeks to enter the United States to work solely:
  - as a minister of religion, or
  - work for the organization in a professional capacity in a religious vocation (baccalaureate degree required to qualify), or
  - work for the organization or a related, tax-exempt entity in another non-professional capacity in a religious vocation or occupation

5,000 visas are available for this sub-category.

D) Employees of the American Consulate in Hong Kong

An "employee of the American Consulate in Hong Kong"is an alien:

- Who was resident in Hong Kong and has been an employee of the U.S. Consulate
- Who has performed faithful service for at least three years

500 visas are available to January 1, 2002.

E) Juveniles Under Court Protection

A "juvenile under court protection" is an alien:

- Who is unmarried
- Who has been the subject of administrative or judicial proceedings
- Who is still a dependent juvenile under the law of the state in which the juvenile court is located
- For whom it has been determined that:
  - it would not be in his or her best interests to be returned to:
  - his or her country of nationality, last habitual residence, or
  - his or her parent's country of nationality or last habitual residence
  - he or she is eligible for long-term foster care
- Who may not pass derivative immigration benefits to their natural parents because of their special immigrant status

Admission Process

Step 1 - Clearing the Job Offer in the United States

Most of these sub-categories do not require a written job offer from a prospective U.S. employer.

Step 2- Clearing the INS in the United States - Initial Petition

The INS is responsible for certifying the eligibility of an alien for preference immigrant status.   *Ref: INA 212(a)(5)(A)*

Where to file a petition varies according to the sub-category. Petitions on behalf of battered spouses are filed with the Vermont Service Center. It may take up to eight weeks to receive the INS Form I-797 Notice of Action.

Because of the diverse nature of this Preference category, there are very precise and very different requirements for supporting document and proof.

There are a number of supporting documents required for these aliens which are common to the various sub-categories. The additional requirements which are unique to an individual sub-category follow later.

Whether or not named in the petition, the child or spouse is entitled to a derivative status corresponding to the classification and priority date of the beneficiary of the petition.   *Ref: 9 FAM 42.32*

Documentation and supporting evidence for all sub-categories includes:
- *INS form*
  - I-360, Petition for Amerasian, Widow(er) or Special Immigrant
- *Fees*
  - filing fee of $110
  - no fee for Amerasians
  - fingerprinting fee of $25, if applicable
- *Civil documents*
  - no birth certificate is required
    (unless relying on a family connection)
- *Employer's evidence to support request*
  - all necessary supporting employment letters, if employment is involved
- *Proof of financial support or solvency*
  - all necessary proof of financial support
  - Form I-864, Affidavit of Support(if relative/relative's entity filed petition)
- *Professional credentials*
  - all necessary professional credentials, if applicable

The unique documentation and filing requirements for each category follow.

A) Amerasian

Any person who is 18 or older, an emancipated minor, or a U.S. corporation may file this petition. If you are filing for Amerasian classification and the person you are filing for is outside the United States, you may file this petition at the INS local office having jurisdiction over the place of residence.

Documentation and supporting evidence includes:

- Copies of evidence that the beneficiary meets the country and date entry criteria including:
  - the full name, date and place of birth
  - present or permanent address of the mother or guardian
  - the signature of the mother or guardian on the release authenticated by a local registrar, court of minors, or a U.S. immigration or consular officer
- If born in Vietnam, a copy of his or her Vietnamese I.D. card, or an affidavit explaining why it is not available
- Copies of evidence establishing the parentage of the person, and of evidence establishing that the biological father was a U.S. citizen such as:
  - birth or baptismal records or other religious documents
  - local civil records
  - an affidavit
  - correspondence or evidence of financial support from the father
  - photographs of the father with the child
  - affidavits from knowledgeable witnesses which detail the parentage of the child and how they know the facts
- A photograph of the person
- A copy of the marriage certificate if the person is married, and
- Proof of any prior marriages
- If the person is under 18 years old, a written statement from his or her mother or legal guardian which:
  - irrevocably releases him or her for emigration and authorizes the placing agencies to make necessary decisions for immediate care until a sponsor receives custody
  - shows an understanding of the effects of the release
  - states whether any money was paid or coercion used prior to obtaining the release

The following sponsorship documents are also required and should be filed with the petition to avoid adding to the overall processing time:

- An affidavit of financial support from the sponsor, with the required evidence of financial ability attached (the original sponsor remains financially responsible if the subsequent sponsor fails)

- Copies of evidence that the sponsor is at least 21 years old and is a U.S. citizen or permanent resident
- Police clearance certificates, as required
- If this petition is for a person under 18 years old, the following documents issued by a placement agency must be submitted:
  - a copy of the private, public or state agency's license to place children in the United States
  - proof of the agency's recent experience in the intercountry placement of children and of the agency's financial ability to arrange the placement
  - a favorable home study of the sponsor conducted by a legally authorized agency
  - a pre-placement report from the agency, including information regarding any family separation or dislocation abroad that would result from the placement
  - a written description of the orientation given to the sponsor and to the parent or guardian on the legal and cultural aspects of the placement
  - a statement from the agency showing that the sponsor has been given a report on the pre-placement screening and evaluation of the child
  - a written plan from the agency to provide follow-up services, including mediation and counseling, and describing the contingency placement plans if the initial placement fails

B) Widow(er)

A widow(er) can file this petition on his or her own behalf. The petition must be filed at the INS regional Service Center having jurisdiction over your place of residence.

Documentation and supporting evidence includes:

- *Civil documents*
  - copy of your marriage certificate to the U.S. citizen
  - proof of termination of any prior marriages of either of you
  - copies of evidence that your spouse was a U.S. citizen, such as:
    - a birth certificate if born in the United States
    - Certificate of Naturalization or Certificate of Citizenship issued by the INS
    - Form FS-240, Report of Birth Abroad of a Citizen of the United States
    - a U.S. passport which was valid at the time of the citizen's death
    - copy of the death certificate of your U.S. citizen spouse who is now deceased and who had been a U.S. citizen

C) Religious Worker

Any person, including the alien can file this petition on Form I-360, Petition for Amerasian, Widow(er), or Special Immigrant.

Documentation and supporting evidence includes:

- *Employer's evidence to support request*
  - letter from the authorized official of the religious organization:
    - establishing that the proposed services and alien qualify as above
    - attesting to the alien's membership in the religious denomination and explaining, in detail:
      - the person's religious work
      - all employment during the past two years
      - the proposed employment
- *Additional evidence*
  - religious organization, and any affiliate which will employ the person is:
    - a bona fide nonprofit U.S. religious organization
    - exempt from taxation under section 501(c)(3) of the Internal Revenue Code of 1986

D) Employees of the American Consulate in Hong Kong

Any person, including the alien can file this petition on Form I-360, Petition for Amerasian, Widow(er), or Special Immigrant.

Documentation and supporting evidence includes:

- A letter from the U.S. Consulate in Hong Kong employing the alien indicating:
  - the length of faithful service
  - circumstances of employment
  - any retirement or termination

E) Juveniles Under Court Protection

Any person, including the alien can file this petition on Form I-360, Petition for Amerasian, Widow(er), or Special Immigrant, for a juvenile under court protection.

Documentation and supporting evidence includes:

- Copies of the court documents upon which the claim to eligibility is based

Step 3 - Processing for Green Card

Option 1 - Adjustment of Status by the INS in the United States

If you have maintained lawful status in the United States and your I-360 petition has been approved making you immediately eligible, you may apply to adjust status to permanent resident by filing with the local INS office having jurisdiction over your place of residence. If you have not maintained lawful status you may no longer pay a $1,000 fine and must be processed in your home country.

Documentation and supporting evidence includes:

- *INS forms*
  - I-485, Application to register Permanent Residence or Adjust Status
  - I-765, Application for Employment Authorization (if required)
- *Fees*
  - I-485 filing fee of $220 for applicants 14 years and over
  - I-485 filing fee of $160 for applicants under 14
  - I-765 filing fee of $100 (if required)
  - fingerprinting fee of $25
- *Passport and photographs*
  - passport valid for six months beyond intended date of entry
  - two identical 1½" (37 mm) square color photographs - 3/4 angle showing right ear
- *Prior approval*
  - copy of approved Notice for immigrant petition making visa number immediately available
- *Current and prior immigration status*
  - copy of Form I-94, if applicable
- *Proof of financial support or solvency*
  - Form I-864, Affidavit of Support (if relative/relative's entity filed petition)
  - evidence of your own assets
- *Civil documents*
  - birth Certificate of principal alien and dependents - long form
  - marriage certificate, if applicable
- *Police clearance*
- *Employer's evidence to support request*
  - employment letter, if applicable

Option 2 - By the Department of State (DOS) Abroad

Aliens living outside the United States may be processed at a U.S. Embassy or Consulate abroad after receiving notification that a visa number is immediately available.

The consular officer shall not issue an immigrant visa to any Fourth Preference Employment-Based immigrant until receiving from the INS:

- A Petition for Immigrant Worker approved in accordance with INA 204, or
- Official notification of such an approval

Documentation and supporting evidence includes:

- *DOS forms*
  - State Department Packet III & IV including:
    - Optional Form 230 Parts I and II
    - G-325A - Biographic information Sheet
- *Fees*
  - visa processing fee of $260
  - visa issuance fee of $65
  - proposed $50 Affidavit of Support review fee (if I-864 required)
- *Passport and photographs*
  - passport valid for at least six months beyond intended date of entry
  - two identical 1½" (37 mm) square color photographs - 3/4 angle showing right ear
- *Prior approval*
  - copy of approved Notice for immigrant petition making visa number immediately available
- *Current and prior immigration status*
  - copy of Form I-94, if applicable
- *Proof of financial support or solvency*
  - Form I-864, Affidavit of Support (if relative/relative's entity filed petition), or
- *Civil documents*
  - birth Certificate of principal alien and dependents - long form
  - notarized offer of employment
  - evidence of your own assets
- *Police clearance*
  - proof of police clearance
- *Medical clearance*
  - Form I-693, proof of medical clearance

If the consular officer is satisfied with the evidence presented, the alien will receive a Fourth Preference Employment-Based visa.

The beneficiary is given a sealed package of documents to carry and give to the INS Immigration Inspector at a U.S. port of entry.

Step 5 - Clearing the INS at a U.S. Port Of Entry

The INS has the final authority to review the documents presented for compliance and make a decision on whether to admit the alien.

Employment-Based Fifth Preference (EB5)

Employment Creation (Investors)

This Preference is for the use of an alien entrepreneur who wishes to establish a new commercial enterprise in the United States and petition for status as a Fifth Preference Employment-Based immigrant.

Applicants are exempt from the requirement to:

- Obtain Labor Certification from the Department of Labor
- Submit a job offer to the INS

Fifth Preference permits the entry of aliens to establish their new enterprise in:

- Areas of low unemployment, or
- Areas of high unemployment

Sub-categories are:

> Fifth Preference (EB5):   Employment Creation (Investors)
>
> Employment Creation (Investors in targeted rural, or high-unemployment centers)

3,000 visas are available for investors in a targeted rural or high-unemployment area. 300 visas are available for regional centers.

Entry Criteria

Both sub-categories require substantial investment with the amount of investment required in a particular area set by regulation. Unless adjusted downward for targeted areas or upward for areas of high employment, the figure shall be $1,000,000. Specific details may be obtained from an INS office or U.S. Embassy or Consulate abroad.

The establishment of a new commercial enterprise may include any of:

- Creation of a new business
- Purchase of an existing business with simultaneous or subsequent restructuring or reorganization resulting in a new commercial enterprise

- Expansion of an existing business through investment of the amount required, so that a substantial change (at least 40 percent) in either the net worth, number of employees, or both, results

Proof is required that you have established a new commercial enterprise:

- In which you will engage in a managerial or policy-making capacity
- In which you have invested or are actively in the process of investing the amount required for the area in which the enterprise is located
- Which will benefit the U.S. economy, and
- Which will create full-time employment for at least 10 U.S. citizens, permanent residents, or other immigrants authorized to be employed, other than yourself, your spouse, your sons or daughters, or any nonimmigrant aliens

The following pages deal with the process as it relates to entrepreneurial applicants.

Admission Process

Step 1 - Clearing the INS in the United States - Initial Petition

The INS is responsible for certifying the eligibility of an alien for preference immigrant status.   *Ref: INA 212(a)(5)(A)*

While Fifth Preference petitioners do not require Labor Certification or a written job offer since they are the employer, there is a requirement for extensive proof about the new commercial enterprise and their involvement in it.

An entrepreneur may file a petition for status as an immigrant to the United States with either the INS regional Service Center in Texas or California depending on where the new commercial enterprise will be principally doing business.

Whether or not named in the petition, the child or spouse is entitled to a derivative status corresponding to the classification and priority date of the beneficiary of the petition.   *Ref: 9 FAM 42.32*

Documentation and supporting evidence includes:

- *INS form*
  - I-526, Immigrant Petition by Alien Entrepreneur
- *Fee*
  - filing fee of $350
  - fingerprinting fee of $25
- *Additional evidence*
  - creation of a new business or the expansion of an existing business which includes:

- evidence that you have created a lawful business entity, or
- evidence that your investment in an existing business has created at least a 40 percent increase in the net worth of the business:
  - copies of articles of incorporation
  - copies of merger or consolidation
  - partnership agreement or certificate of limited partnership
  - joint venture agreement
  - business trust agreement
  - certificate of authority to do business in a state or municipality
- evidence of transfer of capital resulting in a substantial increase in net worth or number of employees such as:
  - stock purchase agreements
  - certified financial reports
  - payroll records
  - agreements or documents as evidence of the investment and resulting substantial change
- if applicable, evidence of the establishment of your enterprise in a targeted employment area such as:
  - an area which has experienced high unemployment of at least 150 percent of the national average rate, or
  - a rural area:
    - not within a metropolitan statistical area, or
    - not within the outer boundary of any city or town having a population of 20,000 or more
  - evidence that you have invested or are actively in the process of investing the amount required for the area in which the business is located:
    - bank statements
    - assets purchased for use in the enterprise
    - money and property transferred from abroad
    - loan, mortgage or security agreements or other evidence of borrowing secured by assets
  - evidence that capital is obtained through lawful means, such as:
    - foreign business registration records
    - tax returns from last five years inside or outside the United States
    - evidence of other sources of capital
    - certified copies of any judgment, pending private or governmental civil or governmental criminal actions against the petitioner from any court within the last 15 years
  - evidence that the enterprise will create at least 10 full-time jobs for U.S. citizens, permanent residents, or aliens lawfully authorized to be employed such as:
    - relevant tax records

- Form I-9 or similar documents, if the employees are already hired, or
- a business plan of when employees are to be hired within the next two years
- evidence that you will be engaged in the management of the enterprise:
  - through day-to-day managerial control, or
  - through policy formulation:
  - statement of your position title
  - complete description of your duties
  - you are a corporate officer, or hold a seat on the board of directors
- if the new enterprise is a partnership:
  - evidence that you are engaged in either direct management or policy-making activities

Step 2 - Processing

Option 1 - Adjustment of Status by the INS in the United States

If you have maintained lawful status in the United States and your I-526 petition has been approved making you immediately eligible, you may apply to adjust status to permanent resident by filing with the local INS office having jurisdiction over the place where the employment is located.

Aliens living in the United States who have not maintained lawful status may no longer pay a $1,000 fine and must be processed in their home country.

Documentation and supporting evidence includes:

- *INS forms*
  - I-485, Application to Register Permanent Residence or Adjust Status
  - I-765, Application for Employment Authorization (if required)
- *Fees*
  - I-485 filing fee of $220 if the applicant is 14 years of age or over
  - I-485 filing fee of $160 if the applicant is under 14 years of age
  - I-765 filing fee of $100 (if required)
  - fingerprinting fee of $25
- *Passport and photographs*
  - passport valid for at least six months
  - two identical 1½" (37 mm) square color photographs - 3/4 angle showing right ear
- *Prior approval*
  - copy of approved Notice for immigrant petition making visa number immediately available

- *Current and prior immigration status*
  - copy of Form I-94, if applicable
- *Proof of financial support or solvency*
  - Form I-864, Affidavit of Support (if relative/relative's entity filed petition)
  - evidence of your own assets, as required
- *Civil documents*
  - birth Certificate of principal alien and dependents - long form
  - marriage certificate, if applicable
- *Police clearance*
- *Employer's evidence to support request*
  - employment letter

Option 2 - By the Department of State (DOS) Abroad

An applicant may be processed at a U.S. Embassy or Consulate abroad after receiving notification that a visa number is immediately available.

The consular officer shall not issue an immigrant visa to any Fifth Preference Employment-Based immigrant until receiving from the INS, a Petition for Immigrant Worker approved in accordance with INA 204, or official notification of such an approval.

Documentation and supporting evidence includes:

- *DOS forms*
  - State Department Packet III & IV including:
  - Optional Form-230 Parts I and II
  - G-325A - Biographic information Sheet
- *Fees*
  - visa processing fee of $260
  - visa issuance fee of $65
  - proposed $50 Affidavit of Support review fee (if I-864 required)
- *Passport and photographs*
  - passport valid for at least six months beyond intended date of entry
  - two identical 1 ½" (37 mm) square color photographs - 3/4 angle showing right ear
- *Prior approval*
  - copy of approved Notice for immigrant petition making visa number immediately available
- *Current and prior immigration status*
  - copy of Form I-94, if applicable
- *Proof of financial support or solvency*
  - Form I-864, Affidavit of Support (if relative/relative's entity filed petition), or
  - evidence of support

- • notarized offer of employment
- • evidence of your own assets
- *Civil documents*
  - • birth Certificate of principal alien and dependents - long form
- *Police clearance*
  - • proof of police clearance
- *Medical clearance*
  - • Form I-693, proof of medical clearance

If the consular officer is satisfied with the evidence presented, the alien will receive a Fifth Preference Employment-Based visa.

Step 3 - Clearing the INS at a U.S. Port Of Entry

The INS has the final authority to review the documents presented for compliance and make a decision on whether to admit the alien.

Step 4 - Removal of Conditional Status

The law has created a two-year trial period during which time permanent residence is conditional. Within 90 days of the end of this period, the investor must file for removal of the conditional status.

The investor must manage the investment personally.

Chapter 11

Diversity (DV) Lottery

A Diversity (DV) Immigrant Visa or Green Card Lottery Program is run each year by the State Department under INA 203(c) to randomly select and provide 50,000 U.S. Green Card immigration opportunities to natives of countries with low rates of immigration to the United States. Another 5,000 visas are currently reserved for use under the Nicaraguan and Central American Relief Act (NCARA).

Sub-categories:
- Diversity immigrant (DV1)
- Spouse of DV1 (DV2)
- Child of DV1 (DV3)

In recent years, the month-long mail-in registration period has been held in October. Entries received before or after this period were disqualified regardless of when they were posted. The October registration period was approximately the same in DV-2000 and DV-2001. This allowed the extra time which the National Visa Center and overseas consulates and embassies needed to process the qualified entries and notify the successful registrants in a timely manner. By law, DV visas may only be issued during the October 1 to September 30 fiscal year, which begins 11 months after the mail-in period ends.

In DV-2000, more than eight million qualified entries were received and another 2.5 million were disqualified for failing to follow the rules. Over 113,000 applicants were registered and notified that they could apply for the 50,000 available visas. Many winners were expected to not pursue their visas.

In this chapter, the DV-2001 lottery is used as an indication of how future lotteries may be structured.

Eligibility

INA 201(a)(3), 201(e), 203(c) and 204(a)(1)(G), taken together, establish an annual numerical limitation of 50,000 visas for distribution among six geographical regions which approximate the continents.

The law provides a mathematical formula for the INS to determine which countries' natives are able to compete for these visas.

In DV-2001, immigrant visas were apportioned so that:

- No country could receive more than 7 percent (3,500 in DV-2000) of the world-wide total of DV visa numbers in any one year
- High and low admission regions and high admission foreign states were identified according to a formula based on total immigrant admissions over the most recent five-year period, and:
  - a greater share of the available visa numbers went to "low admission" countries
  - no Diversity visas were provided for "high admission" countries

Also, DV-2001 entries were not accepted from natives of the following countries: Canada, China (except Hong Kong), Columbia, Dominican Republic, El Salvador, Haiti, India, Jamaica, Mexico, Philippines, Poland, South Korea, Taiwan, United Kingdom and its dependent territories (except Northern Ireland) and Vietnam. Macau natives are no longer eligible. This list has remained relatively stable in recent years.

Program information

As the rules are subject to change each year, it is wise to check before applying.

Sources of information on the Visa Lottery include:

- **Written instructions on how to enter the visa lottery**
  - call the U.S. State Department's Visa Lottery Information Center at (900) 884-8840 (a $5.10 charge applies)
- **DV Lottery Hotline**
  - call the State Department at (202) 331-7199
- **Overseas**
  - contact the nearest U.S. Embassy or Consulate for DV instructions
- **DV-2001 Internet instructions**
  - posted at http://travel.state.gov/visa_services.html

Step 1 - Qualification

Educational or work requirements

- At least a high school education or its 12-year U.S. equivalent, or
- Within the past five years, two years of work experience in an occupation requiring at least two years training or experience

Age requirements

DV-2001 had no minimum age for submission of an application. However, the requirement of a high school education or work experience effectively disqualified most principal applicants under 18.

Nativity

An applicant must be able to claim nativity in an eligible country. Nativity in most cases is determined by the applicant's place of birth. Per INA 202(b)(2) , a person born in an ineligible country may claim the spouse's country of birth. Also, a person may be able to claim one of his or her parent's country of birth if neither parent was born or resided in the ineligible country at the time of the applicant's birth.

Step 2 - Application for Registration

Since DV-2001 applications were required to be received by the National Visa Center between October 4, 1999 and November 3, 1999, Eastern Time, all applications arriving outside this period were disqualified. However, as "winners" are not selected until after the close of each registration period, there is never any advantage to having an application arrive early in the mail-in period. Every properly completed and addressed application received at any time during the one-month period has an equal chance of being selected within its region.

The law requires the filing of a separate application for each year's DV Lottery and persons already registered for an immigrant visa in another category may apply for the current DV registration.

In DV-2001, only one application by or for each person was permitted and disqualification resulted from the detection of more than one entry at either the time of registration or at the visa interview. However, a husband and wife could each submit one application and if either was registered, the other was entitled to derivative status. Each had to include their spouse and unmarried children under age 21.

Regardless of whether an application is submitted by the applicant directly, or assistance provided by someone else, it must be signed personally by the applicant, preferably in his or her native alphabet.

There is no application fee other than postage, although a special DV case processing fee of $75, effective October 1, 1997, is payable at the time of visa processing.

Application format

Recently, the request for registration required information in the following format:

- Typed or clearly printed on a plain sheet of paper in the English alphabet
- Mailed only by regular or air mail from inside or outside the United States
- Sent in an envelope (no postcards):
    - between 6" and 10" or 15 cm and 25 cm wide
    - between 3½" and 4½" or 9 cm and 11 cm high
    - marked on the front top left hand corner:
        - the applicant's native country
        - the applicant's name
        - the applicant's full return mailing address

1. Applicant's Full Name

- Last Name, First Name and Middle Name
- With last name/surname/family name underlined

2. Applicant's Date and Place of Birth
- Date of birth: Day, Month, Year (Example: 15 November 1961)
- Place of birth: City/Town, District/County/Province, Country (use the name by which the country is currently known)

3. Applicant's Native Country if Different from Country of Birth
- *Native* ordinarily means someone born within a particular country
- This item must be completed by applicants claiming chargeability to a native country different from their country of birth including:
  - the country of birth of their spouse
  - the country of birth of a parent (minor child only)
  - the country of birth of either parent (if born in a country of which neither parent was a native or resident at the time of the birth)
- This information must match what is put on the upper left corner of the entry envelope

4. Name, Date and Place of Birth of Applicant's Spouse and Children, if Any
The spouse and child(ren) under 21, not parents, are entitled to the same (derivative) status. To avoid risking disqualification, make sure that full biographic data of all dependents is included.

5. Applicant's Full Mailing Address
The mailing address must be clear and complete, since it is to that address that the notification letter would be sent. A telephone number is optional, but useful.

6. Applicant's Photograph
A recent 1½" (37 m) square photograph of the applicant with his or her name printed on the back of the photograph should be taped, not stapled or paper-clipped, to the application. No photograph is needed for the principal applicant's spouse or child(ren).

7. Applicant's Signature
The applicant must sign the application using his or her normal signature. The signature of the spouse and minor children is not required.

Failure to provide all required information disqualifies an applicant.

Submission of entries
Sending an application to an incorrect address disqualifies the applicant. Entries must be sent to the exact address including Zip (postal) code which corresponds to the applicant's native country or country of chargeability.

Beginning in 2000, all entries must be sent to the new Kentucky Consular Center in Williamsburg, Kentucky rather than the National Visa Center in Portsmouth, New Hampshire as in former years.

Previously, the exact required address could be one of the following geographical areas:

- Asia
- Africa
- North America
- South & Central America & the Caribbean
- Europe
- Oceania

To recap, applications are subject to disqualification if:

- The applicant submits more than one application
- More than one application is in an envelope
- The application is delivered by hand, fax, registered, certified or express mail
- Any special handling is required
- The application is received on a postcard
- The application is sent to other than the specified address
- The application is received outside the one month reception period

The Federal Trade Commission's Bureau of Consumer Protection has issued an annual Consumer Alert to warn against what they called unscrupulous businesses and attorneys who claim that, for a fee, they could increase your chances of winning the Green Card lottery. They cautioned against statements like:

- They are affiliated with the U.S. government
- They have special expertise or there is a special application form
- They have never had a lottery entry rejected
- They can increase the chances of winning

If you think you are the victim of a Green Card Lottery scam, you may call the Federal Trade Commission's DV Lottery Hotline at (212) 264-1406 or the National Consumers League's National Fraud Information Center at (800) 876-7060 during normal business hours or via the internet at http://www.fraud.org.

Step 3 - Selection of "Winners"

In DV-2001, a total of about 100,000 persons, both principal applicants and their spouses and children were registered and notified that they could make application for the 50,000 annually-allocated diversity visas. An additional 5,000 visas were available for use under the Nicaraguan and Central America Relief Act (NCARA).

Each year, all mail received is separated into the proper geographic region and individually numbered. Beginning in 2000, at the end of each application period, a computer at the Kentucky Consular Center in Williamsburg, Kentucky will randomly select "winners" from among all mail received for each geographic region. Within each region, the first randomly selected applicant is the first case registered, and so on.

As a comparison, in the earlier DV-2000 program, the number of registered applicants in each geographical region eligible to "compete" for the 50,000 available visas was:

- Africa   42,422
- Asia   15,990
- Europe   46,051
- North America   36
- Oceania   2,302
- South America, Central America and the Caribbean   6,621
  Total   113,422

As some 100,000 applicants are expected to be registered for the 50,000 available visas, it is important to act quickly, when notified, as "winners" are always processed on a first-come first-served basis. Consequently, each year there is a risk that some could be left out.

Each "selected", or "registered" applicant is immediately sent a notification letter, which provides appropriate visa application instructions and advises of their place on the list. Notification letters are expected to be sent between April and July of the following year. Spouses and unmarried children under 21 may also apply for visas to accompany or follow to join the principal applicant. Applicants not selected are not notified and only one notification letter is sent for each case registered, to the address provided on the application. Therefore, if a "winner" moves, it is important to promptly advise the program administrators of the move by letter or fax according to instructions from the Department of State.

Entitlement to immigrant status in the DV category lasts only through the October 1 to September 30 Fiscal (visa) Year for the which the applicant is selected.

Successful DV-2001 applicants were required to be processed and receive their visas during Fiscal Year 2001 (October 1, 2000 through September 30, 2001). No carry over to the next fiscal year is ever permitted.

Step 4 - Processing

The Kentucky Consular Center will continue to process cases until the point when the "winners" are instructed to make formal application at a U.S. consular office or until those in a legal position to do so may apply for adjustment of status at an INS office in the United States.

It must be emphasized that "winners" should complete and file their visa applications quickly as there is no guarantee of the issuance of a visa due to the number of entries selected and registered greatly exceeding than the number of available immigrant visas.

All registered applicants are informed promptly of their place on the list and visas issued each month according to their registration lottery rank order. Under the law, winners are only entitled to apply for visa issuance and be processed before the end of the fiscal year on September 30. Once the 50,000 visa numbers are used for the current fiscal year, the program ends.

During the visa interview, principal applicants are required to provide documentary proof of a high school education or its equivalent or show two years of work experience in an occupation that requires at least two years of training or experience within the past five years.

Applicants are subject to all grounds of ineligibility specified in the INA with no special provisions for the waiver of any ground of visa ineligibility other than those ordinarily provided in the act.

At the time of visa issuance, DV winners, like all other immigrant visa applicants, have to pay the regular visa fees in addition to the special DV case processing fee of $75, effective October 1, 1997 payable at the time of visa processing.

Ref: IIRIRA96.636

Option 1 - Adjustment of Status by the INS in the United States

Provided they are otherwise eligible to adjust status, registered applicants who are physically present and in status in the United States may apply to the INS for adjustment of status to permanent resident. The INS must complete action on their cases before September 30, when registrations for the applicable fiscal year's DV program terminate.

Ref: INA 245; Department of State Visa Bulletin Number 78A Volume VII

Aliens living in the United States who have not maintained lawful status may no longer pay a $1,000 fine and must be processed in their home country.

Option 2 - By the Department of State (DOS) Abroad

Aliens living outside the United States will be processed at a U.S. Embassy or Consulate abroad in accordance with instructions received from the National Visa Center.

Chapter 12

Refugee/Asylee

The United States was first populated by religious and political refugees. Consequently, many Americans are sympathetic to requests for asylum.

The United States offers asylum and refugee protection based on an inherent belief in human rights and in ending or preventing the persecution of individuals. Claims of persecution must be based on at least one of five internationally-recognized grounds: race, religion, nationality, membership in a particular social group, or public opinion. Some actions under coercive population control programs constitute persecution on account of political opinion and up to 1,000 aliens per fiscal year may be admitted under this provision.

The terms "refugee" and "asylee" are easily confused because both relate to a person who is claiming persecution or fear of persecution in his or her home country and wishes to live in the United States.

Simply stated, a refugee is outside the United States and wants to come in while an asylee is already in the United States or at its borders and wants to stay.

Numerical limitations are established by which the U.S. President with the advice and consent of Congress establishes the total number of refugees which will be admitted in a given year as well as the numerical limit applicable to individual countries or sections of the world. In 1992, President Bush approved 144,000 refugee admissions.

For Fiscal Year 2000, beginning on October 1, 1999, President Clinton authorized 100,000 refugees. This was a 28 percent increase over the previous year and included 57,000 European refugees such as ethnic Albanians.   *Ref:INA 207; 8 USC 1156*

The INS admits that the U.S. asylum system was in crisis in 1993. The system was clogged by people submitting false applications in order to get work authorization. Fraudulent applicants who went through the full INS procedure and were denied were permitted to start the process all over again before an Immigration Judge.

Today, the INS says that its asylum system is a model of fairness and efficiency and that those deserving asylum receive it quickly. During the 1995 calendar year, claims dropped from 123,000 to 53,000. 126,000 cases were completed in 1995 compared to 61,000 in the previous year. Over the same period, the number of persons placed in deportation proceedings jumped from 29,000 to 65,000 and the number of cases completed by Immigration Judges increased from 17,000 to 40,000. The backlog at the end of 1995 stood at 460,000.

Establishing Eligibility

To establish eligibility for refugee or asylee status, an alien must be:

- Outside his or her country of nationality or last habitual residence or have no nationality
- Unable or unwilling to avail himself or herself of the protection of that country because of persecution or a well-founded fear of persecution on account of:
  - race
  - religion
  - nationality
  - membership in a particular social group
  - political opinion

The alien's home country must also:

- Target the alien for punishment
- Be aware of applicant's belief or characteristic
- Have the capacity to punish the applicant
- Have the inclination to punish the applicant

In such special circumstances, the President, after appropriate consultation in accordance with INA 207(e), may specify any person who meets this criteria.

A person who ordered, incited, assisted, or otherwise participated in the persecution of any person on account of race, religion, nationality, membership in particular social group or political opinion. is not eligible.

Denial of employment is not a valid reason for a claim.

A. Refugee

A refugee is a person who is physically outside the United States.

In special circumstances, the President after appropriate consultation and in accordance with the Act, may designate any person as a refugee who is in his or her home country or if without nationality, where he or she habitually resides if he or she meets the criteria for a well-founded fear of persecution. However, the term refugee does not include any person who ordered, incited, assisted, or otherwise participated in the persecution of any other person.

Typically, refugee applicants are interviewed in third countries after having fled their country of persecution. Individuals who consider themselves to be at risk should contact the nearest office of the United Nations High Commissioner for Refugees.

Eligibility for a refugee interview is governed by their nationality and whether they come under one of the processing priorities used to manage the refugee program. The designation of eligible nationalities and processing priorities is decided annually as part of the consultations process. A refugee applicant found to be eligible for a refugee interview should file Form I-590.

The spouses and minor unmarried children of refugees may also enter the United States in refugee status.

In addition, the following family members of persons granted refugee status can apply for parole into the United States:

- Family members who reside in the same household and are part of the same economic unit as the refugee
- Unmarried sons and daughters regardless of age or place of residence

Withholding of removal is available to refugees in the United States who can show a likelihood that their lives or freedom would be threatened if they were returned to the country in question. Withholding of removal is similar to asylum but governed by a higher standard, requiring applicants to establish that it is more likely than not that they would be persecuted. However, once this standard has been met, they may not be returned to their country.   *Ref: INS 10/29/98*

Admission Process

Step 1 - Processing

Application may be made abroad at a U.S. Embassy or Consulate abroad. The INS also maintains refugee offices in embassies and consulates at:

Athens, Greece	Monterrey, Mexico
Bangkok, Thailand	Moscow, Russia
Ciudad Juarez, Mexico	Nairobi, Kenya
Frankfort, Germany	New Delhi, India
Hong Kong	Port-au-Prince, Haiti
Karachi, Pakistan	Singapore
London, England	Soeul, Korea
Rome, Italy	Tegucigalpa, Honduras
Manila, Philippines	Tijuana, Mexico
Mexico City, Mexico	Vienna, Austria

Documentation and supporting evidence includes:

- *INS form*
  - I-590, Registration for Classification as Refugee

If approved, the applicant is issued a Form I-571, Refugee Travel Document which must be presented at a port of entry. After entry, a refugee can apply for his or her spouse and any unmarried children under 21 to join him or her by filing a Form I-730, Refugee/Asylee Relative Petition. After approval the refugee will receive a Notice of Approval and the information will be forwarded to a U.S. Embassy or Consulate abroad which will contact the dependents for processing.

Cuban refugees

The U.S. legal definition of refugee allows for in-country refugee processing in countries so designated by the President. For example, in Fiscal Year 1999, the U.S. refugee program operated in Havana, Ho Chi Minh City and Moscow. U.S. government representatives have provided information on the in-country refugee program to Cubans in safe havens.

A Cuban believing that he or she qualifies for the refugee program should contact the United States Interests Section, U.S.I.N.T. in Havana.

Cubans who may apply for refugee interviews in Havana include:

- Former political prisoners
- Members of persecuted religious minorities
- Human rights activists
- Forced labor conscripts during the period 1965 through 1988
- Persons deprived of their professional status
- Harsh or discriminatory treatment resulting from their perceived or actual political or religious beliefs
- Others who appear to have a credible claim that they will face persecution as defined in the United Nations refugee convention

An annual lottery is open to Cuban citizens who are not eligible for a Green Card in any other manner except through the annual lottery. They cannot have a relative who can file on their behalf. They must also have been employed in Cuba, have an education and be employable in the U.S. 20,000 visas are made available.

In a move to curb illegal emigration from Cuba, the INS and the Department of State have addressed the issue. Effective December 6, 1996, Cubans who enter the United States illegally will be subject to removal:

- Unless they can show that they are targets of political persecution and have valid asylum claims
- If the Cuban government will accept them and they will not be mistreated

Step 2 - Clearing the INS at a U.S. Port Of Entry

The INS has the final authority to review the documents and admit the alien.

Aliens who are admitted become eligible for legal permanent resident status in one year. See Asylee Step 5 for details.

B. Asylum

The Attorney General may grant asylum if an alien is a refugee within the meaning of INA 208. However, the granting of asylum does not mean that permanent residency has been obtained. That is a later step.

To be considered for asylum, an applicant must:

- Be physically present in the U.S. or at a land border or port of entry
- Have been interdicted in international or U.S. waters
- Pay a fee if established by the Attorney General   *Ref: IIRIRA96.604*

If you are applying at a U.S. port of entry on the Canadian border, the INS Immigration Inspector accepts the I-589 and FD-258 Fingerprint Card which are sent to the Vermont Service Center and the asylee remains in Canada until prior authorization has been received by the port of entry.

It is also possible to apply for asylum to the Executive Office for Immigration Review (EOIR), the Department of Justice agency that contains the immigration courts and Board of Immigration Appeals (BIA).

An alien who is in the U.S. and not in immigration proceedings may apply for asylum by filing Form I-589 with the appropriate INS regional Service Center. A receipt notice will be sent the applicant and the application referred to a U.S. asylum office.

For an alien in the U.S. under removal proceedings, it is the Executive Office for Immigration Review which has exclusive jurisdiction. Asylum claims filed before EOIR are a defense against removal. Nevertheless, aliens may be detained for being in the U.S. illegally until an immigration judge rules on their asylum claim.

The new 1996 law IIRIRA mandates that aliens who arrive at a U.S. port of entry without travel documents or who engage in fraud or material misrepresentation be detained and placed in expedited removal. However, aliens who express or indicate a fear of persecution during the expedited removal process receive a "credible fear" interview with an INS asylum officer. Aliens found to have a credible fear are detained and referred for ordinary removal proceedings in which they may apply for asylum before an immigration judge.

INS district directors have discretionary authority to parole, or release an alien in proceedings from detention if the release would serve an urgent humanitarian need or significant public benefit and whether the alien has established his or her identity, poses a threat to the community, demonstrates family ties to the community, presents evidence of a credible asylum claim, or poses a risk of flight.

The INS was behind 500,000 asylum cases at the time of writing. New cases are being processed before older cases which are treated on a "time permitting" basis.

Asylum is not available if the alien:

- May be removed to a safe third country

- Has been in the United States more than one year
- Has previously been denied asylum (unless circumstances have changed)
- Has participated in the persecution of any person on account of race, religion, nationality, membership in a particular social group or political opinion
- Has been convicted of a particularly serious crime (such as an aggravated felony) which constitutes a danger to the U.S. community
- Has committed a serious nonpolitical crime outside the United States
- Is a danger to U.S. security (not subject to judicial review)
- Is inadmissible due to terrorist activity
- Has firmly resettled in another country   *Ref: IIRIRA96.604*
- Is a U.S. citizen
- Is a permanent resident
- Is a conditional resident

An applicant for asylum is not entitled to apply for employment authorization until 150 days after applying for asylum.[INS August 5, 1996] Employment authorization shall not be granted until 180 days after filing the asylum application.
Ref: IIRIRA96.604

Other conditions include:

- Fingerprints and photograph may be required by the attorney General
- Asylum cannot be granted until the identity of the applicant has been checked against the INS and DOS databases
- A frivolous asylum application shall result in permanent ineligibility for benefits under this act
- In the absence of exceptional circumstances:
  - the initial interview or hearing shall commence within 45 days of filing
  - final adjudication shall be completed within 180 days of the filing

If you leave the United States pursuant to advance parole granted under 8 CFR 212.5(e), it shall be presumed that you have abandoned your application if you returned to the country from which you are claiming persecution unless you are able to establish compelling reasons for such return.   *Ref: IIRIRA96.604*

Time spent in the United States is not counted against an alien with a legitimate pending asylum application when determining their liability for the three or ten year reentry bars. Refugees and asylees may be eligible for supplementary assistance.

Special programs

The 1990 ABC settlement provided for different procedures for certain Salvadorans and Guatemalans.

The Haitian Amnesty Bill came into effect as part of the Omnibus Budget bill which was enacted in the fall of 1998. To qualify, a Haitian must have been in the U.S. since 1995 and have:

- Been orphaned, abandoned or an unaccompanied minor when entering the U.S., or
- Had a credible fear of persecution, or
- Applied for asylum before December 31, 1995, or
- Been paroled into the U.S. for emergent or national interest reasons

Temporary Protected Status and employment authorization is available to nationals of foreign states designated by the Attorney General due to armed conflict, environmental disasters and other extraordinary and temporary conditions which prevent the return of nationals in safety to their homelands. The list of participating nations changes frequently. In 2000, natives of Angola, Bosnia, Burundi, Honduras, Kosovo, Liberia, Monserrat, Nicaragua, Serbia-Montenegro, Sierre Leone,Somalia and Sudan who were living in the U.S. were eligible. Applicants file Form I-821, Application for Temporary Protected Status with $50 filing fee and Form I-765, Application for Employment Authorization with $100 filing fee if requesting employment authorization.

Step 1 - Clearing the INS in the United States

Principal alien

If you are currently in deportation or exclusion proceedings, you must file your application with the office of the Immigration Judge having jurisdiction over your case.

If you are not in exclusion or deportation proceedings, you are to mail your application for asylum to the INS regional Service Center having jurisdiction over your place of residence.

To file for asylum, an alien must file Form I-589, Application for Asylum and for Withholding of Deportation.

You must respond to all questions. If any questions do not apply to you, answer "none" or "not applicable".

Behind the original package attach two copies of the items in your original package except photographs. Required documentation must be assembled so that it may be easily separated.

Documentation and supporting evidence includes:

- *INS forms*
    - original signed I-589, Application for Asylum and Withholding of Deportation
    - Form G-28 if represented by an attorney
- *Passport and photographs*
    - copy of every page of the passport and any other U.S. immigration documents for each family member included in your application
    - two ADIT photographs of you and one of every listed family member taken within 30 days of applying:
        - 3/4 frontal profile showing right ear

- head bare (unless headdress is required by your religious order)
- white background, on thin glossy paper
- maximum 2" square
- approximately 1 1/4" from top of head to bottom of chin
- name and A number printed on back
- *Current and prior immigration status*
  - copy of any U.S. immigration documents you possess such as I-94
- *Additional evidence*
  - details of your experiences and/or those of your family which illustrate why you have a well-founded fear of persecution such as:
  - newspaper articles, periodicals, journals, books
  - affidavits of witnesses
  - official documents
  - other personal statements and evidence such as:
    - details of your experiences, events and dates that relate to your claim for asylum
  - original and two copies of any additional sheets and supplementary statements
  - any other supporting documents
- *Civil documents*
  - copy of your birth certificate with adequate translation
  - three copies of any other documentary evidence of relationships to your spouse and unmarried children such as:
  - a birth certificate of the child showing the names of one or both parents if you are applying as the parent(s) plus:
  - certificate of marriage (if applying for your spouse)
  - proof of termination of marriage

If it is not possible to obtain any of the documents, secondary records such as school records, affidavits, photographs, letters, may be submitted for consideration.

You must establish why those incidents or other general information are relevant to your specific circumstances and why you have a well-founded fear of persecution.

Dependents included with principal alien

A spouse or unmarried child under 21 of an asylee, may, if not otherwise eligible for asylum, be granted the same status as the asylee, if accompanying or following to join the asylee. However, dependents may also choose to file separately.

If a dependent spouse and unmarried child is included in your principal alien application, attach one additional package behind your application and the required duplicate packages. In 1998, the INS issued guidelines to evaluate the asylum claims of children.

After being granted political asylum in the United States, an asylee can apply for his or her spouse and any unmarried children under 21 to join him or her by filing a

Form I-730, Refugee/Asylee Relative Petition. After approval the asylee will receive a Notice of Approval and the information will be forwarded to a U.S. Embassy or Consulate abroad which will contact the dependents.

Documentation and supporting evidence includes:

- *Forms*
    - I-730, Refugee/Asylee Relative Petition
    - one copy of Form G-28, if represented by an attorney
- *Photograph*
    - second photograph of each family member stapled to the information about them
- *Additional evidence*
    - one copy of all continuation sheets and supporting evidence submitted with the original application

Dependents - spouse and unmarried children filing separately

If a spouse and unmarried children under the age of 21, were not included as dependents when you obtained your refugee/asylee status, you must file for them if:

- You were granted refugee status under INA 207 or asylum status under INA 208, or
- You were admitted as a refugee or received asylum under the same sections of law and subsequently adjusted, and
- Benefit is available for the spouse and/or child, and
- Your relationship to your spouse or child existed prior to approval of your refugee or asylee status, and
- Your spouse or child have never had U.S. refugee or asylee status

Take a completed application to the INS office having jurisdiction over your place of residence. If filing on behalf of a child under 21, be sure to file in sufficient time for action to be completed and the child receive travel authorization in time to reach the United States before the 21st birthday.

Documentation and supporting evidence includes:

- *INS form*
    - I-730, Refugee/Asylee Relative Petition

Dependents living abroad

If the INS approves your petition, they will send a notice of approval letter to you and the information about your application to the U.S. Embassy or Consulate in the country where your family members are living. They will contact your family with details of their processing.

It usually takes two to three months from the time you receive your notice of approval and your family is contacted for processing.

After processing by the consulate, your family members may proceed to the port of entry where they must apply to the INS for entry.

Married dependents

Married dependents must file a separate Form I-589.

Step 2 - *Judicial Reconsideration Of Denial*

If the case is denied, the applicant will be sent before an immigration judge who will decide the asylum case.

Step 3 - *Application For Employment Authorization*

You may file Form I-765, Request for Employment Authorization, which is available from your local INS office 150 days after filing your asylum application. However, employment authorization shall not be granted until 180 days after filing the asylum application. If you have not received a decision in your case by that time, you will be issued employment authorization. However, any delay that you request or cause in your case will not be counted as part of the 150 or 180 day periods.

There is no fee for filing an initial request for employment authorization.

Ref: INS August 5, 1996

Step 4 - *Processing*

Option 1 - *Adjustment of Status by the INS in the United States*

Aliens may not adjust status to permanent resident (Green Card holder) in the United States if they have not maintained lawful status.

In most cases you become eligible after being physically present in the United States for one year after the granting of asylum if you still qualify as a refugee or as the spouse or child of a refugee. Although there is no limit to the number of persons who can be granted asylum in any given year, the number who can have an adjustment of status to permanent resident has been limited to 10,000 annually, including Fiscal Year 1999.   *Ref: P.L. 100-200, Section 101 (e)*

On an interim basis, asylees and refugees must file their I-485 Application to Adjust Status to permanent resident with the INS regional Service Center in Lincoln, Nebraska if:

- You are living in the United States, and
- You have been granted asylum or refugee status, and
- You are eligible for asylum or refugee adjustment

Documentation and supporting evidence includes:

- *INS form*
  - I-485, Application to Register Permanent Residence or Adjust Status
- *Fees*
  - filing fee of $220 if the applicant is 14 years of age or over
  - filing fee of $160 if the applicant is under 14 years of age

You may expect to:
- File an inquiry sheet
- Have a criminal record check
- Have a check whether you are still a refugee

Spouse and minor children qualify for a Green Card with the applicant as long as:
- They are on a valid visa in the United States
- They are not subject to the two-year HRR requirement of a J-1 or J-2
- Do all paperwork and be processed with the principal applicant

Option 2 - By the Department of State (DOS) Abroad

Documentation and supporting evidence includes:

- *DOS forms*
  - State Department Packet III & IV, or
  - OF 230 - Parts I and II
  - G-325A - Biographic information Sheet
- *Passport and photographs*
  - passport valid for six months beyond intended date of entry
  - two identical 2" square color photographs
- *Prior approval*
  - copy of approved Notice for immigrant petition making visa number immediately available
- *Current and prior immigration status*
  - copy of Form I-94
- *Employer's evidence to support request*
  - employment letter
- *Proof of financial support or solvency*
  - evidence of support
- *Civil documents*
  - birth Certificate

Step 5 - Absences From The United States

Being granted asylum does not prevent an alien from going home. However, since the rationale for the granting of asylum is a well founded fear of persecution, lengthy stays in the home country tend to refute this premise.

Since the INS codes the Green Card to show that asylum was granted, holders sometimes feel it is prudent to leave their Green Card at home when visiting the home country. However, this conflicts with the alien's obligation to produce his or her Green Card when entering the United States after trips abroad.

Part IV

U.S. Citizenship

Akey element of the immigration process is the realization of the dream of U.S. citizenship. Part IV deals with this very important issue.

According to the U.S. Constitution, all people born in the United States and its territories are U.S. citizens. However, children of foreign diplomats born in the United States are excluded.

All people naturalized in the U.S. are citizens. Also, children born abroad who have at least one U.S. citizen parent may be eligible to claim U.S. citizenship by a form of inheritance or derivation.

Any person in the United States who is not a citizen is an "alien" and falls within the following three broad classifications of aliens:

- **Unlawful** or **unauthorized aliens** who have entered illegally and are not *in status*
- **Nonimmigrants** who have entered legally on temporary visas with limited rights
- **Resident aliens** or **permanent residents** who have received Green Cards and can live and work permanently in the United States

Ref: INS ER 806 3-8-94

Since the final step in the process of *Getting In* to the United States is U.S. citizenship, Part IV offers three chapters of insight into the complex issues surrounding the cherished U.S. citizenship as well as help in preparing for the naturalization test which gets you there.

The U.S. passport is covered in Chapter 35 in Book 2.

Chapter 13-Derivative Status

- An examination of how foreign-born dependents of U.S. citizens qualify for citizenship

Chapter 14-Dual Nationality
- An examination of the issues involved with holding citizenship in two countries simultaneously

Chapter 15-Naturalization and Test Questions
- An examination of the bridge from resident alien to citizen with a detailed list of questions which may be expected in a naturalization interview

Qualifying for U.S. Citizenship

U.S. citizens generally fall into one of five categories:
- Born and living in the United States or its possessions
- Born in the United States and living abroad for any length of time
- Born abroad to U.S. parents and living in the United States
- Born abroad to non-U.S. parents and subsequently naturalized
- Living abroad and unaware of a claim to U.S. citizenship

The United States includes:
- The 50 states
- The District of Columbia
- Puerto Rico
- Guam
- The United States Virgin Islands
- The Commonwealth of the Northern Mariana Islands for purposes of determining U.S. citizenship at birth
- The Pacific islands of American Samoa and Swains Island
  - a person born in either of these islands on or after the date of formal U.S. acquisition is a "national" of the United States

A foreign-born child of a U.S. citizen or citizens may have U.S. citizenship depending on the laws in effect in the United States when the child was born and whether citizenship was acquired through a parent or grandparent.

A child born in the United States to foreign diplomats and the foreign parents of a child born in the United States do not qualify for U.S. citizenship.

There has been a dramatic increase in applications for naturalization due to a number of factors such as:
- The three million illegal immigrants who were legalized under the 1986 amnesty law had become eligible to apply for citizenship
- The expiration of pre-1978 Green Cards
- Concern over the loss of benefits following the passing of the welfare reform law in August, 1996 which bans noncitizens from collecting food stamps and Supplemental Security Income.

Rights, Benefits and Responsibilities of U.S. Citizenship

Rights
- Voting
- U.S. passport

Benefits
- Work in Federal, State, local government and national security jobs requiring U.S. citizenship
- Work as an FBI agent or federal judge
- Work as a state police officer or teacher, in some states
- Petition for Green Cards for parents, married children, and brothers and sisters
- Avoiding deportation or exclusion
- Certain scholarships and other federally-funded student aid
- Political office

Responsibilities
- Jury duty

Relinquishing U.S. Citizenship

There is no automatic loss of U.S. citizenship. However, the INA identifies the following ways natural-born or naturalized citizens put their U.S. citizenship at risk:
- Obtaining foreign naturalization
- Taking an oath to a foreign state
- Serving in a foreign army in hostilities against the United States or serving as an officer
- Working for the government of the other country or making a declaration of allegiance to that country
- Formally renouncing U.S. citizenship before a U.S. consular officer
- Formally renouncing U.S. citizenship in the United States in war time
- Conviction for an act of treason   *Ref: INA 349*

A Certificate of Loss of Nationality is issued to former citizens to confirm that they have relinquished their U.S. citizenship.

Information on voluntarily renouncing U.S. citizenship may be obtained from U.S. Embassies or Consulates abroad or from:

Office of Citizens Consular Services   (CA/OCS/CCS)
Room 4811 NS
Department of State
Washington, DC 20520-4818   *Ref: INA 349(5); 8 USC 1481(a)(5)*

Persons wishing to regain lost citizenship may contact the same office.

Chapter 13

Derivative Status

T his chapter is included to offer insight into the concept of derivative status. Anyone who thinks that he or she is entitled to derivative status should contact the U.S. Embassy or Consulate having jurisdiction over their place of residence.

It is not necessary to be born in the United States to obtain U.S. citizenship. Some persons born abroad may qualify for derivative status if they have one or more U.S. citizen parents. Since the rules for obtaining derivative status are complex, it is important to follow all steps very carefully.

Reporting a Birth Abroad

Since most children born outside the United States to U.S. citizen(s) are considered U.S. citizens at birth, it is important that their birth be reported to the nearest U.S. Embassy or Consulate as soon after the birth as possible. Form FS-579/SS-5, Application for Consular Report of Birth Abroad of a Citizen of the United States of America, should be filed with a filing fee of $10. Evidence required includes:

- The child's birth certificate
- Evidence of parent(s)' U.S. citizenship
- Evidence of parents' marriage, if applicable
- Affidavit(s) of parent(s)' physical presence in the United States

Upon approval, a Form FS-240 is given the applicant. This serves as the same proof of citizenship as the Certificate of Citizenship issued by the INS.

Qualifying for Derivative Status

The following may be useful as a general guideline in determining whether a child born outside the United States may have acquired citizenship at birth. It may also be possible to obtain citizenship through a grandparent by filing Supplement A to Form N-600.

The Immigration Corrections bill, passed on October 6, 1994, was intended to clarify derivative status. Generally, if both parents are U.S. citizens, one parent must have lived in the U.S. for at least a total of one year. If only one parent is a U.S. citizen, then that parent must have resided in the U.S. for at least five years, with two of those years after age 14.   *Ref: 8 USC 1401; DHHS Publication No. (PHS) 93-1142*

A child born abroad before May 24, 1934, could be eligible for U.S. citizenship provided that one parent resided in the United States at the time of birth.

A child born between 1934 and 1941, could be eligible for U.S. citizenship provided that:

- At least one parent was a U.S. citizen residing in the United States at the time of birth, and
- The child resided in the United States or its outlying possessions for a total of five years between age 13 and 21 or two continuous years between ages 14 and 28, or
- The citizen parent was employed overseas by a qualifying U.S. organization, in which case no U.S. residence is necessary

A child born between 1941 and December 24, 1952, could be eligible for U.S. citizenship provided that:

- At least one parent was a U.S. citizen residing in the United States or one of its outlying possessions at the time of birth, and
- The citizen parent had resided a total of at least 10 years in the United States including five years after the age of 16, or
- The parent had served in the U.S. armed forces between December 7, 1941 and December 31, 1946 including five years after age 12, or
- The parent had served in the U.S. armed forces between December 31, 1946 and December 12, 1952 and had a total of 10 years of physical presence in the United States including five years after age 14, and
- The child resided in the United States or its outlying possessions for a total of five years between age 13 and 21 or two continuous years between ages 14 and 28, or
- The citizen parent was employed overseas by a qualifying U.S. organization, in which case no U.S. residence is required

A child born between December 24, 1952 and November 14, 1986 could be eligible for U.S. citizenship provided that:

- At least one parent was a U.S. citizen residing in the United States or one of its outlying possessions at the time of the birth, or
- At least one U.S. citizen parent was physically present in the United States or outlying possession for a total of 10 years before the birth, five of which were after age 14

A child born after November 14, 1986 could be eligible for U.S. citizenship provided that:

- At least one parent was a U.S. citizen residing in the United States or one of its outlying possessions at the time of birth, and
- At least one U.S. citizen parent had been physically present in the United States or one of its outlying possessions for a total of at least five years prior to the birth, including two years after age 14

Chapter 14
Dual Nationality

Dual nationality is the simultaneous possession of two citizenships.

As each country makes its own laws on conferring citizenship, dual nationality is a very complex issue. As what follows is a brief introductory overview to the subject, it may be advisable to discuss specific derivative citizenship issues with legal counsel.

In the United States, dual nationality is not looked upon favorably by some INS or State Department officers as the act of accepting the rights and responsibilities of U.S. citizenship implies the waiving of other allegiances and the responsibilities which go with them. These officers tend to prefer the term dual national to dual citizen.

Nevertheless, several U.S. Supreme Court rulings reinforce the ability of a person to retain dual status, including:

- Mandoli v. Acheson, 344 U.S. 133 (1952)
- Kawakita v. U.S.,   343 U.S. 717 (1952)
- Afroyim v. Rusk,   387 U.S. 253 (1967)
- Terrazas v. Vance,   444 U.S. 252 (1980)

As a result of these rulings and a 1990 U.S. law, the United States is not challenging the dual nationality of aliens who take advantage of their original citizenship after being naturalized in the United States. However, the U.S. view is that dual nationals:

- Have no extra status in the United States
- Owe allegiance to the United States
- Are obliged to obey U.S. laws
- Who are required to renounce their U.S. citizenship as part of a foreign country's naturalization process may still retain their U.S. citizenship after:
  - taking a routine oath of allegiance to that foreign country, and
  - being employed in a non-policy level foreign governmental position

Many countries do not recognize the act of renouncing their citizenship even though it is part of the U.S. naturalization process. The old country still considers a dual national as one of its citizens.

Canadian law permits Canadian citizens who are naturalized in the U.S. to retain Canadian citizenship. Some observers believe that as many as 5 percent of Canadians have a claim to U.S. citizenship through U.S. ancestors. In certain cases, citizenship could extend automatically to their children, and possibly to their grandchildren.

Other countries, such as India, do not permit dual citizenship and as a result, the citizenship of children of their nationals may be in doubt.

Potential Loss of U.S. Citizenship

Before a U.S. citizen becomes naturalized in another country, the potential dual citizen should check to ensure that the adopted country is not going to require renunciation of U.S. citizenship. From the U.S. perspective, while swearing allegiance to a foreign country may suggest loss of citizenship, it is difficult to prove that a person knowingly and fully intended to abandon U.S. citizenship.

A dual national may jeopardize his or her U.S. citizenship by:

- Accepting a policy-level position with a foreign government
- Being convicted of treason or engaging in conduct so inconsistent with retention of U.S. citizenship that it compels a conclusion that the dual national intended to relinquish his or her U.S. citizenship

U.S. citizenship may also be lost by a person's statements or actions or by signing a document renouncing it. This was formalized in law in 1986.

Citizens who acquired dual status at birth do not risk loss of their U.S. citizenship if they live abroad or of their foreign citizenship when they reach adulthood. These laws and regulations have been repealed by Congress. Citizenship acquired by birth in the United States is practically impossible to lose.

Passports

If a claim to U.S. citizenship can be documented, a passport application may be filed for a grandchild with a U.S. passport office or at an Embassy or Consulate abroad.

The law requires that you show your U.S. passport when entering the United States. There is no need to mention dual status as it may only raise unnecessary questions and delay processing. Similarly, when leaving, show the airline your U.S. passport.   *Ref: 22 CFR 53*

At passport renewal time, consular offices may require that a dual citizen complete a questionnaire to determine whether there is an intention to renounce U.S. citizenship. Further information is available from the State Department's Office of Citizens Consular Services at (202) 647-4000.

It may not be advisable for dual nationals to take their home country's passport or other identifying documents with them on trips to their native country if their departure was under duress, to avoid the draft or was illegal. In these and most other cases your U.S. passport is your best document. See chapter 35 for further details.

Chapter 15

Naturalization
with Test Questions

Persons 18 years of age or older, who are lawfully admitted permanent resident aliens and meet certain requirements may apply for U.S. citizenship in a process called naturalization. As of April 1996, approximately 5,776,000 legal permanent residents and 687,000 children were considered eligible for naturalization.

The number of applicants exceeded 2,000,000 in Fiscal Year 1998, an increase from 592,000 in Fiscal Year 1994. In Fiscal Year 1997, the INS naturalized 1,049,857 new citizens and undertook to reduce the overall processing time to six months by September 30, 2000.

Obtaining Citizenship

Step 1 - Qualifying Period

An immigrant who did not gain permanent resident status through marriage to a U.S. citizen spouse, U.S. military service or through other special circumstances, becomes eligible for naturalization five years from the date of entry as a lawful permanent resident, provided that he or she has been present in the United States for at least two and a half of those five years and without any continuous absences of one year or more.

Time spent in the U.S. on any form of temporary visa does not count toward the waiting period for naturalization. Only the time after gaining permanent residency counts. The waiting period may not be reduced because of the need for specific skills in a "U.S. Citizen Only" job.

The applicant must have resided for at least the three previous months in the state or service district from which the application was filed.   *Ref: INS N-17*

An immigrant married to and living with a U.S. citizen spouse may apply for naturalization three years from the date of becoming a permanent resident provided that at least one and a half years of the three years have been spent in the U.S. without lengthy absences.

An immigrant who has completed three years or more of U.S. military service may also qualify for naturalization after three years as a Green Card holder if applying while still serving or within six months of an honorable discharge. In such cases, the requirement for physical presence and residence is waived.   *Ref: INA 328*

An immigrant who resided continuously in the U.S. for one year after becoming a legal permanent resident may be eligible to make special application arrangements for naturalization if he or she worked abroad in certain U.S. interests. See Step 2, Form N-470.

Persons working for the CIA may have their one year of continuous physical presence complied with at any time.   *Ref: INA 316*

The Director of Central Intelligence, the Attorney General and the Commissioner of the INS may allow a person to be naturalized after one year of physical presence if they have made an extraordinary contribution to national security or intelligence activities.

Step 2 - Absences During Qualifying Period

Continuity of residence is normally broken by absences from the United States for a continuous period of one year or more after becoming a permanent resident. This break could occur either before or after filing for naturalization. In such cases, the qualifying period usually starts over.

With some exceptions such as military personnel, applicants must have resided in the state or service district from which the application was filed for the previous three months.

Before leaving for an extended period it may be possible to help preserve Green Card status and/or naturalization eligibility by:

- Not being absent for a continuous period of six months or more
- Not being out of the United States for a total of more than 30 months during the last five years
- Filing non-renewable Form I-131, Reentry Permit to allow an absence of up to two years without protecting residency credits for naturalization
- Filing Form N-470, Application to Preserve Residence for Naturalization Purposes with $80 filing fee if employed abroad by:
  - the U.S. government, including the U.S. Armed Forces
  - an American research institute recognized by the Attorney General
  - a recognized U.S. religious organization
  - a U.S. research institution
  - an American firm engaged in the development of foreign trade and commerce of the United States, or

- certain public international organizations involving the U.S.

Ref: INA 316; INA 319

An application is subject to denial if the applicant is on probation following a conviction and must wait until after the probation has been completed.

Step 3 - Application Process

Naturalization application information and N-400 Forms may be obtained on the internet at http://www.ins.usdoj.gov/graphics/services/natz/howapply.htm or by calling (800) 870-3676.

Except for military personnel, filing is at the INS regional Service Center having jurisdiction over the area of residence. It is later forwarded to the appropriate District Office for further processing. If a couple is temporarily separated for job or other valid reasons, permanent residence is governed by where income tax is filed per 316.5 (a), 316.5 (b) (1) (ii). .Military personnel must file the Form N-400 Military Naturalization Packet with the INS regional Service Center in Lincoln, Nebraska.

Other than those who qualify for early naturalization, applications may be filed four years and nine months after obtaining Legal Permanent Resident status, but not before. The countdown to eligibility begins on the date that a person becomes a legal resident as indicated on their Green Card. For a person processed at a U.S. Consulate abroad, the effective date is the date of entry at a U.S. port of entry. Also, when a Green Card is obtained through Adjustment of Status in the U.S., permanent residence begins on the date of INS approval. The passport stamp may come later.

Processing times are now over a year in some states although the INS is aiming for six month processing by September 30, 2000.

Documentation and supporting evidence includes:

- *Form*
  - Form N-400, Application for Naturalization
- *Fees*
  - filing fee of $225
  - fingerprinting fee of $25 (separate check)
- *Photographs*
  - two color photographs in 3/4 frontal profile with right ear showing taken within 30 days of application
- *Additional evidence*
  - copy of I-551 Permanent Resident Card
  - Form G-325B, evidence of military service, if applicable
  - Form N-426, Request for Certification of Military or Naval Service, if application is based on military service

- if application is for a child:
  - copy of child's birth certificate
  - copy of patents' marriage certificate
  - evidence of parents' U.S. citizenship

It is suggested that applications be mailed "Certified" and "Return Receipt Requested".

Submit a separate fingerprinting fee of $25 but no fingerprints with your N-400 application. The INS will advise you by letter when and where to have your fingerprints taken. Fingerprints taken by a Designated Fingerprinting Service are no longer accepted. By 1999, the INS was operating 76 freestanding Application Support Centers (ASCs), 54 sites in INS offices and 38 law enforcement agencies were authorized to do immigration fingerprinting. Questions about fingerprinting may be discussed with an INS officer by calling (888) 557-5398.

To expedite the processing of applications for naturalization, applicants must now file with the N-400 Unit in the INS regional Service Center serving their area. See http://www.ins.usdoj.gov/graphics/services/natz/statemap.htm.

These changes are designed to:
- Reduce processing times for adjudicating applications
- Enable the Service to provide applicants with more information about their case status in a more efficient and expeditious manner
- Limit the number of in-person visits to local INS offices
- Improve the Service's ability to provide service to its customers

Ref:INS 1745-95

There are no restrictions on travel while an N-400 Naturalization application is pending. However, care should be taken to avoid lengthy absences and being out of the U.S. for more than half the period after obtaining the Green Card.

Some states may require the filing of Form N-300, Application to File Declaration of Intention (to obtain naturalization) if you wish to engage in certain occupations or professions or obtain specific licenses.

Documentation and supporting evidence includes:
- *Form*
  - N-300, Application to File Declaration of Intention
- *Fee*
  - filing fee of $50
- *Photographs*
  - two identical 2" square photographs in 3/4 frontal profile showing right ear with full name signature on front not obscuring features
- *Additional evidence*
  - copy of Green Card, or
  - other evidence of permanent resident status

Step 4 - Pre-testing

By April, 1996, there was a backlog of over 800,000 applicants waiting for naturalization tests. To speed up processing and increase the number of applicants who can be processed by an examiner, the INS authorized private contractors to carry out a pre-test of history and government. However, on August 31, 1998, the INS ended private testing and has taken over all naturalization testing.

Study textbooks are available from:

> Superintendent of Documents
> Government Printing Office
> Washington, DC 20402

Form M-132, "Information Concerning Citizenship Education to Meet Naturalization Requirements" is available at INS offices and contains more information about textbooks and courses available by mail.

You may wish to review the test questions reproduced here starting on page 306 before deciding whether you are comfortable enough with the answers to go directly to the interview. Since the INS is making a serious effort to reduce its backlog of applicants, examiners have a very limited number of minutes to spend with each candidate and can, therefore, ask relatively few questions.

Following the passage of the IIRIRA96 and in light of the flood of naturalization applications, the INS has been examining ways to modify the naturalization examination. Before proceeding with your application, make sure that you are prepared for any modifications which may be made to the process.

After reading the test questions in this chapter, you may wish to test your knowledge at the INS internet multiple choice practice self-test site located at http://www.ins.usdoj.gov/graphics/exec/natz/natztest.asp.

Step 5 - Examination

Most applicants are required to pass a naturalization examination. The applicant will be notified when and where to appear. At that time, an interviewer will:

- Test the applicant on his or her:
  - ability to understand, read and write simple English, and
  - knowledge of U.S. history and form of government
    (100 possible questions appear at the end of this chapter)
- Ensure that the applicant has met the requirements for:
  - duration of permanent residency
    - five years in most cases, or
    - three years with a U.S. spouse, or
    - three years in the U.S. military, or
    - other special cases

- good moral character
  - including Selective Service registration (see below)
- three months residency in the state or INS district before filing

Be prepared for questions about the information you have supplied in your original N-400 application. Refresh your memory. Update your list of trips outside the country since filing your N-400 with the reason for and dates of each. Make sure that you can demonstrate that you have been in the United States at least half the time since obtaining permanent resident status.

In an INS study of 7,800 naturalization applications, 48 percent were granted, 43 percent were placed on hold due to missing supporting documents, and eight percent were denied. Of those denied, 44 percent failed the English or civics test, 25 percent did not meet the residency requirements and six percent did not meet the good moral character requirement. 13 percent were denied for other reasons.

All males applying for naturalization who have lived in the U.S. as permanent residents between 18 and 26 years of age must show proof that they registered with Selective Service. See Chapter 21, Selective Service, page 361. However, the INS has instructed its field offices that failure to register bars naturalization only if the applicant knowingly and willfully failed to register during the period for which the applicant must establish good character.   *Ref: INS memorandum, June 18, 1999*

Be sure to study the list of questions about U.S. history and government at the end of this chapter. A minimum of six questions should be answered correctly during the brief interview. However, there is no need to feel intimidated as one interviewer put it, "we try very hard to be compassionate with applicants who try to play by the rules".

The INS says that it is trying very hard. As an example, in order to keep up with the major increase in applications, Miami has processed applicants six days a week at 13 minute intervals and each of the many interviewers handled approximately 22 applicants per day. The interviews were, of necessity, short and barely left time for the minimum six questions.

Permanent residents who are at least 50 years of age with at least 20 years of legal permanent residence or 55 years of age or more with at least 15 years of permanent residence may be exempted from the English language requirement but not the history and government requirement. Also, applicants 65 or older with at least 20 years legal permanent residence may be given special consideration on the test of government and history and tested on a 20-question list.   *Ref: 316.5(b)(1)(2)*

The application for naturalization can be refused for any of the following reasons:
- Membership in any organization preaching and practicing anarchy
- Membership in communist organizations
- Advocating the overthrow of the U.S. government by force, violence or terrorism
- Publishing any material advocating the methods of overthrow

- Refusal to serve in the armed forces of the U.S. (unless exempt)
- Desertion from military forces and draft evasion

Immigrants who fail the English and civics test still might be eligible for naturalization if they show "satisfactory pursuit" of those subjects. This may be demonstrated by producing any of the following evidence:

- A certificate of satisfactory pursuit from an English-Civics program of at least 40 hours, approved by the INS
- U.S. high school diploma
- General equivalency diploma
- Certification from a state-recognized institution for at least one year
- Having passed a proficiency test that demonstrates knowledge equivalent to completing an approved 40 hour course

Ref: Florida Today, January 5, 1996

Step 6 - Naturalization Ceremony

It is possible to have an expedited administration of the oath of allegiance where special circumstances of a compelling or humanitarian nature exist such as illness, disability, advanced age, urgent travel or employment circumstances. In such case, the Certificate of Naturalization, N-550 will be mailed later.   *Ref: 8 CFR 337.3*

Depending on the process being followed in your area, you may be offered the alternative of being sworn in and receiving your Certificate of Naturalization several weeks after your test at either:

- A mass swearing-in ceremony at a regional center, or
- In your county court house

In either case, an oath of allegiance must be sworn.

The standard Oath of Allegiance is as follows:

"I hereby declare, an oath, that I absolutely and entirely renounce and abjure all allegiance and fidelity to any foreign prince, potentate, state, or sovereignty, of whom or which I have heretofore been a subject or citizen; that I will support and defend the Constitution and laws of the United States of America against all enemies, foreign and domestic; that I will bear true faith and allegiance to the same; that I will bear arms on behalf of the United States of America when required by law; that I will perform noncombatant service in the armed forces of the United States of America when required by law; that I will perform work of national importance under civilian direction when required by law; and that I take this obligation freely without any mental reservation or purpose of evasion: so help me God."

A special ceremony with a modified oath is offered for those whose religious beliefs prevent them from promising to bear arms and perform military service. However, the applicant cannot be excused from promising to perform a civilian alternative government service deemed important to the nation.

Persons seeking this exemption are advised to include a letter from their minister written on church letterhead. This letter should explain fully why the applicant desires to take a partial oath of allegiance.

Ref: INS Basic Guide to Naturalization and Citizenship, 1990

Step 7 - Residence After Naturalization

The U.S. no longer requires that newly naturalized citizens remain in the U.S. for one year after naturalization. This was repealed by Congress in October, 1994.

Ref: P.L. 103-416, 108 Stat. 4305

A U.S. passport may be obtained after naturalization. The Certificate of Naturalization must be attached to the application. See Chapter 35 for details.

Naturalization Test - Questions

The test of history and government is based on your understanding of the answers to the following test questions. If you feel comfortable with the answers to these questions you should be able to take your chances in front of an examiner.

States

How many states are there in the United States?	**Fifty (50)**
What are the 49th and 50th states of the Union?	**Hawaii and Alaska**
What is the Capital of your state?	**Your state capital**
What is the head executive of a state government called?	**Governor**
Who is current Governor of your state?	**Your governor**
What is the head executive of a city government called?	**Mayor**
Who is the head of your local government?	**Your mayor**
Can you name the two Senators from your state?	**Your two senators**

History

What is the name of the ship that brought the Pilgrims to America?	**The Mayflower**

Why did the Pilgrims come to America?	**For religious freedom**
Who helped the Pilgrims in America?	**The American Indians (Native Americans)**
What holiday was celebrated for the first time by American colonists?	**Thanksgiving**
What country did we fight during the Revolutionary War?	**England**
What did the Emancipation Proclamation do?	**Freed many slaves**
What is the 4th of July?	**Independence Day**
What is the date of Independence Day?	**July 4th**
Independence from whom?	**England**
What were the 13 original states of the U.S. called?	**Colonies**
Can you name the thirteen original states?	**Connecticut, New Hampshire, New York, New Jersey, Massachusetts, Delaware, Pennsylvania, Virginia, North Carolina, South Carolina, Georgia, Rhode Island and Maryland**
Which countries were our enemies during World War II?	**Germany, Italy and Japan**
Who said "Give me liberty or give me death"?	**Patrick Henry**
Who was Martin Luther King, Jr.?	**A civil rights leader**

Declaration of Independence

Who was the main writer of the Declaration of Independence?	**Thomas Jefferson**
When was the Declaration of Independence adopted?	**July 4, 1776**
What is the basic belief of the Declaration of Independence?	**That all men are created equal**

The Constitution

What is the Constitution?	**The supreme law of the land**
Whose rights are guaranteed by the Constitution and the Bill of Rights?	**Everyone (citizens and non-citizens living in the U.S.)**
In what year was the constitution written?	**1787**
What is the introduction to the Constitution called?	**The Preamble**
Can the Constitution be changed?	**Yes**
What do we call a change to the Constitution?	**Amendments**
How many changes or amendments are there to the Constitution?	**26**
What are the first 10 amendments to the Constitution called?	**The Bill of Rights**
Name one right guaranteed by the first amendment.	**Freedom of speech, press, religion, peaceable assembly, and requesting peaceable change of government**
Where does Freedom of Speech come from?	**The Bill of Rights**

Name three rights or freedoms guaranteed by the Bill of Rights.

1) The right of freedom of speech, press, religion, peaceable assembly and requesting change of government.

2) The right to bear arms (the right to have weapons or own a gun, though subject to certain regulations).

3) The government may not quarter or house soldiers in the people's homes during peacetime without the people's consent.

4) The government may not search or take a person's property without a warrant.

5) **A person may not be tried twice for the same crime and does not have to testify against himself/herself.**
6) **A person charged with a crime still has some rights, such as the right to a trial and to have a lawyer.**
7) **The right to trial by jury in most cases.**
8) **Protects people against excessive or unreasonable fines or cruel and unusual punishment.**
9) **The people have rights other than those mentioned in the Constitution.**
10) **Any power not given to the federal government by the Constitution is a power of either the state or the people.**

Form of Government

What kind of government does the United States have?

Republic

How many branches are there in our government?

Three

What are the three branches of our government?

Legislative, Executive and Judiciary

Executive Branch

What is the executive branch of our government?

The President, cabinet, and departments under the cabinet members

Who was the first President of the United States?

George Washington

Which President is called the "Father of our Country"?

George Washington

Which president was the first Commander in Chief of the U.S.	**George Washington**
Who was President during the Civil War?	**Abraham Lincoln**
Which President freed the slaves?	**Abraham Lincoln**
In what month do we vote for the President?	**November**
In what month is the new President inaugurated?	**January**
Who elects the President of the United States?	**The electoral college**
Who is the President of the United States today?	**Current President**
Who is the Commander in Chief of the U.S. military?	**The President**
Who becomes President of the United States if the President dies?	**Vice-President**
Who becomes President of the United States if the President and the Vice-President should die?	**Speaker of the House of Representatives**
For how long do we elect the President?	**Four years**
How many terms can a President serve?	**Two**
According to the Constitution, a person must meet certain requirements in order to be eligible to become President. Name one of those requirements.	**Must be a natural born citizen of the United States; must be at least 35 years old by the time he/she will serve; must have lived in the United States at least 14 years**
Who signs bills into law?	**The President**
Which special group advises the President?	**The Cabinet**
What is the White House?	**The President's official home**
Where is the White House located?	**Washington, D.C. (1600 Pennsylvania Avenue, N.W.)**
Who is the U.S. Vice-President?	**Current Vice-President**

Legislative Branch

What is the legislative branch of our government?	**Congress**
What is Congress?	**The Senate and the House of Representatives**
Who elects Congress?	**The people**
Who makes the laws in the United States?	**Congress**
What are the duties of Congress?	**To make laws in the United States**
How many senators are there in Congress?	**100**
Why are there 100 Senators in the Senate?	**Two from each state**
For how long do we elect each senator?	**Six years**
How many times may a Senator be re-elected?	**There is no limit**
How many Representatives are there in Congress?	**435**
For how long do we elect the representatives?	**Two years**
How many times may a Congressman be re-elected?	**There is no limit**
Who has the power to declare war?	**The Congress**
Where does Congress meet?	**In the Capitol in Washington, D.C.**

Judiciary Branch

What is the judiciary branch of our government?	**The Supreme Court**
What is the highest court in the United States?	**The Supreme Court**
What are the duties of the Supreme Court?	**To interpret laws**

Who selects the Supreme Court justices?	**Appointed by the President**
How many Supreme Court justices are there?	**Nine**
Who is Chief Justice of the Supreme Court?	**William Rehnquist**

Citizenship

Name one benefit of being a citizen of the United States.	**Obtain federal government jobs; travel with a U.S. passport; petition for close relatives to live in the U.S.**
What is the most important right granted to U.S. citizens?	**The right to vote**

Flag

What are the colors of our flag?	**Red, White and Blue**
How many stars are there in our flag?	**50**
What color are the stars on our flag?	**White**
What do the stars on the flag mean?	**One for each state in the union**
How many stripes are there in the flag?	**13**
What color are the stripes?	**Red and White**
What do the stripes on the flag mean?	**They represent the original 13 states**

General

What are the two major political parties in the U.S. today?	**Democratic and Republican**
What is the national anthem of the United States?	**The Star-Spangled Banner**
Who wrote the Star-Spangled Banner?	**Francis Scott Key**
What is the minimum voting age in the United States?	**18**

What Immigration and Naturalization Service form is used to apply to become a naturalized citizen?

Name one purpose of the United Nations.

Form N-400, "Application to file Petition for Naturalization"

For countries to discuss and try to resolve world problems, to provide economic aid to many countries

Part V

Research Resources

Now that you are aware of the rationale for, and complexities of, the many immigrant and nonimmigrant classifications available to a person considering a new life in America, you may decide to do more research on your own.

Part V is included as an opportunity for the reader to explore some of the resources which are available to help reach a decision on how to proceed with your own immigration project.

This part contains three chapters which introduce some of the resources you may wish to utilize in your research.

Chapter 14-Legal Assistance
- The pivotal role of attorneys in the immigration process

Chapter 15-New Legislation
- The impact of the Illegal Immigration and Immigrant Responsibility Act of 1996 and the American Competitiveness and Workforce Improvement Act of 1998 on the Immigration and Nationality Act of 1952

Chapter 16-U.S. Government Resources
- An examination of resources available for further home study of the INS, the State Department and the Department of Labor

Chapter 16

Legal Assistance

Immigration is a complex subject based on a very delicate fabric of intricate legislation, the Immigration and Nationality Act of 1952 and all the subsequent amending legislation.

Many departments of government are involved and a host of immigration classifications have been created to meet the diverse needs of the alien, industry and government alike.

Because of the complexity of the law, and the differing aspirations and skill sets of intending immigrants, many U.S. attorneys are specializing in immigration cases. If you feel that the amount of detail and sensitivity of your case warrants it, you may wish to consider legal assistance.

Selection of an Immigration Attorney

When selecting a particular immigration attorney, consider whether the attorney:

- Is a member of the American Immigration Lawyers Association (AILA)
- Is active in the local or state bar association's immigration committee
- Is licensed in your state
- Is prohibited from practicing in any state
- Receives a favorable opinion from the local attorney referral service
- Has any unfair business practices on record with the local Better Business Bureau in recent years
- Has a good reputation (one source is the internet)
- Is experienced and has a good success rate with cases like yours
- Makes you comfortable with the terms in your first consultation

An immigration attorney may be especially helpful when preparing your case for presentation to a consular or immigration officer if:

- The case or the rules are complicated
- You are unclear about which facts to emphasize
- Your presentation needs organization
- There are prior legal problems and complications

Attorneys should be chosen carefully. Reports suggest that clients who pay their full fee before services are rendered are sometimes ignored by their attorney. Although clients take great comfort in receiving regular status reports, not all attorneys routinely provide that service.

While you should not expect attorneys to make a case move faster than the system allows, they can be very helpful in making sure that it does not bog down. That may mean something as apparently simple as making sure everything is done right the first time.

If legal counsel is retained, it is not crucial that he or she have an office in your city. Most of the work is done by telephone, fax and mail.

An attorney or other representative must file a Form G-28 signed by the petitioner (8 CFR 103, February 3, 1994) in order to be recognized by the INS. Otherwise, the INS will consider the petitioner to be self-represented and the attorney will not be notified of any action taken.   *Ref: INS Nebraska Service Center*

American Immigration Lawyers Association

A large number of the immigration lawyers in the United States have joined the American Immigration Lawyers Association (AILA).

While we have no connection with the American Immigration Lawyers Association (AILA), we include the address of this association as a reference:

> American Immigration Lawyers Association
> 1400 I Street N.W.
> Suite 1200
> Washington, D.C. 20005
> Phone: (202) 371-9377
> Fax: (202) 371-9449

Free Legal Assistance on the Internet

A number of immigration attorneys respond to general immigration questions in internet news groups. Several maintain informative home pages and offer a formal client relationship at prevailing legal rates.

Other Legal Assistance

Gene McNary, the former Commissioner of the Immigration and Naturalization Service who wrote the Foreword to this book, is typical of the experienced immigration attorneys who are available throughout the United States. He specializes in investor visas and may be contacted at (314) 862-0758 or mms@visalink.com.

Chapter 17

New Legislation

In a story carried by the Associated Press on January 26, 1996, INS Commissioner Doris Meissner was quoted as cautioning against passing laws that reduce benefits for illegal immigrants but urged support for the effort to reduce illegal immigration. She felt that "an effective border patrol backed up by effective enforcement in the workplace would be less disruptive and a far more humane way of enforcing immigration long-term". Her comments came at a time when support is building in Florida for cutting benefits to illegal immigrants following the model introduced in California.

Congress enacted two pieces of important immigration-related legislation in a two year period between the fall of 1996 and 1998. In 1996, it was the Illegal Immigration Reform And Immigrant Responsibility Act Of 1996 (IIRIRA96) and in 1998 the American Competitiveness and Workforce Improvement Act of 1998 (ACWIA98). The main provisions of these bills are enumerated here as a reference. However, because such a wide range of topics is covered, readers should be cautioned that some elements have been canceled, others are being reconsidered or refined and consequently, not all are currently implemented. In the 1998 bill, primary focus was on the H-1B classification.

The Illegal Immigration Reform And Immigrant Responsibility Act Of 1996 (IIRIRA96)

After much discussion, a number of legal and illegal immigration issues were included together in the Illegal Immigration Reform and Immigrant Responsibility Act of 1996 which was signed into law by President Bill Clinton on September 30, 1996.

IIRIRA96 is divided into six Titles or parts and incorporates several key changes to the Immigration and Nationality Act (INA). As these changes are currently being phased in, you should check to see whether any provisions which might affect your case have been implemented.

Title I - Improvements to Border Control, Facilitation of Legal Entry, and Interior Enforcement

Increase in Border Patrol Staff   *Ref: IIRIRA96.101*

- The Attorney General in each of the Fiscal Years 1997, 1998, 1999, 2000 and 2001 may increase by 300 the number of personnel in support of border patrol agents
- The Attorney General shall ensure that additional border patrol agents shall be deployed among INS sectors along the border in proportion to the level of illegal crossing of the U.S. borders measured and anticipated in each sector

Installation of Physical Barriers to Illegal Entry   *Ref: IIRIRA96.102*

- The Attorney General shall take such actions as may be necessary to install additional physical barriers and roads in the vicinity of the U.S. border to deter illegal crossings in the area of high illegal entry into the United States
- A maximum of $12,000,000 is to be appropriated for the construction of fencing and road improvements in the San Diego, California area to extend eastward from the Pacific Ocean along the 14 miles of international land border

Machine-Readable Border Cross Documents   *Ref: IIRIRA96.104*

INA 101(a)(6) is amended:

- After April 1, 1997, border crossing documents must be issued with a machine-readable biometric identifier such as the alien's handprint or fingerprints
- After October 1, 1999, an alien presenting a border crossing identification card will not be permitted to enter the United States unless the biometric identifier (handprint or fingerprint) contained on the card matches the alien's biometric characteristics

Increased Penalties for Illegal Entry   *Ref: IIRIRA96.105*

INA 275 is amended by adding:

- Effective April 1, 1997, penalties for illegal entry (entering or attempting to enter at a time or place other than as designated by immigration officers) shall be subject to a civil penalty of:
  - a minimum of $50 and a maximum of $250 for each such entry or attempted entry
  - twice the amount if an alien has been previously subject to a civil penalty under this subsection

Penalties for High Speed Flights from Immigration Checkpoints

INA 241(a)(2)(A) is amended by adding: *Ref: IIRIRA96.108*

- Any alien who is convicted of fleeing or evading an immigration checkpoint and leading Federal, State, or local law enforcement agents   on a high speed vehicle chase in excess of the legal speed limit shall be fined and/or imprisoned not more than five years and is deportable

Automated Entry and Exit Control System *Ref: IIRIRA96.110*

- By October 1, 1998, the Attorney General must develop an automated entry and exit control system that will:
  - record the exit of every alien and match it to the record of the alien's arrival in the United States
  - through on-line search, identify lawfully admitted nonimmigrants in the United States who have gone out of status
  - integrate information on aliens who have gone out of status into data bases of the INS at ports of entry and State Department consulates abroad
  - be reported annually to the House of Representatives and Senate

Fingerprinting of Illegal or Criminal Aliens *Ref: IIRIRA96.112*

- Additional funds may be appropriated to ensure the INS "IDENT" program is expanded to apply to the fingerprinting of illegal or criminal aliens apprehended nationwide

Pre-Inspection Stations at Foreign Airports *Ref: IIRIRA96.123*

INA is amended by adding new section 235A:

- By October 31, 1998, the INS in consultation with the State Department will establish and maintain pre-inspection stations in at least five of the 10 foreign airports which serve as the last point of departure for the greatest number of inadmissible aliens

Increase in Alien Smuggling and Unlawful Employment Investigators

INA 275 and 275A are amended: *Ref: IIRIRA96.131*

- The INS is authorized to hire an additional 300 staff:
  - in each of Fiscal Years 1997, 1998 and 1999
  - to investigate potential alien smuggling and unlawful employment violations

Increase in Visa Overstayer Investigators *Ref: IIRIRA96.132*

- The INS is authorized to hire an additional 300 staff:
  - in Fiscal Year 1997
  - to investigate visa overstayers

Agreements for State Employees to Perform INS Functions *Ref: IIRIRA96.133*

INA 287 is amended by adding:

- The Attorney General may enter into a written agreement with a state or sub-division of a state to enable a qualified state employee to perform an INS investigation, apprehension and detention function

Allocation of INS Agents to States   *Ref: IIRIRA96.134*

INA 103 is amended by adding:

- The Attorney General shall allocate at least 10 full-time active duty INS agents to each state by January 1, 1997

Title II - Enhanced Enforcement and Penalties Against Alien Smuggling; Document Fraud

Increased Penalties for Alien Smuggling and Hiring   *Ref: IIRIRA96.203*

INA 274A is amended:

- The fines and imprisonment are increased for:
  - alien smuggling
  - hiring illegal aliens

Increase in Assistant U.S. Attorneys to Prosecute Persons Harboring or Bringing In Illegal Aliens   *Ref: IIRIRA96.204*

- The number of Assistant United States Attorneys employed by the Department of Justice may be increased by 25:
  - in Fiscal Year 1997
  - to prosecute persons who harbor or bring illegal aliens into the United States

Increased Penalties for Document Fraud   *Ref: IIRIRA96.211*

INA 1028(b) is amended:

- The penalties are increased for fraud and misuse of government-issued identification documents

Increased Penalties for Improper Document Filing   *Ref: IIRIRA96.212*

INA 274C(a) is amended by adding:

- The penalties are increased for:
  - filing or assisting an alien in the filing of a knowingly false document
  - the improper use of documents before boarding a common carrier, or
  - the failure to present such document to an immigration inspector on arrival

False Claims of Citizenship   *Ref: IIRIRA96.215*

- The law addresses as criminal activity, a false claim of U.S. citizenship with the intent of:
  - obtaining a federal or state benefit or service
  - engaging in unlawful employment
  - registering or voting in any federal, state or local election

Criminal Penalty for Voting   *Ref: IIRIRA96.216*

18 USC 29 is amended by adding:

- Fines and imprisonment of not more than one year for noncitizens voting in an election for federal office

Title III - Inspection, Apprehension, Detention, Adjudication, and Removal of Inadmissible and Deportable Aliens

Admission Criteria and Unlawful Presence   *Ref: IIRIRA96.301*

INA 101(a) is amended:

- A Green Card holder shall not be considered as seeking an admission into the United States unless he or she:
  - has abandoned or relinquished that status
  - has been absent from the United States for a continuous period in excess of 180 days
  - has engaged in illegal activity after having departed the United States
  - has departed from the United States while under legal process seeking removal
  - has committed an offence identified in section 212(a)(2) unless granted subsequent relief
  - is attempting to enter at a time or place other than as designated by immigration officers or has not been admitted to the United States after inspection and authorization by an immigration officer

INA 212(a) is amended:

- An alien is deemed to be unlawfully present in the United States:
  - after the expiration of the authorized period of stay, or
  - without being admitted or paroled
- The alien becomes subject to the following conditions:
  - an alien who is unlawfully present for fewer than 180 days must apply abroad at the U.S. Embassy or Consulate responsible for his or her home country
  - an alien who departed voluntarily is:
    - inadmissible within three years of date of departure if unlawfully present between 180 days and one year
    - inadmissible within 10 years of date of departure if unlawfully present for one year or more
  - an alien ordered removed under INA 235 or 240 is:
    - inadmissible within five years of date of removal unless convicted of aggravated felony
    - inadmissible at any time if convicted of aggravated felony
  - an alien who departed while an order of removal was outstanding is:
    - inadmissible within 10 years of departure
    - inadmissible within 20 years of departure in the case of a second or subsequent removal
    - inadmissible at any time if convicted of aggravated felony

- exceptions permitted in determining the period of unlawful presence include the periods in which an alien:
  - is under the age of 18
  - has a bona fide application for asylum pending
  - is a beneficiary of family unity protection
  - is a battered woman or child
  - within 120 days of the filing of a nonfrivolous application for a change or extension of status before the expiration of the authorized period of stay

Stowaways   *Ref: IIRIRA96.302*

INA 235 is amended:

- A stowaway:
  - is not eligible for admission
  - shall be ordered removed upon inspection by an Immigration Officer unless the alien indicates an intention to apply for asylum
  - shall be referred by the officer for an interview by an asylum officer
  - may not be considered an applicant for admission or eligible for a hearing under INA 240
  - is deemed inadmissible by an immigration officer, the immigration officer shall:
    - either order the alien removed from the United States without further hearing or review, or
    - refer the alien for an interview by an asylum officer if the alien indicates an intention to apply for asylum or a fear of persecution
- If the asylum officer determines that an alien has a credible fear of persecution (a significant possibility that the alien could establish eligibility for asylum under INA 208), the alien shall be detained for further consideration of the application for asylum, or
- If the asylum officer determines that the alien does not have a credible fear of persecution, the officer shall order the alien removed from the United States without further hearing or review, or
- Upon request by the alien, a prompt review by an immigration judge shall be concluded within 24 hours, if possible, but not later than seven days to determine whether the alien has established a credible fear of persecution

Arrest and Detention Pending Removal Decision   *Ref: IIRIRA96.303*

INA 236 is amended:

- The Attorney General may issue a warrant for the arrest and detention of an alien pending a decision on whether the alien is to be removed from the United States
- After arrest and detention, the Attorney General may:
  - continue to detain the alien
  - release the alien

- set bond with approved security of at least $1,500
- approve conditional parole without work authorization unless the alien has:
  - permanent resident status
  - nonimmigrant status which would permit work authorization

Cancellation of Removal of Inadmissible Alien   *Ref: IIRIRA96.304*

INA 239 is redesignated as INA 234 and amended;
INA 240 is redesignated as INA 240C and amended;
INA is amended by adding new section 238:

- The Attorney General may cancel the removal of an inadmissible or deportable alien if the alien:
  - has been lawfully admitted for permanent residence for not less than five years
  - has resided in the United States continuously for seven years after being admitted in any status, and
  - has not been convicted of any aggravated felony
  - has been physically present in the United States for a continuous period of not less than 10 years immediately preceding the date of such application
- The number of adjustments under this paragraph shall not exceed 4,000 for any fiscal year
- The Attorney General may permit an alien voluntarily to depart at his or her own expense in lieu of being subject to removal proceedings if::
  - the alien has been physically present for a period of at least one year
  - the alien has been a person of good moral character for at least five years
  - the alien is not deportable under INA 237 (deportation of aliens excluded from admission or entering in violation of law)
  - the alien has established that he or she has the means to depart and intends to do so
  - the alien was previously permitted to so depart after having been found inadmissible
- Permission to depart voluntarily is valid for a maximum of 60 days

Judicial Review and Fines - Orders of Removal   *Ref: IIRIRA96.306*

INA 242 is amended:

- Section 306 includes such changes as:
  - adding significant restrictions on judicial review of orders of removal
  - establishing fines such as $5,000 for each alien stowaway not removed

Increased Fingerprinting and Registration Authorization *Ref: IIRIRA96.323*

INA 263(a) is amended:

- Aliens who are or have been on criminal probation or criminal parole within the United States are added to the list of groups for which fingerprinting and registration is authorized

Criminal Alien Identification System   *Ref: IIRIRA96.326*

Section 130002 of the Violent Crime Control and Law Enforcement Act of 1994 is amended:

- The Commissioner of the INS is directed to operate a criminal alien identification system to assist Federal, State and local law enforcement agencies in:
  - identifying and locating aliens who may be subject to removal by reason of their conviction of aggravated felonies
  - to provide for the recording in automated fingerprint identification systems of the fingerprint records of aliens who have been previously arrested and removed

Proof of Vaccination of Permanent Residence Applicants *Ref: IIRIRA96.341*

INA 212(a) is amended:

- Aliens seeking adjustment of status to permanent residence are excluded for failing to present documentation of having received vaccination against vaccine-preventable diseases including at least mumps, measles, rubella, polio, tetanus and diphtheria toxoids, pertussis, influenza type B and hepatitis B, and any other vaccinations against vaccine-preventable diseases recommended by the Advisory Committee for Immunization Practices
- This applies to applications for immigrant visas or for adjustment of status filed after September 30, 1996

Exclusion of F-1 Violators   *Ref: IIRIRA96.346*

INA 212(a)(6) is amended:

- An alien who obtains the status of a nonimmigrant F-1 and who violates a term or condition of such status is excludable until the alien has been outside the United States for a continuous period of five years after the date of the violation

Exclusion of Alien Voters   *Ref: IIRIRA96.347*

INA 212(a)(10) is redesignated as Section 301(b) of this title and amended:

- Any alien who has voted in any Federal, State, or local constitutional provision, statute, ordinance, or regulation is excludable

INA 241(a) is redesignated as section 305(a)(2) of this division and amended:

- Any alien who has voted in violation of any Federal, State, or local constitutional provision, statute, ordinance, or regulation is deportable

Deportation of Aliens Convicted of Crimes Against Spouses and Children

INA 241(a) is amended by adding: *Ref: IIRIRA96.350*

- Any alien who at any time after entry is convicted of a crime of domestic violence, a crime of stalking, or a crime of child abuse, child neglect, or child abandonment deportable

Increased Fee for Processing Out of Status Green Card Applicants

INA 245(i) is amended: *Ref: IIRIRA96.376*

- The fee for processing the application of an alien who is out of status and physically present in the United States and who wishes to adjust status to that of an alien admitted for permanent residence is increased to $1,000 from $650 (provision subsequently removed)

Title IV - Enforcement of Restrictions Against Employment

Three Employment Eligibility Confirmation Pilot Programs

Ref: IIRIRA96.403

- The Attorney General shall conduct the following three pilot programs of employment eligibility confirmation to be used in the hiring, recruitment or referral for employment in the United States of each individual covered by this election:
  - the basic pilot program in at least five of the seven states with the highest estimated population of aliens who are not lawfully present in the United States in which the alien will provide:
    - within three days of hiring
    - Social Security Account number
    - INS identification or authorization number
    - the original I-9 form in the manner required for inspection
  - the citizenship attestation pilot program in at least five states that issue driver's license or similar identification document which:
    - contains a photograph of the individual
    - has been determined by the Attorney General to have:
      - security features
      - been issued through application and issuance procedures which make such document sufficiently resistant to tampering, and fraudulent use that it is a reliable means of identification for this section
  - the machine-readable document pilot program in at least five states that issue driver's licenses and similar identification documents issued by the state which include a machine-readable Social Security Account number

Toll-Free or Electronic Identity and Employment Authorization Confirmation
Ref: IIRIRA96.404

The Attorney General shall establish a pilot program confirmation system to receive inquiries made by electing persons and other entities at any time through a toll-free telephone line or toll-free electronic media which provides:

- Within three working days, confirmation or tentative nonconfirmation concerning an individual's identity and authorization to be employed
- Within 10 working days after the date of the tentative nonconfirmation:
- Secondary verification to confirm the validity of information provided, and
- A final confirmation or nonconfirmation

Good Faith Employment Verification
Ref: IIRIRA96.411

INA 274A(b) is amended:

- A person or entity is considered to have complied with the employment verification system notwithstanding a technical or procedural failure to meet such requirement if:
  - there was a good faith attempt to comply, and
  - a period of not less than 10 business days has been given to correct the failure
  - there is no pattern or practice of violations

Social Security Reporting of Aliens Not Authorized to Work *Ref: IIRIRA96.414*

INA 290 is amended:

- If earnings are reported on or after January 1, 1997, to the Social Security Administration on a Social Security account number issued to an alien not authorized to work in the United States, the Commissioner of the Social Security shall provide the Attorney General with information in an electronic form containing:
  - the name and address of the alien
  - the name and address of the person reporting the earnings, and
  - the amount of the earnings

Social Security Authorization to Obtain Alien's Social Security account number for Attorney General or the INS   *Ref: IIRIRA96.415*

INA 264 is amended:

- The Attorney General is authorized to require any alien to provide his or her Social Security account number for purposes of inclusion in any record maintained by the Attorney General or the INS

Limitation on Employment Verification Documentation Proof

INA 274B(a)(6) is amended: *Ref: IIRIRA96.421*

- It is an unfair immigration-related practice to discriminate against an individual by:

- requesting more or different documents than necessary to satisfy the requirements of employment verification
- refusing to honor tendered documents which, on their face, reasonably appear to be genuine

Title V - Restrictions on Benefits for Aliens

State Illegal Aliens' Driver's License Denial Pilot Programs*Ref: IIRIRA96.502*

- All states may conduct pilot programs to determine the viability, advisability and cost-effectiveness of denying driver's licenses to aliens who are not lawfully present in the United States

Denial of Social Security Benefits to Illegal Aliens   *Ref: IIRIRA96.503*

Social Security Act.202 is amended:

- No monthly benefit shall be payable to any alien in the United States for any month during which such alien is not lawfully present in the United States

Proof of Citizenship for Federal Public Benefits   *Ref: IIRIRA96.504*

- The Attorney General in consultation with the Secretary of Health and Human Services shall establish procedures for a person applying for a Federal public benefit to provide proof of citizenship in a fair and nondiscriminatory manner

Eligibility of Illegal Aliens for Postsecondary Education Benefits
Ref: IIRIRA96.505

- Effective July 1, 1998, an alien who is not lawfully present in the United States shall not be eligible on the basis of residence within a state or a political subdivision:
  - for any postsecondary education benefit
  - unless a citizen or national of the United States is eligible for such a benefit in no less an amount, duration or scope, without regard to whether the citizen or national is such a resident

Provision of Personal Information to the INS or DOS   *Ref: IIRIRA96.531*

INA 212(a) is amended:

Factors which are to be considered by the consular officer at the time of the application for a visa or in the opinion of the Attorney General at the time of application for admission or adjustment of status include the alien's:

- Age
- Health
- Family status
- Assets, resources, and financial status
- Education and skills
- Affidavits of support

Affidavit of Support - Public Charge   *Ref: IRIRA96.551*

INA 212(a)(4) and 213A are amended:

- The terms of the Affidavit of Support contract to establish that the alien is not a public charge:
  - must be legally enforceable against the sponsor by the sponsored alien, the Federal Government, any State or political subdivision of the State, or by any other entity that provides a means-tested public benefit
  - are not enforceable with respect to benefits provided after:
    - the date the alien is naturalized, or
    - the completion of the required period of employment
    - the alien has worked 40 qualifying quarters of Social Security coverage
- The sponsor must:
  - demonstrate the means to maintain an average income equal to at least 125 percent of the Federal poverty line
  - be the petitioner and may include an individual who accepts joint and several liability
  - agree to submit to the jurisdiction of any Federal or State court
  - be a citizen, national or a lawfully-admitted permanent resident of the United States
  - be at least 18 years of age
  - be domiciled in a state of the United States, the District of Columbia, or any territory or possession of the United States
  - be petitioning under INA 204
- The Federal poverty line is defined as the level of income equal to the official poverty line, as defined by the Director of the Office of Management and Budget, that is applicable to a family of the size involved
- The Attorney General shall ensure that appropriate information is provided to the system for alien verification eligibility (SAVE) described in Section 1137(d)(3) of the Social Security Act
- Any person who fails to notify the Attorney General and the State of current residence of any change of address within 30 days is subject to a civil penalty of:
  - not less than $250 nor more than $2,000, or
  - not less than $2,000 nor more than $5,000 if the sponsored-alien has received any means-tested public benefits for which he or she is not eligible

Title VI - Miscellaneous Provisions

Parole for Humanitarian Reasons or Public Benefit   *Ref: IIRIRA96.602*

INA 212(d)(5)(A) is amended:

- Authority for parole into the United States is only on a case-by-case basis for urgent humanitarian reasons or significant public benefit

Application for Asylum   *Ref: IIRIRA96.604*
INA 208 is amended:

- An alien may apply for asylum if he or she:
  - is physically present in the United States
  - has arrived in the United States
  - has been interdicted in international or U.S. waters
  - pays a fee if established by the Attorney General
- Asylum is not available if the alien:
  - may be removed to a safe third country
  - has been in the United States more than one year
  - has previously been denied asylum (unless circumstances have changed)
  - has participated in the persecution of any person on account of race, religion, nationality, membership in a particular social group or political opinion
  - has been convicted of a particularly serious crime (such as an aggravated felony) which constitutes a danger to the U.S. community
  - has committed a serious nonpolitical crime outside the United States
  - is a danger to U.S. security (not subject to judicial review)
  - is inadmissible due to terrorist activity
  - has firmly resettled in another country
- Other conditions include:
  - employment authorization shall not be granted until 180 days after filing the asylum application (unless provided under regulation by the Attorney general)
  - fingerprints and photograph may be required by the attorney General
  - asylum cannot be granted until the identity of the applicant has been checked against the INS and State Department databases
  - a frivolous asylum application shall result in permanent ineligibility for benefits under this act
- In the absence of exceptional circumstances:
  - the initial interview or hearing shall commence within 45 days of filing
  - final adjudication shall be completed within 180 days of the filing

Extension and Terms of Waiver of the Two-Year HRR   *Ref: IIRIRA96.622*
Section 220(c) of the Immigration and Nationality Technical Corrections Act of 1994 is amended concerning the Conrad 20 Program:

- The mechanism for requesting a waiver of the two-year foreign country residence requirement with respect to international medical graduates is extended to 2002

- Federally requested waivers are extended to an interested United States Government agency
- The Attorney General shall not grant a waiver in response to a request from an interested State agency or U.S. government agency unless:
  - the government of the alien's home country furnishes the Director of the United States Information Agency with a statement in writing that it has no objection to such waiver
  - the grant of such waiver would not cause the number of waivers to exceed 20 for that state in that fiscal year
  - the alien demonstrates a bona fide offer of full-time employment at a health facility or health care organization, and
  - employment has been determined by the Attorney general to be in the public interest
  - the alien agrees to begin such employment within 90 days of receiving the waiver
  - the alien agrees to continue to work for a total of not less than three years (unless the Attorney General determines that extenuating circumstances exist)
  - in cases other than full-time medical research or training, the alien agrees to practice medicine for not less than three years in the geographic area or areas which are designated by the Secretary of Health and Human Services as having a shortage of health care professionals
- The Attorney General may change the status of an alien who qualifies under this sub-section to that of an H-1B nonimmigrant
- No person who has obtained a waiver and failed to fulfill the terms of the contract with the health care facility shall be eligible to apply for an immigrant visa until it is established that the person has resided and been physically present in the country of his or her nationality or last residence for an aggregate of at least two years following departure from the United States
- The two-year foreign residence requirement shall apply if the alien:
  - ceases to comply with any agreement entered into, or
  - the alien's employment ceases to benefit the public interest at any time during the three-year period

Labor Certification - Professional Athletes   *Ref: IIRIRA96.624*

INA 212(a)(5)(A) is amended for professional athletes:

- An immigrant visa labor certification with respect to a professional athlete shall remain valid after the athlete changes employer, if:
  - the new employer is a team in the same sport as the team which employed the athlete when the athlete first applied for certification
- A professional athlete means an individual who is employed as an athlete by a team that is a member of an association which:

- has six or more professional teams whose total combined revenues exceed $10,000,000 per year
- governs the conduct of its members
- regulates the contests or exhibitions in which its member teams regularly engage

- Any minor league team that is affiliated with such association

F-1 Status - Public Elementary, Secondary and Adult Education

INA 214 is amended: *Ref: IIRIRA96.625*

- An alien may not be accorded status as an F-1 student in order to pursue a course of study at a public elementary school, in a publicly funded adult education program, or at a public secondary school unless:
  - the aggregate period of such status does not exceed 12 months, and
  - the local educational agency has been fully reimbursed
- An alien who has been admitted in F status to study at a private elementary or secondary school or in a language training program that is not publicly funded shall be considered to have violated status and his or her F visa shall be voided by terminating or abandoning those studies to undertake a course of study in:
  - a public elementary school
  - a publicly funded adult education or language training program
  - a public secondary school

Increase in Validity Period of Immigrant Visa   *Ref: IIRIRA96.631*

INA 221(c) is amended:

- The period of validity of an immigrant visa is increased from four to six months from the date of issue by a consular officer
- In the case of aliens who are nationals of a foreign country and who are granted refugee or permanent resident status and resettled in another foreign country, the Secretary of State may prescribe the period of validity of such a visa based upon the treatment granted by that other foreign country to alien refugees and permanent residents, respectively, in the United States

Readmission of Out of Status Aliens   *Ref: IIRIRA96.632*

INA 222 is amended:

- An alien admitted on the basis of a nonimmigrant visa who remained in the United States beyond the period of stay authorized by the Attorney General shall:
  - have his or her visa voided beginning after the conclusion of such period of stay
  - be ineligible to be readmitted to the United States as a nonimmigrant except on the basis of a visa issued in:
    - a consular office located in the country of the alien's nationality, or:

- such other consular office as the Secretary of State shall specify if there is no office in the alien's country of nationality (consulate shopping prohibited)

DOS Nonimmigrant Visa Application Forms   *Ref: IIRIRA96.634*

INA 222(c) is amended:

- At the discretion of the Secretary of State, application forms for the various classes of nonimmigrant admissions may vary according to the class of visa being requested

Extension of Visa Waiver Pilot Program   *Ref: IIRIRA96.635*

INA 217 is amended:

- The Visa Waiver Pilot Program was extended to 1997
- The Visa Waiver Pilot Program becomes the responsibility of the Attorney General who:
  - acts in consultation with the Secretary of State
  - shall place pilot program countries on probation for not more than two full fiscal years if:
    - the program country's disqualification rate is greater than 2 percent, but less than 3.5 percent
  - shall terminate a program country's designation as a pilot program country if:
    - its disqualification rate is 3.5 percent or more
    - after its two-year probationary period:
      - its disqualification rate is greater than 2 percent
      - it has failed to develop a machine-readable passport program

DV Lottery Visa Feè   *Ref: IIRIRA96.636*

- The Secretary of State may establish a fee to be paid by each applicant for an immigrant visa under the terms of the Diversity Immigrant Lottery

Electronic Collection of Alien Student Data   *Ref: IIRIRA96.641*

- The Attorney General in consultation with the Secretary of State and the Secretary of Education shall develop and conduct a program to electronically collect from approved institutions of higher education and designated exchange visitor programs in the United States, information on the alien's:
  - identity and current U.S. address
  - nonimmigrant classification
  - date of visa issue, extension or change of status
  - current academic status
  - full-time student status
  - satisfying the terms and conditions of the program

- disciplinary action and change of program participation as a result of a criminal conviction
- The information shall be provided as a condition of continued:
  - approval of the institution
  - authority to issue documents to demonstrate the alien's eligibility for an F, J or M visa
- An approved institution shall impose on and collect from each alien when the alien first registers with the institution after entering the United States a fee established by the Attorney General which does not exceed $100 (the INS has undertaken a program in five counties from the Atlanta office and there are early indications that the fee will be in the $25 to $75 range)

Marriage Fraud *Ref: IIRIRA96.652*

- The INS estimates that the rate of marriage fraud between foreign nationals and U.S. citizens is 8 percent, a portion of which originates as mail-order marriages
- Each international matchmaking organization is required to:
  - disseminate to recruits, upon recruitment, such information as the INS deems appropriate in the recruits native language including:
    - information concerning conditional permanent residence
    - the battered spouse waiver
    - permanent resident status
    - marriage fraud penalties
    - the unregulated nature of the business
  - pay a penalty of not more than $20,000 for each violation

The American Competitiveness and Workforce Improvement Act of 1998

The Act, included in the Omnibus Budget Bill signed by President Clinton on October 27, 1998, has established a more strict set of rules for"H-1B-dependent" employers with a proportionately larger share of H-1B nonimmigrants in their full-time workforce. At the same time, it has left other employers with a smaller share of H-1B workers with the original less strict rules.

An H-1B-dependent employer is defined as one who has:

- 25 or fewer full-time equivalent employees of whom eight or more are H-1B nonimmigrants, or
- 26 to 50 full-time equivalent employees of whom 13 or more are H-1B nonimmigrants, or
- 51 or more full-time equivalent employees of whom 15 percent or more are H-1B nonimmigrants

The American Competitiveness and Workforce Improvement Act of 1998 is divided into Subtitles A, B and C. While key elements are incorporated into the Immigration and Nationality Act, they are scheduled to terminate on September 30, 2001 because the provisions are meant to act as a temporary measure until permanent solutions can be found for the current shortage of skilled U.S. workers.

Subtitle A - Provisions relating to H-1B Nonimmigrants

Temporary Increase in access to temporary skilled personnel under H-1B program
Ref: Section 411

INA 214(g) is amended:

The INS Fiscal Year " H-1B "numbers" are increased for the following Fiscal Years:

- 115,000 in fiscal year 1999
- 115,000 in fiscal year 2000
- 107,500 in fiscal year 2001
- 65,000 in each succeeding fiscal year

Protection against displacement of United States workers in case of H-1B-dependent employers
Ref: Section 412

INA 212(n)(1) is amended:

On applications submitted between the date the final H-1B regulations are promulgated and October 1, 2001, H-1B-dependent employers must attest that they:

- Did not and will not displace a U.S. worker in the same or essentially equivalent job at the same area of employment within 90 days before or after filing the H-1B visa petition
- Will not place the nonimmigrant with another employer at the other employer's worksite(s) unless assured that the duties were not previously performed by a displaced U.S. worker within 90 days of the placing of the nonimmigrant
- Accept a clear statement of liability if the other employer displaces a U.S. worker
- Have taken good faith steps to recruit, in the U.S. using procedures that meet industry-wide standards and have offered compensation that is at least as great as that required to be offered to H-1B nonimmigrants and U.S. workers for the job in question
- Have offered the job to any equally or better qualified U.S. worker who applies
- Have used relevant legitimate normal and customary selection criteria in a non-discriminatory manner

Changes in enforcement and penalties
Ref: Section 413

INA 212 (n) (2) (C) is amended:

H-1B-dependent employers face new rule changes and penalties, after notice and opportunity for a hearing if:

- The Secretary of Labor finds a failure or a substantial failure to meet a condition, or a misrepresentation of material fact in an application, a maximum $1,000 penalty may be imposed and the Attorney General shall not approve H-1B petitions for that employer for at least one year
- The Secretary finds a wilful failure to meet a condition or wilful misrepresentation of material fact in an application, a civil monetary penalty of up to $5,000 per violation may be imposed and the Attorney General shall not approve H-1B petitions for that employer for at least two years
- The Secretary finds a failure to meet a condition or a wilful misrepresentation of material fact which results in the displacement of a U.S. worker within 90 days before or after the filing of any visa petition and if the placing employer knew or had reason to know of the displacement a monetary penalty not exceeding $35,000 may be imposed and the Attorney General shall not approve H-1B petitions for that employer for at least three years if the employer:
  - discriminates in any way against an employee or former employee who cooperates or seeks to cooperate in the investigation of a possible violation
  - requires that an H-1B nonimmigrant pay a penalty for ceasing employment prior to a mutually agreed date
  - requires that an H-1B nonimmigrant reimburse the employer for any part of the fee for the petition; a maximum $1,000 monetary penalty may be imposed and the amount paid returned to the nonimmigrant
  - places an H-1B nonimmigrant designated as a full or part-time employee in nonproductive status or to fail to pay the nonimmigrant full wages due to a decision by the employer or due to the nonimmigrant's lack of a permit or license (this clause does not apply to non-work-related factors such as the nonimmigrant's voluntary request for an absence or inability to work)
  - fails to offer benefits and eligibility for benefits to an H-1B nonimmigrant on the same basis and criteria as offered to U.S. workers

Collection and use of H-1B nonimmigrant fees for scholarships
Ref: Section 414

INA 214(c) is amended:

The Attorney General shall impose a fee on an H-1B-dependent employer of $500 for each petition on behalf of an H-1B nonimmigrant filed from December 1, 1998 to October 1, 2001 for :

- An initial grant of H-1B status
- An extension of stay
- Change of status

Fees are to be deposited into an H-1B nonimmigrant petitioner account and used for scholarships for low-income math, engineering, and computer science students and job training of U.S. workers who are citizens, Green Card holders or refugees according to the following formula:

- Secretary of Labor - 56.3 percent for demonstration programs and projects to provide technical skills training for employed and unemployed workers
- Director of National Science Foundation - 28.2 percent for scholarships of a maximum of $2,500 per year for low-income students to pursue associate, undergraduate or graduate level degrees in mathematics, engineering, or computer science
- National Science Foundation - 4 percent for merit-reviewed grants for enrollment in year-round academic enrichment courses in mathematics, engineering or science
- National Science Foundation - 4 percent for systemic reform activities
- Attorney General - 1.5 percent for duties related to petitions
- Secretary of Labor - 6 percent for decreasing processing time

Computation of prevailing wage level   *Ref: Section 415*

INA 212 is amended:

In computing the prevailing wage level for an occupational classification in an area of employment in an institution of higher education or a nonprofit research organization or a Governmental research organization the prevailing wage level shall only take into account employees at such institutions and organizations in the area of employment. When the job opportunity for a professional athlete is covered by professional sports league rules or regulations, the wage set forth in those rules shall be considered as not adversely affecting the wages of U.S. workers similarly employed and be considered the prevailing wage.

Improving count of H-1B and H-2B nonimmigrants   *Ref: Section 416*

INA 214(g)(1) is amended:

The attorney General shall take such steps as are necessary to:

- Maintain an accurate count of H-1B and H-2B nonimmigrants
- Revise the forms used for petitions to permit an accurate count of aliens subject to the numerical limitations
- Provide periodic statistical information and background of aliens to Congress

Report on older workers in the information technology field *Ref: Section 417*

The President of the National Academy of Sciences shall conduct a study for Congress to assess the status of older workers in the information technology field - age discrimination, promotion and advancement, working hours, telecommuting, salary, stock options, bonuses, and other benefits and the relationship between rates of advancement, promotion, compensation related to experience, skill level, education and age.

Report on high technology labor market needs; reports on economic impact of increase in H-1B nonimmigrants   *Ref: Section 418*

The Director of the National Science Foundation shall conduct a study for Congress to assess labor market needs for workers with high technology skills during the next ten years - study future training and education needs of high tech companies, improvements in teaching and educational level of American students in math, science, computer science and engineering since 1998, projections on U.S. workers working overseas, relative achievement rates of U.S. and foreign students, cost benefit analysis of foreign high technology workers, needs of high tech sector to adapt products and services to particular local markets abroad

Subtitle B - Special Immigrant Status for certain NATO civilian employees

Special immigrant status for Certain NATO civilian employees
Ref: Section421

Subtitle C - Miscellaneous Provision

Academic honoraria   *Ref: Section 431*

An honorarium and associated incidental expenses may be paid to an alien admitted under INA 101(a)(15)(B) for usual academic activities of not more than nine days at a single institution for the benefit of that institution if the alien has not accepted such payment or expenses from more than five institutions during the previous six months.

Chapter 18

United States Government Resources

The "Big 3" players in the process of U.S. immigration are the Immigration and Naturalization Service of the Department of Justice, the Department of State and the Department of Labor. However, it should be noted that there are also other agencies which play a significant role in the immigration process.

This chapter offers some leads for further research on your own. As you delve into the resources which are made available by each department, you will understand why the immigration process may seem so complex and why such extensive detail had to be incorporated in this book.

Immigration And Naturalization Service (INS)

Forms
The INS provides most of the forms required for the steps covered in this book. Orders may be placed without charge directly from the INS Eastern Forms Center in Williston, Vermont by calling (800) 870-3676. Allow two weeks for delivery. The best time to call is first thing in the morning. If you cannot get the recorded service to take your order, try following the prompts as though you are calling from a rotary telephone.

You may also order or download INS forms from the INS internet website at http://www.ins.usdoj.gov/graphics/exec/forms/index.asp.

INS National Customer Service Center
The INS offers nationwide automated and live telephone information by calling (800) 375-5283. Automated information services are available 24 hours a day, seven days a week.

Live assistance is available with general immigration information from 8 am to 6 pm, Monday to Friday, except holidays. Times vary slightly in Alaska, Hawaii, Puerto Rico and the U.S. Virgin Islands.

The 24-hour menu contains the following recorded information:

- For information on an application that has been filed with the INS
  - for inquiries on the status of your application
  - to update your address on a pending application
  - for assistance on rescheduling an appointment
  - for questions regarding a notice received from the INS
  - for other questions about a pending application
- For information about fingerprinting, your local INS office or for a list of INS authorized doctors
  - for ASC fingerprint location information
  - for INS local office information
  - for a list of doctors in your area authorized to give a medical exam
- For information about forms or applications
  - to place an order for the INS application or forms needed
  - for current application filing fees
  - for information about where to file an application
  - if you have the application but still have questions
- For information on immigration benefits and services
  - for information on how a permanent resident can apply for U.S. citizenship through naturalization
  - for information on how to renew or replace your Green Card
  - for information on bringing a relative, fiancé(e) or orphan to live permanently in the U.S.
  - for immigration services on traveling outside the U.S.
  - for information on immigration benefits available to temporary nonimmigrant visa holders in the U.S.
  - for information on Temporary Protected Status programs
- For information about recent or upcoming changes in immigration programs and procedures
  - for information on changing your address with the INS
  - for changes to fees for applications or petitions
  - for information on changes to Temporary Protected Status
- For information regarding other agencies
  - Social Security
  - Passport Office
    - for visa or entry requirements when traveling to another country, contact their Embassy or Consulate

Internet Information Service

The INS operates a website on the internet. It contains a great deal of information on a variety of subjects with heavy emphasis on immigrant and nonimmgrant status. The INS may be found at http://www.ins.usdoj.gov.

Department of State (DOS)

Visas
The U.S. De Department of State is responsible for the issuance of immigration visas to the United States and U.S. passports. For information on visas call the Department of State's visa office at (202) 663-1225.

Green Card Visa Lottery
For specific information on the State Department Visa Lottery program you may call the Visa Lottery hotline at (202) 331-7199 or (900) 884-8840 ($5.10 charge). Lottery information is available on the internet at http://travel.state.gov/visa_services.html.

Orphan Adoption
Recorded information about orphan adoption in specific countries may be obtained by calling the State Department at (202) 647-3444 or by autofax at (202) 647-3000.

Passports
Information on U.S. passports is available by calling the U.S. Passport Agency at (900)225-5674. The cost is 35 cents per minute to listen to automatic recorded messages or $1.05 per minute to speak with an operator. A live operator is available from 8:30 am to 5:30 pm Eastern time, Monday through Friday. A credit card may be used for a flat rate of $4.95 by calling (888) 362-8668.

For the nearest passport agency office or U.S. Post Office authorized to accept passport applications, check the government listings in your local telephone directory under passport services or U.S. Department of State. Further details are available in Chapter 35.

Internet Service
Like the INS, the DOS Bureau of Consular Affairs operates a website on the internet. It may be found at: http://travel.state.gov.

Department of Labor (DOL)

Forms
Forms may be obtained by calling (202) 219-4369.

Internet Service
The U.S. Department of Labor also operates an internet website. It contains a great deal of information on a variety of labor-related subjects with emphasis on the Employment and Training Administration. Not all the information offered is still valid. The DOL may be found on the internet at http://www.doleta.gov.

Federal Information Center

If you need information about these and other U.S. Government departments or agencies, help is available in most major centers by calling the Federal Information Center at (800) 688-9889. Recorded messages are available 24 hours a day, seven days a week and are updated frequently.

Information specialists may be reached between 9 am and 8 pm Eastern time, Monday though Friday. The specially trained staff will answer your question or direct you to a person with the answer in the U.S. Federal government.

Information is available on:
- Federal taxes
- Federal jobs
- Social Security
- Veterans' benefits
- Sales of property or goods offered by the Federal Government
- Copyright, patent, trademark information
- Government publications
- Federal Communications Commission services, rules and regulations
- Government travel information
  - passports
  - visas
  - travel per diem rates.
- Department of State document authentication services
- Selective Service system
- Savings bonds or default student loans

Other U.S. Government Agencies

The functions and responsibilities of the major U.S. government agencies involved in the post-immigration adjustment process are detailed in the chapters which follow in Book 2.

Book 2

Getting Settled

Adjusting to life in the United States

Book 2

Introduction

Book 2 of **USA Immigration & Orientation** is devoted to demystifying the process of getting settled in the United States. It will help you navigate through the social and administrative experiences which await you after clearing the immigration processes in Book 1.

As your American friends will tell you, life in the United States is both an adventure and a challenge. To assist you in getting adjusted to your new environment, **USA Immigration & Orientation** offers 17 chapters of orientation to a wide range of new social and governmental experiences.

Look for help on these and many other subjects as you settle into your new American home.

Part I - Governmental Procedures

Both the federal and state levels of government have rules to be learned and procedures to be followed.

On the federal side, look for insight into:

- U.S. Customs
- Social Security
- Selective Service

At the state level, read about:

- Automobile ownership
- Driving privileges and responsibilities
- Employee's benefits and obligations

Part II - Finance

Part II includes some tips on the financial side of setting up a new life in the U.S.

The tax system is complex and requires study to take full advantage of your financial position.

Purchasing and financing a home may involve learning a whole new language. Definitions and detailed explanations are provided for the following terms plus many more awaiting the home buyer in the United States:

- Title insurance
- PITI
- Recording fees
- Loan origination fee
- Points

The chapter on banking offers many tips including:

- The legal transfer of funds into the United States
- How to establish your credit rating
- Where to store your valuables

Part III - Insurance

Insurance is a major consideration.

Health insurance can be a big surprise when you find that there is no national government plan to take care of your health needs. To give you a better idea of how the U.S. health care system works, Chapter 29 describes your many options in detail.

Read about a variety of health insurance programs including:

- Medicare
- Medigap
- Managed Health Care
- Fee-for-Service
- Health insurance for expatriates

Home and automobile insurance will also be a necessity. Explanations and definitions are provided for the many new terms you will encounter.

Part IV - Community

A school may be one of the first organizations an alien will encounter in the community. Look for information on:

- Documents needed to register your child in school
- How long a foreign student may attend a public elementary school

Almost every community has a mind-boggling choice of organizations which, when joined, can speed the orientation process.

The institution of marriage is also introduced in chapter 33.

Part V - Post-Naturalization Rights and Responsibilities

Part V offers some insight into the benefits which become available after naturalization such as:

- Who may vote and who must not
- How and where to obtain a passport

Part I

Governmental Procedures

After clearing the formal steps involved with the Departments of Labor, State and Justice, as a newly arrived alien, you still may be faced with a bewildering list of lessons to learn and agencies to satisfy.

Part I of Book 2 offers an in-depth study of the rules and roles of several of the agencies you are likely to encounter and what each expects of you. The following five chapters include information on:

Chapter 19 — U.S. Customs Service
* What you may and may not bring in to the country

Chapter 20 — Social Security
* Who participates
* How to obtain a Social Security Card

Chapter 21 — Selective Service
* Who must register and when

Chapter 22 — Buying or Leasing a Car - License - Registration
* Is leasing a car more economical than buying

Chapter 23 — Employment Benefits and Compensation
* What an employee can expect

Chapter 19

U. S. Customs Service

T he U.S. Customs Service is responsible for the assessment and collection of duties, taxes, and fees on all merchandise entering the United States at ports of entry and along the land and sea borders. In addition to its own laws, Customs also enforces the entry regulations of many other government agencies such as the Environmental Protection Agency, Department of Transportation, Department of Agriculture and Food and Drug Administration.

At the port of entry, you may be interviewed initially by an Immigration (white shirt) or Customs (blue shirt) officer. Make sure to note which agency you are dealing with if there is a problem or if additional contact with either agency is necessary.

Customs randomly selects individuals for inspections to ensure compliance with U.S. laws. Title 19, Section 1582 of the United States Code authorizes Customs Officers to search, inspect, and/or examine all persons, luggage, and merchandise entering the United States from a foreign country. Trained search dogs may assist the officers.

Customs and Immigration officials recommend that you allow sufficient time for clearance and that you have all necessary documents ready for inspection before you approach the officer.

All imported goods are subject to duty unless exempted by law. Certain exemptions are also provided to allow persons moving to the United States, either permanently or temporarily, to bring their personal and household effects.

There is no limit to the amount of money that may be brought into or taken out of the United States. However, if you bring in or take out more than $10,000 in negotiable funds, you must file a Form 4790 with U.S. Customs. Failure to do so can result in civil or criminal penalties. This does not include bank checks, travelers checks or money orders made payable to a named person if they are not endorsed.

When moving to the United States, Customs recommends that you make a list of all furnishings that you are taking into the country, including all items shipped inside a piece of furniture such as in a cabinet. If you send personal goods by commercial movers, fill out a Customs Form 3299, Declaration for Free Entry of Unaccompanied Articles.

Before entering the United States as an immigrant you may find it helpful to contact Customs at your intended point of entry to determine well in advance what the regulations and procedures are.

Automobiles

There is no duty on a car being imported as part of a permanent visa holder's belongings. Information is at http://www.customs.treas.gov/imp-exp2/informal/car.htm.

Be aware that you may have to pay a sales tax on the car when you register it in your new home state. A federal gas-guzzler tax may also be due on certain automobiles over 6,000 lbs that have a low miles-per-gallon rating. There is also an excise tax (luxury tax) of 9 percent on any car over $34,000 but that tax is being phased out by 1 percent each January 1 until it reaches 3 percent in 2002. Then, in 2003, it will be gone altogether.

All imported automobiles must conform to Environmental Protection Agency (EPA) emission requirements and Department of Transport (DOT) safety and bumper standards. Individual state emission requirements, such as are found in California, may exceed those of the federal government. Both federal and state government rules must be satisfied. For more information see http://www.epa.gov/OMSWWW/omshome.htm and http://www.nhtsa.dot.gov/cars/rules/import.

As a legal nonimmigrant, you may import a vehicle duty-free for personal use if the vehicle is imported in conjunction with your arrival. However, it would be dutiable if sold within one year of importation.

A vehicle imported by a legal nonimmigrant for personal use may not need to conform to emission or safety requirements but it must be exported within one year and it must not be sold in the United States.

Many automobiles purchased overseas are not manufactured to comply with U.S. standards and require modification. Both the Department of Transportation and the Environmental Protection Agency advise that although a non-conforming car may be conditionally admitted, the modifications required to bring it into compliance may be so extensive and costly that it may be impractical or impossible to achieve such compliance. You should investigate the procedure and necessary modifications before considering importation.

For the latest information about importing vehicles contact:

U.S. Environmental Protection Agency
Manufacturers Operations Division 6405-J
Investigation/Imports Section
401 M Street S.W.
Washington, D.C. 20460
Phone: (202) 564-9660
Fax: (202) 564-9596

Department of Transportation
Office of Vehicle Safety Compliance (NEF-32)
400 7th Street S.W.
Washington, D.C. 20590
Phone: (202) 366-5313
Fax: (202) 366-1024

Drugs

If you require any medicines containing habit-forming drugs or narcotics (such as cough medicines, diuretics, heart drugs, tranquilizers, sleeping pills, anti-depressants, stimulants), you should:

- Have all medicines and similar products properly identified
- Carry only such quantity as might normally be carried by an individual having a health problem
- Have either a prescription or written statement from your personal physician saying that the medicines are necessary for physical well-being.

The Food and Drug Administration prohibits the importation, by mail or in person, of fraudulent or misbranded prescription and non-prescription drugs and medical devices. These may include unorthodox "cures" for medical conditions. However, the FDA may consider allowing a three-month supply of unapproved new drugs into the country for a serious condition for which effective treatment may not be available domestically, if the product is not considered to represent an unreasonable risk, the patient provides the name and address of the U.S. licensed doctor responsible for the treatment or evidence that treatment began in a foreign country.

Congress approved an amendment to the Controlled Substances Act. This amendment allows a U.S. resident to import up to 50 dosage units of a controlled medication without a valid prescription at an international land border. These medications must be declared upon arrival, be for the person's own use and in their original container. Ref: 21 USC 956(a)

For additional information, contact the nearest FDA office or:

Food and Drug Administration
Division of Import Operations and Policy
Room 12-8 (HFC-170)
5600 Fishers Lane
Rockville, MD 20857
Phone: (301) 443-6553
Fax: (301) 594-0413
http://www.customs.gov/travel/med.htm

Pets

There are controls, restrictions, and prohibitions on entry of animals, birds, turtles, and wildlife.

Endangered species and products made from them are generally prohibited from being imported or exported. This list includes ivory, some animal skins, and whale bone.

For information, contact:

> U.S. Fish and Wildlife Service
> Office of Management Authority
> Department of the Interior
> 4401 N. Fairfax Drive
> Arlington, VA 22203
> Phone: (800) 358-2104
>   (703) 358-2093
> Fax: (703) 358-2281
> http://www.fws.gov

The importation of dogs and cats is regulated by the U.S. Department of Health and Human Services, Center for Disease Control (CDC) in Atlanta, Georgia. In general, cats and dogs must be free of evidence of diseases communicable to man, and dogs must have a health certificate showing that they have been vaccinated for rabies if they come from a country where rabies occurs. This vaccination must have been given at least 30 days, and not more than a year, before the travel date.

For more information and a list of rabies-free areas contact:

> Quarantine Division
> Center for Disease Control
> Atlanta, GA 30333
> Phone: (404) 639-8107
> http://www.cdc.gov/ncidod/dq

Personally-owned pet birds may be entered (limit of two if of the psittacine family), but APHIS (Animal and Plant Health Inspection Service) and Public Health Service requirements must be met, which could include quarantine at an APHIS facility at specified locations, at the owner's expense (approx. $200 per bird per 30 days). Advance reservations are required.

A pet bird coming to the United States from Canada is exempt from quarantine requirements but arrangements must be made for a veterinary inspection at a USDA-designated port of entry. For information call (301) 734-5097.

Non-human primates such as monkeys, apes and similar animals may not be imported as pets.

Check with state, county and municipal authorities about any restrictions and prohibitions before importing a pet.

Hours of service and availability of inspectors will vary from port to port. You are encouraged to check with your anticipated port of entry prior to importing a pet, to be sure it will arrive when the necessary staff are on duty to process it.

For information, contact:

> U.S. Department of Agriculture
> Animal & Plant Health Inspection Service
> 4700 River Road
> Riverdale, MD 20737-1231
> Phone: (301) 734-7830
> http://www.aphis.usda.gov/oa/imexdir.html

Agricultural Items

All agricultural and food items brought into the U.S. must be declared to prevent the entry of pests or crop disease.

Plants, cuttings, seeds, unprocessed plant products and certain endangered species either require an import permit or are prohibited from entering the United States. For information contact:

> U.S. Department of Agriculture
> Plant Health Inspection Service - PPQ
> 4700 River Road, Unit 136
> Riverdale, MD 20737
> Phone: (301) 734-8645
> http://www.aphis.usda.gov/ppq
> http://www.aphis.usda.gov/oa/new/pe.html

Foods

Meats, livestock, poultry and their by-products (such as ham, frankfurters sausage, paté), are either prohibited or restricted from entering the United States, depending on the animal disease condition in the country of origin. Fresh meat is generally prohibited from most countries. Canned meat is permitted if the inspector can determine that it is commercially canned, cooked in the container, hermetically sealed, and can be kept without refrigeration. Canned, cured, or dried meat from most countries is severely restricted.

For information, contact:

>U.S. Department of Agriculture
>Animal and Plant Health Inspection Service - VS
>4700 River Road
>Riverdale, MD 20737-1231
>Phone: (301) 734-8590
>   (301) 734-7834 (Meat and poultry)
>   (301) 734-4401 (Animal products)
>   http://www.aphis.usda.gov/travel/index.html

>Food Safety and Inspection Service
>Import Inspection Division
>Franklin Court
>1099 14th Street, N.W.
>Washington, D.C. 20005
>Phone: (202) 501-7515
>http://www.fsis.usda.gov

"Duty-Free" Shops

Articles bought in "duty-free" shops in foreign countries are free of duty and taxes only for the country in which that shop is located. The articles are intended for export and are not to be returned to the country of purchase. When brought into the United States, they are subject to U.S. customs duty and restrictions but may be included in a personal exemption.

Articles bought in American duty-free shops are subject to customs duty and IRS tax if reentered into the United States.

For further **U.S. Customs** information, contact:

>Department of the Treasury
>U.S. Customs Service
>Washington, DC 20229
>Phone: (202) 927-6724
>http://www.customs.gov

In the United States, you will find Customs listed in the "U.S. Government" section of the local telephone directory under the "Treasury Department" listing.

Chapter 20

Social Security

In 1935, President Roosevelt signed the original Social Security Act into law. The program now covers more than 141 million workers.

Social Security Concept

Employees and employers pay taxes into the system during the employees' working years and employees and members of their families receive monthly benefits when the employee retires or becomes disabled. Survivors also collect benefits upon the employee's death. Social Security is meant to supplement pensions, insurance, savings, and other investments.

Those born before 1938 will be eligible for full Social Security benefits at age 65. However, beginning in the year 2003, the age at which full benefits are payable, will increase in gradual steps from 65 to 67.

Reduced benefits are available as early as age 62, while credit is given to people who delay retirement.

No benefits are payable to anyone illegally present in the United States.

Social Security Tax

Social Security taxes are also used to pay part of Medicare coverage.

The 2000 Social Security tax rate, for employees and employers, would be 7.65 percent each on wages up to $76,200. Of that rate, 6.2 percent pays for Social Security benefits and 1.45 percent finances Medicare's hospital insurance program.

The payroll deduction may be labeled "FICA" on a pay slip. FICA is the Federal Insurance Contributions Act, the law that authorized the Social Security payroll tax.

In 2000, an employee would earn one credit for each $780 in earnings up to a maximum of four credits per year. Most people need 40 credits (10 years of work) to qualify for benefits.

The self-employed pay 15.3 percent of taxable income into Social Security, up to $76,200. Those earning more than $76,200 in 2000 would continue to pay 2.9 percent for the Medicare portion of the Social Security tax on the rest of their earnings.

Social Security Number

The Social Security number is used to track earnings during working days and to track benefits once Social Security checks begin.

In addition to its official uses, some businesses and government agencies use the number for record keeping purposes.

The nine-digit Social Security number is divided into three parts. The first three numbers generally indicate the state of residence at the time a person applies for the first card. The middle two digits have no special significance and the last four represent a straight numerical progression of assigned numbers.

Social Security Card

Social Security services are free. To obtain a card, an application must be filed at the local Social Security office. The card will be mailed to the applicant.

Three types of Social Security cards are issued.

One has been issued since 1935 and shows the person's name and Social Security number and lets a person work without restriction. It is issued to U.S. citizens and permanent resident aliens.

Green card holders applying for a Social Security card should make sure that the Social Security agent who accepts the application puts a "Y" in the box marked PRA (Permanent Resident Alien). This should ensure that they issue a Social Security card without restriction. If the agent is not familiar with this box, the authority comes from the *Social Security POMS Manual RM00203.570C.2B*.

Social Security began issuing a second type of card in 1992. It shows the words, "VALID FOR WORK ONLY WITH INS AUTHORIZATION" and is issued to people who are admitted to the U.S. on a temporary basis and who require INS authorization to work.

The third type of card shows the words, "NOT VALID FOR EMPLOYMENT". Social Security assigns it to people from other countries who are admitted to the United States on a temporary, non-working basis.

Lawfully admitted aliens with permission to work in the U.S. need a Social Security number and should take their INS documents to the local Social Security office to apply.

Lawfully admitted aliens without permission to work who need a Social Security number must provide original documents showing age, identity and lawful alien status. They must also provide a letter from the government agency that requires the alien's Social Security number. The letter must be on letterhead stationery (no form letters or copies). The letter must identify the alien as the applicant, cite the law requiring a Social Security number and indicate that the alien meets all the agency's requirements, except having the Social Security number.

If an alien is assigned a Social Security number for non-work purposes, he or she cannot use it to work. If the alien does use it to work, the Social Security Administration may inform the INS.

Schools are not authorized to use students' Social Security numbers and will assign internal numbers. A student applying for the SAT, ACT, GRE or other tests does not need a Social Security number to take the test.

The Social Security Administration no longer assigns non-work numbers to aliens who request them for banking, income tax or monetary transaction purposes. The Internal Revenue Service assigns individual taxpayer identification numbers (ITIN) for tax purposes to non-citizens who do not qualify for Social Security numbers.

Aliens who need individual taxpayer identification numbers may request IRS Form W-7 from the local IRS office or write to IRS, Philadelphia Service Center, ITIN Unit, P.O. Box 447, Bensalem, PA 19020 or call (800) 829-3676.

Supplemental Security Income (SSI)

SSI is run by Social Security but is financed by U.S. Treasury tax revenues. Generally, monthly checks are paid to qualified people who have low income and few assets and are:

- Age 65 or older, or
- Blind, or
- Disabled
- Living in the U.S. or on the Northern Mariana Islands
- A U.S. citizen
- Certain noncitizens in the U.S. or receiving SSI on August 22, 1996, or
- Certain refugee or asylee-type noncitizens during first seven years, or
- Lawful permanent resident with 40 work credits, or
- Certain noncitizens with a military service connection, or
- Certain American indians

Local Social Security offices determine SSI eligibility.

Local social services or public welfare offices have information about all the services available in the community. Some non-profit agencies may provide assistance without regard to citizenship.

Household Workers

In 2000, a household worker would earn Social Security credit only for wages of at least $1,100 from any single employer.

The employer should deduct Social Security and Medicare taxes from the wages, pay the taxes to the Internal Revenue Service, and report the wages to the Social Security Administration. If these wages are not reported, there may not be enough credit for the employee's benefits, or the benefits may be less.

Earnings for household workers (such as baby sitters) under age 18 are exempt from the Social Security tax unless household employment is the worker's primary occupation.

Social Security and Visas

Neither Social Security nor Medicare taxes apply to students in F, J, or M status or International Cultural Exchange Visitors in Q status. Form 843 may be filed for a refund of FICA (Social Security tax) collected while on a student visa. However, Social Security Tax does apply to H-1 visa holders.

Social Security Benefits Outside The United States

It is not necessary to reside in the United States or to have a U.S. visa to receive benefits. A Social Security benefit can be paid at age 65 to any person who has paid the required amount of Social Security tax each year for at least 10 years.

A person who maintains Permanent Residence for 10 years, then leaves the U.S. and abandons Permanent Resident status, may still be eligible for a Social Security retirement benefit. For more information, refer to the Social Security pamphlet, "Your Social Security Checks While You are Outside the United States".

Reciprocal Agreement between U.S. and Canada

On August 1, 1984, an Agreement on Social Security between the U.S. and Canada went into effect to help protect people who:

- Work or have worked in both countries
- Would not be eligible for monthly retirement, disability, or survivor's benefits under the Social Security System of one or both countries
- Have earned Canadian Social Security credits based on residence in Canada
- Would otherwise be required to pay Social Security taxes to both countries for the same work

The agreement covers retirement, disability, and survivors insurance benefits. However, it does not cover benefits under the U.S. Medicare program or the Supplemental Security Income (SSI) program. For Canada, the agreement applies to both the Old-Age Security program and the Canada Pension Plan. Each country pays its own benefits.

A certificate of coverage issued by one country now serves as proof of exemption from Social Security taxes on the same earnings in the other country. Generally, a certificate is needed only if employment lasts more than 183 days in a calendar year.

Totalization

Under the 1984 reciprocal agreement, the concept of totalization, or combining Social Security credits from both countries, was introduced. It enables immigrants from Canada and the United States to combine Social Security credits from both countries. An immigrant from Canada who has a minimum amount of U.S. credit can transfer his credits from the Canadian system in order to build up enough credits to qualify for U.S. Social Security benefits. In the reverse situation, a U.S. immigrant to Canada may also use credits from both countries to meet the eligibility requirements for Canadian Social Security benefits.

To be eligible to combine U.S. and Canadian credits, it is necessary to have earned a minimum of six credits (one and a half years) in the U.S. or one year in Canada provided that all the basic requirements under one country's system are met.

For a U.S. worker, a benefit is determined based on U.S. earnings as if the entire career had been completed under the U.S. system. This initial benefit is then reduced or discounted because some of the credits were transferred from the Canadian system. The amount of that reduction depends on the number of U.S. credits: the more U.S. credits, the smaller the reduction; and the fewer U.S. credits, the larger the reduction.

There are different ways to obtain U.S. and/or Canadian benefits including:
- Regular benefits from both countries (without combining credits).
- Regular benefits from one country (without combining credits) plus totalization benefits from the other country (with combined credits).
- Totalization benefits from both countries (by combining credits if you do not have enough credits in either country to get a benefit).
- Regular or totalization benefits from one country and no benefits from the other country.

Actual benefit entitlement depends on work history and meeting all the basic requirements of both systems.

Application

Application for benefits under this agreement may be made in the U.S. or Canada.

If this is your first application for U.S. benefits, it may be necessary to submit certain proofs including:

- U.S. Social Security and Canadian Social Insurance numbers
- Proof of age
- Evidence of U.S. earnings in the past 24 months
- Information about coverage under the Canadian system

Further information may be obtained from either:

Social Security Administration
Office of International Policy
P.O. Box 17741
Baltimore, MD 21235

Department of National Health and Welfare
Income Security Programs
International Operations Directorate
Ottawa, ON Canada K1A 0L4.   *Ref: SSA Pub. 05-10198, Rev. June, 1996*

Pamphlets Available

- Social Security - Understanding the Benefits
  (SSA Publication # 05-10024)
- Your Social Security Checks While You Are Outside The United States
  (SSA Publication # 05-10137)
- Agreement on Social Security Between The U.S. and Canada
  (SSA Publication # 05-10198)
- When You Get Social Security Retirement or Survivors Benefits
  (SSA Publication # 05-10077)
- SSI - Supplemental Security Income
  (SSA Publication # 05-11000)
- Social Security - How You Earn Credits
  (SSA Publication # 05-10072)
- Survivors
  (SSA Publication # 05-10084)
- Social Security For Newborns
  (SSA Publication # 05-10023)
- If You're Self-Employed
  (SSA Publication # 05-10022)

The above pamphlets may be found at any local Social Security office or ordered by calling (800) 772-1213. You may speak to a representative at that number any business day from 7:00 am to 7:00 pm, Eastern Time. Social Security information is also available to users of the Internet: http://www.ssa.gov.

Chapter 21

Selective Service

The Selective Service System is a government agency which will provide personnel for the Armed Forces in the event of a national emergency.

Conscription

Compulsory enrollment into the armed forces is termed conscription.

Congress passed the Selective Service Act in 1948, thus instituting a peacetime form of conscription in order to maintain the strength of the armed forces. Since 1973, with the beginning of the All Volunteer Force, it has been in a "standby" position. The purpose of registration is to allow immediate response in time of war or national emergency.

Legal penalties may apply to those who fail to register. Conviction of this felony may result in imprisonment for up to five years and/or fines of not more than $250,000.

Registration Requirements

All male U.S. citizens, permanent resident aliens, dual national U.S. citizens, refugees, parolees and asylee aliens and undocumented (illegal) aliens are required by law to register with the Selective Service System within 30 days of their 18th birthday or after their arrival in the USA. No one may register after age 26.

The INS sends a tape of all new Green Card holders to Selective Service so that they may send a letter to males between 18 and 26. All males in this age group must register with Selective Service.

When a male applies to become a U.S. citizen after five years as a Green Card holder, he must provide proof, during his naturalization interview, that he has registered with Selective Service. Otherwise, he risks citizenship delays or denials. A non-registrant must show substantial evidence that he did not knowingly and purposely fail to register.

If a male did not register and is now 26 or older, he may be denied eligibility for such benefits as Federal student financial aid, Federal job training or Federal employment. He should explain to the official handling his case the reasons for failure to register.

Males are not required to register with Selective Service while they are:

- Members of the Armed Forces on active duty
- Students at certain military schools
- Lawfully admitted aliens in nonimmigrant status
- Diplomatic and consulate personnel (including their families)
- Foreign students in valid student status
- Tourists with unexpired visas or border crossing documents
- Special agricultural workers with I-688A documents
- Incarcerated
- Hospitalized or institutionalized for medical reasons

Upon being released from an institution or the armed forces, a man must register within 30 days or before reaching age 26, whichever is earlier.

For women to be required to register for Selective Service, Congress would have to amend the law which now refers to "male persons". Currently, women are excluded from the draft by the Department of Defense and by policy from front line combat.

Currently aliens cannot volunteer for the military unless they have permanent resident alien status.

Registration Procedure

Eligible males may register by picking up a SSS Form 1M at any U.S. Post Office and mailing the completed form to Selective Service for processing.

U.S. citizens and Green Card holders living or visiting overseas at the time they are required to register, should do so at the nearest U.S. Embassy or Consulate office.

Registration may also be carried out online at http://www.sss.gov.

The registrant should receive a Registration Acknowledgment within 90 days and keep it as evidence of his registration. He must report any change in registration information. This includes legal name, mailing address, phone number, and so on.

Changes may be reported on the Correction/Change of Information Form (SSS Form 3B) provided with the Registration Acknowledgment or on a preaddressed Change of Information Form (SSS Form 2) available at any U.S. Post Office, U.S. Embassy or U.S. Consulate.

Military Inductions

Because there have been no induction draft orders issued since 1973, there are no classifications of eligibility for registrants or local boards who deal with claims for reclassification or postponement. The only requirement is registration.

Should the President and Congress authorize inductions into military service, the Secretary of Defense will request men for the Armed Forces. Selective Service will:

- Conduct a lottery to determine the order of selecting registrants for induction beginning with men whose 20th birthday falls within the calendar year
- Assign each registrant the Random Sequence Number (RSN) drawn by lottery for his date of birth
- Select and order registrants for examination and induction beginning with RSN 1

Postponement or Reclassification

Should a registrant be ordered to report for induction, he must either report or file a claim for postponement or reclassification.

An alien whose other country of nationality has a reciprocal agreement with the U.S. may be exempt from induction or receive credit for military service in that country.

An alien or dual national who has served on active duty in certain countries may qualify for reclassification with the proper documentation. He should first check all regulations with Selective Service to be sure that reclassification is in his best interests.

A word of warning to aliens who are nationals of certain countries. It is important to understand that, if an application for exemption from military training and service in the U.S. Armed Forces is granted, the registrant will be classified as a Treaty Alien and will henceforth be barred from U.S. citizenship.

Ref: SSS, Information For Registrants Oct 1988, Part II, Section B,
Classifications, 14

For further information, contact:
Selective Service System
Registration Information Office
P.O. Box 94638
Palatine, IL 60094-4638
Phone: (847) 688-6888 (an operator comes on line at the end of the menu)
http://www.sss.gov

Chapter 22

Buying or Leasing a Car - License & Registration

If you like to negotiate, you'll love buying or leasing a car. Increasing numbers of dealers have set prices with no room to negotiate. However, most expect a battle of wits.

Buying a Car

Buying a car requires plenty of time to do research. Libraries have magazines like Motor Trend and Consumer Reports. Also, there is help at: www.intellichoice.com, www.autoconnect.com, www.nhtsa.dot.gov, www.cars.com and www.kbb.com.

Satisfied car buyers recommend that you know as much as possible about the vehicle you are buying beforehand. Try to determine the dealer's costs for the vehicle and options and how much room you have for bargaining.

It is also recommended that you talk to drivers of that model and find out how satisfied they are.

If you have a car to trade in, figure out from buyer's guides, what it should be worth before haggling with the dealer. Most of the dealers' profits are said to come from used car sales rather than new, so obviously it is in their best interest to offer you less than the car may be worth.

The Federal Trade Commission advises that you read an advertised special carefully and call or visit the dealer to find out about all the terms and conditions of the offer. While these advertisements may help you shop, finding the best deal requires careful comparison among several dealers.

Experts say you should first negotiate the price of the car; second, discuss the financing; third, discuss the value of your trade in. Keep each deal separate. Before signing, be sure that you really want any of the dealer's high profit add-ons such as extended warranties and service contracts.

Because new cars are so expensive, the demand for used cars has increased greatly as have their prices. The steepest rate of depreciation occurs in the first two years of a car's life (approximately 50 percent). It then levels off considerably.

Buying a used car from a private individual is usually less expensive than from a dealer. However, the dealer may provide service and support afterward. You will have to decide whether cost or service is more important.

Car Loan

If you are planning to buy a car, chances are you will need a loan. Car dealers will do anything they can to make sure you get financing. However, the loan they find for you might not be the best one available. You should first check on loans from such sources as credit unions (you must be a member), financial institutions and loan companies.

Leasing a Car

Some people find that leasing a new or used car is preferable to investing a large amount of money into buying one. You do not own the leased vehicle. Instead, a lease grants you the right to use the vehicle for a fixed period of time. Your lease payments cover the cost of the vehicle's depreciation over the length of the term of the lease instead of the actual purchase price.

The short term costs are lower. However, if you want to keep a car for five to ten years, leasing can cost more in the long term. Also, if you drive many miles per year (over 15,000), leasing may not be a good option as you have to pay extra (approximately 10-15 cents per mile) when you exceed the mileage limit.

Leasing may enable you to drive a more expensive car than you can afford to own. If used for business purposes, leasing offers a greater tax write-off than owning.

You can pay for the use of the car for 24 to 60 months, then return it to the dealer and lease a new model. The lease may include an option to purchase the car at the end of that period. However, leasing could end up being more expensive than financing in that case.

Read the fine print and find out any hidden costs. There are many details you should understand before signing the lease. They include:
- Monthly payment amounts and how they are calculated
- Retail price of the car
- Security deposit
- Down payment
- Lease fee
- Fee if payment is late
- Fee for early termination of the lease

- Mileage limit
- Price per mile over limit
- Purchase option at end of lease
- Warranties
- Definition of wear and tear to know how much is considered normal
- Permission for transferring the lease to someone else
- Sales and use tax
- Acquisition Fee - charges for preparation of car and the lease
- Disposition Fee - charges for preparing the car for resale at end of lease
- Residual Value - projected value of vehicle at end of lease

You are responsible for adequate automobile insurance and regular mechanical maintenance whether you lease or buy.

Experts recommend that you negotiate the price of the vehicle before negotiating a lease agreement. Some components of the lease may be negotiable. Shop around and be sure to compare leases on the same model of vehicle with the same options. A good leasing agent will explain all the components of the lease and answer questions.

Used lease cars are available and provide another option for purchasing a vehicle.

Driver's License

You must have a driver's license in order to legally drive a motor vehicle on public streets or highways. You will need a commercial license in order to drive a commercial vehicle such as a truck or bus.

If you are a temporary resident, you may not be required to get a new license if you have a valid one from another state or country.

It is a good idea to check with the driver's and motor vehicle license offices to find out the rules of your state. If a new license is needed, ask what documents and fees they expect from applicants. Also ask what method of payment they require. Also, if you have an out-of-state driver's license, be prepared to give it up in exchange for the new license.

The driver's license office should have a handbook available showing safe driving tips and rules of the roads in your state.

The driving examination may include any or all of the following: vision and hearing tests, written test on traffic rules, road sign identification, vehicle inspection and a driving test.

When applying for a license for the first time, you must show proof of registering your vehicle in the state. You may also be required to complete a traffic law and substance abuse education course before you will be issued a license.

Before you learn to drive, you must take a test for a restricted license (learner's license). The restrictions may include driving during daylight hours only and having a licensed driver at least 18 years old (21 in some states) sit to the right of the driver.

In an attempt to reduce the rate of teen driving deaths, many states are introducing graduated licensing. Teens must take driver's education courses at school or through a private company. Then, by working their way through the levels of requirements, by age 17, they may be eligible for an unrestricted license. However, they must have passed all the courses and tests, completed the hours of supervised driving and be accident- and violation-free for a specified period.

At least one state (Florida) demands that persons who are 15 to 17 years of age show proof of school enrollment from the school administration office or proof of graduation from high school. Those who drop out of school before becoming 18 or graduating, will have their license suspended.

Illegal Aliens and Driver's Licenses

Within six months of its enactment, The Immigration Act of 1996 requests the states to begin conducting pilot programs to determine the viability, advisability, and cost-effectiveness of denying driver's licenses to aliens who are not lawfully present in the United States.   Ref: IIRIA96.502

Jury Duty

In some areas, jurors will be randomly selected from a list provided by the driver's license office. However, only U.S. citizens may serve as jurors.

Car Registration

A vehicle must be registered and licensed in the state of residence. The cost of the license plate may depend on the age, type, weight or cost of the car, depending on state law. The vehicle must always have a current license plate and the driver must always have the registration in the vehicle. Some states also collect a yearly tax of as much as several hundred dollars. In addition, many states require that all vehicles have an annual inspection.

Any car imported to the United States must meet the U.S. highway safety and emission standards. Research should be done in advance if contemplating importing a car. (See Customs Procedures, chapter 19)

Chapter 23

Employment Benefits and Compensation

T he various levels of government ensure that there are uniform standards of benefits available to employees in the United States. This chapter provides a cursory overview of some of the more important aspects.

Minimum Wage

A bill, passed by Congress on August 2, 1996, raised the minimum wage from $4.25 an hour to $4.75, effective October 1, 1996 and to $5.15 on September 1, 1997.

Workers who receive tips still receive a minimum of $2.13 an hour. The employer must pay more if the employees don't collect enough tips to earn the minimum wage. The "training wage" for the first 90 days on the job remains at $4.25 for employees younger than 20.

Legal Public Holidays

The following are legal holidays for federal government employees. Private businesses may vary in which of these holidays they observe.

New Year's Day	January 1
Birthday of Martin Luther King, Jr.	Third Monday in January
Presidents Day	Third Monday in February
Memorial Day	Last Monday in May
Independence Day	July 4
Labor Day	First Monday in September
Columbus Day	Second Monday in October
Veterans Day	November 11
Thanksgiving Day	Fourth Thursday in November
Christmas Day	December 25

Vacations

Many businesses allow an employee at least a week's paid vacation after a year of employment. The vacation entitlement generally increases slowly over the years to a set maximum, while the employee remains with the company. Vacation time tends to be shorter in the United States than in many other countries.

Health Insurance

Employers generally pay all or part of health insurance premiums for their employees. More information on health insurance options may be found in Chapter 29.

Social Security

Employers and employees share the payments to Social Security. See chapter 20.

Unemployment Insurance

Unemployment insurance is temporary income for eligible workers who become unemployed through no fault of their own and who are ready, willing, able to work and have built up sufficient weeks of credit and wages in previous covered employment.

An employer must provide unemployment insurance coverage for most types of work. This takes the form of a separate employer-paid tax which is used to pay for the employee's benefits.

To be eligible for unemployment benefits, you must be available for work and actively seeking employment while you are claiming benefits. You must keep a written record of all your efforts to find employment.

You should file a claim for unemployment insurance benefits in person at your local Department of Labor office which accepts claims. You will need to take a valid original Social Security card, a second form of identification with your signature and photograph on it and a copy of your Record of Employment which should be given to you by your employer.

Worker's Compensation

The employer pays into this state fund and the benefits are for workers who have suffered a work-related injury.

Disability Insurance

These policies are designed to replace a portion or all of your income if you become disabled and cannot work. The level of coverage depends on the plan and premium.

Welfare

The U.S. welfare bill, signed by President Clinton in August of 1996 and effective June, 1997, set a lifetime limit of five years of welfare for a family. Welfare recipients are required to find work within two years.

Food stamp funding is reduced and Medicaid will be denied to adults who lose welfare by refusing to work. States may provide education assistance for those lacking a suitable background for work.

As a result of the welfare reform as well as the immigration act of 1996, Supplemental Security Income (SSI), housing assistance and food stamps are restricted for most people who are not U.S. citizens. Illegal immigrants are ineligible for a wide range of public benefits.

However, according to USA Today of July 30, 1997, disability and Medicaid benefits are restored to legal immigrants. Provisions in the new budget allow disabled and elderly noncitizens already on SSI or Medicaid to continue to receive payments. Immigrants who were in the United States when the welfare law was signed in August, 1996, will be eligible for SSI if they become disabled in the future.

On June 23, 1998, President Clinton signed a bill to restore food stamp benefits to immigrants who lawfully resided in the USA as of August 22, 1996 who are at least 65 years of age or disabled or under 18 years of age.

Pensions

In recent years, 401(k) savings plans are being offered by many employers. They provide separate tax-deferred accounts to which workers and sometimes their employers contribute. Employees make the investment choices and can take the proceeds with them if they leave. Still, many businesses offer no pensions at all and most of those that do, offer no portability.

Part II

Finance

Part II of Book 2 deals with the inescapable issue of money. As was the case in Part I, several agencies and institutions will be involved in your financial life when you settle in the United States.

USA Immigration & Orientation offers an introduction to these financial subjects. Much of the information contained in the following chapters may be new to you. In some cases, it is the terminology, in others it is the process or the obligation which is different from the way things are done back home. So, take a deep breath and read carefully. We hope you will come away with a better understanding of not only how things are done, but why.

The four chapters which follow deal with:

Chapter 24 — Taxation
- Some basic principals, advantages, and responsibilities of the U.S. tax system

Chapter 25 — Banking and Financial Transactions
- A brief introduction to U.S. banking and credit

Chapter 26 — Buying or Renting a Home
- An introduction to the process of buying or renting

Chapter 27 — Mortgages
- Home mortgage programs and terms

Chapter 24

Taxation

This chapter offers many basic financial principles which will give you some appreciation of the advantages and responsibilities of the U.S. tax system. It is advisable to consult a tax advisor for help in dealing with your particular case. You may also wish to contact the IRS at (215) 574-9900 for more information.

U.S. citizens and permanent resident aliens living in the United States are U.S. taxpayers and required to file U.S. income tax returns on their worldwide income. April 15 is the annual deadline for the filing of Form 1040, U.S. Individual Income Tax Return.

U.S. citizens who do not live in the United States on a full time basis, and some temporary resident aliens may not be required to file an annual return.

If you spend at least 122 days in the United States in a calendar year, you may have to file a 1040NR Non-Resident Income Tax return with:

Internal Revenue Service
Philadelphia, PA 19255

However, this may not be necessary if:

- You spend fewer than 183 days in the United States, and
- Can show a "closer connection" to your home country" than to the United States

To obtain a determination on your "closer connection" status, you must file IRS Form 8840 Closer Connection Exemption Statement with your answers to such questions as:

- The location of your personal belongings, furniture and bank organizations with which you are connected
- The country in which you are covered for "national" health care insurance
- Where your tax home is
- Whether you are being taxed as a resident

Some of the exemptions which may be available include:

- $250,000 in profits from the sale of an individual's residence ($500,000 for a couple) once every two years
- A general exemption from estate taxes by U.S. citizens equal to the first $675,000 (in 2000 and 2001) of net assets owned at the time of death. As a result of the 1997 budget, the individual exemption rises gradually to $1 Million after 2005. For couples, the exemption goes from $1.2 million to $2.6 million. Family businesses and farms could qualify for a $1.3 million exemption effective in 1998
- A general exemption from estate taxes by non-residents equal to the first $60,000 of net assets owned at the time of death
- A surviving non-U.S. citizen may be eligible for deferral of the tax if a Qualified Domestic Trust has been established with at least one U.S. citizen trustee or a domestic corporation

Other advantages include:

- Deferral until withdrawal of tax on interest earned on foreign investment such as Canadian RRSPs
- Deduction of mortgage interest and property taxes

Canadian Tax

Canadians who reside in the United States and are U.S. taxpayers, have 15 percent of their Canadian pensions withheld at the source. However, their Canada Pension Plan and Old Age Security payments are tax exempt in Canada but must be declared on their U.S. Income Tax return.

Because of the reciprocal nature of the U.S.-Canada Tax Treaty, a foreign tax credit may be claimed when filing the annual U.S. Income Tax return. This should greatly reduce the potential for double taxation.

Canadians who move to the United States and become U.S. taxpayers and even U.S. citizens are not automatically relieved of their obligation to pay full Canadian income tax on their world-wide income. The Canada Customs and Revenue Agency (CCRA), formerly called Revenue Canada, may make a unilateral determination that a person is still a Canadian resident for tax purposes many years after they have left Canada.

The following is only a partial list of "indicators", any combination of which, if retained in Canada, could point to Canadian residency and cause the CCRA to rule that a U.S. resident is still a Canadian resident for tax purposes:

Residence:	home, vacation property, mailing address, telephone
Family:	Canadian resident spouse, other family ties
Personal property:	clothing, furniture, automobile, boat, airplane
Financial:	bank and investment accounts, pension, credit cards
Legal documents:	provincial health card, driver's licence, will, burial plot
Formal contacts:	voter's list, business, directorship, professional affiliation

Ref: Tax Court decisions - Cited 95 DTC

The CCRA also considers the amount of time spent in Canada each year after departure. Some factors are weighted more heavily than others.

If an individual is deemed to be a resident of both countries then the CCRA applies a series of tiebreaker rules:

First: a permanent home	(available for use on trips to Canada)
Second: the individual's center of vital interests	(see indicators above)
Third: the individual's habitual abode	(time spent in Canada)
Fourth: the individual's citizenship	(Canadian or dual citizenship)

Ref: Canada-U.S. Tax Convention

If the residence of an individual cannot be determined by these tests, the competent authority of the countries will settle the question by mutual agreement.

To avoid the risk of continued Canadian taxation and legal costs, tax experts recommend that persons moving to the United States sever their ties to Canada before their official date of departure. Of particular importance is the sale of what has been their principal residence before the date of departure to a non-family buyer. The sale of a property in Canada after departure requires a CCRA clearance which could initiate a review of the seller's residency indicators and result in a demand by the CCRA for the filing of annual Canadian tax returns and payment of back taxes on world-wide income back to the date of departure. Also, because of the CCRA's couples in tandem' rule, it is important to ensure that both spouses sever their Canadian ties at the same time, before leaving.

Filing for a CCRA Determination of Residency Status when departing is the best way to obtain CCRA clearance. This filing requires detailed answers to the above list of indicators, and more.

If a Canadian return must be filed, at least a portion of the tax paid in Canada may be deducted from the U.S. return because of a reciprocal tax treaty. Nevertheless, the possibility of paying tax at a higher Canadian rate and some double taxation is a real possibility.

Chapter 25

Banking and Financial Transactions

B anking and financial transactions can, of course, be complicated and bewildering. This chapter will outline some of the more common monetary decisions you will be required to make.

Transfer of Funds from Outside the U.S.

Instant withdrawals from a foreign bank account may be made by using automated teller machines (ATMs) affiliated with Cirrus or The Plus. Depending on the nature of the foreign account and the limits on the U.S. ATM, you can usually bring in between $300 and $1,000 per day. You may be charged a transaction fee in either or both countries.

For larger amounts, your foreign bank can wire funds to a specific account in a U.S. bank or other financial institution. The money should be available within a day from many countries. There may be fees of $30-$65 at both ends. It may cost less if you are a customer of the bank.

A foreign bank may also prepare and mail a bank draft to your U.S. bank on a one time or on a regular basis. There is usually a fee at the foreign end with no guarantee when it will arrive.

Money orders from a foreign country drawn on a U.S. bank will clear much faster than those drawn on a foreign bank. Normally, you cannot withdraw that money until your bank has received the cleared funds.

Transfer of Funds for Real Estate Transactions

When buying real estate, you may avoid delays by determining well in advance in what form the closing agent wants the funds. An out-of-country cashier's check or money order could cause a delay in a real estate closing. Ask your bank how long it will take to clear funds from your home country. It simplifies the closing if the money is transferred and deposited into your U.S. bank account in advance so that it is cleared and available when needed.

Legal Entry of Funds to the United States

There is no limit to the amount of money which may be brought into or taken out of the country. However, if you receive, transfer or arrange the transfer of more than $10,000 (U.S. or foreign equivalent or combination) of **negotiable funds** on any occasion, you are to file a Form 4790 with U.S. Customs. This includes money in the following forms: coin, currency, traveler's checks, money orders, personal or cashier's checks, stocks or bonds. Failure to file the required report or to report the total amount may lead to seizure of all the money and may result in civil and criminal penalties.

Ref: 31 USC (1101, et seq.)

Withdrawal of Funds

If you withdraw or deposit a large amount at your bank, be prepared to explain why you are making the transaction. Banks are required, under federal law, to report all cash transactions over $10,000 to the Internal Revenue Service.

Bank Accounts

There are many types of accounts in which to deposit your money. For instance, some do not have fees but pay no interest. Others give you some interest and allow you to write a certain number of checks. In some accounts, a penalty is assessed if your monthly balance falls below a certain amount. There are also accounts with special privileges for seniors. Bank employees will help you select the kind most suitable for you.

Banks in United States are local, state or regional. Dealing with them may seem very slow or complicated if you are from a country with large national institutions. You may not be able to deposit funds electronically from one bank to an account in another branch of the same major U.S. bank in an adjoining state.

Do not be surprised if bank policy states that cash or other deposits, made after 2:00 pm, are not credited to your account until the next business day.

The Federal Deposit Insurance Corporation (FDIC) protects your deposits to a maximum of $100,000 per institution.

Becoming Known to Your Banker

You may be asked for photo identification when you go to a bank teller. Until they get to know you, they want to be sure they are not letting an imposter make transactions in your account. When you have become established at a bank, they can be very helpful with your financial affairs. While an automated tell machine (ATM) is convenient, you do not become known to bank employees.

Automatic Deposit/Withdrawal

Arrangements may be made with some employers to have all pay checks automatically deposited into your bank account.

You also may arrange with some businesses such as utilities and credit card companies to automatically withdraw the amount owing on their bills. They normally send the bill to you for your information before the money is withdrawn.

Check Cashing Fees

If you are not a customer of a bank and want to cash a check, be prepared for a check-cashing fee. In some cities they may also require fingerprinting on the back of the check. Banks are protected because if the check proves fraudulent, the print can be used by police to help identify the person who cashed it.

PC Banking

Many banks are introducing personal computer service using software available from them. With a computer, modem and the software, you can access account information, pay bills, transfer funds, and so on. There may be a charge.

Paying for Goods and Services

In addition to paying for a purchase by cash, credit card, or check, you may also pay by **debit card** through a Point-of-Sale (POS) terminal. You swipe the card through the machine in a store, type in your code (Personal Identification Number - PIN) and the money is taken immediately from your bank account. The shopper and the retailer both pay a fee for the service. Be aware that the retailer may block several times the amount of the purchase price from your bank account.

Cash cards provide a safe, low-cost way to carry money that can be changed into local currency 24 hours a day, can't be used by anyone else, and will be replaced promptly if lost. They combine the safety of traveler's checks with the convenience of ATM cards. The bank sells you the amount of money you wish on the card. Then you may withdraw local currency from any compatible ATM worldwide. You enter a pre-assigned code (Personal Identification Number - PIN) to use the card at an ATM.

Non-resident Withholding Tax

If you are a non-resident, you can submit Form W-8 to the bank. It will let them know that you are a non-resident alien and, therefore, exempt from withholding tax on the interest earned on your account. If tax has already been withheld, you may file for a refund on Form 1040NR (U.S. Nonresident Alien Income Tax Return) by April 15 with: Internal Revenue Service
            Philadelphia, PA 19255

Establishing Credit

It takes time to establish credit. If possible, credit reports may be obtained from your home country when you apply for a loan. A bank letter of credit may also help with the loan application.

If you are planning to be in the United States for a long period, it is important to build a reputation. One way of accomplishing this would be to apply for a store credit card. Stores may have a higher risk tolerance but charge high interest rates for accounts not paid by the due date each month. However, they may be prepared to offer a card with a low credit limit to get you started. If you pay your bills on time and appear to have stability to your life, such as a home, job, and family, the large credit card companies and lenders may look favorably upon your application.

Independent credit bureaus provide credit reports to organizations who want to know your credit history. You may wish to check your own credit to see what information is being supplied. Two of the credit bureaus that supply reports are:
            Equifax - (800) 685-1111
            Experian - (800) 682-7654

Fees vary by state but are usually no more than $8 plus tax. Credit bureaus may provide a free report if you have just been denied credit.

Safe Deposit Boxes

Banks have vaults containing a variety of sizes of boxes - Safe Deposit Boxes. For a yearly fee, you can rent a box where you may keep important documents, jewelry or other valuables. Your key and the bank's must both be used to get into the box.

Notary Public

Many U.S. documents must be notarized. U.S. notaries can authenticate papers, such as financial and legal, very economically and quickly. Some banks provide this service without charge. You must have proper identification, usually a photo I.D.

Many businesses have staff who are licensed to notarize documents for staff members while others will sign and stamp papers for the public at a fee of several dollars. Look for a "Notary" sign at the front of the store.

The requirement for notarization can become more complicated and expensive if the documents must be signed in a country where there are no notaries. It may be necessary to hire a lawyer to witness your signature.

Accountant

For tax and estate-planning advice, you may contact a certified public accountant (CPA). Talk to several to be sure you are comfortable with one's approach to financial matters. Ask for referrals from people you trust or contact the local CPA organization for names of accountants in your area who specialize in the service you require or contact: American Institute of Certified Public Accountants
201 Plaza 3
Jersey City, NJ 07311-3881
Phone: (201) 938-3000 or (800) 862-4272

Financial Planners

If you require assistance with financial matters, especially in two countries, be sure to find a cross-border planner who is knowledgeable in the services that apply to you. Do not hire a financial planner who is learning at your expense.

Ask for referrals or contact IAFP who will refer you to member planners in your area.   International Association for Financial Planning
5775 Glenridge Dr. NE
Atlanta, GA 30328
Phone: (404) 845-0011 or (800) 945-4237

Chapter 26

Buying or Renting a Home

Buying a home in the United States can be confusing since the rules and practices may be very different from those found in other countries.

This chapter sets out some of the terms a home buyer may encounter. Hopefully, by learning the "language" of U.S. home purchasing, you will avoid some of the misunderstandings.

Read all contracts, both front and back, to be sure that you understand and agree to all terms before signing. Even if you have the expertise of a real estate agent and attorney, only you know your wishes.

Real estate and relocating literature will have lists of points you should consider when looking for a home. Here are some additional considerations to keep in mind:

- Proximity to shopping, recreation, places of worship, fire station, police, ambulance, medical facilities, post office, schools
- Access to expressways, city center, airport
- Attractiveness of the neighborhood
- Future use of vacant land in the area
- Traffic noise
- Public transportation
- Land in designated flood zone or land elevation conditions that could result in flooding
- Crime rate
- Land in area which qualifies for Homeowner's Insurance
- Erosion protection, if on water (Check history of annual rate of erosion and what types of protection are allowed by government agencies)
- Garbage pickup available
- Sewers and other utilities available
- Local restrictions on house design, use of land, and so on
- Tax rate

Useful sources are http://www.realtor.com, http://www.homeadvisor.msn.com and http://www.owners.com.

Condominium

- History of, or prediction of, special assessments for such costs as common area repairs, improvements, upkeep
- Maintenance fees - good value, artificially low, or overpriced
- Noise-proof units
- Tolerable rules and regulations
- Do owners actually own amenities such as pool and tennis courts, or must they purchase them from the developer in the future

Buying a New Home

Investigate the builder thoroughly. Talk to the Better Business Bureau and any other organizations that keep track of builders' records in your area. See if any complaints have been lodged against the builder and, if so, how the builder addressed these complaints.

A spokesperson for the U.S. National Association of Home Builders, has been widely quoted as suggesting a visit to communities where the company recently built homes similar to the one you're interested in. They suggest that you go on a Saturday morning when everyone is doing yard work. Talk to several homeowners and ask what their experience has been with their builder. Ask if they have had any problems and if they were fixed promptly and properly.

They also counsel you to read the contract carefully. If you don't understand any part, consult a lawyer or real estate expert. The builder may say it's a standard contract, but, anything in a contract is negotiable and may be changed if both sides agree. Just because a contract is preprinted does not mean that you can't cross out and change provisions.

Real estate experts caution you to get everything that is important to you in writing. Oral statements are difficult to prove and enforce. You should put in writing all complaints and problems during and after construction and keep copies.

The most common methods of buying property are:

- The payment of the full amount of money, or
- The combination of a downpayment with a **mortgage** for the remaining amount

When paying cash, you avoid the costs connected with a loan but still have **closing costs**. Whether you are buying or selling a home, **closing costs** are a major expense. In spite of local custom, you may negotiate who pays which of the costs involved.

Home Buying Definitions

The following definitions are included as a guide to help prepare a buyer for the complexities of buying a home. Before signing any documents or depositing any money, an attorney should be consulted to ensure that the buyer's rights are properly protected.

Note:

- A bold typed word appearing within a definition indicates that the word appears in the list of definitions in this chapter or in Chapter 27, Mortgages.
- Some terms may have different meanings in another context.
- The definitions are general, non-technical and short.
- State laws, as well as local custom and usage may change the meanings in various regions.

Abstract (Of Title) A summary of the public records of the **title** to a particular piece of land. An attorney or **title insurance** company reviews an abstract of title to determine whether there are any problems which must be cleared up before a buyer can purchase clear, **marketable** and insurable **title**.

Adjustments between Buyer and Seller At **settlement** time, it is necessary to pro-rate all bills such as insurance, taxes and utilities, to determine the adjustments necessary between the buyer and seller. For example, if the taxes have been paid in advance for a year by the seller, credit is given to the seller for the period of the year that he is not occupying the home.

Agreement of Sale Known by various names, such as **contract of purchase**, **purchase agreement,** or **sales agreement,** according to location or jurisdiction, is a contract in which a seller agrees to sell and a buyer agrees to buy. Certain specific terms and conditions are spelled out in writing and signed by both parties. The agreement should include the sale price of the home, method of payment, date for taking possession, what fixtures, appliances, and personal property are to be sold with the home. It should also set out which party pays for specific settlement costs, home inspections, and other items involved in the sale. Attention should be paid to deadlines in the contract for any action that has been agreed upon such as repairs to be made by the seller. Proposed modifications to price and details may be handwritten and initialed on the contract until both parties are satisfied. If real estate brokers are involved they usually carry the **counter offers** between the buyer and the seller. Before signing, both parties may want their own lawyers to review the agreement. If a party does not know a local attorney, he should consult the bar association referral service or a neighborhood legal service office. Be careful. In some areas, once signed, the contract is binding on both the buyer and the seller.

Appreciation Increase in value or worth of property.

Assessed Value Value placed on property as a basis for levying **property taxes**.

Attorney's Fees Fees which may be paid for legal services such as examining the title, providing closing services.

Bathroom - Numerical Descriptions

- Full bath - Toilet, sink and tub
- One-half bath - Toilet and sink
- Three-quarter bath - Toilet, sink and shower stall

Binder (Offer to Purchase) A preliminary agreement accompanied by the payment of **earnest money**, between a buyer and seller as an offer to purchase real estate. A binder secures the right to purchase real estate upon agreed terms for a limited period of time. If the buyer changes his mind or is unable to purchase, the earnest money may be forfeited unless the binder expressly provides that it is to be refunded.

Broker Person licensed by the state to represent another for a fee in real estate transactions.

Building Code Local government regulations setting out standards for building.

Building Line or Setback Distances from the ends and/or sides of the lot beyond which construction may not extend. The building line may be established by a filed **plat** of subdivision, by **restrictive convenants** in **deeds** or leases, by **building codes**, or by **zoning ordinances.**

Certificate of Title Certificate issued by a **title** company or a written opinion rendered by an attorney that the seller has good marketable and insurable title to the property which he is offering for sale. A certificate of title offers no protection against any hidden defects in the title which an examination of the records could not reveal. The issuer of a certificate of title is liable only for damages due to negligence.

Chattel Personal property.

Closing or **Settlement** A procedure which occurs at the end of the home buying process when the title to the property is formally transferred from the seller to the buyer. In some areas, the buyer and seller meet with the closing agent and sign the papers. In other cases, they sign the papers in advance and an agent gets everything in order.

Closing Agent (**Settlement Agent**) Closing practices vary from locality to locality. They may be conducted by such businesses as lending institutions, title insurance companies, real estate brokers, or attorneys.

Closing Costs (Settlement Costs) The numerous expenses which buyers and sellers normally incur to complete a transaction in the transfer of ownership of real estate. One business day before **closing**, the settlement form should be available for inspection. It should itemize all services and fees being charged. These costs are in addition to the price of the property and are items paid on the **closing day**.

The agreement of sale negotiated previously between the buyer and the seller may state in writing who has agreed to pay each of the following applicable costs:

Closing fee to **Settlement Agent**   **Document Preparation**
Notary   **Home Inspection**
Escrow Fees   **Appraisal**
Survey   Attorney or Paralegal Fee
Title Search & Examination   **Commission**
Title Insurance   **Termite Inspection**
Recording & Transfer Charges   **Documentary Stamps**

Closing Day The day on which the formalities of a real estate sale are concluded. The final closing merely confirms the original agreement reached in the **agreement of sale**.

Cloud (On Title) An outstanding claim or **encumbrance** which adversely affects the **marketability of title**.

Commission Money paid to a real estate agent or broker by the seller as compensation for finding a buyer and completing the sale. Usually it is a percentage of the sale price - for example, 6 percent to 7 percent on houses, 6 percent to 10 percent on land. Percentages may be negotiated in some cases.

Conditional Offer Purchase offer in which the buyer proposes to purchase only after certain occurrences such as the sale of another home or securing financing.

Condominium Individual ownership of a dwelling unit within a multi-unit project and access to the common areas and facilities which serve the project.

Contract of Purchase See **Agreement of Sale**.

Contractor In the construction industry, a contractor is one who hires and co-ordinates sub-contractors for each phase of construction such as heating, electrical, plumbing, air conditioning, roofing and carpentry.

Cooperative Housing An apartment building or a group of dwellings owned by a corporation, the stockholders of which are the residents of the dwellings. It is operated for their benefit by their elected board of directors. Expenses are paid by the shareholders in proportion to the number of shares owned and may include a portion of the mortgage payments, maintenance and taxes.

Counteroffer An amendment or new offer made in response to an offer.

Deed A formal written document by which **title** to real property is transferred from one owner to another. The deed should contain an accurate description of the property being purchased, should be signed and witnessed according to the laws of the state where the property is located and should be delivered to the purchaser on **closing day**. There are two parties to a deed: the **grantor** (seller) and the **grantee** (buyer).

Deed of Trust Like a mortgage, a security instrument whereby real property is given as security for a debt. However, in a deed of trust there are three parties: the borrower, the **trustee**, and the lender, (or beneficiary). In such a transaction, the borrower transfers the legal **title** for the property to the trustee who holds the property in trust as security. If the borrower pays the debt as agreed, the deed of trust becomes void. If, however, he **defaults** in the payment of the debt, the trustee may sell the property at a public sale. In most jurisdictions where the deed of trust is in force, the borrower is subject to having his property sold without benefit of legal proceedings. A few states have begun in recent years to treat the deed of trust like a **mortgage.**

Deed Restriction (Restrictive Covenant) Provision placed in a deed to control use and occupancy of the property by future owners.

Depreciation Decline in value of a house due to wear and tear, adverse changes in the neighborhood, or any other reason.

Document Preparation Fee A fee which covers preparation of final legal papers such as a **mortgage, deed of trust,** note, or **deed.**

Documentary Stamps A state tax, in the form of stamps, required on **deeds** and **mortgages** when real estate **title** passes from one owner to another. The amount varies with each state.

Downpayment The amount of money to be paid by the purchaser to the seller upon the signing of the **agreement of sale**. The downpayment may not be refundable if the purchaser fails to buy the property without good cause. If the purchaser wants the downpayment to be refundable, he should be sure there is a clause in the agreement of sale specifying the conditions under which the deposit will be refunded. If the seller cannot deliver clear **title**, the agreement of sale usually requires the seller to return the downpayment and to pay **interest** and expenses incurred by the purchaser.

Duplex A structure with two dwelling units.

Earnest Money The deposit money given to the seller or his agent by the potential buyer upon the signing of the agreement of sale to show that he is serious about buying the property. If the sale goes through, the earnest money is applied against the **downpayment**. If the sale does not go through the earnest money may be forfeited or lost unless the **binder** or **offer to purchase** expressly provides that it is refundable.

Easement Rights Right-of-way granted to a person or company authorizing access to or over the owner's land. An electric or telephone company with a right-of-way across private property is a common example.

Encroachment An obstruction, building, or part of a building that intrudes beyond a legal boundary into neighboring private or public land, or a building extending beyond the **building line**.

Encumbrance A legal right or interest in land that affects a good or clear title, and diminishes the land's value. It can take numerous forms, such as **zoning ordinances, easement rights**, claims, **mortgages, liens**, charges, a pending legal action, unpaid taxes, or **restrictive convenants**. An encumbrance does not legally prevent transfer of the property to another. A **title search** is all that is usually done to reveal the existence of such encumbrances, and it is up to the buyer to determine whether he wants to purchase with the encumbrance, or what can be done to remove it.

Fiduciary Person in a position of trust or responsibility with specific duties to act in the best interest of the client.

General Warranty Deed A deed which conveys not only all the seller's interests in and **title** to the property to the buyer, but also warrants that if the title is defective or has a "**cloud** on it (such as mortgage claims, tax **liens**, title claims, judgments, or **mechanic's liens** against it) the buyer may hold the seller liable.

Grantee That party in the **deed** who is the buyer or recipient.

Grantor That party in the **deed** who is the seller or giver.

Hazard Insurance (Homeowner's Insurance) Helps pay for damage caused to property by fire, windstorms, and other common hazards.

Home Inspection Home inspectors determine whether the basic elements of a house are in sound condition. They inspect such features as the heating and cooling system, plumbing, appliances, floors, roof and the electrical system.

Home Warranties

New-Home Warranties
Warranties for new homes generally supplement the builder's warranty and have a deductible, which the homeowner pays when a claim is made.

Typically, new-home warranties cover:
- Workmanship and materials for 1 year
- Major systems, such as heating, cooling, electrical and plumbing for two years
- The foundation for 10 years

New-home warranties do not cover:
- Appliances (covered by manufacturer's warranty)
- "Acts of God" such as hurricanes, floods, earthquakes

Existing-Home Warranties
May be sold by real estate agents, usually to sellers.

Warranties for existing homes cover:
- Appliances such as dishwashers, water heaters, stoves
- Major systems such as heating, air conditioning, electrical and plumbing

Existing-home warranties do not cover:
- "Acts of God"
- Air-conditioning systems and pool equipment (may be optional)

Homeowner's Insurance Several kinds of insurance together in one package - theft, disaster, liability.

HUD Homes (U.S. Department of Housing and Urban Development) Properties that are deeded to HUD/FHA (Federal Housing Administration) by mortgage companies who foreclose on FHA-insured mortgage loans. HUD must sell these homes quickly. The listing price of a HUD property is based on an estimate of its fair market value. Anyone who has the money or can qualify for the mortgage financing can purchase a HUD Home. They are marketed on a competitive basis with sealed bid offers being submitted through any participating licensed real estate broker. The "offer period" is usually a 10-day period. At the end of the period, all bids received on the home will be opened at a public event. When an offer has been accepted, the broker will be notified within 48 hours. Sometimes HUD will accept an offer that is less than the listing price and sometimes buyers make bids higher than the listing price, depending on market conditions.

Joint Tenancy Ownership by two or more persons, each with an undivided ownership; if one dies, the property automatically goes to the survivor.

Lease An agreement that conveys the right to use property for a period of time.

Lessee Tenant.

Lessor Landlord.

Lien A claim by one person on the property of another as security for money owed. Such claims may include obligations not met or satisfied, judgments, unpaid taxes, materials, or labor (See also **special lien** and **mechanic's lien**).

Listing Agreement Contract between a property owner and a real estate broker, authorizing the broker to find a buyer.

Maintenance Fees Fees a property owner is required to pay in a multiple-owner property which cover such expenses as maintenance and repair of common buildings and property.

Market Value The highest price that a buyer would pay and the lowest price a seller would accept on a property.

Marketable Title A **title** that is free and clear of objectionable **liens, clouds,** or other title defects. A title which enables an owner to sell his property freely to others and which others will accept without objection.

Mechanic's Lien Claim placed against property by unpaid workers or suppliers.

Mobile Home Manufactured home moved by truck and set upon a permanent foundation, usually in a mobile home park where utilities, security, recreation facilities, may all be available.

Multiple-Listing Service (MLS) Many different real estate companies in an area working together to sell properties and share the resulting commissions.

Notary A licensed person who signs and seals documents verifying the signature of the parties.

Plat A map or chart of a lot, subdivision or community drawn by a surveyor, showing boundary lines, buildings, improvements on the land, and **easements**.

Power of Attorney A legal document authorizing one person to act on behalf of another.

Property Taxes Taxes are levied according to the value of the property. The funds are used to support schools, street maintenance, fire, police, and so on.

Purchase Agreement See **agreement of sale**

Quitclaim Deed A deed which transfers whatever interest the seller may have in the particular parcel of land. A quitclaim deed is often given to clear the title when the grantor's interest in a property is questionable. By accepting such a deed the buyer assumes all the risks. Such a deed makes no warranties as to the title, but simply transfers to the buyer whatever interest the grantor has. (See **deed**.) A **title insurance** policy may provide comfort to the buyer.

Real Estate Broker Person licensed to act independently in conducting real estate brokerage business.

Seller's agent
- Is obligated to tell the seller anything known about the buyer that would benefit the seller
- Advises seller on how to make property more saleable

- Researches the market to assist seller in setting the selling price
- May list property with **MLS (Multiple Listing Service)**
- Advertises property for sale
- Shows interested clients through home and makes arrangements for other agents to do the same
- Advises and assists in the contract negotiations
- Usually attends the closing
- Takes a predetermined fee from the sale of the home, usually 6 percent to 7 percent

Buyer's agent
- Represents the buyer's interests in looking for property
- Shows the buyer available properties
- Assists and advises with contract negotiations
- Shares with the seller's agent, the predetermined commission, paid by the seller
- May assist the buyer in finding a lender for the mortgage

Real Estate Salesperson   Person employed by a **real estate broker** to list and negotiate the sale, lease or rental of real property under the guidance of the employing broker.

Realtor   Registered name for a member of the National Association of Realtors, sworn to abide by the code of ethics.

Realtor Associate   Salesperson associated with a broker who is a member of a Board of Realtors.

Recording Fees   Money paid for recording a home sale with the local authorities, thereby making it part of the public records.

Restrictive Covenants   Clauses placed in **deeds** and **leases** to control how owners and **lessees** may or may not use the property. For example, restrictive covenants may limit the number of buildings per acre, regulate size, style or price range of buildings to be erected, or prevent particular businesses from operating in homes in a given area.

Sales Agreement   See **Agreement of Sale**.

Settlement Agent/Costs   See **Closing Agent/Costs**.

Special Assessments   A special tax imposed on property, individual lots or all property in the immediate area, for such expenses as road or sidewalk construction, sewers, or street lights.

Special Lien   A lien that binds a specified piece of property, unlike a general **lien**, which is levied against all one's assets. It creates a right to retain something of value belonging to another person as compensation for labor, material, or money expended in that person's behalf. In some localities it is called "particular" lien or "specific" lien.

Special Warranty Deed A deed in which the seller (**grantor**) conveys title to the buyer (**grantee**) and agrees to protect the buyer against title defects or claims asserted by the seller and those persons whose right to assert a claim against the title arose during the period the seller held title to the property. In a special warranty deed the seller guarantees to the buyer that he has done nothing during the time he held title to the property which has, or which might in the future, impair the buyer's title.

State Stamps See **Documentary Stamps**.

Survey A map or **plat** made by a licensed surveyor showing the results of measuring the land with its elevations, improvements, boundaries, and its relationship to surrounding tracts of land. A survey is often required by the lender to assure him that a building is actually sited on the land according to its legal description. In some areas the buyer may contact the previous surveyor and request an update. Usually the buyer pays the fee.

Termite Guarantee or Bond In termite-prone areas, pest control technicians treat the base of the home at construction then make an annual inspection outside the house and apply any additional treatment found necessary. A more expensive annual fee includes an annual inspection, necessary treatment and a limited repair guarantee for any termite damage to the wooden structure.

Timesharing A method of dividing up and selling living units for specified lengths of time each year. The buyer may occupy a unit for a certain number of days yearly. The timeshare must be paid in advance and an annual maintenance fee is required.

Title As generally used, the rights of ownership and possession of particular property. In real estate usage, title may refer to the instruments or documents by which a right of ownership is established (title documents), or it may refer to the ownership interest one has in the real estate.

Title Company Searches for hidden problems that might affect the title and provides an insurance policy. May also conduct **closings**.

Title Insurance A form of insurance policy to protect against loss if any problem ever occurs which results in a claim against ownership. Examples of title defects include a forged will or deed, undisclosed heirs, invalid divorces. If a claim is made against the property, the company may either fight the claim in court or pay the loss. If the insurance company decides to fight, the title insurance will, in accordance with the terms of the policy, assure a legal defense and pay all court costs and legal fees. Also, if the claim proves valid, the owner will be reimbursed for the actual loss up to the face value of the policy. Some insurers offer coverage with inflation endorsements. Coverage may be purchased from Title Insurance Companies or attorneys.

The premium is paid only once (usually .5 to 1 percent of the property cost). There are no renewal premiums and there is no expiration date on the policy. Coverage lasts as long as the owner or his heirs retain an interest in the property.

In some areas, there may be no need for a full historical title search if the property has recently changed hands. Some title insurance companies may reissue a policy at a lower premium.

Title Search or Examination A detailed examination of the historical records concerning a property, generally at the local public records, to make sure the buyer is purchasing a house from the legal owner and there are no **liens**, overdue **special assessments,** or other claims or outstanding **restrictive covenants** filed in the record, which would adversely affect the seller's right to transfer ownership.

Townhouse A row of dwelling units with shared walls.

Transfer Charges Recording Fees for documents, including the **deed** or **deed of trust**.

Triplex A structure containing three dwelling units.

Trustee A party who is given legal responsibility to hold property in the best interest of or "for the benefit of" another. The trustee is one placed in a position of responsibility for another, a responsibility enforceable in a court of law (See **deed of trust**).

Walk-through A final inspection of the property just prior to settlement.

Zoning Ordinances The acts of an authorized local government establishing building codes and setting forth regulations that control the specific use of land.

Utilities

Before moving into a home, arrangements must be made with the local utility companies in order to have all equipment functioning when you move in. Some utilities have a waiting list so it is wise to contact them in advance.

Once the initial fees are paid, you are then responsible for the monthly charges which will be billed to you. Some utility companies accept payment electronically with Automatic Funds Transfer. The bill is sent to you for your review and then the amount owing is automatically withdrawn from your bank account before the due date.

Utility requirements will vary from area to area. The following are samples in one city:

Utility	Deposit	Connect Fee	Advance Notice
Electric	$125-$175*	-	1 business day
Natural Gas	$75	-	2 business days
Telephone	**	$42.75 (1 jack)	3 business days
Cable TV	-	$15-$85 to install	4-7 business days
Water & Sewer	$105	-	2 business days

*Waived with good credit from previous power company
**Waived with good credit

Property Taxes

Property taxes are collected each year to provide such municipal services as schools, police, fire, sewer, garbage collection, street lighting, street repair, senior citizen and community centers.

Taxes are based on a percentage of the property's assessed value. In at least one state (Florida) a Homestead Tax Exemption of $25,000 may be deducted from the assessed value of the property. To qualify, the owner must:

- Be living on the property
- Hold title to the property
- Be a legal and permanent resident of the state and the U.S.

You may want to check on any similar exemption in your state.

Rental Accommodation

Real estate offices usually handle house and condominium rentals. Apartments will normally have a rental office on site.

Some apartment rental leases can be short-term, but condominiums and houses usually have a longer minimum rental period. Most units are unfurnished.

Once you have selected the rental accommodation, you will likely be asked to fill out an application form. There could be an application fee of an amount something like $25. The agent will verify your background and financial history.

By law, you cannot be turned down on the basis of race, religion, color, national origin, sex, handicap or having children.

You will be expected to sign the agreement and to pay the first and perhaps the last month's rent at the beginning of the lease. A deposit is also required but it will be returned to you after you move away at the end of your lease, providing you have caused no damage in excess of the usual wear and tear. If there is damage, the amount of money it takes to make the repair will be deducted before the deposit is returned.

Many apartment complexes offer amenities such as swimming pools, saunas, tennis courts, and fitness equipment.

The apartment unit should have a stove and refrigerator. It may also have a dishwasher and garbage disposal. A heating system is required and air conditioning is a necessity in the southern United States.

There usually are large centrally located laundry rooms with coin-operated washers and dryers for the use of all the renters in the complex. Some apartment units have washer and dryer connections so that the renter can supply those two appliances.

Pets may be prohibited or restricted as to size. There could be a maximum weight which an animal can be, such as 20 or 50 lbs. There also will probably be a pet deposit (may be non-refundable) and a monthly payment. For instance, one complex demands a $500 deposit plus $30 per month.

Points to consider when renting:

- Inspect the unit carefully and report any pre-existing damage.
- Read all rules and regulations applying to the unit.
- Check to see how much advance notice must be given before moving out.
- Determine the owner's obligation to make the necessary repairs.
- Renter and tenant should have a clear written agreement, including which utilities each will pay.
- Renters of some houses are expected to do the yard maintenance.
- Keep a copy of the lease or agreement.
- Determine clean-up requirements for when you move out. Most clean-up costs can be deducted from the security deposit if instructions are not followed.
- Check on prohibitions against sub-letting should you wish to leave before the lease has expired.
- Any oral agreements should be indicated on the contract and signed by both parties.
- It is important to always pay the rent on time.

Chapter 27

Mortgages

$\mathbf{A}$ real estate agent should know what financing programs are available in your area and should be an excellent resource. Agents advise that you start your home financing process well in advance of your offer to purchase by getting a mortgage pre-approval. However, you can't apply for the actual mortgage until you have signed a sales contract.

Mortgage Lenders

Financial information a lender may require includes:
- W-2s for prior years
- List of assets and liabilities
- List of all income
- Proof of employment
- Year-to-date pay check stubs
- Bank statements
- Signed sales contract
- Verification of the source of the down payment

Most mortgage lenders will help you determine how much home you can afford.

Experts suggest comparing several lenders. Mortgage information is available at www.financenter.com, www.mortgage.com, www.homeadvisor.com and www.lendingtree.com. If you plan to stay in the house two or three years, pay attention to your short-term costs such as closing costs (including points), downpayment, appraisal and attorney's fees. If you are going to be a long-term owner, then pay attention to the total interest cost on the life of the loan. You may also want to consider **biweekly mortgage payments**.

When looking at the projected mortgage payment and existing debt, some lenders might use ratios such as "28" and "36" to determine whether the applicant qualifies for the loan. The "28" refers to the percentage of gross income (before taxes) that may be spent on housing expenses, (including principal and interest on the mortgage, real estate taxes and insurance). The "36" refers to the percentage of gross income that may be spent for payments on all debts (including the mortgage); the monthly payments on outstanding debts, when added to the monthly housing expenses, may not exceed 36 percent of the gross income.

Additional points to consider when looking for a mortgage loan include:

- Where to go for a mortgage? Banks, savings and loans, mortgage companies, mortgage brokers, credit unions, home sellers, internet.

- What types of loans are available to you? Lenders can tell you exact mortgage limits for which you qualify.

- What length of loan is best for you? For example, 30-year fixed rate, 15-year fixed, one-year ARM and so on.

- Does the lender make privately or federally insured or guaranteed loans? (Some lenders offer mortgage loans backed by a federal agency such as the Federal Housing Administration (FHA loans) or the Department of Veterans Affairs (VA loans). Loans that are not government-insured are called **conventional mortgages**. Insured mortgages may be more attractive than conventional mortgages in some ways - such as lower downpayment requirements. They may be more restrictive in other ways. For example, they may be available only for certain kinds of homes, or for properties whose value is below a specified price.

- The downpayment required by the lender. The longer the term and the larger the downpayment, the smaller the monthly payments.

- The interest rate. In some cases the amount of the downpayment will influence the interest rate - the larger the downpayment, the lower the interest rate.

- Interest rates and fees may vary among lenders. Differences of as little as a quarter of a percent can mean thousands of dollars in the difference of total payments over the life of the loan.

- Penalties may apply for **refinancing** the mortgage.

- The length of the approval process. In some cases, be prepared for a wait of 30-45 days or longer from the date the lender receives all the information with the application.

- Mortgage interest payments are deductible from federal income tax.

Lenders generally charge lower initial interest rates for **adjustable rate loans** (ARMs) than for **fixed-rate mortgages**. There is a risk that interest rates will increase, leading to higher monthly payments. If you don't plan to keep the property many years, rising interest rates are not of concern.

With most ARMs, the interest rate and monthly payment change every year, every three years, or every five years. The time when one rate period ends and the next begins is called the **adjustment period**.

Discuss the **margin** with your lender. To determine the interest rate on an ARM, lenders add to the **index** rate a few percentage points called the **"margin"**. The amount of the margin can differ from one lender to another but it is usually constant over the life of the loan.

Index rate + Margin = ARM interest rate.

To choose among **fixed-rate** mortgage loans, you should compare interest rates, monthly payments, fees, **prepayment** penalties, and **due-on-sale** clauses.

If a lender refuses a loan, federal law requires the lender to tell the applicant, in writing, the specific reasons for the denial. Some companies have stricter credit standards than others. It pays to keep looking.

Items Payable in Connection with Loans may include:

- **Loan Origination Fee**
- **Points**
- **Appraisal**
- **Credit Report**
- **Mortgage Insurance Application Fee**
- **Assumption Fee**
- Lender's **Home Inspection**

Items that may be required by the lender to be paid by borrower in advance:

- **Accrued Interest**
- **Mortgage Insurance**
- Taxes
- **Hazard Insurance**

Mortgage Definitions

The following are some terms that you may encounter when arranging a mortgage in order to purchase property. Those words in bold print are defined elsewhere in the following list or in Chapter 26, Buying of Renting a Home. Customs and interpretations of terms may vary from region to region.

Acceleration Clause A condition in a **mortgage** that may require the balance of the loan to become due immediately, if regular mortgage payments are not made or other conditions of the mortgage are not met.

Accrued Interest Interest from the date of settlement to the beginning of the period covered by the first monthly payment.

Adjustable-mortgage Loan See **Adjustable-rate Mortgage**.

Adjustable-rate Mortgage (ARM) Interest rate fluctuates with changes in prevailing rates throughout the life of the loan. Initially the interest rate may be lower than a fixed-rate mortgage. ARMS may also be referred to as **AMLs** (adjustable mortgage loans) or **VRMs** (variable-rate mortgages).

Adjustment Interval In an **adjustable-rate mortgage**, the time between changes in the interest rate and/or monthly payment, is typically, one, three or five years, depending on the index.

Amortization A gradual process enabling the borrower to reduce his debt gradually through monthly payments that cover both interest and **principal**. As payments are made to the lender each month, the size of the mortgage debt, or principal, declines in most cases.

Annual Percentage Rate (APR) A measure of the cost of credit expressed as a yearly rate. It includes interest as well as other charges. Because all lenders follow the same rules to ensure the accuracy of the annual percentage rate, it provides consumers with a good basis for comparing the cost of loans, including mortgage plans.

Appraisal An expert judgment or estimate of the quality or value of real estate as of a given date.

Assumable Mortgage A mortgage that is transferable from seller to buyer.

Assumption Fee A fee which is charged for processing papers for cases in which the buyer takes over the payments on the prior loan of the seller.

Assumption of Mortgage An obligation undertaken by the purchaser of the property to be personally liable for payment of an existing **mortgage**. In an assumption, the purchaser is substituted for the original **mortgagor** in the mortgage agreement and the original **mortgagor** is released from further liability under the mortgage. Since the **mortgagor** is to be released from further liability in the assumption, the lender's consent is usually required.

The original **mortgagor** should always obtain a written release from further liability if he desires to be fully released under the assumption.

Balloon Mortgage Low fixed-rate payments as though for a 30-year term, but has a short term such as five to seven years at the end of which is a single large payment (the "balloon").

Biweekly Mortgage Payments Payments are made every two weeks rather than monthly (They may even be automatic withdrawals from the homeowner's account.) There are 26 half payments or the equivalent of 13 monthly payments. The extra payment serves to build equity faster and reduce interest costs. Payments are scheduled for a 30-year loan, but the extra payment each year means the loan is paid off in just under 20 years.

Buydown See **Seller Buydown**.

Cap Limit by which an adjustable mortgage rate may be raised at any one time. By law, virtually all ARMs must have an overall cap. Many have a periodic interest-rate cap. Periodic caps limit the interest-rate increase from one adjustment period to the next. Overall caps limit the interest-rate increase over the life of the loan. Payment caps don't limit the amount of interest the lender is earning, so they may cause **negative amortization**.

Ceiling (Lifetime Cap) Limit beyond which an adjustable mortgage rate may never be raised.

Community Reinvestment Act (CRA) Federal law requiring banks to lend to modest-income consumers.

Construction Loan A short-term interim loan for financing the cost of construction. The lender advances funds to the builder at periodic intervals as the work progresses.

Conventional Mortgage A **mortgage** loan not insured by **HUD** or guaranteed by the **VA**. It is subject to conditions established by the lending institution and state statutes. The mortgage rates may vary with different institutions and between states. (States have various interest limits).

Conversion Clause A provision in some **ARMs** that allows you to change the ARM to a fixed-rate loan at some point during the term.

Credit Report A summary which is compiled by a credit reporting agency for the lender. The report shows the buyer's credit history and general reputation. This fee is generally paid by the buyer.

Debt-to-Income Ratio The ratio, expressed as a percentage, which results when a borrower's monthly payment obligation on long-term debts is divided by his or her net income (FHA/VA loans) or gross monthly income (conventional loans). See **Housing expenses-to-income ratio**.

Deed of Trust See **Mortgage**.

Default Failure to make mortgage payments as agreed to in a commitment based on the terms and at the designated time set forth in the **mortgage** or **deed of trust**. In the event of default, the **mortgage** may give the lender the right to accelerate payments, take possession and receive rents, and start **foreclosure**. Defaults may also come about by the failure to observe other conditions in the **mortgage** or **deed of trust**.

Deferred Interest See **Negative Amortization**.

Delinquency Failure to make mortgage payments on time. This can lead to foreclosure.

Department of Veterans Affairs (VA) An independent agency of the federal government which guarantees long-term, low- or no-downpayment mortgages to eligible veterans.

Discount Points See **Points**.

Discounted Rate Some lenders offer initial **ARM** rates that are lower than the sum of the **index** and the **margin**. Discounted rates are often combined with large initial loan fees (**points**) and with higher **interest** rates after the discount expires.

Downpayment When a buyer is using a mortgage for the purchase of the property, the downpayment is the money paid to make up the difference between the purchase price and the mortgage amount. Downpayments usually are 10 percent to 20 percent of the sales price on conventional loans, and no money down up to 5 percent on FHA and VA loans.

Due-on-Sale-Clause A provision in a mortgage or deed of trust that allows the lender to demand immediate payment of the balance of the mortgage if the mortgage holder sells the home.

Equal Credit Opportunity Act (ECOA) Prohibits lenders from discriminating against credit applications on the basis of race, color, religion, national origin, sex, marital status, age, or receipt of income from public assistance programs.

Equity The value of a homeowner's unencumbered interest in a piece of real estate. Equity is computed by subtracting from the property's fair market value the total of the unpaid mortgage balance and any outstanding liens or other debts against the property. A homeowner's equity increases as he pays off his mortgage and/or as the property appreciates in value. When the mortgage and all other debts against the property are paid in full the homeowner has 100 percent equity in his property.

Escrow Funds paid by the buyer to a third party (the escrow agent) to hold until the occurrence of a specified event, after which the funds are released to a designated individual. In FHA mortgage transactions an escrow account usually refers to the funds a mortgagor pays the lender at the time of the periodic mortgage payments. The money is held in a trust fund, provided by the lender for the buyer. Such funds should be adequate to cover anticipated yearly expenditures for **mortgage insurance premiums**, taxes, **hazard insurance premiums,** and **special assessments**.

Fannie Mae See **Federal National Mortgage Association**
Fannie Mae 3 percent down payment mortgages are available to low income and minority home buyers.

Federal Home Loan Mortgage Corporation (FHLMC) Also called "**Freddie Mac**", a quasi-governmental agency that purchases conventional mortgages from insured depository institutions and HUD-approved mortgage bankers.

Federal Housing Administration (FHA) A division of the Department of Housing and Urban Development. Its main activity is the insuring of residential mortgage loans made by private lenders. FHA also sets standards for underwriting mortgages.

Federal National Mortgage Association (FNMA) Also known as, "**Fannie Mae**", a tax-paying corporation created by Congress that purchases and sells conventional residential mortgages as well as those insured by FHA or guaranteed by VA. This institution, which provides funds for one in seven mortgages, makes more affordable mortgage money available.

FHA Loan Loan insured by the Federal Housing Administration open to all qualified home purchasers. While there are limits to the size of FHA loans, they are generous enough to handle moderate-priced homes almost anywhere in the country.

Fixed-rate mortgage Same interest rate with the same monthly payment for the term of the loan. The longer the loan term, the lower the monthly payment but the higher the ultimate cost.

Foreclosure (Also known as repossession of property) A legal process by which the lender or the seller forces the sale of a mortgaged property because the borrower has not met the terms of the mortgage.

Freddie Mac See **Federal Home Loan Mortgage Corporation (FHLMC)**.

Ginnie Mae See **Government National Mortgage Association (GNMA)**.

Good Faith Estimate When an application for a loan is filed, the lender must provide a Good Faith Estimate of settlement service charges that will occur.

Government National Mortgage Association (GNMA) Also known as **Ginnie Mae**, provides sources of funds for residential mortgages, insured or guaranteed by **FHA** or **VA**.

Government Recording and Transfer Charges Charges for legally recording the new deed and mortgage. City, county and /or state tax stamps may have to be purchased as well.

Graduated Payment Mortgage (GPM) A type of flexible payment mortgage where the payments increase for a specified period of time and then level off. This type of mortgage has negative amortization built into it.

Gross Monthly Income The total amount the borrower earns per month, before any expenses are deducted.

Guaranty A promise by one party to pay a debt or perform an obligation contracted by another if the original party fails to pay or perform according to a contract.

Housing Expenses-to-Income Ratio The ratio, expressed as a percentage, which results when a borrower's housing expenses are divided by his effective income (FHA/VA loans) or gross monthly income (conventional loans). See **debt-to-income ratio.**

HUD Department of Housing and Urban Development.

Impound See **Reserves**.

Index A published interest rate against which lenders measure the difference between the current interest rate on an adjustable rate mortgage and that earned by other investments (such as one, three, and five-year U.S. Treasury security yields, the monthly average interest rate on loans closed by savings and loan institutions, and the monthly average cost-of-funds incurred by savings and loans), which is then used to adjust the interest rate on an **adjustable mortgage** up or down.

Interest A charge paid for borrowing money (see **Mortgage Note.**)

Lending Institutions Lend money to the buyer at either a set or fluctuating interest rate. Lending institutions include commercial banks, mutual savings banks, savings and loan associations and mortgage companies. Settlement charges and fees vary among the lenders. Some local newspapers publish a weekly shopper's guide to mortgage interest rates.

Loan Application Application which asks for information such as the borrower's place of employment, assets, and liabilities. False information can lead to severe penalties and loss of the property.

Loan Commitment Lender's promise to make a loan available in a specific amount at a future time.

Loan Discount See **Points**.

Loan Origination Fee A fee to cover the lender's administrative costs in processing the loan. It is often expressed as a percentage of the loan and varies among lenders and localities. It could amount to 1 percent to 2 percent of the loan.

Loan-to-Value Ratio The relationship between the amount of the mortgage loan and the appraised value of the property expressed as a percentage.

Lock-in A lender's promise to hold a certain interest rate and certain number of **points** for a specified period of time, while the loan is processed.

Margin The number of percentage points the lender adds to the index rate to calculate the **ARM** interest rate at each adjustment. For example, if the index rate is 9 percent and the margin is 3 percent, then the fully-indexed rate is 12 percent.

Mortgage (Deed of Trust or Security Deed) A loan of money which allows the buyer to purchase property. A **lien** or claim against real property is given by the buyer to the lender as security for money borrowed. Under government-insured or loan-guarantee provisions, the payments may include **escrow** amounts covering taxes, **hazard insurance,** and **special assessments**. There are many types of mortgages usually running from 10 to 30 years, during which time the loan is to be paid off.

Mortgage Broker Agent who represents many mortgage lenders.

Mortgage Commitment A written notice from the bank or other lending institution saying it will advance mortgage funds in a specified amount to enable a buyer to purchase a house.

Mortgage Insurance Application Fee A fee which covers processing the application for private mortgage insurance which may be required on certain loans. It may cover both the **appraisal** and application fee.

Mortgage Insurance Protects the lender from loss due to payment default by the borrower. With this insurance protection, the lender may be willing to make a larger loan, thus reducing downpayment requirements.

Mortgage Life Insurance Insurance designed to pay off a mortgage in the event of physical disability or death of the borrower.

Mortgage Loan Fee See **Loan Origination Fee**.

Mortgage Note A written agreement to repay a loan. The agreement is secured by a **mortgage**, serves as proof of an indebtedness, and states the manner in which it will be paid. The note states the actual amount of the debt that the mortgage secures and renders the **mortgagor** personally responsible for repayment.

Mortgage (Open-End) Mortgage with a provision that permits borrowing additional money in the future by **refinancing** the loan or paying additional financing charges. Open-end provisions often limit such borrowing to no more than would raise the balance to the original loan figure.

Mortgagee The lender in a mortgage agreement.

Mortgagor The borrower in a mortgage agreement.

Negative Amortization Occurs when the monthly payments are not large enough to pay all the interest due on the loan. This unpaid interest is added to the unpaid balance of the loan. The danger of negative amortization is that the home buyer ends up owing more than the original amount of the loan.

No Cost Mortgage The up-front loan fee is included in a higher interest rate. This loan is often used by buyers who plan to keep their home only a few years.

Nonassumption Clause A statement in a mortgage contract forbidding the assumption of the mortgage without the prior approval of the lender.

Origination Fee The fee charged by the lender to prepare loan documents, make credit checks, inspect and sometimes appraise a property, usually computed as a percentage of the face value of the loan.

PITI Abbreviation for principal, interest, taxes and insurance, elements that commonly make up a borrower's payment on a loan.

Points Sometimes called "**discount points**." A point is one percent of the amount of the mortgage loan. Lenders frequently charge points in both **fixed-rate** and **adjustable-rate** mortgages in order to increase the yield on the mortgage and to cover loan closing costs. These points usually are paid at closing. Buyers are prohibited from paying points on **HUD** or **VA** guaranteed loans (sellers can pay, however). On a **conventional mortgage**, points may be paid by either buyer or seller or split between them.

Preapproval Letter Lender's letter giving approval for a mortgage up to a certain amount, contingent upon appraisal of the property.

Prepayment Payment of mortgage loan, or part of it, before due date. Mortgage agreements often restrict the right of prepayment either by limiting the amount that can be prepaid in any one year or charging a penalty for prepayment. The Federal Housing Administration does not permit such restrictions in FHA insured mortgages.

Prequalification Letter Potential lender's or broker's estimate whether the buyer qualifies for a loan before shopping for property. This is not necessarily a firm commitment to give a loan.

Primary Mortgage Market Lenders making mortgage loans directly to borrowers, such as savings and loan associations, commercial banks and mortgage companies. These lenders sometimes sell their mortgages into the secondary mortgage markets such as FNMA or GNMA.

Principal The basic amount of money borrowed. In other words, principal is the amount upon which interest is paid.

Refinancing The process of the mortgagor paying off one loan with the proceeds from another loan.

Renegotiable Rate Mortgage See **Adjustable Rate Mortgage**

Reserves Deposited with Lender (Reserves, Escrow, or Impound Accounts) Funds held in an account by the lender to assure future payment for such recurring items as real estate taxes and hazard insurance, mortgage insurance or homeowners fees. At settlement, an initial amount may have to be paid by the buyer to start the reserve. A portion of the regular monthly payments will be added to the reserve account.

Secondary Mortgage Market The place where primary mortgage lenders sell the mortgages they make to obtain more funds to originate more new loans.

Security Deed See **Mortgage**.

Seller Buydown The seller pays an amount to the lender so the lender can give the buyer a lower rate and lower payments early in the mortgage term. The seller may increase the sales price of the home to cover the cost of the buydown.

Term Mortgage See **Balloon Mortgage**.

Title Insurance Title insurance may be issued to either the **mortgagor**, as an "owner's title policy," or to the **mortgagee**, as a "lender's title policy." Insurance benefits will be paid only to the "named insured" in the title policy.

If the buyer is satisfied that the title is clear, he may choose not to purchase a policy for himself. However, he will normally be asked to pay for the lender's policy.

Truth in Lending A statement which is prepared by the lender to set out the annual percentage rate, fees and other credit costs.

Underwriting The decision whether to make a loan to a potential home buyer based on credit, employment, assets, and other factors and the matching of this risk to an appropriate rate and term or loan amount.

VA Loan A long-term, low- or no-downpayment loan guaranteed by the Department of Veterans Affairs. Restricted to individuals qualified by military service or other entitlements.

Variable Rate Mortgage (VRM) See **Adjustable Rate Mortgage**.

Verification of Deposit (VOD) A document signed by the borrower's financial institution verifying the status and balance of his financial accounts.

Verification of Employment (VOE) A document signed by the borrower's employer verifying his position and salary.

Part III

Insurance

Insurance is a major consideration in the United States.

Part III explores the complex subject of insurance for home, health and automobile.

Home insurance covers the structure, its contents and liability protection. Renter's insurance covers the contents. See chapter 28.

Health insurance is an examination of the many kinds of medical coverage in the United States. Millions of U.S. residents are either uninsured or underinsured. Millions more are covered because of their low income level, governmental affiliation or access to insurance through their employer or through their own financial resources. Chapter 29 provides a major insight into this important aspect of getting settled in the United States.

As with residential insurance, there is a need for protection from the liabilities associated with driving a car or truck in the United States. Chapter 30 offers an introduction to this special insurance need.

Insurance company ratings may be found in publications in local libraries. Included are A.M. Best and Standard and Poor's (S&P), Weiss Research and Moody's Investors Service.

Chapter 28 — Homeowners' Insurance

- Insurance programs to provide compensation for damage or loss of your home and replacement of contents

Chapter 29 — Health Insurance

- Insurance Programs to provide compensation for sickness or injury requiring hospital and/or medical assistance and treatment

Chapter 30 — Automobile Insurance

- Insurance programs to provide compensation for losses due to automobile accidents

Chapter 28

Homeowner's Insurance

Homeowner's insurance helps pay to repair or rebuild your home and replace personal possessions affected by perils such as theft, fire or other disasters. The policy may also include such coverage as Personal Liability and Medical Payments which offer protection against a claim or lawsuit resulting from bodily injury or damage to property of others.

Homeowner's/Liability insurance is not generally required by law unless your local government demands it. However, it is highly recommended that all homeowners purchase a policy.

The amount of insurance needed should be sufficient to protect the structure and contents (personal possessions), not the land the house is on. An insurance industry standard is to write homeowner's policies for at least 80 percent of replacement cost.

Homeowner's insurance is available from insurance agents in your area.

Check out limitations to determine whether additional coverage is needed on potential damage not covered by the homeowner's policy. For example, items such as jewelry and antiques have value limits within the policy. This coverage can be added at extra cost.

The policy may provide either "replacement" or "cash value" coverage. For example, suppose you bought a bed for $200. Ten years later it was destroyed by a fire If you were insured for actual cash value, you would not be paid $200 by the insurance company but rather a lower figure that reflected the depreciated value of the bed - such as $100. If you were insured for replacement cost, and it cost $250 to replace the bed, you should have been reimbursed $250 from the insurance company.

A homeowner's policy may cover wind-driven rain damage and certain other water damage but not the rising water of flooding. If you live in a flood-prone area, talk to your agent about flood insurance.

Most homeowner's policies cover damage caused by windstorm and hail. However, in some areas, mostly coastal, this coverage is excluded. In these cases, coverage may be purchased through a separate agency such as the Florida Windstorm Underwriting Association which insures property in that state. Contact a local insurance agent for information.

Most mortgage lenders require homeowner's insurance coverage in the loan contract to protect their interest in the property.

Before purchasing property, especially in high-risk areas, make sure that you are able to find suitable insurance.

After several years of major disasters, many insurance companies in Florida have stopped writing or reduced the number of new policies. Premiums have risen dramatically, some as much as 100 percent in a year. Florida homeowners have access to the Market Assistance Plan for help in finding available, but not necessarily affordable, insurance. For more information call Market Assistance Plan (MAP) FL at (800) 524-9023.

Florida has a private risk pool of companies that still write insurance. It is a program authorized by the Florida Legislature to provide residential insurance for people who are unable to find coverage for their homes elsewhere. It is sold through regular insurance agents. Coverage costs much more than the average cost of other carriers in Florida. It is a short-term solution to a crisis caused by natural disasters.

Be aware of any changes to local ordinances or building codes that affect the home. Check with your agent because the insurance company may not be responsible for paying the cost of upgrading the home to meet these changes.

Renter's or tenant's insurance is available for contents of a rented property. Insurance options are also available for the owner to cover the structure of the rented building.

If you are a condominium resident, you should find out exactly what portion of the property is covered by the condominium association insurance and what portion is the homeowner's responsibility.

Check with the agent about discounts for fire and burglary safeguards.

Make a list of belongings. Save receipts showing the year the item was purchased and the amount paid. Dated photographs or video tapes of your possessions are a good idea. Store all records in a safe deposit box or other secure place.

Inform the agent of any additions or major improvements to the home. Each year, check with the agent and make sure the policy provides adequate coverage.

Homeowner's Insurance Definitions

The following is a list of terms which you are likely to encounter when arranging for home insurance:

Additional Living Expense (Loss of Use) Coverage that pays for the extra, above-normal expenses such as food and lodging incurred while the policyholder's home is being repaired.

Adjuster Person who is licensed and professionally trained to assess damage.

All-Risk Policy or "Special Form" A policy that covers the loss of property or damage that results from any peril, except those that are specifically excluded in the contract.

Cancellation Termination of an insurance policy by the insurance company or policyholder before it expires.

Claim A request for reimbursement for a loss covered by the policy.

Condominium Insurance An owner's insurance which covers any items not insured by the condominium association's policy.

Deductible The amount a policyholder must pay per claim or loss before the company will begin paying. (It is a fixed amount set out in the policy. The higher the deductible, the lower the premium.)

Endorsement A change added to an insurance policy that alters the original terms.

Floater Additional coverage added to an insurance policy to cover special items.

Inflation Guard The coverage limit increases annually by a certain percentage that reflects inflation trends.

Insured Loss A loss (theft, damage) that the insurance policy will pay in full or in part.

Liability Legal obligation.

Licensed Agents and Companies Agents and companies that are approved and monitored by the state insurance department.

Limit The maximum amount an insurance policy will pay in the event of a loss.

Medical Payments Payment for medical expenses of visitors accidentally injured in your home.

Mobile Home Insurance Policy similar to homeowners' policy but specifically for a mobile home.

Mortgage Insurance Pays off the mortgage on your home in the event of your death.

Peril The cause of a loss to a policyholder (theft, fire, windstorm).

Personal Liability Protects against a claim or lawsuit resulting from (non-automobile) bodily injury or property damage to others.

Premium Regular periodic payments made by the policyholder for insurance coverage.

Renters' Insurance Insures renters' household contents against perils.

Risk The chance of loss to insured persons.

Chapter 29

Health Insurance

In many countries, the government provides a national health insurance program for all residents. However, in the United States, over 1,500 insurance companies offer coverage.

Because of the major differences in approach, this chapter has been included to give readers some insight into their health insurance options when they arrive in the United States.

Group insurance is usually available to employees. Furthermore, the employer may pay for all or part of the premiums.

Individuals such as the self-employed, early retirees, part-time workers, immigrants, and those with pre-existing conditions may have difficulty affording or obtaining health insurance. In fact, according to the Census Bureau's annual survey released October 4, 1999, more than 44 million people are uninsured. Others are underinsured. Many are not poor enough to qualify for Medicaid and not rich enough to afford adequate health insurance.

To better understand how the system works, examine the four sections of this chapter:
- Health care legislation
- Points to consider when choosing health insurance
- Options for health insurance coverage
- Summary of health insurance definitions

Health Care Legislation

The Health Insurance Portability and Accountability Act

In 1996, Congress attempted to address some of the nation's concerns about health care with a new piece of legislation, the Health Insurance Portability and Accountability Act.

The Act mandates that:

- Tax deductions be allowed for long-term care
- Insurers sell to companies with between two and 50 employees (employers are prohibited from excluding employees based on health status)
- Income tax exemptions for the self-employed increase to 80 percent by 2006
- A four-year experiment be established to test tax-deductible medical savings accounts (MSAs)
- Private health insurance coverage for certain employees and individuals be available and renewable
- Employees not be excluded from a new group plan longer than 12 months (18 months for late enrollees) for pre-existing conditions diagnosed within six months of enrollment (states may impose shorter periods)
- Either:
  - states implement laws that allow eligible individuals who leave group coverage plans to purchase individual insurance policies, <u>or</u>
  - all issuers in the individual market must offer individual coverage to all eligible persons moving from group to individual coverage after exhausting their coverage under COBRA or other state programs
- Employees can take their health insurance eligibility with them when they change jobs, providing the new employer offers coverage. It is their eligibility that is portable, not the insurance
- For individuals moving within the group market or from individual to group, the period of pre-existing condition exclusion is reduced by the total of periods of creditable coverage that individual had

The act does not limit the pre-existing condition restrictions in the individual policies, except for eligible people who move from group to individual coverage. It also does not limit waiting periods that plans may impose before an individual is eligible for coverage, although any waiting period must run concurrently with any pre-existing condition restriction period.

People who cannot afford the premiums are not guaranteed coverage and it is not clear how affordable the individual policies will be since the Act does not limit the premiums.

Other Legislation

In 1996, Congress also passed two other health reform measures. One requires that insurance companies cover at least 48-hour hospital stays, when requested, for mothers and newborns (96 hours, after a Caesarean Section).

The other measure requires businesses with more than 50 workers to make annual and lifetime caps for mental illness equal to the limits for physical illness.

According to the November 19, 1996 issue of USA Today, some insurance companies were mandating that a mastectomy be an outpatient procedure. More federal measures may be introduced if insurance companies continue to restrict doctors' control of their patients' care.

The Balanced Budget Act of 1997 created Medicare+Choice which provides several additional health care options for Medicare beneficiaries. However, not all options are likely to be offered in all parts of the country.

Points to Consider When Choosing Health Insurance Providers

For individual coverage, find an insurance agent who is interested in getting the most appropriate insurance to meet your needs.

Setting Your Priorities

When choosing a health insurance provider, set your priorities by considering the importance of the following:

- The insurance company:
  - its reputation
  - level of satisfaction of its clients
  - promptness with which it processes claims, if traditional-style insurance
  - speed with which treatment approval is obtained
  - financial rating of the company
  - state in which the company is licensed (Does that state regulate rates)
  - accreditation by review organizations

- The participating doctors:
  - percentage of plan's doctors who are board certified (served residency and passed exam in that field)
  - method of payment to doctors (salaried or per patient basis)
  - physician access (much of the routine care may be handled by nurse practitioners, not doctors)
  - procedure and cost to see a specialist inside and outside the plan
  - length of wait for an appointment
  - pre-set limit to the doctor's bill
  - doctors accessible by phone
  - office hours

- Preventive medical care:
  - immunizations
  - physical examinations
  - mammograms
  - prenatal care

- Additional coverage:
  - prescription drugs, dental or optical visits

- substance abuse and mental health treatment
- injuries during sports activities
- injuries in private aircraft
- pre-existing conditions

Choosing a Plan

When researching, make sure:

- Comparison of insurance premiums is based on the same benefits (Beware, the cheapest is not always the best).
- The hospitals in the plan are appropriate for you.
- Coverage can be arranged if you are out of town, out of the state or out of the country.
- You determine the plan's rules on emergency care. You should be able to go to any hospital in an emergency.
- What symptoms create an emergency situation -
  Suppose you have chest pains, suspect a heart attack and go to the emergency room, only to be diagnosed as having indigestion. (Find out whether the company's payment will be based on the final diagnosis or on the fact that a prudent person had legitimate symptoms)
- You understand the plan's policy on treatments or procedures that are considered experimental, and therefore, not covered.
- You know the plan's review procedures for monitoring your care.
- You know the plan's procedures for appealing decisions about your care and whether an outside board is available.
- You do not over-insure because you cannot collect on the same claim twice.
- You find the type of plan that is right for you. If you are concerned about a limited choice of doctors and less control over treatment decisions, then an HMO may not be the answer.

Choosing a Doctor or Dentist

Contact the local dental or medical association. You may also find some referral agencies which only refer you to professionals who pay for the service. Be sure you understand whether the referral service provides the names of all suitable practitioners or only those who subscribe to their referral service.

Try to determine the names of those who specialize in the area of importance to you. Ask health professionals such as nurses or pharmacists which doctors or dentists they see. Friends, neighbors or co-workers may also have suggestions. Medical libraries and large public libraries have directories listing doctors' educational background and board-certified specialty.

Consider your first visit as a tryout of the office, staff and medical professionals.

Options For Health Insurance Coverage

Three basic options exist for those seeking primary health care insurance in the United States:

- Option 1 - Medicare
- Option 2 - U.S. Private Insurance Companies
- Option 3 - Insurance Companies Offering Coverage to Expatriates

Option 1 - Medicare

Medicare is a two-part federal health insurance program for:

- People 65 or older
- People of any age with permanent kidney failure
- Certain disabled people under 65

Medicare is administered by the Health Care Financing Administration (HCFA), a federal agency in the Department of Health and Human Services.

The Social Security Administration provides information, collects premiums, and handles enrollment. Various commercial insurance companies are under contract to process and pay Medicare claims.

Aliens must be lawfully admitted permanent residents and must have lived in the United States for five years before they can enroll in Medicare.

Medicare Structure

Medicare - Part A

Part A is hospital insurance which provides coverage of inpatient hospital care, skilled nursing facility care, home health care and hospice care.

Medicare provides coverage within the United States only, except in a specific emergency where a Canadian or Mexican hospital is substantially closer than a U.S. hospital.

Medicare - Part B
      Part B is medical insurance which pays a portion of doctors' services, outpatient hospital services, home health visits, flu shots, mammography and Pap smear, prostate and colorectal cancer screening, diagnostic X-Rays, laboratory and other tests. There are new plans to phase in home health care.

Medicare - Eligibility and Enrollment

      Those eligible to receive Social Security benefits are automatically enrolled in Medicare when they turn 65. Part B may be declined.

      The initial enrollment window is seven months starting three months before the 65th birthday. Those who are not automatically enrolled, should be aware that penalties and delays may apply if the deadline is missed. Social Security will help sort out the regulations.

      As employees work and pay taxes, they earn Social Security credits. Most people need 40 credits to qualify for benefits such as premium-free Part A Hospital Insurance. In 2000, employees earn one credit for each $780 in earnings - up to a maximum of four credits per year.

      Those who don't have the 40 work credits may still qualify for hospital insurance by paying a monthly premium. If the employee or spouse has 30-39 credits, the premium for Part A in 2000 is $166 per person per month. For anyone with fewer than 30 Social Security credits, the monthly premium for Part A in 2000 is $301.

      The 2000 premium for Part B is $45.50 a month for all applicants.

      For additional information, visit a local Social Security office or call (800) 772-1213.

Choice of Medicare Providers

      Medicare beneficiaries may choose to receive their hospital, doctor and other health care services covered by the program, either through traditional fee-for-service or some form of managed care.

Medicare via Traditional Fee-for-Service Plan
      This traditional plan allows patients to be treated by any doctor or hospital. However, the patient should ask if a medical provider "accepts assignment" (participates in the Medicare plan). If they do, they will accept the amount Medicare approves for a particular service and will not charge more than the 20 percent coinsurance. Federal law prohibits a doctor from charging more than 15 percent above Medicare's approved amount. Some states are even more strict.

Medicare does not limit the premiums that private fee-for-service plans may charge. This means that some enrollees may be paying a premium in addition to the standard medicare premium.

With the fee-for-service plan, the patient must deal with the insurance claims, pay deductible and co-insurance and also pay the medigap premiums. The patient can choose any licensed healthcare provider certified by Medicare. The following expenses will be encountered:

Part A (Hospital) Deductible and Co-insurance - In 2000 the patient pays:
- One-60 days, a single deductible of $776
- 61-90 days, co-insurance of $194 per day
- Over 90 days, co-insurance of $388 per day (to a lifetime maximum reserve of 60 days)
- After 60 day reserve is spent, all costs

Part B (Medical) Deductible and Co-insurance - The patient paid:
- A single $100 annual deductible
- Remaining amount after Medicare paid 80 percent of a set fee for medical services (co-insurance)

Medigap Insurance

Most people in the fee-for-service Medicare plan also purchase private insurance called "Medigap" to supplement their Medicare coverage. Medigap is designed to fill in some of the gaps in Medicare coverage, created because Medicare generally pays less than 100 percent of the cost of covered services, and does not cover some services at all.

Medicare via Managed Care

In some states, many Medicare beneficiaries join managed care plans, most of which are health maintenance organizations (HMOs). Medicare prepays the HMOs and enrollees may be required to pay the HMO a nominal monthly premium and/or co-payment and must continue to pay Medicare Part B premiums.

In most cases HMO enrollees do not need Medigap supplemental insurance because their plan may offer all or most of the Medigap benefits. Many plans also provide benefits beyond those which Medicare pays, such as prescription drugs, hearing aids and eyeglasses.

Most Medicare HMOs have become established in areas where Medicare pays the highest rates for their enrollees. Consequently, these plans are not found in every state

Medicare+Choice

The Balanced Budget Act of 1997, provides additional options for Medicare beneficiaries. The old-style fee-for-service and HMOs are still available but so are these more flexible forms of managed care:

- **Point of Service (POS)** allows members to receive care outside the HMO network, but at a higher cost
- **Preferred Provider Organization (PPO)** members pay more to go outside this network of health care providers, less restrictive than a POS
- **Provider Sponsored Organization (PSO)** is owned by doctors or other providers and is operated like HMOs.
- **Medical Savings Account (MSA)** is offered to about one percent of Medicare beneficiaries on an experimental basis. They choose a private insurance policy with a high deductible to cover catastrophic expenses. Medicare pays the premium and deposits money in a savings account which is used to pay medical expenses until the deductible is reached

Benefits vary from plan to plan and patients should read each description to determine which plan has the most appropriate benefits.

For information on Medicare, contact:

The Health Care Financing Administration
Baltimore, MD 21235.
Phone: (800) 772-1213
Internet: http://www.hcfa.gov
    http://www.medicare.gov

Pamphlets available from local Social Security offices, or by calling the above phone number, include:

- Medicare (SSA Publication # 05-10043)
- Your Medicare Handbook (HCFA Publication # 10050)
- Guide to Health Insurance for People with Medicare (HCFA Publication # 02110)
- Managed Care Plans (HCFA Publication # 02195)

Option 2 - U.S. Private Insurance Plans

Health insurance coverage is available to groups and individuals.

"Group" insurance provides coverage for a group of people under a single policy issued to their employer or organization with which they are affiliated.

"Individual" (Personal) insurance policies are sold to individuals and families.

Health plans can vary substantially in their organizational structure, depending on who sponsors the plan, what state laws govern them and what their individual contracts stipulate.

Common Insurance Plans

Some common insurance plans which are available to U.S. citizens and some legal aliens are:

- Traditional Fee-for-Service Payment System
- Managed Care -
  - Health Maintenance Organization (HMO)
  - Point of Service Plan (POS)
  - Preferred Provider Organization (PPO)
  - Exclusive Provider Organization (EPO)
- Medical Savings Account (MSA)
- Single Employer Plan

Here is how these models operate.

Traditional Fee-for-Service Payment System

These insurance companies collect premiums (payments) from clients and put the money into a fund from which they pay patients' eligible medical expenses. They issue an ID card and instructions on how to make a claim.

If an illness or injury is covered by the policy, the company evaluates the claim, checks the usual charge for the service in the patient's home area, then determines how much it will pay. In some cases the company pays the medical provider directly and in others, it partially or entirely reimburses the patient. There may be a great amount of paper work to deal with after making a claim.

The patient may choose from a range of annual deductibles. After paying the annual deductible, the patient usually must pay a co-insurance portion of the eligible charges to a set maximum (stop-loss). After that maximum limit is reached, the insurer pays to the policy limit. The patient is responsible for any extra charges that the insurer does not cover.

Conditions, situations and services which are not covered are called exclusions. Common exclusions are:

- Pre-existing conditions
- Routine physicals
- Pregnancy
- Mental disorders
- Declared and undeclared war (such as IRA bombings)
- Aviation (except as a passenger in a commercial aircraft)

It is suggested that a patient contact a claims person in an insurance company if unable to determine whether a condition is on the list of exclusions. A sales representative may explain the coverage from the sales perspective, but the claims expert knows what is really covered.

These traditional health insurance plans are becoming more and more unpopular as the costs become more prohibitive.

Health Maintenance Organization (HMO)

HMO networks consist of doctors, hospitals and other health care providers who have joined together in a geographical area to provide a unified service.

HMOs may be sponsored by employers, insurance companies or doctors.

The patient or employer provides a fixed, prepaid premium. There is usually no deductible. The amount of the co-payment, if any, will likely depend on the plan and premium chosen. There is little or no paper work for the patient to file.

The patient must choose a primary care physician (gatekeeper) who is responsible for directing and coordinating the complete medical care for covered services. When deemed necessary by the physician, the patient will be referred to other participating providers for X-rays, laboratory tests and hospitalization. Often the primary care physician makes all referrals to specialists. Only the medical providers on the list of that particular HMO may be used.

Preventive care, such as annual physical exams and prenatal care, is generally included while some HMOs may also include life, disability, vision and dental insurance.

A suitable plan should provide satisfactory preventive, chronic and acute care.

The company may have an arrangement for emergency medical care for patients who become ill outside the local HMO area. They should check before traveling and make arrangements accordingly.

Point of Service Plan (POS)

POS plans are the most rapidly growing form of managed care. These are essentially HMOs that allow enrollees to use services outside the HMO's network by paying an additional amount (usually a higher deductible and co-payment). It is estimated that over 20 percent of the insured population is now enrolled in such plans, up from 9 percent in 1993.

Preferred Provider Organization (PPO)

PPOs are networks of physicians and other health-care providers who negotiate with employers, insurance companies or other organizations and agree to give discounts when servicing the plan's members. If the patients use these providers, a greater portion of their health-care cost will be covered by the plan than if they use other providers outside the network.

There may be deductibles and co-insurance, similar to a traditional medical plan. PPOs give patients freedom to go without referral to any provider.

Exclusive Provider Organization (EPO)

EPO is another way employers can offer benefits and control costs. An EPO is a smaller, select group of PPO physicians and hospitals. The network is comprised of both primary and specialty care providers. Employees may choose providers based on the way the specific EPO network and benefit design is structured. Patients are discouraged from going outside the network.

Medical Savings Account (MSA)

MSA is a special account in which a worker, or an employer on his or her behalf, sets aside tax-free dollars for ordinary medical costs while covering major expenses with a high-deductible plan.

Single Employer Plan

Under guidelines of the federal Employee Retirement Income Security Act (ERISA), an employer establishes a health plan and pays the employees' health care and/or other benefits.

The self-insured employer might hire an insurance company to administer the plan, but the employer is responsible for paying the claims. The plan may also be fully insured by the insurance carrier.

Option 3 - Insurance Providers to Non-Citizens and Residents
Availability of Coverage

Some companies refuse to insure non-U.S. citizens and some will only cover certain immigrants, depending on the medical history of their home country.

Independent health insurance brokers should be able to offer options suited to your particular situation. You may have to check with more than one as they don't all represent the same companies.

Rules may be interpreted differently:

- From patient to patient
- From company to company
- From state to state

Even if a company agrees to insure a person, it may exclude coverage of a pre-existing condition for a period of time. These pre-existing conditions represent some of the greatest concerns for those looking for individual health insurance. One alien said she would never have moved to the United States if she had known how devastating her health insurance problems would be.

As one agent put it, "Insurance companies don't want to buy trouble." They prefer not to insure anyone who is apt to make a claim. The people who need coverage the most are often the ones who are the least likely to qualify.

When applying for health insurance coverage, list all pre-existing conditions as required. If the company should find that information is incorrect, they might deny a claim and could cancel the policy.

You could be an undesirable health insurance applicant if you have pre-existing medical problems such as:

- Heart disease
- Cancer
- Diabetes

- Epilepsy
- Depression
- High blood pressure

Some policies restrict coverage of a condition if the dosage of the prescribed medication for that condition has recently been changed.

Insurance brokers advise not to be discouraged by a negative response from an insurer. Keep trying. Some companies will try to work with you to provide answers to your insurance problems.

Anyone with a serious health problem who is unable to find coverage from private insurers should check to see if there is a state fund that guarantees membership.

Canadians who are in the United States under six months per year receive partial coverage for emergency medical services from their provincial plans but must obtain supplementary insurance to help pay the difference. These policies are available from insurance companies in their home province.

Anyone who qualifies for both U.S. Medicare and Canadian health coverage and spends half of the year in each country, may wish to check into the feasibility of using both plans.

Since health insurance for non-U.S. citizens may be difficult to obtain, we have included brief descriptions of the health insurance programs offered by some of the more prominent companies specializing in the alien community.

Some policies are limited to a short term for those intending to return to their home country, while other plans are renewable for a number of years. Some are available to U.S. citizens, only if they are living outside the United States.

For information and assistance on insurance laws, rights and companies, contact your state insurance office or http://www.insure.com.

The British United Provident Association Ltd. (BUPA)

BUPA International is based in England and offers a choice of health insurance plans to expatriates in the United States and U.S. citizens in other countries.

BUPA has established a service partnership with a U.S. health care company, to provide support for members needing to arrange treatment and settle claims. Medical providers are paid directly on behalf of the patient.

Three optional **Lifeline** plans are offered for acute illness or injury necessitating the services of a specialist related to the patient's condition (payment for the services of non-specialist practitioners is at the company's discretion)

International Health Insurance danmark a/s (IHI)

IHI is a Danish company which:

- Specializes in comprehensive worldwide health insurance
- Accepts applications from people of all nationalities who have not yet reached the age of 75
- Offers guaranteed lifetime renewability to accepted clients

International Medical Group, Inc. and WASA International (UK) Insurance Company, Ltd. (IMG)

These two companies are partners in providing IMG Global and Patriot Medical health insurance to expatriates, irrespective of nationality, occupation or current country of residence. These short- and long-term insurance programs are administered by IMG in the United States.

John Ingle Insurance Group Inc.

John Ingle of Canada offers Nomad Plan Two which is designed especially for Canadians (under age 80) who are no longer eligible for coverage under a provincial government health insurance plan in Canada, or who are awaiting other insurance coverage in the country in which they are residing.

Petersen International Insurance Brokers

Petersen is a U.S. company which holds a contract from Lloyd's of London for underwriting disability, life, medical and such other special insurance coverage as kidnap, professional athlete disability and event cancellation.

Petersen offers International Major Medical Insurance which provides medical coverage for expatriates up to age 75, with consideration given up to age 85.

They also offer The Bridge Plan which is an individual Major Medical Plan for senior age individuals while in the United States. It is designed like Medicare and may be purchased with both A and B, just A, or just B. It covers:

- New U.S. permanent residents waiting for Medicare eligibility
- U.S. citizens without Medicare Part A or Part B
- U.S. residents/citizens waiting for Medicare eligibility (who missed the enrollment period and must wait for the next enrollment opportunity)

Specialty Risk International, Inc. - SRI

SRI is a private U.S. wholesale broker that designs and develops international insurance programs.

SRI administers and services:

- Approved International travel medical insurance for J-1/J-2 visa holders
- AAA Medical Insurance (medical insurance for foreign nationals visiting the U.S.)
- U.S. Assist (emergency travel assistance program)
- Accident and health coverage for expatriates, under age 80, outside their home country for 6-12 months, renewable to three years
- Medical and accidental death coverage to foreigners visiting the United States from two weeks to 12 months

Health Insurance Definitions

Application A signed statement of facts that an insurance company uses to determine whether to issue coverage. It may ask questions about the patient's age, medical history, and will become part of the health insurance contract.

Assignment A document signed by a policyholder authorizing a company to pay benefits directly to the policyholder's hospital, doctor or other health care provider.

Assignment (Medicare) Arrangement whereby a doctor or other medical provider agrees to accept the amount Medicare approves for a particular service under Part B and will not charge more than the 20 percent coinsurance after the $100 deductible has been paid.

Benefit Period Period an illness or injury is covered before the patient becomes responsible for all of the costs.

Broker Sales and service representative selling insurance of various kinds for several companies.

Capitation Method of payment for health services in which a hospital or physician is paid a fixed, per capita amount for each person served, regardless of the actual number of services provided to each.

Carrier Insurance company responsible for processing claims.

Catastrophic Policy Pays covered expenses from an extremely costly illness or accident after a patient pays a high deductible.

Claim Reporting of medical expenses to an insurance company by the insured person to request reimbursement.

COBRA (Consolidated Omnibus Budget Reconciliation Act) Under certain circumstances, after leaving a job, COBRA allows an employee to continue coverage for a period of time under the former employer's plan by self-paying all premiums and an administration fee.

Comprehensive Major Medical Insurance Basic plan plus **major medical** insurance.

Conversion Policy An individual policy that replaces a group policy when a policyholder is no longer eligible for group coverage.

Coinsurance Percentage of covered expenses (in addition to the deductible) that a patient must pay. Many policies require the patient to pay 20 percent up to a certain amount.

Co-payment A specified dollar amount the patient pays, as a subscriber to a managed-care plan, for covered health care services. It is paid to the medical provider at the time the service is rendered.

Cost Contract Medicare patient is allowed to go to providers outside the managed care plan but must pay Medicare's coinsurance and deductibles and other charges, similar to fee-for-service.

Cost Shifting Occurs when hospitals charge paying patients extra money for their stay in the hospital. This offsets the cost of caring for the non-paying or indigent patients.

Custodial Care Care not requiring a nurse that is provided in a nursing home or private home. Includes help with activities such as bathing, dressing, eating or taking medicine. Care must be recommended by a doctor.

Deductible The specified amount the patient must pay per illness or per year before an insurance company begins to pay - the higher the chosen deductible, the lower the monthly premium.

Disability Insurance Replaces a portion of an employee's income if he becomes disabled and cannot work.

Dread Disease Policy Pays benefits for only a specified illness, such as cancer.

Eligible Expenses Procedures that are covered by the insurance policy and costs that are within limits set by the insurance company - not necessarily the full amount of the medical bill.

Elimination Period Length of time a policyholder has to wait before receiving benefits after a covered illness begins.

Emergency A medical condition, manifesting itself by acute signs or symptoms, which could seriously endanger an insured person's health if immediate medical attention is not provided (interpretation may vary among policies).

Emergency Evacuation Transportation is provided to an appropriate hospital if timely treatment for a serious illness or injury is not available locally.

Exclusion Rider Policy excludes coverage for specific ailments, either for a specified period or as long as the policy is in force.

Exclusions Conditions, services or treatments which are not covered.

Exclusive Agent Sells insurance for one company for a commission.

Expatriate A person who has left the home country and is living in another country for either a short or long term.

Fee-for-Service (Traditional) Patient or insurer pays medical provider for each service.

Gatekeeper See **Primary Care Physician (PCP)**

Home Country (Country of Residence) The country where a person has a permanent home to which he has the intention of returning.

Home Health Care Intermediate or custodial care received at home from a nurse, therapist or home health aide under a doctor's supervision.

Hospital-Indemnity Policy Covers a fixed limit of daily or weekly hospital expenses.

Hospital Insurance Usually pays a portion of room and board and some eligible hospital services such as operating room use and X-Rays.

Independent Agent Represents several insurance companies who pay the agent a sales commission.

Independent Physician Association (IPA) An organization that manages the contracting and claims process for a single group of physicians organized into a medical group or multiple medical groups. The IPA will contract with various insurance plans for the healthcare provided by these groups.

Inflation Protection Benefits are automatically increased each year by a specified percentage to stay in line with the increasing cost of long-term health care.

Inpatient A person who is an overnight patient of a hospital, using and being charged for room and board.

Long-term Care Care an individual needs in the event of a chronic illness or disability - services may be on an inpatient (such as nursing home), outpatient or at-home basis.

Major-Medical Policy Covers inpatient and outpatient hospital stays and physicians' services. Patient pays a deductible and co-insurance. Policy costs more and provides more benefits than basic policy.

Medicaid State assistance plan for Medicare patients with low income and few assets.

Medically Necessary A medical procedure or treatment that is necessary to maintain or resume good health. Many policies will not pay for non-essential procedures such as cosmetic surgery.

Medicare A national health insurance program for people 65 years of age or older and certain younger disabled people.

Medigap Insurance Policies sold by private insurance companies to help pay health care expenses not fully covered by Medicare.

Nurse Practitioner - Registered Nurse who has additional training and is able to perform functions such as ordering tests and prescribing medication.

Outpatient A person who receives medically necessary treatment for injury or illness which does not require an overnight stay in hospital.

Physician/Hospital Organization (PHO) A formal organization in which a physician group(s) join with a hospital(s) in a managed-care venture to provide comprehensive healthcare services.

Physician's Assistant Has advanced medical training but is not a Medical Doctor. May order tests, write prescriptions, and do physical exams.

Policy Limits Specific dollar limits on the amount that the company will pay for each service, per policy period, or lifetime.

Portability Allows a covered person to meet the waiting period for a pre-existing condition only once, even if the individual changes employer or insurer.

Precertification Before the patient receives medical treatment, the insurance company is contacted to get clarification and approval on what medical expenses the company is prepared to cover.

Pre-existing Condition A health condition that existed a specific period before the insurance coverage began. Sometimes companies refuse to cover such a condition and its consequences or they may demand a waiting period before allowing coverage of that condition.

Premium A periodic payment a policyholder must make for insurance coverage. Premiums help the insurance company pay policyholders' claims and other expenses, such as commissions to agents, taxes and administrative expenses.

Prepaid Dental Plan A managed care system which requires periodic premium payments. It involves a combination of co-payments and no-charge benefits. Routine examinations, cleanings and X-Rays are provided at no charge. Major services have predetermined co-payments.

Primary Care Physician (PCP) HMO doctor selected by a subscriber to provide or authorize all medical treatment and referrals.

Provider Any physician, hospital or other institution, person or organization that furnishes health care services and is licensed or authorized to practice in the state.

Repatriation Return of body or ashes to a home country.

Rider An attachment to an insurance policy that specifies conditions or benefits the policy covers in addition to the original contract benefits.

Risk Chance of making a claim.

Risk Contract Medicare patient is generally locked into receiving all covered care through a certain managed care plan or through referrals by the plan. The only exceptions are for emergency charges or POS services.

Skilled Nursing Care Twenty-four-hour, daily nursing and rehabilitative care performed by or under the supervision of a registered nurse or a doctor.

State Insurance Pool State-sponsored organization providing health coverage for residents of the state who, by reason of the existence or history of a medical condition, are unable to acquire or afford coverage for the condition.

Stop-loss Limit Provision which limits the amount of coinsurance to a definite amount per individual or per family.

Supplemental Insurance Policy Provides coverage beyond or in addition to what is provided by a basic policy - not a substitute for basic medical insurance.

Underwriter Either a company that receives premiums and fulfills the contract, or the company employee who decides which applicants they will insure.

Usual, Reasonable and Customary Expenses The most common charge for similar services, medicines, or supplies within the area in which the charge is incurred as determined by the Plan Administrator.

Utilization Review Process for deciding whether to approve treatment or referrals recommended by doctors.

Waiting Period Length of time an insured must wait from the date of enrollment to the date the insurance is effective.

Waiver Agreement attached to a policy that exempts certain conditions from coverage.

Chapter 30
Automobile Insurance

W hen purchasing a car, you should determine the auto insurance requirements in your state. An insurance agent can help sort out the insurance companies that are available.

Factors to Consider When Shopping for Automobile Insurance

Although not all companies use the same criteria, several common factors may affect the premium. These factors include: kind of car, age of driver, driving record, car's safety equipment, deductible amount, and geographic location.

When you buy a car, keep in mind that premiums are usually higher for cars that are more expensive to repair or have less passenger protection from accidents. Likewise, cars that are favorite targets of thieves, such as sports cars, are more expensive to insure.

It is wise to shop around and compare coverages and get price quotes. The cheapest is not always the best.

Be sure to purchase at least the minimum limits of coverage as required by state law.

Check with trusted friends, an attorney, or state insurance consumer office to get assistance. Read the policy and ask questions.

The agent should provide a binder which should show the name of the agent and insurance company, lienholders (if any), policy effective date and time, and the coverage purchased. It should also be signed by the agent.

Try to pay insurance premiums by check or money order. Always get a detailed receipt. The policy should be issued within 60 days of its effective date.

Keep copies of all insurance records in a safe place. Have proof of insurance in your car at all times.

If coverage is not maintained on a financed car, the financial institution may purchase insurance to protect its own interest. It may be more expensive coverage and inadequate but the owner will have to pay the premiums.

In changing coverage or companies, make sure that your new coverage is in effect before the old policy is canceled.

Keep track of the names of the agent, the insurance company and the insurance agency. They may all be different.

Ask the agent about the company's policy for renewal and premium rate increases following accidents.

Automobile Insurance Definitions

The following is a brief description of some of the terms that may be found when searching for an automobile insurance policy:

Accidental Death and Dismemberment Coverage up to the policy limit for death or dismemberment (loss of limb) in an auto accident.

Adjuster A person licensed and professionally trained to assess damage.

Agent Local representative who sells and services insurance policies.

At-fault The person who is charged with causing the accident is considered to be at fault.

Binder The contract a policyholder receives once an insurance application is signed. It provides proof of insurance until the permanent policy is issued.

Bodily Injury Liability Coverage of serious and permanent injury or death to others when the insured's car is involved in an accident in which he is at fault.

Claim A request for financial reimbursement on an insured loss.

Collision Coverage of repairs to a car if it collides with another vehicle, crashes into an object or turns over.

Comprehensive Coverage of some losses from incidents other than a collision. Examples could be fire, theft, windshield breakage, windstorm, vandalism, flood or hitting an animal.

Deductible The amount which a policyholder must pay per claim or accident, before an insurance company pays its share. The higher the deductible, the lower the premium.

Dismemberment Loss of Limb (arm or leg).

Exclusion A provision in an insurance policy which denies coverage for certain losses.

Identification Card A wallet-sized card issued by an insurance company indicating policy number and coverage.

Insured The persons and items covered under an insurance policy.

Insurer The company that provides the insurance.

Liability Any legally enforceable obligation.

Liability Insurance Insurance covering the policyholder's legal liability for injuries to other persons or damage to their property.

Licensed Agents and Brokers Certification issued by the Department of Insurance which verifies that a company is qualified to sell insurance in the state.

Limit The maximum benefit that the insurance company will pay in the event of a loss.

Loss An occurrence or event resulting in damage or loss of property, or injury or death.

Medical Payments Coverage of medical expenses resulting from accidental injury, up to the limits of the policy.

Personal Injury Protection (PIP)(No-Fault) A system in which the insured is compensated for his loss according to the terms of the policy, regardless of who is responsible for causing the accident.

Policy A written contract between the insurance company and the insured person.

Premium The amount paid for coverage. This is based on the type and amount of policy chosen.

Property Damage Liability Coverage of damage to other people's property.

Rental Car Coverage Collision coverage or property damage liability may apply to rental cars, depending on the terms and conditions of the policy.

Rental Reimbursement Coverage Reimbursement for car rental if insured car is in an accident and not driveable.

Towing Towing and road service up to a certain limit.

Uninsured Motor Vehicle Fee This does not provide insurance coverage but allows a driver to operate a vehicle for a certain period of time.

Uninsured/Underinsured Motorist Benefits for injury or death caused by an uninsured or underinsured driver who is at fault.

Emergency Road Service

Emergency road service offers you protection for problems that are not typically handled by your auto insurance.

Among the benefits you receive are:

- A certain number of miles of free towing to a repair facility
- Emergency fuel delivery
- Lock service to get you into your locked car if the keys are left inside
- Flat tires changed
- Battery boosts
- Trip routing and maps

This coverage is available from various insurance companies, stores such as Sears, and travel clubs such as the American Automobile Association (AAA).

Part IV

Community

P art IV explores some of the important social encounters which often tend to be taken for granted or even overlooked.

The following chapters provide a basic explanation of some important social issues you will meet upon entering your new U.S. community.

Chapter 31 — Primary and Secondary Education
- A brief introduction to the U.S. pre-university/college education process

Chapter 32 — Social Activities
- An overview of some of the customs, organizations, and activities awaiting the new resident

Chapter 33 — Marriage Procedures
- A brief introduction to U.S. marriage laws, customs, and procedures

Chapter 31

Primary and Secondary Education

Each state governs its own education system and each local school board is in charge of the schools in its area. Therefore, regulations and traditions vary across the nation. In addition to public education, there are many private schools throughout the country. These cover diverse levels of tuition and facilities.

School Attendance

When you reside in a school district, the property taxes, which you or your landlord pay, give you the right to send your children to a public school without additional charge. If you choose to send your children to private schools, you must pay that tuition but you or your landlord are not exempt from tax for the public school system.

Generally, school is mandatory for all children, age five to 16.

Each district has its own age cut-off date to enroll for a school year. For example, in some school boards, a child must be five years of age on or before September 1 in order to qualify for kindergarten for that school term.

A child's English proficiency will be assessed and classes in English for Speakers of Other Languages (ESOL) should be offered free of charge to those in need of instruction.

In order to register at school the following will be required:
- Birth Certificate (for initial entry)
- Proof of Residence - suggested documents:
  - driver's license
  - current utilities statements
  - county voter registration card
  - current deed, rental or lease agreement

- Proof of the required immunizations and physical examinations (unless exempt for medical or religious reasons)
- All information documenting previous education (if transferring)

Students must be at school each day and on time. They may stay home because of illness or family emergency but must have a note from a parent, guardian or doctor, explaining their absence.

Sample hours for schools in one district:
- Elementary   - 9:00 am - 3.30 pm
- Junior High   - 7:55 am - 2:45 pm
- High   - 7:15 am - 2:05 pm

The following are two methods of dividing the grade levels:
- Elementary   - Kindergarten through fifth grade
- Middle   - sixth through eighth
- High   - ninth through 12th

- Elementary   - Kindergarten through sixth grade
- Junior High   - seventh through ninth
- High   - 10th through 12th

Normally, textbooks are supplied free of charge but the student is responsible for pens, pencils, and notebooks. Participation in after-school activities may involve additional expenses.

The United States Department of Agriculture (USDA) regulates a food service program which provides meals at reasonable or reduced prices, or free, depending on the student's family size and income. There is also the option of taking a lunch from home.

Don't be surprised if students are not allowed to leave their school for lunch, unless picked up by a parent. Schools claim that they are concerned for the health and safety of the students.

The Pledge of Allegiance to the U.S. flag occurs daily. However, students of other nationalities may just stand quietly.

Prayer in public schools has been held unconstitutional but there is some provision for students to have silent reflection inside or to lead prayers off campus. Parochial schools have religious training and prayer within the school.

Dress Code

Schools usually have standards of appearance for students. Many schools are introducing uniforms.

Parent-Teacher Association (PTA)

A good way to learn about your child's school is to get involved with the PTA. It is an organization that supports the school by such activities as fund raising, assisting in class, etc.

Foreign Student

An alien may be given status as a nonimmigrant in order to attend a public elementary or secondary school, or adult education program, not to exceed 12 months. The student must pay the per capita cost of the education.

Attendance at private schools is permitted but transfer from a private to a public school is not. For details, see Chapter 17, New Legislation.   *Ref: IIRIRA96.625*

Choosing a Neighborhood

The following are some issues which should be considered when choosing an area to live.

Boundaries

The school boundaries may not be the same for the three levels so you can't assume that because you live in a certain elementary school area you will automatically be within the boundaries of a nearby junior high or high school district.

Some school boards allow students to attend schools other than in their area, while others may charge tuition for the privilege.

School Term

School terms vary from county to county. For example, one board may have classes from August 12 to May 23 while another may run from September to June. Many schools are also experimenting with year-round classes.

Busing

School boards have varying rules on busing. One may provide free transportation to all students who live two miles or more from the school. Another may insist that all students ride a bus no matter where they live. They may be concerned about children crossing busy streets near the school or cars stopped on the busy streets to pick up children.

Public schools in some parts of the country have overcrowding or racial inequality and their school boards redistribute the population. To accomplish that end they bus a number of students to schools outside of their home district. Alternatively, parents have the option of sending their children to private schools at considerable cost. It is wise to investigate school policies to be sure that you are comfortable with the potential school placement of your children before settling in an area.

Chapter 32

Social Activities

T he social side of U.S. living holds many surprises and traditions. This chapter offers a little insight into what you can expect.

The Pledge of Allegiance

Many activities start off with everyone standing, facing the flag, holding the right hand over the heart, and reciting the Pledge of Allegiance.

Non-citizens may just stand at attention. The pledge states, "I pledge allegiance to the flag of the United States of America and to the Republic for which it stands, one nation under God, indivisible, with liberty and justice for all".

Organizations "Welcoming" Newcomers

Don't be surprised if you find that some community organizations are more welcoming than others. One organization which exists for the purpose of giving new residents in the community opportunities to get together also has a firm rule that each member must have a Voter's Registration card. This means that all members must be citizens of the United States and have proven residency in that particular county. By definition that eliminates all newcomers from other nations. It saves time and embarrassment if you determine their rules up front.

Social Customs in the United States

Many traditions and customs may be different from other countries. For example, here are three common situations that could cause concern for newcomers:

Standing in line is usually very orderly and you will be expected to go to the end of the line and wait your turn. You will find great resentment if you cut in front of others who were there before you.

Social interpretations of being on time vary among the regions of the country. However, you will be expected to be prompt for all business appointments.

It is very normal to say sir or ma'am in the southeast. In fact, it is expected. However, some people in the north are uncomfortable when addressed in that manner.

These are examples of behavior that should be considered when you arrive in the U.S. You will find books in the library that will give tips on social manners. Hopefully, your new acquaintances will be able to answer questions you may have.

Voluntary Service

Work on a volunteer basis is performed by millions of people in their communities. Volunteers come from all social and economic environments and all age groups right across the country.

If your visa doesn't allow you to work, consider volunteering. It's an opportunity to meet people, get work experience, and find great personal satisfaction. You won't be paid, but you will be getting exposure to U.S. society and culture and gaining the satisfaction of helping others.

You may also make contacts that will be of benefit in the workplace if your status changes and you are permitted to work.

However, it is suggested that satisfying volunteering requires patience, flexibility, independence, and perhaps most of all, a sense of humor.

Examples of volunteer jobs:
- Hospital volunteers staffing mobile libraries, providing support to patients, or offering clerical help
- Police office volunteers involved in administrative work or police-trained citizen forces
- Parent-teacher associations supporting schools and school activities

Examples of other areas where volunteers are needed:
- Alcohol and drug addiction
- Assistance for the elderly
- Animal welfare
- Blood and organ/tissue donations
- Youth organizations
- Disease and disability support groups
- Disaster assistance
- Food and housing for the poor
- Veterans affairs

- Museums
- Art galleries
- Zoos
- Theaters
- Libraries

You may contact a volunteer organization directly or check the phone book listings for an office such as a Volunteer Bureau or Volunteer Information and Referral service. These offices have information on organizations in need of volunteers.

Community Activities

Most communities have sports facilities and organized sports activities for children as well as adults.

Social organizations also offer you a chance to get involved with the community. Some examples:

- Churches usually have youth and adult groups as well as worship services.
- Private clubs such as tennis, golf and health clubs are available for a fee.
- Ethnic groups represent nationalities such as Indian, German, Greek and many others.
- Social service organizations exist for all kinds of causes. Some examples are Red Cross, Cancer Society and Big Brothers/Big Sisters.
- Such public service clubs as Kiwanis and Lions provide fellowship for the members and social benefits for the community.

Chapter 33

Marriage Procedures

Marriage laws are set by the state where you wish to be married.

Age

Most states require that both the bride and groom be at least 18. In Nebraska and Wyoming you must both be over 19, while in Mississippi you must be 21. A few states allow you to marry before the age of 16, with parents' consent.

You will need to provide proof of age. This can be done with your birth certificate, immigration record, adoption record or passport.

License

You must have a marriage license. The fee varies by location. Some states require a waiting period of three to five days between the application for a license and the marriage. In many areas you must also have a medical examination and blood test before getting a license.

Ceremony

The wedding may be a religious ceremony, performed in a house of worship or it may be in the form of a civil ceremony, performed anywhere by a civil official such as a judge.

Some states require couples to announce their intention to marry a certain length of time before the ceremony. Many couples follow this practice, started by the Roman Catholic Church, by having their engagements announced in church for several Sundays. These announcements are called "banns".

Other Laws

Some states prohibit marriage by persons with certain mental or physical limitations.

If you were not born in the United States, be prepared to show proof of your immigration status.

A common requirement is that both parties freely consent to the marriage. If it can be shown that either the bride or groom was threatened or forced, the marriage may be declared void.

State laws do not permit a person who has been married once to marry again while the first marriage is still in effect. Marrying a second time in such a case constitutes the crime of bigamy, and the second marriage is considered void.

You will need a copy of your divorce decree, if applicable.

Some states acknowledge common-law marriages as valid. These are informal marriages in which the parties have not complied with the legal requirements for a license or ceremony. They simply carry out an agreement to live as husband and wife. The community recognizes them as a married couple. In some states where an agreement to live together is all that is necessary, marriages by mail or telephone may be possible.

A marriage by proxy is common in some countries and may be recognized in some states. In this ceremony, one of the parties is not present. Someone else substitutes as the absent person's proxy.

A marriage is usually considered valid according to the laws of the state where the ceremony was performed. Two persons who are not qualified to marry under the laws of one state may go to another state where the laws are different, have the ceremony performed, and then return. However, the couple's home state may, and often does, refuse to recognize the validity of the marriage.

Same-sex Marriages

According to CNN on December 3, 1996, a Hawaiian state court upheld the right of same-sex couples to be legally wed, five years after a gay couple first filed suit against Hawaii for denying them a marriage license.

The ruling makes Hawaii the first state to recognize that gay and lesbian couples are entitled to the same privileges as heterosexual married couples. However, the case is far from over since both sides promised to appeal should the verdict be against them.

The case has been closely watched, as it could set a landmark precedent throughout the United States.

Many states have taken up efforts to outlaw same-sex marriages and some have actually passed laws banning such marriages.

Congress passed the Defense of Marriage Act in September of 1996. The measure would not bar states from legalizing same-sex marriages, but states would not be obligated to recognize such marriages performed in another state.

Divorce

Divorce laws vary from state to state. There are various grounds for divorce, such as irreconcilable differences, adultery or extreme cruelty.

Find an attorney who is competent in divorce/family law to help you.

Part V

Post-Naturalization Rights

As was explained in Book 1, Getting In, the final step in the immigration process is becoming a United States citizen.

With the responsibilities of citizenship come certain benefits.

Clearly the right to vote is the major privilege of U.S. citizenship. After spending several years on the fringe of American society, many Green Card holders look forward to the final step in their transition–citizenship and the right to participate fully in American society.

Chapter 34 — Voting
- Details about the most cherished right of citizenship

Chapter 35 — Passport
- Foreign travel as a U.S. Citizen

Chapter 34

Voting

In order to participate in any U.S. election, voters in all states, except North Dakota, must register in advance.

The Federal Registration Act which took effect in 1995, regulates all states. Although each has its own laws regarding registration and deadlines, all states have to pass legislation to make the provisions of the act applicable to federal, state and local elections.

The act requires states to register voters in three specified ways in addition to any other procedures the state uses for voter registration:

- Simultaneous application for driver's license and voter registration
- Mail application for voter registration
- Application in person at designated government agencies, including public assistance agencies and agencies that provide services to people with disabilities

You may leave the completed form with the state agency or public office and the application should be submitted for you. Or, you can mail or deliver it in person to your local registration office. In many states the deadline is 30 days before an election.

To register in most states, you must:

- Be a U.S. citizen (Severe penalties apply to aliens who vote illegally)
- Be at least 18 years of age at the time of the next election
- Be a resident of the state where registering
- Not be mentally incapacitated
- Not have been convicted of a felony without civil rights having been restored
- Not claim the right to vote in another county or state

If you are living outside the United States, you will find Federal Postcard Applications for registration at military bases, U.S. embassies or consular offices.

There is no statutory requirement to show proof of age, citizenship, or residency, but the Supervisor of Elections has the right to ask, if in any doubt. Therefore, it is advisable to take proof if applying in person.

In about half the states, you must register with a party if you want to take part in that party's primary election, caucus, or convention. You can still vote in general elections and nonparty primary elections even if you have no party preference.

If you do not want to register with a party, write "no party" or leave the box blank. Do not write in the word "independent" if you mean "no party" because this might be confused with the name of a political party in your state.

The application must be signed as an oath that all information is true. If it is not true, you can be convicted of a felony of the third degree.

You should receive a voter's registration card in the mail within a couple of weeks of applying.

If you move from one state to another, you must register in the new state.

You fill out the box that asks where you last were registered and the new state should notify the previous location that you have moved.

Absentee ballots are available for voters who will be out of town on election day or are physically unable to get to the poles.

The county Supervisor of Elections office will answer questions about the registration process. Assistance will also be given to anyone who has a problem understanding the ballot or voting procedure.

There is no legal prohibition against a U.S. citizen voting in a foreign election. This was struck down by Afroyim v. Rusk, 387 U.S. 253 in 1980 and in 1986 repealed by Congress.

Jury Duty

The right of a trial by jury is a privilege of every person in the United States. This right is guaranteed by the U.S. Constitution. Therefore, jurors are essential to the administration of justice.

Once your name is on the voters' list, you may receive notice at any time that you must report for jury duty. However, in some areas, jurors will be selected randomly from a list provided by the driver's license office.

Jurors must be U.S. citizens. Certain people such as those under prosecution for a crime, convicted felons and lawyers may be disqualified.

Generally, at least in one state, the following may be excused from jury duty if they wish:

- Persons who have been summoned for jury duty within one year
- Expectant mothers
- Parents with custody of a young child, meeting specific conditions
- Persons 70 years or older
- Persons responsible for the care of someone mentally or physically incompetent
- Persons with physical or medical impairment

Running for Political Office

Once you are qualified to vote, you may be interested in running for office. Without significant financial resources or a political organization to help you through the process, it is difficult to win an election.

In spite of the stress of public office, it also can provide an exciting, challenging and gratifying life.

Many political offices require that you be a registered voter over 18 years of age. However, the minimum age requirement for the U.S. Senate is 30 and for the U.S. Congress the minimum is 25. You must be born in the United States in order to run for president.

A declaration of candidacy is the document you sign in order to start the process of becoming a candidate. You "declare" yourself as a candidate for a particular office and if you wish to run as a party candidate, you "declare" yourself to be a member of that party also.

Check for details with the appropriate level of government where you are considering running.

Chapter 35

Passport

P assports are issued to U.S. citizens and nationals by the Passport Office of the Department of State's Bureau of Consular Affairs. They are a symbol of the government and excellent proof of citizenship and identity.

Dual Citizens may be required to show the passport of their other country of citizenship when entering and leaving that country.

Application (in person)

Most Passport Agencies now have an automatic telephone appointment system and will accept only those individuals with appointments.

Some Passport Agencies are now issuing passports only to customers traveling within 14 calendar days or who need extra time because they require visas. You must phone for an appointment, then must arrive at the agency not more than 15 minutes prior to, and not later than, your scheduled time. In addition to the normal required documents, you must provide proof of travel within 14 days (airline ticket, confirmed airline-generated itinerary, or a travel letter from an employer for business travel). In addition to the regular passport fee, you will pay a $35 expedite fee for each application. A completed passport may be returned by overnight delivery for an additional cost.

First-time applicants may also apply at one of the designated post offices, clerks of court, municipal offices or public libraries authorized to accept passport applications. You will receive your passport in the mail within 25 business days from receipt of completed applications by the passport agency. Expedited service, plus the two-way overnight delivery option, are also available for the additional $35 fee, plus delivery costs. Together, these generally ensure receipt of passports in 7 to 10 business days.

A list of locations accepting applications may be accessed on the Bureau of Consular Affairs home page on the internet at http://travel.state.gov. That site also has information on application requirements and passport application forms for downloading.

It is a good idea to phone first to find which agency in your area accepts passport applications. Also check what form of payment they require.

Minors under 13 are not required to sign and do not need to appear. However, all persons, including newborn infants, must obtain their passports in their own names.

Documents required include:

- *Forms*
  - DSP-11 Application form filled out (using black ink but **not** signed until instructed to do so by the agent)
- *Proof of citizenship*
  - if born <u>in</u> the U.S.
    - previous U.S. passport, or
    - certified copy of your birth certificate issued by the state, county, or city of birth (A certified copy has a registrar's raised, embossed, impressed, or multicolored seal and the date the certificate was filed with the registrar's office)
  - if <u>not</u> born in the U.S.
    - previous passport, or
    - Certificate of citizenship, or
    - Certificate of naturalization (Note: An Attestation of Naturalization is not acceptable documentation of citizenship when applying for a passport)
  - if claiming citizenship through birth abroad to U.S. citizen parent(s) submit:
    - Certificate of Birth (Form FS-545 or DS 1350) or
    - Consular Report of Birth (Form FS-240) or
    - foreign birth certificate, parents' marriage certificate, proof of parents' citizenship, and affidavit of U.S. citizen parent(s) showing all periods and places of residence/physical presence in the U.S. and abroad before your birth
  - if claiming citizenship through naturalization of parent(s), submit:
    - Certificate of Naturalization of your parent(s)
    - your foreign birth certificate
    - proof of your admission to the U.S. for permanent residence
- *Proof of identity*
  - generally acceptable documents with signature and physical description or photographs such as:
    - previous U.S. passport, or
    - Certificate of Naturalization or citizenship, or
    - valid driver's license, or
    - government, military or corporate ID

- *Photographs*
  - two identical passport photographs (2" square) taken within the past six months in color or black and white
  - Note:
    - passport photographers should have the specifications
    - newspaper, magazine and most vending machine prints are not acceptable
    - head coverings are only acceptable if worn for religious reasons
    - Passport Services encourages photographs of relaxed and happy applicants
- *Fee*
  - $60 for a 10-year passport
  - $40 for a five-year passport for persons under 16
  - Note:
    - these amounts include a $15 service fee
    - verify the method of payment required by the application agency you choose
    - a check, bank draft, or money order payable to Passport Services may be acceptable except when dealing with a court, embassy or consulate abroad
    - cash, in the exact amount, may also be accepted by passport agencies and some, but not all, post offices and courts
- *Social Security Number*
  - if you have not been issued a Social Security number, enter zeroes in box #6

According to the Passport Application, Section 6039E of the Internal Revenue Code of 1986 requires that a passport applicant provide name, mailing address, date of birth and social security number. In turn, Passport Services, provides this information to the Internal Revenue Service. An IRS spokesperson stated that the IRS wants to be sure that everyone who has proven to be living and working legally in the U.S.A., is also paying taxes. Any applicant who fails to provide the required information is subject to a $500 penalty enforced by the IRS. Any questions on this matter should be referred to the nearest IRS office.

Application (by mail)

You may apply for renewal by mail if you:

- Are a U.S. citizen with a passport issued within the past 12 years
- Were over 16 years old at the time it was issued

- Have the same name as on the most recent passport or have had your name changed by marriage or court order and can submit proper documentation

If your name has been changed, enclose the court order, marriage certificate or divorce decree and Form DSP-19 Passport Amendment/Validation Application. If your name is changed by any other means, you must apply in person. If you just want to change the name on your passport, there is no charge.

Application Process

Pick up and fill out (in black ink) a DSP-82 "Application For Passport By Mail" available from a specified post office, courthouse or a U.S. Consulate or Embassy abroad. Phone first to be sure where forms are available and to determine the procedure if an expedited passport renewal is required. Forms may also be downloaded from the internet. See the address under "Information".

Attach
- Your most recent passport
- Two identical passport photographs, taken within the last six months
- $40 fee. Make personal check or money order payable to Passport Services (The $15 service fee is waived for those eligible to apply by mail)
- If applicable, a $35 fee for urgent service plus delivery costs

Mail

The completed DSP-82 application and attachments (in a padded envelope, if possible) should be mailed to:

National Passport Center
P.O. Box 371971
Pittsburgh, PA 15250-7971

U.S. citizens residing abroad cannot submit this form to this address. They should contact the nearest U.S. Embassy or Consulate for information.

If you wish to use an overnight service that will not deliver to a post office box, send it to:

Passport Services - Lockbox
Attn: Passport Supervisor 371971
3 Mellon Bank Center, Room 153-2723
Pittsburgh, PA 15259-0001

Include the appropriate fee for overnight return of your passport. Overnight service will not speed up processing time unless the $35 payment for expedited service is also included.

Your previous passport will be returned with your new passport.

Certain acts or conditions may need to be explained as part of your application. For instance, if, since acquiring U.S. citizenship, you have worked for a foreign government or entered into the armed forces of a foreign state, a supplementary explanation under oath may be necessary. Information is on the back of the application.

Information

Helpful information and instructions are found on the back of the Passport Application forms available at any court or post office which deals with passport applications, a passport office, U.S. Embassy or Consulate abroad.

Application forms may be downloaded at http://travel.state.gov/get_forms.html.

The Federal Information Center has passport information at (800) 688-9889.

For general information on passports or to check on the status of an application, phone The National Passport Information Center (NPIC) at (900) 225-5674. Callers of the 900 number will be charged 35 cents per minute to listen to the automated messages, and $1.05 per minute to speak with an operator. A live operator is available from 8:30 am to 5:30 pm, Eastern Time, Monday through Friday. A credit card call may be made for a flat rate of $4.95 to (888) 362-8668.

Passport Agencies are located at:

Boston Passport Agency
Thomas P. O'Neill Federal Building
Room 247, 10 Causeway Street
Boston, MA 02222-1094
Information: (617) 565-6990*
Region: ME,MA,NH,RI,Upstate NY,VT

New York Passport Agency **
Federal Office Building
376 Hudson Street, New York
Only for travel within 14 days
Appointment: (212) 206-3500
Region: New York City and Long Island

Chicago Passport Agency
Suite 380
Kluczynski Federal Office Bldg
230 South Dearborn Street
Chicago, IL 60604-1564
Appointment: (312) 341-6020
Region: IL,IN,MI

Philadelphia Passport Agency **
U.S. Customs House
200 Chestnut Street, Room 103
Philadelphia, PA 19106-2970
Appointment: (215) 418-5937
Region: DE,NJ,PA,WV

Honolulu Passport Agency

1st Hawaiian Tower
1132 Bishop St., Ste 500
Honolulu, HI 96813-2809
Information: (808) 522-8283*
Region: American Samoa, Federated
States of Micronesia, Guam, HI,
North Mariana Island

Houston Passport Agency

Suite 1400
Mickey Leland Federal Building
1919 Smith Street
Houston, TX 77002-8049
Appointment: (713) 751-0294
Region: KS,OK,NM,TX

Los Angeles Passport Agency

Suite 1000
11000 Wilshire Blvd.
Los Angeles, CA
90024-3615
Appointment: (310) 575-5700
Region: CA (all counties south of &
including San Luis Obispo, Kern &
San Bernardino & NV (Clark county only)

Miami Passport Agency

3rd Floor, Claude Pepper
Federal Office Building
51 S.W. 1st Avenue
Miami, FL 33130-1680
Appointment: (305) 539-3600
Region: FL,GA,PR,SC,USVI

San Francisco Passport Agency

95 Hawthorne St., 5th floor
San Francisco, CA 94105-3901
94105-3901
Appointment: (415) 538-2700
Region: AZ, CA (all counties
north of & including Monterey,
Kings, Oulare & Inyo, NV (except
Clark County), UT

Seattle Passport Agency

Room 992, Federal Office Bldg.
915 2nd Avenue
Seattle, WA 98174-1091
Information: (206) 220-7788
                (206) 220-7777*
Region: AK,CO,ID,MN,MT,NE,ND,
SD,OR,WA,WY

Stamford Passport Agency

One Landmark Square
Broad and Atlantic Street
Stamford, CT 06901-2767
Appointment: (203) 969-9000
Region: CT, Westchester Co.(NY)

Washington Passport Agency

1111 19th St. N.W.
Washington, D.C. 20524
Appointment: (202) 647-0518
Region: MD, northern VA (including
Alexandria, Arlington
County, Fairfax County), D.C.
Also accepts applications for diplomatic,
official and No-Fee passports

New Orleans Passport Agency

One Canal Place
365 Canal Street, Suite 1300
New Orleans, Louisiana
70113-1931
Information: (504) 589-6728*
              (504) 589-6161/2
Region: AL,AR,IA,KY,LA,MS,MO,NC,
OH,TN, VA (except D.C. suburbs),WI

*This is a 24-hour information line that includes general passport information, passport agency location and hours of operation and information regarding emergency passport services during non-working hours.

**Customers must make an appointment and be traveling within 14 calendar days.

Effective May 15, 2000, the Department of State will refund the passport application fee and the fee for executing an application for a passport only in cases when the fee was collected in error from persons exempted from payment by law, or the fee collected was in excess of the prescribed fee.

In cases where an application for issuance of a passport is denied on the sole ground of inadequate documentation or a reason that can be cured by the provision of further documentation, a new application fee should not be required when the applicant provides acceptable documentation in a timely manner so that a passport is issued. An applicant's denied application for a passport may be reconsidered without the payment of an additional application fee by the submission of adequate documentation within 90 days of a notice of denial.

The Department of State will not refund the fee paid for a passport application when, after processing, it is determined that the applicant will not be issued a passport.

Ref: 65 FR 14212

Appendix A

Immigration And Naturalization Service (INS) Forms and Fees

Effective October 13, 1998

Form No.	Form Name/Description	Fee
I-17	Petition for Approval of School for Attendance by Nonimmigrant Students	$200
I-90	Application to Replace Permanent Resident Card	$110
I-102	Application for Replacement/Initial Nonimmigrant Arrival Departure Document	$85
I-129	Petition for a Nonimmigrant Worker	$110
I-129F	Petition for Alien Finance(e)	$95
I-129	Petition with Unnamed Beneficiaries (per petition)	$110
I-129	Petition with Named Beneficiaries (per petition)	$110
I-130	Petition for Alien Relative	$110
I-131	Application for Travel Document	$95
I-140	Immigrant Petition for Alien Worker	$115
I-191	Application for Advance Permission to Return to Unrelinquished Domicile	$170
I-192	Application for Advance Permission to Enter as a Nonimmigrant	$170
I-193	Application for Waiver of Passport and/or Visa	$170
I-212	Application for Permission to Reapply for Admission into the U.S. After Deportation or Removal	$170
I-360	Petition for Amerasian, Widow(er), or Special Immigrant (except for a petition seeking classification as Amerasian)	$110
I-485	Application to Register Permanent Residence or Adjust Status	
	• if 14 years of age or older	$220
	• if under 14 years of age	$160
I-526	Immigrant Petition by Alien Entrepreneur	$350
I-539	Application to Extend/Change Nonimmigrant Status (plus $10 per co-applicant)	$120
I-600	Petition to Classify Orphan as an Immediate Relative	$405
I-600A	Application for Advance Processing of Orphan Petition	$405
I-601	Application for Waiver of Grounds of Excludability	$170
I-612	Application for Waiver of the Foreign Residence Requirement	$170
I-751	Petition to Remove the Condition on Residence	$125

I-765	Application for Employment Authorization	$100
I-817	Application for Voluntary Departure Under Family Unity Program	$120
I-821	Application for Temporary Protected Status	$50
N-300	Application to File Declaration of Intention	$50
N-400	Application for Naturalization	$225
N-565	Application for a Certificate of Naturalization	$135
N-470	Application to Preserve Residence for Naturalization Purposes	$80
N-565	Application for Replacement Naturalization/Citizenship Document	$135
N-600	Application for Certificate of Citizenship	$160
N-643	Application for Certificate of Citizenship - Behalf of Adopted Child	$125
N-644	Application for Posthumous Citizenship	$80

Appendix B

Affidavit of Birth

If it is not possible to obtain a birth certificate to satisfy entry criteria, it will be necessary to submit alternative documentation. In such cases, it may be acceptable to file an affidavit of birth such as the following sample.

An affidavit should be completed and sworn sworn before a Notary Public. The following sample affidavit is provided as a guideline only.

Affidavit of Birth

I, (name of relative), being duly sworn, do depose and say that:

(1) I presently reside at _____.

(2) I am a citizen of _____.

(3) I was born on _____ at_____.

(4) I am the (state relationship to the person whose birth is being verified)

(5) I know that (name of person) was born on _____ at _____.

(6) A request has been made with the proper authorities for (name of person)'s birth certificate.

_____
Signed

Sworn to and subscribed to before me this _____ day of _____ (YEAR), at _____.

_____
Notary Public

My commission expires:_____.

Appendix C

Information Telephone Numbers

American Institute of Certified Public Accountants	(800) 862-4272
American Immigration Lawyers Association	(202) 371-9377
Citizenship Test Program - Florida	(800) 667-3271
Community Home Buyer's Program - Information	(800) 732-6643
Consumer Outreach	(800) 357-2099
Customs	(202) 927-6724

Department of Labor -
Forms	(202) 219-4369
Stats - Sliplaws	(202) 219-7316

Department of State -   (202) 647-4000
American Citizen Consular Information Line	(800) 529-4410
FAM	(202) 647-6575
National Visa Center(Immigrant Visa Inquiries)	(603) 334-0700
Nonimmigrant Visa Appointments	(888) 840-0032
Nonimmigrant Visa Cancellations	(888) 611-6676
Office of Citizen Consular Services	(202) 647-4000
Orphan Adoption	(202) 647-3444
Passport Agency	(202) 647-0518
Visa Information	(202) 663-1225
Visa Information - Officer - 2-4 pm Eastern Time	(202) 663-1213
Visa Lottery Hotline (900) 884-8840	(202) 331-7199
Visa Priority Date Information	(202) 663-1541
(800) and (900) visa information line listings	(800) 283-4356

Dictionary of Occupational Titles - Inquiry	(919) 733-7917
Employment Discrimination Complaints (Office of General Counsel)	(800) 253-7688
Equifax - Credit Report	(800) 685-1111
Experian - Credit Report	(800) 682-7654

Fannie Mae Lenders	(800) 7FANNIE
FBI - Fingerprint inquiry	(304) 625-5590
Federal Election Commission	(800) 424-9530
Federal Information Center	(800) 688-9889
Florida Windstorm Underwriting Association	(904) 354-3302
Government Printing Office	
Order Line	(202) 783-3238
Charge Orders	(202) 512-1800
HUD Housing Hotline - Fair Lending Laws	(800) 669-9777
Immigration and Naturalization Service (INS)	
INS- Recorded and in-person information	(800) 375-5283
800 Recorded Information Service	(800) 755-0777
Fingerprint inquiries	(888) 557-5398
Form Orders	(800) 870-3676
Insurance Consumer Hotline FL	(800) 342-2762
International Association for Financial Planning	(800) 945-4237
Internal Revenue Service (IRS)	
Information	(800) 829-1040
Tax Forms	(800) TAX-FORM
Market Assistance Plan (MAP) FL	(800) 524-9023
Medicare Hotline	(800) 638-6833
National Flood Insurance Program	(800) 638-6620
National Passport Information Center	
Passport Status or Passport Technical Info	(900) 225-5674
Selective Service	(708) 688-6888
Social Security	(800) 772-1213
State Department	(202) 647-4000
List of J-1 Exchange Visitor Programs	(202) 485-7979
Exchange Visitor Hotline	(202) 260-3038
Visa Lottery Hot Line (900) 884-8840	(202) 331-7199
Visa Priority Date Information Line	(202) 663-1541

Appendix D

Credential Evaluators

Employment related visas often require analysis of education and work experience to prove that the applicant's background is relevant to the position offered.

The INS may ask for an academic credential evaluation from an approved consulting service to determine the equivalent educational level.

Many post-secondary institutions and professional associations prepare their own assessments.

However, if you need assistance, the following is a list of some of the organizations that evaluate credentials. They are members of the National Association of Credential Evaluation Services (NACES) and affiliate members of the American Association of Collegiate Registrars and Admissions Officers (AACRAO). It would be wise to check with INS to be sure that they require a professional evaluation and will accept the appraisal of the specific one you choose, before hiring the company.

Center for Applied Research, Evaluation and Education, Inc
P.O. Box 20348
Long Beach CA 90801
Phone: (213) 430-1105

Education Evaluators International, Inc.
P.O. Box 5397
Los Alamitos CA 90720-5397
Phone: (310) 431-2187
FAX: (310) 493-5021

Education International, Inc
29 Denton Road
Wellesley MA 02191
Phone: (617) 235-7425
FAX: (617) 235-6831

Educational Credential Evaluators, Inc.
P.O. Box 514070
Milwaukee WI 53202
Phone: (414) 289-3400
FAX: (414) 289-3411
Email: eval@ece.org

Evaluation Services, Inc
P.O. Box 1455
Albany NY 12201
Phone: (518) 672-4522
Email: esi@capital.net

Foundation for International Services
200 West Mercer Street, Suite 503,
Seattle WA 98119-3958
Phone: (206) 298-0171
Fax: (206) 298-0173

International Consultants of Delaware, Inc.
109 Barksdale Professional Center
Newark DE 19711
Phone: (302) 737-8715
FAX: (302) 737-8756

International Education Research Foundation, Inc.
P.O. Box 66940
Los Angeles CA 90066
Phone: (310) 390-6276
FAX: (310) 397-7686

World Education Services, Inc.
P.O. Box 745
Old Chelsea Station NY 10113-0745
Phone: (800) 937-3895
Email: info@wes.org

The documents you submit must be in English, or be translated accurately. The translator doesn't have to be a professional, but should be competent in both languages.

The translator must attach the following statement:

"I certify that I am competent to translate this document from (insert foreign language) to English and that this translation is accurate and complete to the best of my knowledge and ability.

Signature

                                Date

Appendix E

Dictionary of Occupational Titles (DOT)

Three-digit Occupational Group Codes

Professional, Technical, and Managerial Occupations and Fashion Models

Occupations in Architecture, Engineering, and Surveying

001 Architectural

002 Aeronautical Engineering

003 Electrical/Electronics Engineering

005 Civil Engineering

006 Ceramic Engineering

007 Mechanical Engineering

008 Chemical Engineering

010 Mining and Petroleum Engineering

011 Metallurgy and Metallurgical Engineering

012 Industrial Engineering

013 Agricultural Engineering

014 Marine Engineering

015 Nuclear Engineering

017 Drafters

018 Surveying/Cartographic

019 Other Architecture, Engineering and Surveying

Mathematics and Physical Sciences

020 Mathematics

021 Astronomy

022 Chemistry

023 Physics

024 Geology

025 Meteorology

029 Other Mathematics and Physical Sciences

Computer-Related Occupations

030 Systems Analysis and Programming

031 Data Communications and Networks

032 Computer System User Support

033 Computer System Technical Support

039 Other Computer-Related

Occupations in Life Sciences

040 Agricultural Sciences
041 Biological Sciences

045 Psychology
049 Other Life Sciences

Occupations in Social Sciences

050 Economics
051 Political Science
052 History

054 Sociology
055 Anthropology
059 Other Social Sciences

Occupations in Medicine and Health

070 Physicians and Surgeons
071 Osteopaths
072 Dentists
073 Veterinarians
079 Other Medicine and Health

074 Pharmacists
076 Therapists
077 Dieticians
078 Medical and Dental Technology

Occupations in Education

090 College and University
    Education
091 Secondary School Education
092 Preschool, Primary School
    and Kindergarten Education

094 Education of Persons with
    Disabilities
096 Home Economists and Farm Advisors
097 Vocational Education

099 Other Education

Occupations in Museum, Library and Archival Sciences

100 Librarians
101 Archivists

102 Museum Curators and Related
109 Other Museum, Library, and Archival
    Sciences

Occupations in Law and Jurisprudence

110 Lawyers
111 Judges

119 Other Law and Jurisprudence

Occupations in Religion and Theology

120 Clergy

129 Other Religion and Theology

Occupations in Writing

131 Writers

132 Editors: Publication,
   Broadcast and Script

139 Other Writing

Occupations in Art

141 Commercial Artists: Designers
   Illustrators, Graphic Arts

142 Environmental, Product, and
   Related Designers

149 Other Art

Occupations in Entertainment and Recreation

152 Music

159 Other Entertainment and Recreation

Occupations in Administrative Specializations

160 Accountants, Auditors and
   Related

161 Budget and Management
   Systems Analysis

162 Purchasing Management

163 Sales and Distribution
   Management

164 Advertising Management

165 Public Relations Management

166 Personnel Administration

168 Inspectors and Investigators,
   Managerial and Public Service

169 Other Administrative

Managers and Officials

180 Agriculture, Forestry and
   Fishing Industry Managers
   and Officials

181 Mining Industry Managers
   and Officials

182 Construction Industry
   Managers and Officials

183 Manufacturing Industry
   Managers and Officials

184 Transportation,
   Communication, and Utilities
   Industry Managers and Officials

185 Wholesale and Retail Trade
   Managers and Officials

186 Finance, Insurance, and Real
   Estate Managers and Officials

187 Service Industry Managers and
   Officials

188 Public Administration Managers
   and Officials

189 Miscellaneous Managers and
   Officials

Miscellaneous Professional, Technical, and Managerial Occupations

195 Social and Welfare Work

199 Miscellaneous Professional, Technical, and Managerial

Sales Promotion Occupations

297 Fashion Models

Ref: FR Doc. 95-1394, January 18, 1995

Appendix F

Department of Labor - Employment and Training Administration (ETA) Regional Offices - Regional Certifying Officers

Region I   J.F. Kennedy Federal Building
Room E-350
Boston, MA 02203
Phone: (617) 565-4446
Fax: (617) 565-2158
Tone-Talker: (617) 565-2267

Serving: Connecticut, Maine, Massachusetts, New Hampshire, Rhode Island, and Vermont.

Region II   201 Varick Street
Room 755
New York, NY 10014
Phone: (212) 337-2186
Fax: (212) 337-1342
Tone-Talker: (212) 337-2193

Serving: New York, New Jersey, Puerto Rico, and the Virgin Islands.

Region III   3535 Market Street
Room 13450
Philadelphia, PA 19104
Phone: (215) 596-6363
Fax: (215) 596-0480
Tone-Talker: (215) 596-5033

Serving: Delaware, Maryland, Pennsylvania, Virginia, West Virginia, and the District of Columbia.

Region IV   Sam Nunn Federal Center
            61 Forsyth Street, S.W.
            Suite 6M-12
            Atlanta, GA 30303
            Phone: (404) 562-2115
            Fax: (404) 562-2152
            Tone-Talker: (404) 562-2131
Serving: Alabama, Florida, Georgia, Kentucky, Mississippi, North Carolina, South Carolina, and Tennessee.

Region V   230 South Dearborn Street
            Room 605
            Chicago, IL 60604
            Phone: (312) 353-1550
            Fax: (312) 353-1509
            Tone-Talker: (312) 353-1059
Serving: Illinois, Indiana, Michigan, Minnesota, Ohio, and Wisconsin.

Region VI   525 Griffin Street
            Room 317
            Dallas, TX 75202
            Phone: (214) 767-4989
            Fax: (214) 767-4788
            Tone-Talker: (214) 767-4975
Serving: Arkansas, Louisiana, New Mexico, Oklahoma, and Texas.

Region VII 1100 Main Street
            Suite 1050
            Kansas City, MO 64105
            Phone: (816) 426-3796
            Fax: (816) 426-2729
Serving: Iowa, Kansas, Missouri, and Nebraska.

Region VIII 1999 Broadway
            Suite 1780
            Denver, CO 80202-5716
            Phone: (303) 844-1668
            Fax: (303) 844-1685
            Tone-Talker: (303) 844-1674
Serving: Colorado, Montana, North Dakota, South Dakota, Utah, and Wyoming.

Region IX   Mail address - P.O. Box 193767
             Courier address - 71 Stevenson Street
             Room 830
             San Francisco, CA 94119-3767
             Phone: (415) 975-4601
             Fax: (415) 975-4612
             Tone-Talker: (415) 975-4617
Serving: Arizona, California, Guam, Hawaii, and Nevada.

Region X   1111 Third Avenue
             Suite 900
             Seattle, WA 98101-3212
             Phone: (206) 553-8037
             Fax: (206) 553-2069
Serving: Alaska, Idaho, Oregon, and Washington.

Note: Tone-Talker, the ETA's automated telephone information service, is available in most regional ETA offices.

Glossary

Accompanying Relatives Spouse and unmarried children under age 21 coming with visa holder

Adjudicate To legally judge a document or case

Admission/Admitted Lawful entry of an alien into the United States after inspection and authorization by an immigration officer

Advance Parole Person is granted advance parole if it is necessary to leave the U.S. temporarily before getting a visa

Alien Any person in the United States who is not a citizen or a national is an "alien".

The three broad classifications of aliens include:

- **unlawful, unauthorized, undocumented or illegal aliens** who have entered illegally or violated the terms of their visas
- **nonimmigrants** who have entered on temporary visas with limited rights
- **resident-aliens** or **permanent residents** who have received Green Cards and can live and work permanently in the United States

Ref: INS ER 806 3-8-94

Alien Registration Receipt Card Former name of Permanent Resident Card

Appeal To request a new hearing in a higher court

Application A formal request for immigration admission status or for permission or compliance in connection with a government regulation

Asylee An alien who applies for and receives asylum within the United States and must prove a well-founded fear of persecution or physical danger upon return to the home country

Attestation Sworn statement made by employer assuring the U.S. Department of Labor that the job offer meets DOL specifications to protect the U.S. labor force

Attestation of Citizenship Temporary document proving that the alien has been sworn in as a citizen. Does not replace the Certificate of Citizenship

Beneficiary Person who is being sponsored in a petition for a green card or visa

Border Crossing Cards Special, limited approval for Canadians and Mexicans who have legal status to cross the border on a regular basis

Citizens According to the Constitution of the U.S., all people born in the United States and its territories are U.S. citizens except children of foreign diplomats born in the United States who are excluded

All people naturalized in the U.S. are citizens. Also, children born abroad who have at least one U.S. citizen parent may be eligible to claim U.S. citizenship by a form of inheritance or derivation

Consul Department of State representative abroad, responsible for processing nonimmigrant and immigrant applications. A Consul also represents the interests of citizens abroad who are currently within their jurisdiction

Consulate Office of the Consul and government representatives (branch office of U.S. Embassy)

Embassy Office of the Ambassador and representatives of a government in a foreign country, traditionally based in a capital city

ESL English as a Second Language. Students are taught English skills from basic to advanced. At the advanced level they should be able to make oral presentations at university and write essays and reports

Excludability Condition preventing a visa applicant from being allowed into the United States

Foreign National A person who is a citizen of a country other than where residing

Green Card Term used to describe an I-551 Permanent Resident Card issued to permanent resident aliens

High Commission Office of the representative of a commonwealth government in the capital city of another commonwealth country

Immigrant An alien who has a permanent visa allowing him or her to live in the United States permanently (Permanent Resident Alien)

Immigrant Visa Entry permit issued to a permanent resident alien. The Green Card is not issued until after entry into the U.S.

Inadmissable Alien Any alien present in the United States without being admitted or paroled, or who arrives in the United States at any time or place other than as designated by the Attorney General

Labor Certification Official acceptance by the DOL that no U.S. residents are available for the job offered to a foreigner

Legal Alien An alien who has permission to live in or work in the United States

National Could be either a citizen of the United States or a person, who although not a citizen of the United States, still owes permanent allegiance to the country

National Visa Center (NVC) Department of State unit which receives and processes Green Card applications and sends out forms

Naturalization A process which converts permanent resident aliens into citizens

Nonimmigrant Alien An alien who has a visa giving permission to travel, study or work for a fixed period of time

Parolee Someone who does not meet the technical visa requirements but is allowed to come to the United States, without a visa, for humanitarian purposes

Petition Proves eligibility for a green card or visa

Permanent Resident Alien An alien who has received an immigrant visa from the INS and has been granted permission to may live and work permanently in the United States

Permanent Resident Card Green Card, formerly called Alien Registration Receipt Card

Petitioner A person who sponsors a foreign national for a Green Card or visa

Political Asylum Status is granted to someone who has entered the United States as a nonimmigrant or illegal alien and has a well-founded fear of persecution in the home country

Preconceived Intent Process of applying for a visa but intending to change that status in the future to a more favorable one

Preference Family-sponsored and Employment-Based visas each have several preference categories, with close relatives of U.S. citizens and aliens with extraordinary qualifications having the highest preference

Priority Date Date of first filing of an application for a Green Card

Qualified Alien Category created by 1996 welfare reform consists of lawful permanent residents, refugees (including conditional entrants), asylees, and persons who have had their deportation withheld, parolees admitted for at least one year, and certain battered aliens and alien parents of battered children; all other categories are considered "not qualified aliens"

Quota Number of immigrants who can enter the United States in a year, including a certain number from any particular country

Refugee Person who has a well-founded fear of persecution in the home country, receives permission to come to the United States in refugee status before arriving

Regional Certifying Officer The official (in the Employment and Training Administration) (ETA) in a Department of Labor regional office who is authorized to act on labor certifications and employment attestations on behalf of the Secretary of Labor

Registration Letter sent as entry in a Green Card lottery (diversity) program

Sponsor (in relation to a sponsored alien) means an individual who executes an Affidavit of Support with respect to the sponsored alien, is a citizen or national of the United States or a lawfully admitted permanent resident and meets all criteria of sponsorship

Status Privileges given to aliens who are allowed entry in the United States

Temporary Visa (Nonimmigrant visa) allows an foreigner to visit the United States for a specific purpose and for a certain length of time

TOEFL Test of English as a Foreign Language is a test to measure reading and listening comprehension and writing recognition

TSE Test of Spoken English

TWE Test of Written English

Undocumented Alien An alien whose visa has expired or who has entered the country illegally

Visa An entry document, either on a separate piece of paper or in a passport issued outside the U.S.

Visa Number A number which is immediately available to an intending immigrant for entry in a pre-selected preference category

Visa Waiver Program Tourists from certain countries may come for 90 days without a visa

References

Books

Carroll, Andrew. *Volunteer USA.* New York: Ballantine Books, 1991.

Cutright, Melitta J. *The National PTA Talks to Parents: How to Get the Best Education for Your Child.* New York: Doubleday, 1989.

Daughters of the American Revolution. *DAR Manual for Citizenship.* rev. ed. Washington, DC: National Society, Daughters of the American Revolution, 1993.

Dresser, Norine. *Multicultural Manners.* New York: John Wiley & Sons, 1996.

Harwood, Bruce M. *Real Estate Principles.* 4th ed. Englewood Cliffs, NJ: Prentice-Hall, 1986.

Hogue, Kathleen; Jensen, Cheryl; and McClurg Urban, Kathleen. *The Complete Guide To Health Insurance: How to Beat the High Cost of Being Sick.* New York: Walker Publishing, 1988.

Government Publications

Code of Federal Regulations. Title 8. Aliens and Nationality. Washington, DC, 1997.

_____. Title 20. Employees' Benefits. Washington, DC, 1996.

_____. Title 22. Foreign Relations. Washington, DC, 1996.

Federal Register. Vol. 57, No. 181. 20 CFR Part 655, September 17, 1992.

_____. Vol. 59, No. 243. 20 CFR Part 655. 29 CFR Part 507, December 20, 1994.

_____. Vol. 60, No. 12. 20 CFR Part 655, 29 CFR Part 506, January 19, 1995.

Florida Department of Insurance. Consumer Outreach and Education. *Automobile Insurance Consumers' Guide.* Tallahassee, FL, 1997.

_____. *Health Insurance Consumers' Guide.* Tallahassee, FL, 1997.

_____. *Health Maintenance Organization Consumers' Guide.* Tallahassee, FL, 1997.

_____. *Insuring Your Home Consumers' Guide.* Tallahassee, FL, 1997.

Public Law. *Health Insurance Portability and Accountability Act.* (PL 104-191, August 21, 1996).

_____. *Illegal Immigration Reform and Immigrant Responsibility Act of 1996.* (PL 104-208, September 30, 1996).

_____. *Immigration and Nationality Act of 1952.* (PL 82-414, 1952).

_____. *Immigration Act of 1990.* (PL 101-649, November 29, 1990).

_____. *International Organizations Immunities Act.* (PL 79-291, 1946).

_____. *North American Free Trade Agreement Implementation Act.* (PL 103-182, December 8, 1993).

Selective Service System. *Information for Registrants.* Fort Worth, TX, 1988.

U.S. Code, Title 8. Aliens and Nationality. Washington, DC, 1994.

_____. Title 22. Foreign Relations and Intercourse. Washington, DC, 1994.

_____. Title 29. Labor. Washington, DC, 1994.

U.S. Department of Health and Human Services. Health Care Financing Administration. *Managed Care Plans.* Washington, DC. Publication No. CDFA-02195.

_____. *Your Medicare Handbook.* Baltimore, MD. Publication No. HCFA-10050, 1996.

U.S. Department of Health and Human Services. Health Care Financing Administration and the National Association of Insurance Commissioners. *Guide to Health Insurance for People with Medicare.* Baltimore, MD. Publication No. HCFA-02110, 1996.

_____. Social Security Administration. Agreement on Social Security Between the U.S. and *Canada.* Washington, DC. Publication No. 05-10198, 1990.

_____. *Medicare.* Baltimore, MD. Publication No. 05-10043, 1996.

_____. *Social Security–Household Workers.* Washington, DC. Publication No. 05-10021, 1997.

_____. *Social Security–How You Earn Credits.* Washington, DC. Publication No. 05-10072, 1997.

_____. *Social Security Numbers for Newborns.* Washington, DC. Publication No. 05-10023, 1995.

_____. *Social Security Retirement Benefits.* Washington, DC. Publication No. 05-10035, 1997.

_____. *Social Security–Understanding the Benefits.* Washington, DC. Publication No. 05-10024, 1997.

_____. *Social Security: When You'll Get Your Benefit.* Washington, DC. Publication No. 05-10031, 1997.

_____. *Your Social Security Number.* Washington, DC. Publication No. 05-10002, 1993.

_____. *Your Social Security Payments While You Are Outside The United States.* Washington, DC. Publication No. 05-10137, 1995.

U.S. Department of Housing and Urban Development. *The HUD Home Buying Guide.* Washington, DC. Publication No. HUD-1507-SFPD, 1997.

_____. Office of Housing. *Settlement Costs.* Washington, DC. Publication No. HUD-398-H(3), 1997.

U.S. Department of Justice. Immigration and Naturalization. *Service Law Books.*

_____. *Naturalization Requirements and General Information.* Form N-17, 1992.

_____. Eastern Regional Office. *Basic Guide to Naturalization and Citizenship.* Burlington, VT. Publication No. ER 721.

_____. *Guide to the Immigration and Naturalization Service.* Burlington, VT. Publication No. ER 806. March 8, 1994.

U.S. Department of Labor. Employment and Training Administration. *Policy Guidance on Alien Labor Certification Issues.* Field Memorandum 48-94. May, 1994.

_____. *Instructions for Filing Applications for Alien Employment Certification for Permanent Employment in the United States.* Washington, DC.

_____. Pension and Welfare Benefits Administration. *Health Benefits Under the Consolidated Omnibus Budget Reconciliation Act (COBRA).* Washington, DC.

U.S. Department of State. Bureau of Consular Affairs. *Passports: Applying for them the Easy Way.* Washington, DC. Publication No. 10049.

_____. *Foreign Affairs Manual.* 22 CFR, Vol. 9, Sub chapter E - Visas, April 1, 1997.

U.S. Department of the Treasury. U.S. Customs Service. *Importing A Car.* Washington, DC. Publication No. 520, 1995.

_____. *Know Before You Go.* Washington, DC. Publication No. 512, 1994.

_____. *Pets and Wildlife.* Washington, DC. Publication No. 509, 1995.

_____. *Tips for Visitors.* Washington, DC. Publication No. 521-A, 1993.

U.S. Federal Reserve Board. Office of Thrift Supervision. *Consumer Handbook on Adjustable Rate Mortgages.* Washington, DC. Publication No. FRB9-200,000-0892-C.

_____. *A Consumer's Guide to Mortgage Lock-Ins*. Washington, DC. Publication No. FRN 5-30,000-0993-C.

_____. *Home Mortgages: Understanding the Process and Your Right to Fair Lending*. Washington, DC. Publication No. FRB 2-250,000-493C.

U.S. Federal Trade Commission. *Buying A Used Car*. Washington, DC.

_____. *Facts for Consumers–Solving Credit Problems*. Washington, DC. Publication No. F002472, 1994.

Index

A – Senior Government Official 183
   admission process 183
   ambassadors, public ministers,
      diplomats or consular officers 183
   change to other status 187
   employment authorization 186
   extension/change of status 184

APHIS (Animal and Plant Health Inspection
   Service) 352

Accountant 133, 379, 458

Admissions 14, 203

Advance Parole 46, 207, 287

Affidavit of Birth 457

Affidavit of Support 159, 165, 328, 472

Alien in Transit 42, 188

American Competitiveness and Workforce
   Improvement Act 333

American Immigration Lawyers
   Association (AILA) 315

American Indians born in Canada 211

American Institute of Certified Public
   Accountants 379

Application for Employment 22

Asylee 206, 281, 285
   adjustment of status 290
   admission 287
   criteria 285
   dependents 288
   employment authorization 290
   establishing eligibility 286
   statistics 286

Athlete 105, 148, 330
   Minor League Professional - H-2B... 105
   Internationally-Recognized
      Athlete and Entertainer – P . . 148

Attorney General 7, 8

Automobile Insurance 366, 428
   definitions 429
   emergency road service 430

Automobiles 350

B – Visitor for Business or Pleasure 33

Banking 375

Border Crossing Card 40
   Canada 41
   Mexico 40

Business Professionals 90
   Treaty Trader or Investor – E 91
   Professional, Temporary Worker
      or Trainee – H 99
   Intracompany Transferee - L 123
   Treaty NAFTA - TN 132

C-1– Alien in Transit 42
   admission process 42

C-2/C-3 – Alien in Transit to U.N. &
      Foreign Government Official . 188
   admission process 188

Canada . . 20, 26, 41, 115, 132, 215, 358, 373

Canadian citizens/permanent residents . . 32
   border crossing card 41
   temporary visitor for business or
   pleasure 36

Car 364
   buying 364
   driver's license 366
   importing 350
   importing (see US Customs) 350
   insurance 428
   leasing 365
   loan 365
   registration 367
   used cars 364

Center for Disease Control 352

Change of Address 22, 206

Citizenship 292

Community Activities 439

Condominium 381

Conrad 20 Program 78, 83, 329

Credential Evaluators 460

Crew member, Sea or Air–D 42

Cultural Exchange Program
      Participant – Q-1 167

Customs
   see U.S. Customs Service 349

D – Crew member, Sea or Air 42
   admission process 42
   Crewman's Landing Permit - Land
     or Sea 42
   Department of Labor attestation .. 43

Definitions
   automobile insurance 429
   health insurance 424
   home buying 382
   homeowner's insurance 406
   mortgage 396

Dentist 135, 414

Department of Agriculture 349, 353

Department of Justice 8
   Attorney General 8

Department of Labor 8, 10, 204, 225, 340, 367
   internet 340
   labor certification 8, 107, 204
   Labor Condition Application 8, 105

Department of State 7
   Bureau of Consular Affairs 7
   internet 340
   orphan adoption 340
   passports 340, 447
   visa lottery program 274

Department of the Treasury 355

Department of Transportation   349, 350, 351

Derivative Status 228, 230, 233, 295
   birth abroad 295
   qualifying 295

Disability Insurance 370

Diversity (DV) Lottery 274

Divorce 441, 442

Doctor . 79, 107, 111, 135, 244, 247, 413, 414

Doctrine of Dual Intent . 101, 116, 124, 132

Driver's License 366

Dual Nationality 297
   passport 298
   risk of Loss of U.S. citizenship 298
   status of U.S. dual nationals 297
   U.S. Supreme Court rulings 297

Duty 349, 350, 354

E–Treaty Trader or Investor 91

Education 50, 433

Educational Classifications 50
   academic student – F 51
   Exchange Visitor - J 65

vocational or non-academic 30
   student – M 84

Emergency Road Service 430

Employment
   benefits and compensation 368
   holidays 368, 369
   minimum wage 368

Employment Authorization 55, 105, 204, 225

Employment-Based Preferences 224
   admission process 225
   Consular interview 231
   eligibility and waiting period 224
   entry criteria 225
   labor certification 225
   medical examination 230
   numbers available 224
   preference categories 224
   retaining your Green Card 232

Employment-Based
   First Preference – EB1 233
   admission process 234
   entry criteria 233

Employment-Based
   Second Preference – EB2 . . . 242
   admission process 245
   entry criteria 243
   labor certification 245
   National Interest Waiver . . . 244, 253

Employment-Based
   Third Preference – EB3 242
   admission process 245
   entry criteria 244
   labor certification 245

Employment-Based
   Fourth Preference – EB4 . . . 260
   admission process 262
   Amerasians, widow(er)s, religious
   workers 264

employees of U.S. Consulate in
   Hong Kong 265
   entry criteria 260
   juveniles under court protection . . . 265

Employment-Based
   Fifth Preference – EB5 268
   admission process 269
   employment creation (investors) . . 268
   entry criteria 268

Entertainer
Internationally-Recognized
   Athlete and Entertainer – P . . 148

Environmental Protection Agency . 349, 350

ETA Regional Offices 466

Extraordinary Ability–Sciences, Arts,
   Education, Business – O 141

Extraordinary/Internationally
   Recognized Classifications . . . 140

F – Academic Student 51
   admission process 52
   curricular practical training 57
   employment/training 55
   Illegal Immigration Reform and
      Immigrant Responsibility
      Act of 1996 54
   internship with an international
      organization 56
   optional practical training 58
   severe economic hardship
      employment 60

Family-Sponsored Preferences 216
   admission process 218
   Consular interview 222
   dependents 218, 220
   eligibility and waiting period 216
   employment authorization 223
   entry criteria 217
   medical examination 221
   numbers available 216

police clearance 221
preference categories 216
sponsorship 217

Fiancé(e) of U.S. Citizen 159

Financial Planner 379

Fingerprints 18, 20, 28
204, 207, 210, 221, 301, 319, 323

Food and Drug Administration . . 349, 351

Food stamps 293, 370

Foreign Government and Organization
Representative 181
Government Representative to
International Organization– G189
International Organization
Family Member – N 195
Representative of Member
State – NATO 197
Senior Government Official – A . . 183

Foreign Government Representative
Classifications 14

Fulbright-Hays Act of 1961 65

G – Government Representative to
International Organization . . 189
admission process 189
change to other status 194
dependent employment
authorization 193
extension/change of status 191
"Howe Letter" 190

Glossary 469

Government Official
Foreign Government Official – C-3   188
Senior Government Official – A . . 183

Government Official – A 183

Green Card Lottery 274
application 276

Diversity (DV) Lottery 274
entry criteria 275
processing 279
qualification 275, 276
quotas 275
selection of "winners" 201

Green Cards 188
absences from the United States . . 198
admission process 190
advance parole 193
Diversity (DV) Lottery 192
employment-based petitions 192
employment-based preferences 209
family-sponsored preferences . 191, 201
interviews 194
overview 189
refugees/asylees 192
replacement Green Card 197
statistics 190

H – Professional, Temporary Worker or
Trainee 99
admission process 102
Aliens in Specialty Occupations and as
Fashion Models – H-1 99
blanket application 104
Dictionary of Occupational Titles . 106
doctrine of dual intent 101, 116
H-1B-dependent employers 101, 108, 333
Labor Condition Application . . 105, 118
mechanisms for enforcement 108
nurses 99, 104, 105, 106
. . . . 112, 118, 119, 135, 227
Other Temporary Workers – H-2B . . . .
105, 109, 115, 118
revalidation/extension or change of status
. . . . 117
Special Education Exchange
Visitor – H-3 99, 111, 112, 115, 117
Spouse and Minor Children – H-4 . . . .
. . . . 99, 101, 111, 115, 117, 120
Temporary Agricultural Service
Workers – H-2A 105, 108, 115, 118

Temporary Trainee – H-3 110, 112, 115

H-2A – Temporary Agricultural Service
 Workers 105, 108, 115, 118

H-2B – Other Temporary Workers
 . . . . 105, 109, 115, 118

H-3 – Special Education Exchange
 Visitor 99, 111, 112, 115, 117
H-3 – Temporary Trainee . . . 110, 112, 115

H-4 – Spouse and Minor Children . . . .
 . . . . . 99, 101, 111, 115, 117, 120

Health Care Financing Administration 415

Health Insurance 410
 aliens 415
 definitions 424
 EPO 420
 fee-for-service 416, 419
 group 418
 HMO 420
 individual 419
 insurance plans 419
 insurance providers to non-citizens
  and residents 421
 legislation 411, 412
 Medicare 415
 Medigap 417
 MSA 421
 POS 418, 420
 PPO 418

History of Immigration Laws 3

Home Residence Requirement (HRR) . . 74

Home
 buying 380, 381
 definitions 382
 rental accommodation 339

Homeowner's Insurance 406
 definitions 408

Humanitarian Parole 180

I – Foreign Information Media
 Representative 156
 revalidation/extension 157

Illegal Aliens 1, 320, 327, 367, 469

Illegal Immigration Reform and
 Immigrant Responsibility
 Act of 1996 . . . . 3, 54, 317
 employment verification practices . . 23

Immigration Act of 1990 3

Immigration and Nationality
 Act of 1952 . . . . 3, 7

Immigration and Naturalization
 Service 9, 316
 "Ask Immigration" 338
 Commissioner 9
 forms 338, 340
 forms and fees 455
 internet 338, 340
 mission 9
 toll-free 800 information service . . . 339

Immigration Process 9
 overview 9

Information Telephone Numbers 458

INS Regional Service Centers 24
 Vermont Service Center 24
 Nebraska Service Center 25
 Texas Service Center 24
 California Service Center 24

Insurance
 automobile 428
 health 410
 home 406
 title 390, 404

Internal Revenue Service 358, 372

International Association for Financial
 Planning 379

International Organization Family
    Member – N 195

Internationally-Recognized   Athlete   and
    Entertainer – P 148

Intra-Company Transferee – L 123

Investor – E 91

Irish Peace Process Cultural and Training
    Program Participant - Q-2 167

J – Exchange Visitor 65
    J-1 (HRR) 74
    approval of programs 67

Journalists 156

Jury Duty 445

K – Fiancé(e) of U.S. Citizen 159
    adjustment of status 163
    admission process 159
    after marriage 161. 162
    before marriage 159, 162
    conditional status 165, 166
    Green Card interview 164
    Marriage Fraud Act of 1986 165

L – Intra-Company Transferee 123
    admission process 124
    blanket petition 124
    citizens of Canada and Mexico . . . 128
    revalidation/extension or change of
        status 128

Labor Certification . . . 8, 107, 204, 225, 227
    National Interest Waiver 228
    other temporary workers - U.S.
        workers are not available . . . 107
    schedule A occupations 226
    schedule B occupations 227
    sheepherders 226
    temporary agricultural service
        workers 108

Labor Condition Application (LCA) . . . 105

registered professional nurses 106

Legal Assistance 315
    American Immigration Lawyers
        Association 316
    legal assistance on the Internet . . . 316
    selection of an immigration
        attorney 315

M – Vocational or Non-Academic Student   84
    acceptance by an accredited
        institution 84
    admission process 84
    employment authorization 87
    Illegal Immigration Reform and
        Immigrant Responsibility
        Act of 1996 87
    revalidation/extension 89

Machine-Readable Visa (MRV) 19

Marriage Procedures 440

Media – I 156

Medicaid 370, 426

Medical Insurance
    see health insurance 410

Medicare 415, 416

Mexican nationals 33
    border crossing card 36, 40
    temporary visitor for business or
        pleasure 33

Mortgages 394
    definitions 396

Multinational Executives and Managers   233

N– International Organization Family
        Member 195
    admission process 195

NAFTA – Professional – TN 132

NATO – Representative of Member
        State 197

admission process 198

Naturalization with Test Questions . . 299
    absences during qualifying period 300
    application process 300
    examination 303
    naturalization ceremony 305
    naturalization test - questions . . . 306
    pre-testing 302
    qualifying period 299

New Legislation 317

Newcomers Organizations 437

Notary Public 379, 457

Nurses 99, 104, 105, 106, 112
    . . . . 118, 119, 135

O – Extraordinary Ability–Sciences, Arts,
    Education, Business 141
    admission process 142
    aliens in the motion picture or television
    industries 142
    aliens in the sciences, arts, education,
    business or athletics 142
    revalidation/extension or change of
    status 146
    union consultation 144

Out of Status 12, 22, 207
    filing limits 119
    rebuttal evidence 63
    renewals 131

P – Internationally-Recognized Athlete
    and Entertainer 148
    admission process 148
    athlete 148
    entertainer 149
    revalidation/extension or change of
    status 152
    union consultation 150

Passport 158, 447
    agencies 452

application (by mail) 449
application (in person) 447
information 451

Permanent Resident Alien 471

Physician 79, 107, 111, 135, 244,247, 413, 414

Pledge of Allegiance 434, 437

Political Office 446

Port of Entry 10, 349

Priority Workers – Extraordinary Ability 233

Professor and Researcher 234

Property Taxes 392

Property, buying 381

Q-1/Q-2–International Cultural Exchange/
    Irish Peace Process Cultural and
    Training Program Participant 167
    admission process 168
    revalidation/extension or change of
    status 170

R – Alien in a Religious Occupation 172
    admission process 173
    ministers of religion 172
    religious workers 172
    renewal/extension/ change of status..172

Reduction in Recruitment (RIR) 251

Re-entry Permit . 24, 47, 213, 214, 215, 300

Refugee 47, 206, 281
    establishing eligibility 282, 283
    processing 283
    statistics 281

Religious Occupation Alien – R 172

Renewal or Change of Status 23
    visa information 26

Rental Accommodation 392

Research Resources 338

Retirement Visa 180

S – Alien Witness and Informant 178
   admission process 178
   certification by the Attorney
      General 178
   certification by the Secretary of
      State and Attorney General . 179

Violent Crime Control and Law

Enforcement Act of 1994 178

Schools 50, 433

Selective Service 361
   military inductions 362
   postponement 363
   reclassification 363
   registration 361
   treaty alien 363

Social Activities................... 437

Social Customs in the United States .. 437

Social Security 326, 355, 418
   application 359
   benefits 358
   Canada-U.S. agreement 358
   number and card 356
   credits 355
   household workers 358
   Medicare 355
   tax 355
   Supplemental Security
      Income (SSI) 357
   visas – F, J, M, Q 358

Special Purpose Classifications 155
   Alien in a Religious Occupation – R 172
   Alien Witness and Informant – S . 178
   Fiancé(e) of U.S. Citizen – K 159
   Foreign Information Media
      Representative – I 156
   Humanitarian Parole 180
   International Cultural Exchange

Program Participant – Q 167
   Retirement Visa 180
Student
   Academic – F 51
   Exchange Visitor – J 65
   Vocational or Non-Academic
      Student –M 84

Supplemental Security Income(SSI) ... 357

TN–Treaty NAFTA Professional 132
   admission process 133
   Mexico 136
   physicians 132
   revalidation/change of status 139

Taxation 372

Temporary Protected Status 287

Temporary Status 12
   admission process 14
   application for employment 22
   business professionals classifications 13
   educational classifications 13
   extraordinary/internationally-recognized
      classifications 13
   foreign   government   representative
      classifications 14
   grounds for denial 18
   renewal or change of status 23
   special purpose classifications 13
   visitor classifications 13

Temporary Visitor for Business or
      Pleasure – B 33
   admission process 34
   Canadians 36
   Mexicans 36
   revalidation/extension or change of
      status 38
   Visitor for Business – B-1 33
   Visitor for Pleasure – B-2 33
Third-Country Nationals (TCNs) ... 25, 114
   visa processing in Canada/ Mexico .. 25

Transit Alien – C-1 42

Treaty Trader or Investor – E 91

Two-year Home Residency Requirement
   (HRR) 74
   exceptional hardship 80
   Interested Government Agency . . . 78
   No Obligation to Return – NORI . . 77
   Fear of persecution 80

TWOV – Transit WithOut Visa 49
   application process 49

U.S. Citizenship 292
   derivative status 295
   dual nationality 297
   naturalization with test questions 299
   non-citizen aliens 292
   qualifying 293
   relinquishing U.S. citizenship . . . 294
   rights, benefits and responsibilities 294

U.S. Consulates in Mexico and Canada . 27

U.S. Customs Service 349
   agricultural items 351
   automobiles 350
   drugs 351
   duty 349
   duty-free shops 354
   endangered species 351
   foods 353
   medicines 351
   negotiable funds 349
   personal goods 349
   pets 351
   plants 353
   port of entry 353

U.S. Department of Agriculture 353

U.S. Fish and Wildlife Service 352

Unemployment Insurance 369

United Nations 188
   Alien in Transit – C-2 188

Representative –G 189

United States Code 6

United States Congress 5
   Code of Federal Regulations (CFR) . . 6
   Federal Register (FR) 6
   Foreign Affairs Manual (FAM) 6
   how a bill becomes law 5
   public and private bills 5
   publishing laws 6
   Slip Law 6
   Statutes at Large 6
   United States Code (USC) 6

United States Government Resources . . 338
   Department of Labor (DOL) 340
   Department of State (DOS) 340
   Federal Information Center 341
   INS 378

Utilities 391

Vacations 369

Violent Crime Control and Law
      Enforcement Act of 1994 . 178, 324

Visa Waiver Pilot Program – VWPP 30
   participating countries 31
   tourist visas and passports 30

Visitor for Business or Pleasure – B 33

Visitor Classifications 29
   Exchange Visitor 65
   Visa Waiver Pilot Program 30

Vocational or Non-Academic - M 84

Voluntary Service 438

Voting 444

Waiver of Inadmissibility 21, 204

Welfare 370

Witness and Informant - S 178

Worker's Compensation 369

Order Form - USA Immigration & Orientation

Phone Orders: (have credit card ready)	(888) US-VISA9, (888) 878-4729
Fax:	(321) 779-3333
Internet orders:	orders@wellesworth.com
Website:	http://www.wellesworth.com
Postal Address:	Wellesworth Publishing P.O. Box 372444 Satellite Beach, FL, 32937-2444
Enclose:	$US 39.95 per book _____

Sales Tax (6% for Florida addresses only): $US 2.40 _____

Priority Shipping

   Enter shipping charge (See following
   page for charges to your destination)   _____

                                   Total: _____

Cash ____   Check____

American Express ____   Discover____   Mastercard____   Visa ____

Card Number: _____

Name on Card: _____ Exp. Date: ____/_____

Signature: _____

Name: _____

Address: _____

             _____

City/State/Prov.: _____

ZIP/Postal Code: _____

Country: _____

Telephone: _____

Email: _____

SHIPPING CHARGES

Priority Mail shipping within the United States is $US 3.20.

Global Priority Mail shipping to Canada and Mexico (Guadalajara, Mexico City and Monterrey) is $US 7.00.

Global Priority Mail shipping to the following cities and countries is $US 9.00:

Australia	Germany	Malaysia	South Africa
Austria	Hong Kong	Monaco	South Korea
Belgium	Hungary	Netherlands	Spain
Brazil (a)	Iceland	New Zealand	Sweden
Chile (b)	India	Norway	Switzerland
China (c)	Ireland	Philippines	Taiwan
Colombia	Israel (d)	Poland	Thailand
Denmark	Japan	Portugal	United Kingdom
Finland	Liechtenstein	Saudi Arabia (e)	Vietnam
France	Luxembourg	Singapore	

(a) São Paolo and Rio de Janeiro only
(b) Santiago, Valparaiso and Viña del Mar only
(c) Beijing, Chongqing, Dalian, Guangzhou, Nanjing, Qingdao, Shanghai, Shenyang, Shenzhen, Suzhou, Tianjin, Wuhan, Wuxi, Xiamen, Xian and Zhuai only
(d) Haifa, Jerusalem and Tel Aviv only
(e) Riyadh, Jeddah and Damman only

For shipping charges to other destinations, contact Wellesworth Publishing at (888) USVISA9 or info@wellesworth.com.